AF713514

Networks in the Early History of Capitalism

Drawing on a detailed examination of Venetian commerce in the Middle Ages, this book explores the business practices and structures that enabled merchants to compete in a challenging international market.

Contributing to the literature on the early history of capitalism, this book demonstrates how Venetian merchants combined innovation with traditional methods to maintain their edge in a competitive world, providing valuable lessons on resilience and strategic planning in commerce. Small- and mid-sized commercial companies operating across borders and geographies in the early Renaissance period faced numerous challenges, including identifying profitable sectors and businesses, developing effective business strategies, dealing with peers and subordinates, managing the flow of information, and assessing risks and potential rewards. The chapters explore a range of topics in this context, including the roles of family-based firms, the strategic deployment of agents, and the impact of state policies on private enterprise. Readers are introduced to the ways Venetian merchants managed capital, adapted to market demands, and overcame obstacles like wars and resource shortages.

This book will be of significant interest to historians and social scientists researching economic history, the history of trade, the history of capitalism, medieval and Renaissance history, and historical network analysis.

Stefania Montemezzo is an economic and social historian with a keen interest in the Renaissance period in Italy. She received her PhD in Economic History from the University of Verona. Her professional experience includes research fellowships at the University of Bologna, Aalto University in Helsinki, the University of Padua, and I Tatti, The Harvard University Center for Italian Renaissance Studies.

Routledge Explorations in Economic History

Edited by Lars Magnusson, Uppsala University, Sweden

The Sustainability and Development of Ancient Economies
Analysis and examples
Clement A. Tisdell and Serge Svizzero

The Economy of Classical Athens
Organization, institutions and society
Emmanouil M.L. Economou

The Political Economy of Interwar Foreign Investment
Economic nationalism and French capital in Poland, 1918–1939
Jerzy Łazor

The Development of European Competition Policy
Social democracy and regulation
Edited by Brian Shaev and Sigfrido Ramírez Pérez

Economic History of the European Energy Industry
Lighting up western Europe, 19th to 21st centuries
Alberte Martínez-López, Jesús Mirás-Araujo and Nuria Rodríguez-Martín

Economy of Ancient Egypt
State, administration, institutions
Mahmoud Ezzamel

For more information about this series, please visit: www.routledge.com/Routledge-Explorations-in-Economic-History/book-series/SE0347

Networks in the Early History of Capitalism

Merchant Practices in Renaissance Venice

Stefania Montemezzo

Routledge
Taylor & Francis Group
LONDON AND NEW YORK

First published 2025
by Routledge
4 Park Square, Milton Park, Abingdon, Oxon OX14 4RN

and by Routledge
605 Third Avenue, New York, NY 10158

Routledge is an imprint of the Taylor & Francis Group, an informa business

© 2025 Stefania Montemezzo

The right of Stefania Montemezzo to be identified as author of this work has been asserted in accordance with sections 77 and 78 of the Copyright, Designs and Patents Act 1988.

All rights reserved. No part of this book may be reprinted or reproduced or utilised in any form or by any electronic, mechanical, or other means, now known or hereafter invented, including photocopying and recording, or in any information storage or retrieval system, without permission in writing from the publishers.

Trademark notice: Product or corporate names may be trademarks or registered trademarks, and are used only for identification and explanation without intent to infringe.

British Library Cataloguing-in-Publication Data
A catalogue record for this book is available from the British Library

ISBN: 9781032628134 (hbk)
ISBN: 9781032628172 (pbk)
ISBN: 9781032628103 (ebk)

DOI: 10.4324/9781032628103

Typeset in Times New Roman
by codeMantra

To my husband, whose intellect, dedication, and companionship have enriched every aspect of my personal and academic journey.

To my family, whose support and encouragement have been a source of strength over the years.

Contents

Figures and tables

Figures

Tables

About the Author

Stefania Montemezzo is an economic and social historian with a keen interest in the Renaissance period in Italy. Her research primarily investigates the extensive trade networks of late medieval Venice, focusing on how these networks managed conflicts and facilitated trade across the Mediterranean. She also examines the material culture of the time, particularly the consumption patterns and everyday life of the lower social strata. Stefania received her PhD in Economic History from the University of Verona. Her professional experience includes research fellowships at the University of Bologna, Aalto University in Helsinki, the University of Padua, and I Tatti, The Harvard University Center for Italian Renaissance Studies. Her work integrates thorough archival research with a nuanced understanding of historical economic and social structures.

Acknowledgements

This book owes its existence to the invaluable support of colleagues and friends encountered throughout my journey. While it is impossible to individually acknowledge all those to whom I owe gratitude, I must highlight those who significantly influenced various stages of this volume's research and writing.

First and foremost, I extend heartfelt thanks to Andrea Caracausi for his unwavering support, diligent manuscript reviews, and insightful feedback that substantially enriched my work. My deep gratitude also goes to Giuseppe Gullino, whose guidance was instrumental in mastering archival complexities and understanding the art of research. Over the years, numerous colleagues have offered me guidance and support. Among them, I am profoundly indebted to Francesco Ammannati, Catia Antunes, Francisco Apellaniz, Andrea Berto, Francesco Guidi Bruscoli, Flavio Miranda, Sheilagh Ogilvie, Mathieu Schermann, and Francesco Vianello. I am also grateful to all who provided valuable feedback on my papers during seminars, workshops, and conferences, as well as to the anonymous referees whose insightful comments have enriched this volume. Special thanks are extended to Hannelore Zug Tucci for facilitating the publication of this volume, made possible by the 'Tucci Prize' awarded by the Istituto Veneto di Lettere, Scienze e Arti in Venice.

The University of Padua played a crucial role in advancing my studies, notably through the STARS grant scheme. Additionally, I am grateful for the generous support provided by I Tatti, The Harvard University Center for Renaissance Italian Studies, the University of Bologna, and the University of Verona, where I pursued my doctoral research under the supervision of Edoardo Demo and Renzo Sabatini.

Finally, I would like to express my gratitude to Rufo Iannelli for his translation of the first draft of the manuscript.

Acronyms and Abbreviations

ASVe	Archivio di Stato di Venezia
cc	cartae
ff	folios
GrM	Archivio privato Gradenigo rio Marin
MdC	Miscellanea di carte non appartenenti ad alcun archivio
MG	Miscellanea Gregolin
Reg	register
SM	Senato Mar

Note on Transcription, Citations, and Units of Measurements

Transcription and Reference Guidelines

Fifteenth-century Venetian writing was not standardized and could exhibit significant stylistic variations. Therefore, in transcribing sources, certain criteria have been applied to make the text more comprehensible while preserving its original form, including spelling, syntax, and morphological inconsistencies. Corrections have been made only where clear errors could obstruct understanding, introducing the most probable intended wordings. The application of capitalization (pertaining to names of individuals and places) and the use of punctuation have been adapted to align with the conventions of contemporary Italian style. Apostrophes and accents are utilized where necessary to enhance understanding. All abbreviations have been expanded following conventional practice, aligning with common spelling or the text's intent in cases of ambiguity or when the same abbreviation is used for different terms, ensuring clarity and readability while maintaining scholarly precision.

In delineating the methodology for document citation, distinctive approaches have been articulated, contingent upon the nature of the source material. For accounting documents, the schema for page numeration diverges from that typically applied to registers, which utilize a recto and verso system. This variance arises due to the layout of accounts across adjacent pages, with debits positioned on the left (*dare*, Arabic numeral) and credits on the right (*avere*, Roman numeral), accompanied by their respective entries and counter-entries. Consequently, citations referring to an entry will only identify the page number. In instances where reference is made to an individual record, the citation will further specify the page side. Pertaining to the citation of letters, the Marco Bembo collection does not adhere to a page numbering protocol. To streamline scholarly referencing and augment the legibility of citations, the method employed will specify the recipient, destination and its date. This approach is intended to ensure both clarity and accuracy in the identification and utilization of these documentary sources.

Coinage, Weights, and Measures[1]

In the medieval period, the diversity in currencies, weights, and measures was a notable feature, with variations even among closely situated cities. To face these complexities, merchants of the time turned to commercial manuals and tariffs.[2]

These invaluable guides provided detailed information on the exchange rates and measurement systems applicable in various markets. Additionally, merchants received timely updates from their intermediaries and agents. These updates served two crucial purposes: they kept the merchants informed about any changes in the markets, and they offered conversion ratios to aid their correspondents in making accurate calculations.

For the purposes of this volume, unless specifically stated otherwise, Venetian standards for coins and measurements will be employed. Should there be any deviation from these standards, detailed explanations will be provided in the footnotes to ensure clarity and maintain consistency across the text.

The Venetian Monetary System

The account currency utilized in the ledger, known as the '*lira di grossi a oro'* (gold *grossi* pound), adheres to a fixed exchange rate, both within its own structure and in relation to minted currencies. The relationship between these account currencies (*lira, denari, soldi*, and *piccoli*) is systematically outlined as follows: 1:20:12:32

In terms of minted currency, the gold *grossi* pound was equivalent to 10 ducats or 240 *soldi grossi.* A single ducat could be converted to 6 *lire* and 4 *soldi piccoli*, or directly to 124 *soldi piccoli.*

Measures

In medieval Venice, measurements were specifically tailored to the nature of each commodity and the context of sale, whether retail or wholesale. This section succinctly outlines the metrics pertinent to the discussions presented in this volume.

Weight Measures: Venice utilized two primary weight standards: the *libbra sottile* (light pound) and *libbra grossa* (heavy pound), designed to accommodate the grading of goods. Each consisted of 12 ounces, with the light pound equating to approximately 300 grams and the heavy pound to 477 grams, establishing a conversion ratio of 100 heavy pounds to 158 light pounds. For dry commodities like grain, the measurement of choice was the *moggio*, divisible into four *staia.*

Volume Measures: Liquid volumes, particularly wine, were measured differently depending on the transaction type, either retail or wholesale. For wholesale transactions, the standard was the amphora, divided into four *bigonci.* However, the records also reference other measures identifying the container, such as barrels (*botte*, while buckets were typically used in retail trade), with the former being equivalent to two *carratelli*, and the latter accommodating approximately six buckets. Oil, while also a liquid, was measured using its own unit, the *mier*, consisting of 40 *miri.* In the Michiel ledger, the quantity of oil is frequently indicated alongside the number of barrels, a method not documented in traditional mercantile manuals. This discrepancy, along with the undefined capacity for a barrel and its prevalent use in calculating freight charges, has led to the interpretation of barrels as containers rather than precise measurements for oil volume. Oil from Apulia was measured in Apulian *miera* or thousands, which were equivalent to the Venetian measure.

Length Measures for Fabrics: The Venetian *braccio* had two variations: wool (approximately 68 centimetres) and silk (about 63 centimetres), both subdivided into 4 *quarte* or 12 ounces.

Software Tools Used for Data Visualization

In the elaboration of charts and diagrams for this book, I utilized three software tools, each chosen for their unique capabilities in handling complex data and visualizing it effectively. *RawGraphs*, developed by the Politecnico di Milano, was instrumental for visual representations of data in charts and treemaps.[3] *Palladio*, developed by Stanford's Humanities + Design Lab, was used for mapping and exploring relational data, which was essential for illustrating the connections and patterns within historical trade networks.[4] Lastly, *Gephi*, an open-source network analysis tool, was used to construct detailed network graphs that demonstrate the interdependencies among various mercantile agents and locations.[5]

Notes

1 Giacomo Badoer, *Il libro dei conti (Costantinopoli 1436-1440)*, ed. Umberto Dorini and Tommaso Bertelè (Roma: Istituto poligrafico dello Stato, Libreria dello Stato, 1956); Bartholomeo Di Pasi, *Tariffa de pexi e mesure. Qui comincia la utilissima opera chiamata taripha la qual tracta de ogni sorte de pexi e misure conrispondenti per tuto il mondo* (Venice: Albertin da Lisona Vercellese, 1503); Franco Borlandi, ed., *El libro di mercatantie et usanze de'paesi* (Torino: S. Lattes & c., 1936); Frederic C. Lane and Reinhold C. Mueller, *Money and Banking in Medieval and Renaissance Venice*, vol. 1. Coins and Moneys of Account (Baltimore, MD: The Johns Hopkins University Press, 1985); Reinhold C. Mueller, *Money and Banking in Medieval and Renaissance Venice, 2. The Venetian Money Market: Banks, Panics, and the Public Debt, 1200-1500* (Baltimore, MD: The Johns Hopkins University Press, 1997); Peter Spufford, *Handbook of Medieval Exchange* (London: Royal Historical Society, 1986); Peter Spufford, *Money and Its Use in Medieval Europe* (Cambridge: Cambridge University Press, 1988); Alessio Sopracasa, *Venezia e l'Egitto alla fine del Medioevo: le tariffe di Alessandria* (Alexandrie: Centre d'études alexandrines, 2013).

2 Such as Di Pasi, *Tariffa de pexi e mesure*; Francesco Balducci Pegolotti, *La pratica della mercatura*, ed. Allan Evans (Cambridge, MA: Mediaeval Academy of America, 1936).

3 'Rawgraph' (Density Design, Politecnico di Milano, 2013), https://www.rawgraphs.io/; Michele Mauri et al., 'RAWGraphs: A Visualisation Platform to Create Open Outputs', *Proceedings of the 12th Biannual Conference on Italian SIGCHI Chapter*, 18 September 2017, 1–5, https://doi.org/10.1145/3125571.3125585.

4 Stanford University Humanities + Design, 'Palladio', 2013, https://hdlab.stanford.edu/palladio/.

5 'Gephi' (Association Gephi, 2008), https://gephi.org/; Mathieu Bastian, Sebastien Heymann, and Mathieu Jacomy, 'Gephi: An Open Source Software for Exploring and Manipulating Networks', *Proceedings of the International AAAI Conference on Web and Social Media* 3, no. 1 (19 March 2009): 361–62, https://doi.org/10.1609/icwsm.v3i1.13937.

References

Badoer, Giacomo. *Il libro dei conti (Costantinopoli 1436-1440)*. Edited by Umberto Dorini and Tommaso Bertelè. Roma: Istituto poligrafico dello Stato, Libreria dello Stato, 1956.

Balducci Pegolotti, Francesco. *La pratica della mercatura*. Edited by Allan Evans. Cambridge, MA: Mediaeval Academy of America, 1936.

Bastian, Mathieu, Sebastien Heymann, and Mathieu Jacomy. 'Gephi: An Open Source Software for Exploring and Manipulating Networks'. *Proceedings of the International AAAI Conference on Web and Social Media* 3, no. 1 (19 March 2009): 361–62. https://doi.org/10.1609/icwsm.v3i1.13937.

Borlandi, Franco, ed. *El libro di mercatantie et usanze de' paesi*. Torino: S. Lattes & c., 1936.

Di Pasi, Bartholomeo. *Tariffa de pexi e mesure. Qui comincia la utilissima opera chiamata taripha la qual tracta de ogni sorte de pexi e misure conrispondenti per tuto il mondo*. Venice: Albertin da Lisona Vercellese, 1503.

'Gephi'. Association Gephi, 2008. https://gephi.org/.

Humanities + Design, Stanford University. 'Palladio', 2013. https://hdlab.stanford.edu/palladio/.

Lane, Frederic C., and Reinhold C. Mueller. *Money and Banking in Medieval and Renaissance Venice*. Vol. 1. Coins and Moneys of Account. Baltimore, MD: The Johns Hopkins University Press, 1985.

Mauri, Michele, Tommaso Elli, Giorgio Caviglia, Giorgio Uboldi, and Matteo Azzi. 'RAWGraphs: A Visualisation Platform to Create Open Outputs'. *Proceedings of the 12th Biannual Conference on Italian SIGCHI Chapter*, 18 September 2017, 1–5. https://doi.org/10.1145/3125571.3125585.

Mueller, Reinhold C. *Money and Banking in Medieval and Renaissance Venice, 2. The Venetian Money Market: Banks, Panics, and the Public Debt, 1200-1500*. Baltimore, MD: The Johns Hopkins University Press, 1997.

'Rawgraph'. Density Design, Politecnico di Milano, 2013. https://www.rawgraphs.io/.

Sopracasa, Alessio. *Venezia e l'Egitto alla fine del Medioevo: le tariffe di Alessandria*. Alexandrie: Centre d'études alexandrines, 2013.

Spufford, Peter. *Handbook of Medieval Exchange*. London: Royal Historical Society, 1986.

Spufford, Peter. *Money and Its Use in Medieval Europe*. Cambridge: Cambridge University Press, 1988.

Introduction

Marco Bembo, Giovanni Foscari, and Alvise Michiel, three Venetian merchants who lived in the second half of the 15th century, are the central figures of this book. Like many of their contemporaries, they engaged in commerce across a network of trading ports and emporiums. Their careers were marked by a mix of successes and failures, a common experience among merchants of their time. With the varying outcomes of their ventures, Bembo, Foscari, and Michiel exemplify the medieval international merchant. Their extensive activities across diverse commercial hubs positioned them as crucial observers and active participants in the economic landscape of their era. Their experiences, as chronicled through their surviving records, provide invaluable insights into the dynamics, challenges, and triumphs of trade during the Medieval and Renaissance periods.

The profession of merchants was marked by its complexity and sophistication, situated at the intersection of Western and Eastern cultures. The aspiration to comprehend and control the circumstances that may have an influence on their interests encouraged the development of tools such as memories, letters, charts, receipts, and administration records, which turned out to be extremely useful for their own activities, and for our knowledge. Mastery in this field required not only a profound understanding of accounting and arithmetic but also a keen expertise in diverse mercantile techniques. Additionally, a comprehensive knowledge of foreign institutions and, on occasion, multiple languages was essential. These practices have been the fundamentals of Italian merchants' success in ports across the Mediterranean Sea and in Europe and have been the key to their competitiveness even in the least favourable situations. Nevertheless, the impact of their work extended beyond individual success; it spurred the generation of wealth, catalysed the growth of local industries, and fostered the development of a robust service sector. These contributions were central, playing a crucial role in the economic and cultural flourishing of many Renaissance cities.[1] The Ragusean trader, Benedetto Cotrugli, in 1468 described very well the role of merchants within the society and economy of the time:

> But trade, if properly cultivated and conducted, is not only useful but, more than that, quite vital to human operations, and therefore it is the noblest activity. On this subject Cicero said: 'merchant(s) are the resources of the State',

DOI: 10.4324/9781032628103-1

> speaking of the better sort, expert and well-educated. For the same reason, Aristotle maintains that one of the principal and most necessary ornaments of the city is commerce, on which all other activities proliferate, as from a pure spring, until it deteriorates and fails. And it is a difficult occupation, being, as we have said, so various, and for this reason one hears often the common saying: 'More goes into the making of a merchant than a High Court judge', because every science has its rules and regulations, by following which a man becomes expert therein. Only trade demands such a probing of one's natural intellectual ability, which is daily and hourly put to the test.[2]

The role and prominence of trade, a noble profession that can be elevated to the status of art according to Cotrugli, take on an even greater significance within the urban economy when considering merchants' operations in cities such as Venice, a context distinguished by its role as a mediator between diverse cultural and economic realms.[3] Historically, this strategic location facilitated Venice's role as a crucial hub, significantly shaping the patterns of economic and cultural exchanges across these hemispheres.

This research is focused on exploring the world of Renaissance trade, particularly through the activities of Venetian family firms. It aims to unravel how these merchant companies, especially those of small and medium scale, navigated and achieved success in foreign markets during that era. The study seeks to provide insights into the strategies and practices that enabled these firms to flourish in the competitive and diverse international trade environment of the Renaissance period. It aims to shed light on their adaptive mechanisms in the face of external adversities, such as abrupt market closures and the adverse impacts of warfare on commerce. Additionally, the study examines the organizational methods these firms implemented to manage the flow of merchandise, ensuring a steady supply of goods in the markets they served and maintaining the active engagement of their international partners and agents. This book is structured into five chapters, each dedicated to exploring a distinct aspect of the commercial practices of Renaissance Venetian businesses. Chapter 1 focuses on business forms and partnerships, offering an in-depth look at their corporate structures and operational methodologies. Chapter 2 delves into the dynamics between commercial enterprises and public institutions, highlighting aspects such as public navigation systems, tax regimes, and economic incentives. In Chapter 3, attention shifts to commercial strategies, providing insights into the everyday operations, market challenges, and goods trading. Chapter 4 examines capital management, including its turnover, the mechanisms for monitoring and managing financial resources, and strategies for investment. Chapter 5 investigates the flow of information and the tools employed for business oversight, and a detailed analysis of the function and impact of agents and intermediaries within the commercial network, focusing on their hierarchical roles and the importance of trust and control in these relationships.

This book delves into the regulatory mechanisms of trade during crises, focusing on three Venetian merchants, Marco Bembo, Giovanni Foscari, and Alvise Michiel, during the turbulent times of the first conflict between Venice and the Ottoman

Empire (1463–79) and the War of Ferrara (1482–84). Their stories, while individually distinct, offer insights into the varied responses and strategies employed by Venetian merchants in navigating the challenges of their era. Marco Bembo (1465–84 ca.), the younger son of Girolamo and Caterina Barbarigo, assumed responsibility for the family business in conjunction with his brother Lorenzo until the latter's demise. Thereafter, Marco assumed sole control and relocated to Venice. His extensive commercial letters, which span his time as a traveling clerk to his years as a Venice-based merchant, document his wide-ranging travels across Europe and the Mediterranean for business, highlighting both his commercial acumen and his role in managing his brother's estate.[4] Giovanni Foscari (1440–79 ca.), a nephew of Doge Francesco Foscari and a member of one of Venice's most notable families, chose to distance himself from politics. Instead, he focused on trade, often collaborating with his wife's family, the Grittis. Despite the limited and fragmented records resulting from the controversy surrounding his uncle's '*dogado*', surviving accounting books and letters provide evidence of Foscari's activities as a merchant, agent, and patron across various European and Mediterranean ports.[5] Alvise Michiel (1430–82), also from a noble family and adopting a non-political stance, faced challenges in managing his family business alone, especially after his son Silvestro's death. Like Bembo, Michiel adapted by appointing the members of his extended family network, his brothers-in-law, as agents. His master ledger, documenting trade activities between 1470 and 1480—a period marked by the Ottoman-Venetian War—reveals his adeptness at identifying new trade opportunities to navigate through times of crisis.[6] Together, the experiences of Bembo, Foscari, and Michiel illustrate the resilience and adaptability of Venetian merchants in the face of geopolitical and familial challenges and their use of commercial, financial, and management tools, contributing to our understanding of trade dynamics during a fundamental period in Venetian history.

The Economy of the Renaissance

In this book, we will firstly discuss Venetian merchants, a small group of individuals operating within a privileged context, in the context of the Renaissance Italian economy. From the 13th century, Venetian merchants played a crucial role in linking Asia and Europe, making Venice a key hub for Eastern trade well into the Modern Era. Their long-distance trade routes brought spices, textiles, and gems to Europe's wealthy, while exporting woollen fabrics and minerals to Byzantium, Syria, and North Africa. By the 15th century, Venice's trade system had reached its peak, supported by a strong network across Europe and Asia, diplomatic ties, and a state-controlled navigation system.[7] This legal environment favoured trade, protecting merchants, while the arsenal and private docks efficiently served both state and commercial shipping needs.[8] This century, balancing medieval traditions and emerging modernity, is more accurately understood within the context of the Renaissance, challenging the traditional separation between the Middle Ages and the early modern era. Beginning in the 19th century, with Jacob Burckhardt's foundational work,[9] discussions about the Renaissance, particularly from the late

14th to the 17th centuries—considering the 'long Renaissance'[10]—have evolved to concentrate on its economic aspects. This shift in focus has aimed to unravel the distinct economic dynamics characterizing this transformative period.[11] Scholars like Carlo Maria Cipolla, Roberto Sabatino Lopez, and Harry Miskimin in *The Economic History Review* discussed varying perspectives,[12] with Cipolla advocating a regional approach to economic trends, countering the 'catastrophist' views of a generalized crisis. Contributions from Armando Sapori, Michel Mollat, and others enriched the debate, emphasizing the medieval era's innovations and the Renaissance's international dominance in trade.[13] The discourse highlights the difficulty in declaring a systemic crisis, instead pointing to a diversification of production systems and traffic that significantly altered global economic balances.[14] Key factors in this era's decline, where applicable, included conditions of European commercial expansion, demographic stagnation, failures in Italian commerce and finance, and the decline of the Flemish textile industry, agricultural downturns, and monetary instabilities.[15] Building on this perspective, Lopez proposed that during the Renaissance, there was a notable shift in the patterns of mercantile and manufacturing investments. Traditional production sectors, indeed, witnessed a shift in capital towards the acquisition of art and books, as well as increased funding in artistic patronage, as culture emerged as a vital status symbol for the nobility in Renaissance Italy. This evolution reflects a broader transformation in the allocation of resources and cultural priorities during the period.[16] Nevertheless, such a theory can be only partially confirmed within Venetian society, where 'culture had never been used to ascend society, as access to power was only granted through the privilege of birth'.[17] In Venetian society, particularly between the 15th and 16th centuries, there was a notable reallocation of noble resources and capital towards the mainland (*Terraferma*), where agriculture and emerging manufacturing sectors awaited investment.[18]

Although reaching a definitive conclusion about a general economic trend during the Renaissance proved elusive, it became apparent to many scholars that significant geographic variations existed, necessitating a comprehensive analysis that included trade, capital, as well as demographic, societal, and labour factors.[19]

The Interplay of Private Interests and Public Policy

Another focal point of this book will be the interplay between the interests of Venetian family commercial enterprises and those of the public sector. Who controlled whom? Historians and economists have often posited that in historical societies, public authorities were generally unable to enforce institutional rules on economic activities effectively, necessitating private institutions to create their own networks and regulations to maintain economic functionality. Furthermore, public institutions have been scrutinized based on their capacity to either stimulate or stifle economic growth.[20] However, the delineation between formal and informal institutions, along with the interplay between public and private interests, appears to be more subtle than previously understood, emphasizing the importance of investigating the collaboration between public institutions and private enterprises.

This perspective is particularly illuminated by examining how the Venetian state strategically supported its businesses to ensure their competitiveness on the international stage, with a deliberate policy of intervention. The galley system's development, aimed at securing the Rialto market's position at the heart of the Mediterranean trading system, serves as a prominent example.[21]

Accordingly, Venetian economic strategies were compelled to consider both domestic and international influences. By the end of the 15th century, international relations had created a complex scenario due to changing dynamics in the Mediterranean, with Ottoman expansion, and in Italy, with the Spanish crown extending its influence over the Peninsula. Venetian nobility continued to focus on the Levant and other areas that had historically contributed to its success, by securely tying its own fortunes to a capillary State control of the trading system.[22] After Constantinople's conquest by the Ottomans, the Saint Mark's government employed a large part of its resources to preserving its commercial activities in the area, by strenuously attempting to stipulate treaties that could grant its merchants some degree of safety for their trading.[23] The Venetian government, comprising the nobility at the heart of international commerce, served as a conduit for addressing the needs of Venetian family-owned trading firms. As explored in further chapters of this book, the implementation of various mechanisms—ranging from public navigation systems and assigning remunerated positions on galleys exclusively to Venetian nobles, to mandating that all merchandise be routed through Venice or providing subsidies for the importation of specific goods—illustrates how the noble and mercantile class promoted their own interests.[24] This approach, often at the expense of free market principles and affecting prices in certain instances, effectively merged public and private interests.[25]

The evolving dynamics of the international chessboard and the political turmoil, from the wars with the Ottomans to the Italian Wars of the early 16th century, were paralleled by significant internal transformations within Venetian institutions, encompassing both political and economic dimensions. Venice came out of the 15th century deeply changed in its mercantile groups, the trading structures, and its institutions (like the courts and State voyages).[26]

Since the latter 15th century, the trading landscape, once dominated by Venetian patricians and their businesses, began to change as citizens gained control of Europe-Asia trade routes. This shift, which became widespread in the Italian Peninsula by the 16th century, saw the nobility investing more in land, facilitated by state-influenced favourable conditions for acquiring territories. This move not only served as a risk diversification strategy but also aimed to safeguard their wealth, reflecting how Venetian nobles leveraged state mechanisms to support their economic interests across different sectors.[27]

Family Businesses and Competitive Markets

Besides public policies and private interests, this volume focuses on the activities of small- and medium-sized enterprises that, despite operating at one of the international trade's focal points, remained small businesses facing cyclical challenges, such as wars, making their ingenuity their strength. During the Medieval period, Italian merchant organizations faced an escalating flow of goods and capital amidst an increasingly complex European and Mediterranean socio-economic landscape. To navigate the challenges of long-distance commerce, these enterprises innovated with new mechanisms that enhanced control over their operations and efficiency of resources, including the adoption of double-entry bookkeeping, financial instruments, and novel corporate forms. This era marked the beginning of a significant shift in business structures, eventually leading to the emergence of joint-stock companies and the advent of financial markets.[28]

The tools that allowed Venetian, and Italian, merchants to succeed in business were accounting, business organization, and credit methods.[29] Accounting, in the form of double-entry bookkeeping, allowed for monitoring the operations carried out by the company, through the simple concept of balancing all entries, thus enabling an immediate verification of the progress of each single deal. Another essential factor for the success of Italian companies in the rest of Europe and the Mediterranean ports was business organization. Particular types of contracts, such as the *commenda*, financed long-distance trade, commissioning merchants with insufficient financial means for the venture to ship and sell goods at foreign ports, generating a profit that was then shared with the investors who financed the voyage.[30] Companies of the Renaissance were essentially based on the institution of family. This was particularly true, despite the fact that since the 13th century the structure of companies involved in international trade started evolving towards more complex forms, in relation to the creation of branches of the company abroad and entrusting part of the decision-making responsibility to factors, agents, and other types of representatives in distant markets.[31] While this evolution was taking place in Genoa and Florence,[32] trade in Venice remained deeply rooted in traditional family businesses, the '*fraterne*', up until the 16th century, with joint-stock companies developing to a lesser extent compared to other regions of the Peninsula. Although these partnerships operated on the division of shares and managed substantial capitals, they never became permanent fixtures in the Venetian Renaissance economy. Instead, they retained a temporary nature, often limited to a single venture or journey.[33]

Against this backdrop of change, the Republic of Venice's seeming lack of evolution presents a striking contrast to the period's broader economic dynamism. This raises a critical question: how were Venetian family-owned firms able to compete with larger partnerships? The forthcoming analysis in this book will address this question by examining the activities of three Venetian family firms. It will delve into how the synergy of institutional interventions—including flag navigation, trade treaties, incentives, and consular support—and Venice's social structure, particularly regarding the preservation of family wealth, might have eliminated the necessity for Venetian merchants to form long-lasting corporate entities.[34] This premise suggests that comprehensive backing from public institutions, along with the mechanisms at their disposal, could have rendered short-term, goal-specific ventures (often centred on a single transaction) a viable method for navigating intricate trade dealings and reducing risks. Consequently, this leads to the exploration of whether the family firms consciously bypassed major internal restructuring or the pursuit of external funding, leveraging instead the state-facilitated resources for maintaining competitiveness in the international market.

Business and Capitalist Practices

Finally, through the letters of Marco Bembo and the records of Alvise Michiel and Giovanni Foscari, this book will explore small businesses and their capitalistic practices. However, why employ the term 'capitalistic practices' rather than 'capitalism', especially when Venice, along with the Italian Peninsula, could be termed the cradle of capitalism?[35] The answer begins with the origin of the term itself. While discussing capitalism in its nascent forms, it is crucial to remember that contemporaries did not coin the term, whether they were Roman *negotiatores* or medieval and modern merchants.[36] Instead, it emerged in the 19th century, primarily to describe industrial capitalism, carrying a materialistic connotation.[37] The fortunes of the term 'capitalism' have fluctuated throughout the 20th century (with a resurgence in prominence following the crisis of 2008), such that it appears different, and significantly less defined, compared to its usage in the late nineteenth and early 20th centuries.[38]

Viewing capitalism from a historical perspective—thus considering corporate individualism and profit, advanced credit instruments, and speculation among others—it becomes clear that the Middle Ages already exhibited capitalistic attitudes or practices, even though it existed within a society that featured capitalists[39] but lacked a capitalistic societal configuration.[40] This distinction arises because the capitalistic mindset, especially when linked to trade involving 'distant trade movements and to the complicated arrangements for credit, was a sophisticated art, open only to a few initiates at most'.[41] Yet, these 'few', shielded by the state through the granting of privileges and the establishment of monopolies, managed to amass wealth that disrupted the feudal balance, propelling the medieval economy to a different level.[42] Immanuel Wallerstein defines this new plateau as the world economy, noting a significant shift in European economies from the end of the 15th century. These economies were not confined to local and regional markets but were part of a network of economic ties that transcended state borders, connecting distant and diverse areas, the so-called European world economy.[43] Wallerstein suggests that capitalists' primary goal was to grow their capital by building relationships, frequently with labourers, which would lead to producing and selling products at prices above production costs across varied market levels. This strategy was designed to generate profits for potential reinvestment.[44] With this framework in mind, the scenario in late medieval Venice reveals that international merchants lacked complete oversight over both production and sales, a trend that would only emerge in subsequent decades. Their efforts were mainly concentrated on marketing, while the production aspect was delegated to other actors like artisans. These artisans were subject to the governance of guilds, which managed labour relations, browsed information asymmetries, and monitored market interactions.[45] In such an ecosystem, it becomes apparent that the individuals who secured the highest profit margins were those adept in commercial strategies and who engaged the most effective intermediaries. This success often hinged on the ability to control information and gain access to the most profitable markets, in an environment characterized by wide price fluctuations and, as a result, varying profit margins.

Considering Venice and Italy during the late Middle Ages, it's not accurate then to describe their economic systems as fully capitalist in terms of production, commodification, commercialization, and the management of the economy. Instead, it is more apt to speak of capitalistic practices implemented by capitalists operating within a predominantly non-capitalist setting. They navigated the market by responding to its signals, adjusting resource allocation in line with demand dynamics and price changes. Therefore, a detailed micro analytic examination of individual commercial firms' activities is crucial for understanding these practices, which, in the Venetian context, were deeply intertwined with family structures.[46] To grasp these capitalistic dynamics and the evolution of commerce fully, examining Venice's financial and credit systems is crucial, especially the methods bankers employed in the Rialto market to finance international trade. This included facilitating long-distance payments via bills of exchange, extending payment terms, offering loans, and engaging in speculation on prices and interest rates.[47] These tools, and effectively, this mercantile culture, enabled even the small- and medium-sized Venetian companies to compete on the international stage alongside large firms and limited liability partnerships.[48] Credit and payment mechanisms were complemented by the availability of formal institutions, such as contracts, courts, and trading corporations, as well as informal institutions, like trust, mutual support, and personal connections, all of which became cornerstones of international trade cooperation. The security provided by these instruments, particularly in terms of pursuing cheaters, was crucial for small merchant enterprises that, on their own, could never chase down debtors, especially outside their network and jurisdiction.[49]

Notes

1 Kirti N. Chauduri, 'Reflections on the Organizing Principles of Premodern Trade', in *The Political Economy of Merchant Empires. State, Power and World Trade, 1350–1750*, ed. James D. Tracy (Cambridge: Cambridge University Press, 1991), 421–43.

2 Benedetto Cotrugli, *The Book of the Art of Trade*, ed. Carlo Carraro and Giovanni Favero (Cham: Palgrave Macmillan, 2017), 25. See also: Benedetto Cotrugli, *Il libro dell'arte di mercatura*, ed. Ugo Tucci (Venezia: Arsenale, 1990).

3 Cotrugli aimed to elevate the status of the merchant's craft from a mechanical to a liberal art, seeking to confer a nobler distinction upon it. During the Renaissance, as commerce became less associated with the noble classes, it was often categorized as a mechanical art. Ugo Tucci, 'La psicologia del mercante veneziano', in *Mercanti, navi e monete nel Cinquecento veneziano* (Bologna: Edizioni Il Mulino, 1981), 43–94; Ugo Tucci, 'Il patrizio veneziano mercante e umanista', in *Mercanti, navi e monete nel Cinquecento veneziano* (Bologna: Edizioni Il Mulino, 1981), 15–42; Andrea Zannini, 'Il "pregiudizio meccanico" a Venezia in Età moderna. Significato e trasformazioni di una frontiera sociale', in *Le regole dei mestieri e delle professioni. secoli XV-XIX*, ed. Maria Grazia Meriggi and Alessandro Pastore (Milano: Franco Angeli, 2000), 36–51.

4 The letters under consideration are those written by a resident merchant between 1482 and 1484, addressed to agents in the Mediterranean and Europe. These are preserved in a manuscript copybook housed in the State Archive of Venice (hereafter ASVe), *Miscellanea di carte non appartenenti ad alcun archivio* (hereafter MdC), folder 29, reg. 2. Freddy Thiriet, 'Les lettres commerciales des Bembo et le commerce venitien dans l'Empire Ottoman a la fin du XVe siecle', in *Studi in onore di Armando Sapori*, vol. II (Milan: Istituto Editoriale Cisalpino, 1957), 911–33; Alessio Sopracasa, 'Les marchands vénitiens à Constantinople d'après une tariffa inédite de 1482', *Studi veneziani* 63 (2011): 49–220; Alessio Sopracasa, 'Passage au Levant. Le «voyage» de Candie-Constantinople de la compagnia Bembo dans la seconde moitié du xve siècle: organisation et séjour', *Cahiers d'études italiennes*, no. 25 (2017), https://doi.org/10.4000/cei.3499.

5 The two ledgers, preserved in ASVe, *Gradenigo rio Marin* (hereafter GrM), folder 250, reg. 2, have been published in Stefania Montemezzo, *Giovanni Foscari. Viaggi di Fiandra 1463–1464 e 1467–1468* (Venice: La Malcontenta, 2012). Information on the family and the activities of Giovanni Foscari: Giuseppe Gullino, *La saga dei Foscari: storia di un enigma* (Verona: Cierre, 2005); Stefania Montemezzo, 'Galley Routes and Merchant Networks between Venice and the North Sea in the Fifteenth Century', in *Commercial Networks and European Cities, 1400–1800*, ed. Andrea Caracausi and Christof Jeggle (London: Pickering & Chatto, 2014), 153–69; Stefania Montemezzo, 'Ships and Trade: The Role of Public Navigation in Renaissance Venice', in *Reti marittime come fattori dell'integrazione europea / Maritime Networks as a Factor in European Integration*, vol. 50, Atti delle «Settimane di Studi» e altri Convegni (Florence: Firenze University Press, 2019), 473–84.

6 The ledger is preserved in ASVe, *Miscellanea Gregolin* (hereafter MG), folder 15, reg. 2 (a note from 1587 indicates it was submitted to the procurators' court for the litigation involving Ottaviano Contarini). Stefania Montemezzo, 'Strategie familiari e commercio internazionale: i Michiel da San Barnaba', *Studi storici Luigi Simeoni* 65 (2015): 29–40; Stefania Montemezzo, 'Fra pubblico e privato: la fraterna veneziana nel commercio del secondo Quattrocento', *Ricerche di Storia Economica e Sociale* III (2017): 7–34.

7 Paola Lanaro, 'Reinterpreting Venetian Economic History', in *At the Centre of the Old World. Trade and Manufacturing in Venice and the Venetian Mainland, 1400–1800*, ed. Paola Lanaro (Toronto: CRRS, 2006), 19–69; Andrea Mozzato, 'The Production of Woollens in Fifteenth- and Sixteenth-Century Venice', in *At the Centre of the Old World. Trade and Manufacturing in Venice and the Venetian Mainland, 1400 – 1800*, ed. Paola Lanaro (Toronto: CRRS, 2006), 73–107; Andrea Mozzato, 'I drappieri di Venezia incontrano i lanaioli di Terraferma. Per una storia del lanificio veneto nel Quattrocento (prima parte)', *Studi Storici Luigi Simeoni* LX (2010): 47–60; Mozzato.

8 Frederic Chapin Lane, *Venice, a Maritime Republic* (Baltimore, MD: Johns Hopkins University Press, 1973), 44–48, 66–81; Benjamin Arbel, 'Venice's Maritime Empire in the Early Modern Period', in *A Companion to Venetian History, 1400–1797*, ed. Eric R. Dursteler, (Leiden, Boston: Brill, 2013), 125–253. On the Arsenal: Ennio Concina, *L'Arsenale della Repubblica di Venezia: tecniche e istituzioni dal medioevo all'età moderna* (Milano: Electa, 1988); Robert C. Davis, *Shipbuilders of the Venetian Arsenal Workers and Workplace in the Preindustrial City* (Baltimore, MD: Johns Hopkins University Press, 1991).

9 Jacob Burckhardt, *The Civilisation of the Renaissance in Italy* (London: Sonnenschein, 1892).

10 Peter Burke, *The Renaissance* (Houndmills, Basingstoke, Hampshire: Palgrave Macmillan, 1997).

11 Henri Pirenne, *Histoire économique et sociale du moyen âge*, ed. Hans van Werveke, first published in 1933 (Paris: Presses universitaires de France, 1963).

12 Roberto S. Lopez and Harry A. Miskimin, 'The Economic Depression of the Renaissance', *The Economic History Review* 14, no. 3 (1962): 408–26; Carlo M. Cipolla, 'Economic Depression of the Renaissance? I', *The Economic History Review* 16, no. 3

(1964): 519–24; Robert S. Lopez, 'Economic Depression of the Renaissance? II', *The Economic History Review* 16, no. 3 (1964): 525–27; Harry A. Miskimin, 'Economic Depression of the Renaissance? III', *The Economic History Review* 16, no. 3 (1964): 528–29. The impact of this debate on economic history and other disciplines is analyzed by: Judith C. Brown, 'Prosperity or Hard Times in Renaissance Italy?', *Renaissance Quarterly* 42, no. 4 (1989): 761–80.

13 Armando Sapori, 'Medioevo e Rinascimento: Spunti per una diversa periodizzazione', *Archivio storico italiano* 115, no. 2 (414) (1957): 135–64; Michel Mollat, 'Y-a-t-il une economie de la Renaissance?', in *Actes du Colloque sur la Renaissance, 3, De Pétrarque à Descartes*, ed. Pierre Mesnard (Paris: J. Vrin, 1958), 37–54; Ruggiero Romano, 'La storia economica. Dal secolo XIV al Settecento', in *Storia d'Italia. Dalla caduta dell'Impero romano al secolo XVIII*, ed. Ruggiero Romano and Corrado Vivanti, vol. II (Torino: Einaudi, 1974), 1811–1931; Maurice Aymard, 'La transizione dal Feudalesimo al Capitalismo', in *Storia d'Italia, Annali, I, Dal Feudalesimo al Capitalismo*, ed. Ruggiero Romano and Corrado Vivanti (Torino: Einaudi, 1978), 1158–92; Federigo Melis, *Tracce di una storia economica di Firenze e della Toscana in generale dal 1252 al 1550. Appunti raccolti alle lezioni del Prof. Federigo Melis*, ed. Bruno Dini (Firenze: Università degli Studi di Firenze, 1965).

14 An extensive analysis of the historiography on the Italian Renaissance and various theories of crisis can be found in Franco Franceschi and Luca Molà, 'L'economia del Rinascimento: dalle teorie della crisi alla 'preistoria del consumismo', in *Il Rinascimento italiano e l'Europa, v. I, Storia e storiografia*, ed. Marcello Fantoni (Treviso: Colla Editore, 2005), 185–246. The authors draw attention to the evolving perception of the Renaissance in the 1970s, observing that its increasing definition as a transitional period in historical scholarship led to a reluctance to use the term 'Renaissance' in many works discussing the 13th to 16th centuries, p. 193.

15 Pirenne, *Histoire économique et sociale du moyen âge*, 406–32; Richard A. Goldthwaite, *The Building of Renaissance Florence: An Economic and Social History* (Baltimoe and London: Johns Hopkins University Press, 1980), 422–25. For an overview of the Renaissance Northern Italian economy: Paolo Malanima, *The Economy of Renaissance Italy* (Abingdon, Oxon, New York: Routledge, 2022), 147–53.

16 Robert Sabatino Lopez, 'Hard Times and Investment in Culture', in *The Renaissance: A Symposium (February 8–10, 1952)*, ed. Metropolitan Museum of Art (New York: Metropolitan Museum of Art, 1953) reprinted in *The Renaissance: Six Essays*, (New York: Harper Torchbooks, 1962), 29-54; William Caferro, *Contesting the Renaissance* (Malden, MA: Wiley Blackwell, 2011), 126–55.

17 Ugo Tucci, *Mercanti, navi e monete nel Cinquecento veneziano* (Bologna: Edizioni Il Mulino, 1981), 36.

18 Stuart J. Woolf, 'Venice and the Terraferma: Problems of the Change from Commercial to Landed Activities', in *Crisis and Change in the Venetian Economy in the Sixteenth and Seventeenth Century*, ed. Brian Pullan (London: Methuen & Co, 1968), 175–203; James C. Davis, *A Venetian Family and Its Fortune, 1500–1900: The Donà and the Conservation of Their Wealth* (Philadelphia, PA: American Philosophical Society, 1975), 32–37.

19 Malanima, *The Economy of Renaissance Italy*, 147–53. For a historiographic overview of Venice and Florence in the Renaissance, until 1860s: Gene Brucker, 'Tales of Two Cities: Florence and Venice in the Renaissance', *The American Historical Review* 88, no. 3 (1983): 599–616.

20 Frederic C. Lane, 'The Role of Governments in Economic Growth in Early Modern Times', *The Journal of Economic History* 35, no. 1 (1975): 8–17. The debate surrounding formal and informal institutions is extensive, but the essential readings for the commercial sector specifically include: Avner Greif, Paul Milgrom, and Barry R. Weingast, 'Coordination, Commitment, and Enforcement: The Case of the Merchant Guild', *Journal of Political Economy* 102, no. 4 (1994): 745–76; Sheilagh Ogilvie, '"Whatever

Is, Is Right"? Economic Institutions in Pre-Industrial Europe', *The Economic History Review* 60, no. 4 (2007): 649–84; Avner Greif, 'Reputation and Coalitions in Medieval Trade: Evidence on the Maghribi Traders', *The Journal of Economic History* 49, no. 4 (1989): 857–82; Avner Greif, *Institutions and the Path to the Modern Economy: Lessons from Medieval Trade* (Cambridge: Cambridge University Press, 2006); Sheilagh Ogilvie, *Institutions and European Trade: Merchant Guilds, 1000–1800* (Cambridge: Cambridge University Press, 2011); Jeremy Edwards and Sheilagh Ogilvie, 'Contract Enforcement, Institutions, and Social Capital: The Maghribi Traders Reappraised', *The Economic History Review* 65, no. 2 (2012): 421–44.

21 For some preliminary conclusions on the economic role of privileges: Andrea Caracausi, Giovanni Favero, and Paola Lanaro, 'A Political Economy? Some Preliminary Thoughts on Economic Privileges in Early Modern Venice', in *Die ökonomie des privilegs, Westeuropa 16.-19. jh./L'économie du privilege, Europe Occidentale XVIe-XIX siecles.*, ed. Guillaume Garner (Frankfurt am Mainz: Vittorio Klostermann, 2016), 365–95. See also: Jean Jean Claude Hocquet, 'Les routes maritimes du commerce vénitien au XVe et XVIe siècles', in *Atti del V Convegno internazionale di studi colombiani, navi e navigazione nei sec. XV e XVI*, ed. Graziella Galliano and Ausilia Roccatagliata (Genova: Civico Istituto Colombiano, 1990), 581–605. ; Claire Judde de Larivière, *Naviguer, commercer, gouverner: économie maritime et pouvoirs à Venise (XVe-XVIe siècles)* (Leiden, Boston: Brill, 2008), 44–61; Montemezzo, 'Ships and Trade'. While galley trade represented the public will to invest in commerce, the bulk of Venetian goods actually traveled on private ships. For a recent study on the private sector, refer to: Renard Gluzman, *Venetian Shipping: From the Days of Glory to Decline, 1453–1571* (Leiden, Boston: Brill, 2021).

22 Robert Sabatino Lopez, *Su e giù per la storia di Genova* (Genova: Università di Genova. Istituto di paleografia e storia medievale, 1975), 35–42; Jacques Heers, *Gênes au XVe siècle: activité économique et problèmes sociaux* (Paris: SEVPEN, 1961), 363–507; Quentin Van Doosselaere, *Commercial Agreements and Social Dynamics in Medieval Genoa* (Cambridge, New York: Cambridge University Press, 2009), 46–60; Michel Balard, 'L'amministrazione genovese e veneziana nel Mediterraneo orientale', in *Genova, Venezia e il Levante (secc. XII-XIV)*, ed. Gherardo Ortalli and Dino Puncuh (Venice: Istituto Veneto di Scienze, Lettere ed Arti, 2001), 201–28; David Jacoby, 'Mercanti genovesi e veneziani e le loro merci nel Levante crociato', in *Genova, Venezia e il Levante (secc. XII-XIV)*, ed. Gherardo Ortalli and Dino Puncuh (Venice: Istituto Veneto di Scienze, Lettere ed Arti, 2001), 229–56.

23 Lane, *Venice, a Maritime Republic*, 144–46; Daniel Goffman, *The Ottoman Empire and Early Modern Europe* (Cambridge: Cambridge University Press, 2002), 138.

24 Frederic Lane famously described the Venetian Senate ad a 'board of governors' that regulated the activity of the big joint stock company represented by the entire city's commercial class. Frederic C. Lane, *Andrea Barbarigo. Merchant of Venice* (Baltimore, MD: Johns Hopkins University Press, 1944), 48.

25 Lane, 45–84; Jean-Claude Hocquet, *Le sel et la fortune de Venise. I. Production et monopole*, 2nd edition (Villeneuve-d'Ascq: Publications de l'Université de Lille III, 1978), 241–77; Jean-Claude Hocquet, *Le sel et la fortune de Venise. II. Voiliers et commerce en Mediterranée* (Villeneuve-d'Ascq: Publications de l'Université de Lille III, 1978), 434–86.

26 Lane, *Venice, a Maritime Republic*, 251–73.

27 Tucci, *Mercanti, navi e monete nel Cinquecento veneziano*; Lane, *Andrea Barbarigo. Merchant of Venice*; Paola Lanaro, 'Flexibilité et diversification: les investissements du patriciat de Venise et de la Terre Ferme (XVe-XVIIIe siècles)', *Revue d'histoire moderne et contemporaine* 59, no. 1 (2012): 62–82; Giuseppe Gullino, 'Quando il mercante costruì la villa: le proprietà dei veneziani nella Terraferma', in *Storia di Venezia, VI, Dal Rinascimento al Barocco,* ed. Gaetano Cozzi and Paolo Prodi (Roma: Istituto della Enciclopedia Italiana, 1994), 875–924.

28 This topic has been addressed through the study of merchant company operations in various Italian contexts: Raymond De Roover, *The Rise and Decline of the*

Medici Bank, 1397–1494 (Cambridge: Harvard University Press, 1963); Heers, *Gênes au XVe siècle: activité économique et problèmes sociaux*; Edwin S. Hunt, *The Medieval Super-Companies. A Study of the Peruzzi Company of Florence* (Cambridge: Cambridge University Press, 1994); Lopez, *Su e giù per la storia di Genova*; Francesco Guidi Bruscoli, 'I rapporti con il Nord-Europa', in *Francesco di Marco Datini: l'uomo, il mercante*, ed. Giampiero Nigro (Firenze-Prato: Firenze University Press, Fondazione Istituto internazionale di storia economica "F. Datini, 2010), 407–28; Sergio Tognetti, *Il banco Cambini: affari e mercati di una compagnia mercantile-bancaria nella Firenze del XV secolo* (Firenze: L.S. Olschki, 1999); Van Doosselaere, *Commercial Agreements and Social Dynamics in Medieval Genoa*.

29 Angela Orlandi, 'The Emergence of Double-Entry Bookkeeping in Tuscan Firms of the Thirteenth and Fourteenth Centuries', *Accounting History* 26, no. 4 (2021): 534–51; Richard A. Goldthwaite, 'The Practice and Culture of Accounting in Renaissance Florence', *Enterprise & Society* 16, no. 3 (2015): 611–47; Carlo Antinori, 'La contabilitità pratica prima di Luca Pacioli: origine della partita doppia', *De Computis. Revista espanola de historia de la contabilidad* 1, no. 1 (2004): 4–23; Claudio Marsilio, *Dove il denaro fa denaro: gli operatori finanziari genovesi nelle fiere di cambio del 17. secolo* (Novi Ligure: Città del silenzio, 2008). The efficacy of double-entry bookkeeping in contributing to the success of merchant enterprises has been challenged by Northern European historical scholarship. Francesco Guidi Bruscoli, 'Le techiche bancarie', in *Rinascimento italiano e l'Europa. Commercio e cultura mercantile*, ed. Franco Franceschi, Richard A. Goldthwaite, and Reinhold C. Mueller (Treviso: A. Colla, 2007), 555n.

30 Harry A. Miskimin, *The Economy of Early Renaissance Europe, 1300–1460* (Englewood Cliffs, NJ: Prentice-Hall, 1969), 117–18.

31 Edwin S. Hunt and James M. Murray, *A History of Business in Medieval Europe, 1200–1550* (Cambridge, New York: Cambridge University Press, 1999), 31–33.

32 Recent studies on medieval and modern Florence indicate that limited partnerships were less prevalent in the economic landscape than previously thought: Francesca Trivellato, 'Renaissance Florence and the Origins of Capitalism: A Business History Perspective', *Business History Review* 94, no. 1 (2020): 242–47.

33 Frederic C. Lane, 'Family Partnerships and Joint Ventures in the Venetian Republic', *The Journal of Economic History* 4, no. 2 (1944): 178–96. For a recent contribution that addresses the theme of social mobility within the Renaissance Italian commercial world, see Sergio Tognetti, 'Uomini d'affari e mobilità sociale in Italia tra metà Trecento e primo Cinquecento', *Archivio storico italiano* 175, no. 1 (2017): 119–50.

34 Lane, *Andrea Barbarigo. Merchant of Venice*, 45–52.

35 Luciano Pezzolo, 'The via Italiana to Capitalism', in *The Cambridge History of Capitalism, I, The Rise of Capitalism: From Ancient Origins to 1848*, by Larry Neal and Jeffrey G. Williamson (Cambridge: Cambridge University Press, 2014), 266–313.

36 Jairus Banaji, *A Brief History of Commercial Capitalism* (Chicago, IL: Haymarket Books, 2020), IX–XVII, 4–5; Thomas Max Safley, *Family Firms and Merchant Capitalism in Early Modern Europe: The Business, Bankruptcy and Resilience of the Hoechstetters of Augsburg* (Abingdon, Oxon, New York: Routledge, 2019), 15–19.

37 This reference pertains to the Marxist concept of capitalism, as subsequently modified by Weber and Sombart. Robert Fredona and Sophus A. Reinert, 'Italy and the Origins of Capitalism', *Business History Review* 94, no. 1 (2020): 7; Maarten Prak, 'Introduction', in *Early Modern Capitalism. Economic and Social Change in Europe, 1400–1800*, ed. Maarten Prak (Abingdon, Oxon, New York: Routledge, 2001), 1–21.

38 For an overview on the use of the term capitalism: Neal Harris and Gerard Delanty, 'What Is Capitalism? Toward a Working Definition', *Social Science Information* 62, no. 3 (2023): 329–34.

39 Henri Pirenne, 'The Stages in the Social History of Capitalism', *The American Historical Review* 19, no. 3 (1914): 494–515.

40 Fredona and Reinert, 'Italy and the Origins of Capitalism'a 9; Rebecca Jean Emigh, *The Undevelopment of Capitalism: Sectors and Markets in Fifteenth-Century Tuscany*, Politics, History, and Social Change (Philadelphia, PA: Temple University Press, 2009), 1–10. For an analysis based on the criteria for distinguishing feudal societies from capitalist ones as proposed by Marx, see Richard Britnell, 'Commerce and Capitalism in Late Medieval England: Problems of Description and Theory', *Journal of Historical Sociology* 6, no. 4 (1993): 359–76.
41 Fernand Braudel, *Civilization and Capitalism, 15th–18th Century, Volume I, The Structures of Everyday Life: The Limits of the Possible* (New York: Harper and Row, 1979), 24.
42 Prak, 'Introduction', 1–4.
43 Immanuel Maurice Wallerstein, *The Modern World-System. I, Capitalist Agriculture and the Origins of the European World-Economy in the Sixteenth Century*, First published in 1974 (Berkeley: University of California Press, 2011), 15–36.
44 Immanuel Wallerstein, *Historical Capitalism* (London, New York: Verso Editions, 1988), 13–15.
45 Sheilagh Ogilvie, *The European Guilds: An Economic Analysis* (Princeton, NJ: Princeton University Press, 2019); Andrea Caracausi, 'Information Asymmetries and Craft Guilds in Pre-Modern Markets: Evidence from Italian Proto-Industry', *The Economic History Review* 70, no. 2 (2017): 397–422.
46 About the relationship between the history of capitalism and business history, see: Trivellato, 'Renaissance Florence and the Origins of Capitalism', 229–35.
47 Richard T. Rapp, 'Real Estate and Rational Investment in Early Modern Venice', *The Journal of European Economic History* 8, no. 2 (1979): 269–90; Reinhold C. Mueller, *Money and Banking in Medieval and Renaissance Venice, 2. The Venetian Money Market: Banks, Panics, and the Public Debt, 1200–1500* (Baltimore, MD: The Johns Hopkins University press, 1997), 288–355; 453–87; John H. A. Munro, 'The Monetary Origins of the 'Price Revolution' : South German Silver Mining, Merchant Banking, and Venetian Commerce, 1470 - 1540', in *Global Connections and Monetary History, 1470 - 1800*, ed. Dennis O. Flynn, Arturo Giraldez, and Richard Von Glahn (Aldershot: Ashgate, 2003), 1–34.
48 For recent works and related bibliography, see: Greif, *Institutions and the Path to the Modern Economy*; Francesca Trivellato, *The Familiarity of Strangers: The Sephardic Diaspora, Livorno, and Cross-Cultural Trade in the Early Modern Period* (New Haven, CT, London: Yale University Press, 2009).
49 David Hancock, *Citizens of the World.London Merchants and the Integration of the British Atlantic Community, 1735–1785* (Cambridge: Cambridge University Press, 1997), 104–14; Francesca Trivellato, 'Juifs de Livourne, Italiens de Lisbonne, hindous de Goa', *Annales. Histoire, Sciences Sociales* 58, no. 3 (2003): 581–603; David J. Hancock, 'L'émergence d'une économie de réseau (1640–1815)', *Annales. Histoire, Sciences Sociales* 58, no. 3 (2003): 649–72; Manuel Herrero Sanchez and Klemens Kaps, 'Connectors, Networks and Commercial Systems: Approaches to the Study of Early Modern Maritime Commercial History', in *Merchants and Trade Networks in the Atlantic and the Mediterranean, 1500–1800. Connectors of Commercial Maritime Systems*, ed. Manuel Herrero Sanchez and Klemens Kaps (Abingdon, Oxon: Routledge, 2017), 1–36.

Bibliography

Antinori, Carlo. 'La contabilitità pratica prima di Luca Pacioli: origine della partita doppia'. *De Computis. Revista española de historia de la contabilidad* , no. 1 (2004): 4–23.

Arbel, Benjamin. 'Venice's Maritime Empire in the Early Modern Period'. In *A Companion to Venetian History, 1400–1797*, edited by Eric R. Dursteler, 4:125–253. Leiden, Boston: Brill, 2013.

Aymard, Maurice. 'La transizione dal Feudalesimo al Capitalismo'. In *Storia d'Italia, Annali, I, Dal Feudalesimo al Capitalismo*, edited by Ruggiero Romano and Corrado Vivanti, 1158–92. Torino: Einaudi, 1978.

Balard, Michel. 'L'amministrazione genovese e veneziana nel Mediterraneo orientale'. In *Genova, Venezia e il Levante (secc. XII-XIV)*, edited by Gherardo Ortalli and Dino Puncuh, 201–28. Venice: Istituto Veneto di Scienze, Lettere ed Arti, 2001.

Banaji, Jairus. *A Brief History of Commercial Capitalism*. Chicago, IL: Haymarket Books, 2020.

Braudel, Fernand. *Civilization and Capitalism, 15th–18th Century, Volume I, The Structures of Everyday Life: The Limits of the Possible*. New York: Harper and Row, 1979.

Britnell, Richard. 'Commerce and Capitalism in Late Medieval England: Problems of Description and Theory'. *Journal of Historical Sociology* 6, no. 4 (1993): 359–76.

Brown, Judith C. 'Prosperity or Hard Times in Renaissance Italy?' *Renaissance Quarterly* 42, no. 4 (1989): 761–80.

Brucker, Gene. 'Tales of Two Cities: Florence and Venice in the Renaissance'. *The American Historical Review* 88, no. 3 (1983): 599–616.

Burckhardt, Jacob. *The Civilisation of the Renaissance in Italy*. London: Sonnenschein, 1892.

Burke, Peter. *The Renaissance*. Houndmills, Basingstoke, Hampshire: Palgrave Macmillan, 1997.

Caferro, William. *Contesting the Renaissance*. Malden, MA: Wiley Blackwell, 2011.

Caracausi, Andrea. 'Information Asymmetries and Craft Guilds in Pre-Modern Markets: Evidence from Italian Proto-Industry'. *The Economic History Review* 70, no. 2 (2017): 397–422.

Caracausi, Andrea, Giovanni Favero, and Paola Lanaro. 'A Political Economy? Some Preliminary Thoughts on Economic Privileges in Early Modern Venice'. In *Die Ökonomie Des Privilegs, Westeuropa 16.-19. Jh./L'économie Du Privilège, Europe Occidentale XVIe-XIX Siècles.*, edited by Guillaume Garner, 365–95. Frankfurt am Mainz: Vittorio Klostermann, 2016.

Chauduri, Kirti N. 'Reflections on the Organizing Principles of Premodern Trade'. In *The Political Economy of Merchant Empires. State, Power and World Trade, 1350–1750*, edited by James D. Tracy, 421–43. Cambridge: Cambridge University Press, 1991.

Cipolla, Carlo M. 'Economic Depression of the Renaissance? I'. *The Economic History Review* 16, no. 3 (1964): 519–24.

Concina, Ennio. *L'Arsenale della Repubblica di Venezia: tecniche e istituzioni dal medioevo all'età moderna*. Milano: Electa, 1988.

Cotrugli, Benedetto. *Il libro dell'arte di mercatura*, edited by Ugo Tucci. Venezia: Arsenale, 1990.

Cotrugli, Benedetto. *The Book of the Art of Trade*, edited by Carlo Carraro and Giovanni Favero. Cham: Palgrave Macmillan, 2017.

Davis, James C. *A Venetian Family and Its Fortune, 1500–1900: The Donà and the Conservation of Their Wealth*. Philadelphia, PA: American Philosophical Society, 1975.

Davis, Robert C. *Shipbuilders of the Venetian Arsenal Workers and Workplace in the Preindustrial City*. Baltimore, MD: Johns Hopkins University Press, 1991.

De Roover, Raymond. *The Rise and Decline of the Medici Bank, 1397–1494*. Cambridge: Harvard University Press, 1963.

Edwards, Jeremy, and Sheilagh Ogilvie. 'Contract Enforcement, Institutions, and Social Capital: The Maghribi Traders Reappraised'. *The Economic History Review* 65, no. 2 (2012): 421–44.

Emigh, Rebecca Jean. *The Undevelopment of Capitalism: Sectors and Markets in Fifteenth-Century Tuscany*. Politics, History, and Social Change. Philadelphia, PA: Temple University Press, 2009.

Franceschi, Franco, and Luca Molà. 'L'economia del Rinascimento: dalle teorie della crisi alla 'preistoria del consumismo'. In *Il Rinascimento italiano e l'Europa, v. I, Storia e storiografia*, edited by Marcello Fantoni, 185–246. Treviso: Colla Editore, 2005.

Fredona, Robert, and Sophus A. Reinert. 'Italy and the Origins of Capitalism'. *Business History Review* 94, no. 1 (2020): 5–38.

Gluzman, Renard. *Venetian Shipping: From the Days of Glory to Decline, 1453–1571*. Leiden, Boston: Brill, 2021.

Goffman, Daniel. *The Ottoman Empire and Early Modern Europe*. Cambridge: Cambridge University Press, 2002.

Goldthwaite, Richard A. *The Building of Renaissance Florence: An Economic and Social History*. Baltimore and London: Johns Hopkins University Press, 1980.

Goldthwaite, Richard A. 'The Practice and Culture of Accounting in Renaissance Florence'. *Enterprise & Society* 16, no. 3 (2015): 611–47.

Greif, Avner. *Institutions and the Path to the Modern Economy: Lessons from Medieval Trade*. Cambridge: Cambridge University Press, 2006.

Greif, Avner. 'Reputation and Coalitions in Medieval Trade: Evidence on the Maghribi Traders'. *The Journal of Economic History* 49, no. 4 (1989): 857–82.

Greif, Avner, Paul Milgrom, and Barry R. Weingast. 'Coordination, Commitment, and Enforcement: The Case of the Merchant Guild'. *Journal of Political Economy* 102, no. 4 (1994): 745–76.

Guidi Bruscoli, Francesco. 'I rapporti con il Nord-Europa'. In *Francesco di Marco Datini: l'uomo, il mercante*, edited by Giampiero Nigro, 407–28. Firenze-Prato: Firenze University Press, Fondazione Istituto internazionale di storia economica "F. Datini, 2010.

Guidi Bruscoli, Francesco. 'Le techiche bancarie'. In *Rinascimento Italiano e l'Europa. Commercio e cultura mercantile*, edited by Franco Franceschi, Richard A. Goldthwaite, and Reinhold C. Mueller, 543–66. Treviso: A. Colla, 2007.

Gullino, Giuseppe. *La saga dei Foscari: storia di un enigma*. Verona: Cierre, 2005.

Gullino, Giuseppe. 'Quando il mercante costruì la villa: le proprietà dei veneziani nella Terraferma'. In *Storia di Venezia: dalle origini alla caduta della Serenissima. VI. Dal Rinascimento al Barocco*, edited by Gaetano Cozzi and Paolo Prodi, 875–924. Roma: Istituto della Enciclopedia Italiana, 1994.

Hancock, David. *Citizens of the World. London Merchants and the Integration of the British Atlantic Community, 1735–1785*. Cambridge: Cambridge University Press, 1997.

Hancock, David J. 'L'émergence d'une économie de réseau (1640–1815)'. *Annales. Histoire, Sciences Sociales* 58, no. 3 (2003): 649–72.

Harris, Neal, and Gerard Delanty. 'What Is Capitalism? Toward a Working Definition'. *Social Science Information* 62, no. 3 (2023): 323–44.

Heers, Jacques. *Gênes Au XVe Siècle: Activité Économique et Problèmes Sociaux*. Paris: SEVPEN, 1961.

Herrero Sanchez, Manuel, and Klemens Kaps. 'Connectors, Networks and Commercial Systems: Approaches to the Study of Early Modern Maritime Commercial History'. In *Merchants and Trade Networks in the Atlantic and the Mediterranean, 1500–1800. Connectors of Commercial Maritime Systems*, edited by Manuel Herrero Sanchez and Klemens Kaps, 1–36. Abingdon, Oxon: Routledge, 2017.

Hocquet, Jean Claude. *Le sel et la fortune de Venise. I. Production et monopole*. 2nd edition. Villeneuve-d'Ascq: Publications de l'Université de Lille III, 1978.

Hocquet, Jean Claude. *Le sel et la fortune de Venise. II. Voiliers et commerce en Mediterranée*. Villeneuve-d'Ascq: Publications de l'Université de Lille III, 1978.

Hocquet, Jean Claude. 'Les routes maritimes du commerce vénitien au XVe et XVIe siècles'. In *Atti del V Convegno internazionale di studi colombiani, navi e navigazione nei sec. XV e XVI*, edited by Graziella Galliano and Ausilia Roccatagliata, 581–605. Genova: Civico Istituto Colombiano, 1990.

Hunt, Edwin S. *The Medieval Super-Companies. A Study of the Peruzzi Company of Florence*. Cambridge: Cambridge University Press, 1994.

Hunt, Edwin S., and James M. Murray. *A History of Business in Medieval Europe, 1200–1550*. Cambridge, New York: Cambridge University Press, 1999.

Jacoby, David. 'Mercanti genovesi e veneziani e le loro merci nel Levante crociato'. In *Genova, Venezia e il Levante (secc. XII-XIV)*, edited by Gherardo Ortalli and Dino Puncuh, 229–56. Venice: Istituto Veneto di Scienze, Lettere ed Arti, 2001.

Judde de Larivière, Claire. *Naviguer, commercer, gouverner: économie maritime et pouvoirs à Venise (XVe-XVIe siècles)*. Leiden, Boston: Brill, 2008.

Lanaro, Paola. 'Flexibilité et diversification: les investissements du patriciat de Venise et de la Terre Ferme (XVe-XVIIIesiècles)'. *Revue d'histoire moderne et contemporaine* 59, no. 1 (2012): 62–82.

Lanaro, Paola. 'Reinterpreting Venetian Economic History'. In *At the Centre of the Old World. Trade and Manufacturing in Venice and the Venetian Mainland, 1400–1800*, edited by Paola Lanaro, 19–69. Toronto: CRRS, 2006.

Lane, Frederic C. *Andrea Barbarigo. Merchant of Venice*. Baltimore, MD: Johns Hopkins University Press, 1944.

Lane, Frederic C. 'Family Partnerships and Joint Ventures in the Venetian Republic'. *The Journal of Economic History* 4, no. 2 (1944): 178–96.

Lane, Frederic C. 'The Role of Governments in Economic Growth in Early Modern Times'. *The Journal of Economic History* 35, no. 1 (1975): 8–17.

Lane, Frederic Chapin. *Venice, a Maritime Republic*. Baltimore, MD: Johns Hopkins University Press, 1973.

Lopez, Robert S. 'Economic Depression of the Renaissance? II'. *The Economic History Review* 16, no. 3 (1964): 525–27.

Robert Sabatino Lopez, 'Hard Times and Investment in Culture', in *The Renaissance: A Symposium (February 8–10, 1952)*, edited by the Metropolitan Museum of Art. New York: Metropolitan Museum of Art, 1953. Reprinted in *The Renaissance: Six Essays*, 29–54. New York: Harper Torchbooks, 1962.

Lopez, Robert Sabatino. *Su e giù per la storia di Genova*. Genova: Università di Genova. Istituto di paleografia e storia medievale, 1975.

Lopez, Roberto S., and Harry A. Miskimin. 'The Economic Depression of the Renaissance'. *The Economic History Review* 14, no. 3 (1962): 408–26.

Malanima, Paolo. *The Economy of Renaissance Italy*. Abingdon, Oxon, New York: Routledge, 2022.

Marsilio, Claudio. *Dove il denaro fa denaro: gli operatori finanziari genovesi nelle fiere di cambio del 17. secolo*. Novi Ligure: Città del silenzio, 2008.

Melis, Federigo. *Tracce di una storia economica di Firenze e della Toscana in generale dal 1252 al 1550. Appunti raccolti alle lezioni del Prof. Federigo Melis* , edited by Bruno Dini. Firenze: Università degli Studi di Firenze, 1965.

Miskimin, Harry A. 'Economic Depression of the Renaissance? III'. *The Economic History Review* 16, no. 3 (1964): 528–29.

Miskimin, Harry A. *The Economy of Early Renaissance Europe, 1300–1460*. Englewood Cliffs: Prentice-Hall, 1969.

Mollat, Michel. 'Y-a-t-il une economie de la Renaissance?' In *Actes du Colloque sur la Renaissance, 3, De Pétrarque à Descartes*, edited by Pierre Masnard, 37–54. Paris: J. Vrin, 1958.

Montemezzo, Stefania. 'Fra pubblico e privato: la fraterna veneziana nel commercio del secondo Quattrocento'. *Ricerche di Storia Economica e Sociale* III (2017): 7–34.

Montemezzo, Stefania. 'Galley Routes and Merchant Networks between Venice and the North Sea in the Fifteenth Century'. In *Commercial Networks and European Cities, 1400–1800*, edited by Andrea Caracausi and Christof Jeggle, 153–69. London: Pickering & Chatto, 2014.

Montemezzo, Stefania. *Giovanni Foscari. Viaggi di Fiandra 1463–1464 e 1467–1468*. Venice: La Malcontenta, 2012.

Montemezzo, Stefania. 'Ships and Trade: The Role of Public Navigation in Renaissance Venice'. In *Reti marittime come fattori dell'integrazione europea / Maritime Networks as a Factor in European Integration*, 50:473–84. Atti delle «Settimane di Studi» e altri Convegni. Florence: Firenze University Press, 2019.

Montemezzo, Stefania. 'Strategie familiari e commercio internazionale: i Michiel da San Barnaba'. *Studi storici Luigi Simeoni* 65 (2015): 29–40.

Mozzato, Andrea. 'I drappieri di Venezia incontrano i lanaioli di Terraferma. Per una storia del lanificio veneto nel Quattrocento (prima parte)'. *Studi Storici Luigi Simeoni* LX (2010): 47–60.

Mozzato, Andrea. 'The Production of Woollens in Fifteenth- and Sixteenth-Century Venice'. In *At the Centre of the Old World. Trade and Manufacturing in Venice and the Venetian Mainland, 1400–1800*, edited by Paola Lanaro, 73–107. Toronto: CRRS, 2006.

Mueller, Reinhold C. *Money and Banking in Medieval and Renaissance Venice, 2. The Venetian Money Market: Banks, Panics, and the Public Debt, 1200–1500*. Baltimore, MD: The Johns Hopkins University press, 1997.

Munro, John H. A. 'The Monetary Origins of the 'Price Revolution' : South German Silver Mining, Merchant Banking, and Venetian Commerce, 1470 - 1540'. In *Global Connections and Monetary History, 1470 - 1800*, edited by Dennis O. Flynn, Arturo Giraldez, and Richard Von Glahn, 1–34. Aldershot: Ashgate, 2003.

Ogilvie, Sheilagh. *Institutions and European Trade: Merchant Guilds, 1000–1800*. Cambridge: Cambridge University Press, 2011.

Ogilvie, Sheilagh. *The European Guilds: An Economic Analysis*. Princeton, NJ: Princeton University Press, 2019.

Orlandi, Angela. 'The Emergence of Double-Entry Bookkeeping in Tuscan Firms of the Thirteenth and Fourteenth Centuries'. *Accounting History* 26, no. 4 (2021): 534–51.

Pezzolo, Luciano. 'The via Italiana to Capitalism'. In *The Cambridge History of Capitalism, I, The Rise of Capitalism: From Ancient Origins to 1848*, edited by Larry Neal and Jeffrey G. Williamson, 266–313. Cambridge: Cambridge University Press, 2014.

Pirenne, Henri. *Histoire économique et sociale du moyen âge*, edited by Hans van Werveke. First published in 1933. Paris: Presses universitaires de France, 1963.

Pirenne, Henri. 'The Stages in the Social History of Capitalism'. *The American Historical Review* 19, no. 3 (1914): 494–515.

Prak, Maarten. 'Introduction'. In *Early Modern Capitalism. Economic and Social Change in Europe, 1400–1800*, edited by Maarten Prak, 1–21. Abingdon, Oxon, New York: Routledge, 2001.

Rapp, Richard T. 'Real Estate and Rational Investment in Early Modern Venice'. *The Journal of European Economic History* 8, no. 2 (1979): 269–90.

Romano, Ruggiero. 'La storia economica. Dal secolo XIV al Settecento'. In *Storia d'Italia. Dalla caduta dell'Impero romano al secolo XVIII*, edited by Ruggiero Romano and Corrado Vivanti, II:1811–1931. Torino: Einaudi, 1974.

Safley, Thomas Max. *Family Firms and Merchant Capitalism in Early Modern Europe: The Business, Bankruptcy and Resilience of the Hoechstetters of Augsburg*. Abingdon, Oxon, New York: Routledge, 2019.

Sapori, Armando. 'Medioevo e Rinascimento: Spunti per una diversa periodizzazione'. *Archivio storico italiano* 115, no. 2 (414) (1957): 135–64.

Sheilagh Ogilvie. '"Whatever Is, Is Right"? Economic Institutions in Pre-Industrial Europe'. *The Economic History Review* 60, no. 4 (2007): 649–84.

Sopracasa, Alessio. 'Les marchands vénitiens à Constantinople d'après une tariffa inédite de 1482'. *Studi veneziani* 63 (2011): 49–220.

Sopracasa, Alessio. 'Passage au Levant. Le « voyage » de Candie-Constantinople de la compagnia Bembo dans la seconde moitié du xve siècle: organisation et séjour'. *Cahiers d'études italiennes*, no. 25 (2017). https://doi.org/10.4000/cei.3499.

Thiriet, Freddy. 'Les lettres commerciales des Bembo et le commerce vénitien dans l'Empire Ottoman à la fin du XVe siècle'. In *Studi in onore di Armando Sapori*, II:911–33. Milan: Istituto Editoriale Cisalpino, 1957.

Tognetti, Sergio. *Il banco Cambini: affari e mercati di una compagnia mercantile-bancaria nella Firenze del XV secolo*. Firenze: L.S. Olschki, 1999.

Tognetti, Sergio. 'Uomini d'affari e mobilità sociale in Italia tra metà Trecento e primo Cinquecento'. *Archivio storico italiano* 175, no. 1 (2017): 119–50.

Trivellato, Francesca. 'Juifs de Livourne, Italiens de Lisbonne, hindous de Goa'. *Annales. Histoire, Sciences Sociales* 58, no. 3 (2003): 581–603.

Trivellato, Francesca. 'Renaissance Florence and the Origins of Capitalism: A Business History Perspective'. *Business History Review* 94, no. 1 (2020): 229–51.

Trivellato, Francesca. *The Familiarity of Strangers: The Sephardic Diaspora, Livorno, and Cross-Cultural Trade in the Early Modern Period*. New Haven, CT, London: Yale University Press, 2009.

Tucci, Ugo. 'Il patrizio veneziano mercante e umanista'. In *Mercanti, navi e monete nel Cinquecento veneziano*, 15–42. Bologna: Edizioni Il Mulino, 1981.

Tucci, Ugo. 'La psicologia del mercante veneziano'. In *Mercanti, navi e monete nel Cinquecento veneziano*, 43–94. Bologna: Edizioni Il Mulino, 1981.

Tucci, Ugo. *Mercanti, navi e monete nel Cinquecento veneziano*. Bologna: Edizioni Il Mulino, 1981.

Van Doosselaere, Quentin. *Commercial Agreements and Social Dynamics in Medieval Genoa*. Cambridge, New York: Cambridge University Press, 2009.

Wallerstein, Immanuel. *Historical Capitalism*. London, New York: Verso Editions, 1988.

Wallerstein, Immanuel Maurice. *The Modern World-System. I, Capitalist Agriculture and the Origins of the European World-Economy in the Sixteenth Century*. First published in 1974. Berkeley: University of California Press, 2011.

Woolf, Stuart J. 'Venice and the Terraferma: Problems of the Change from Commercial to Landed Activities'. In *Crisis and Change in the Venetian Economy in the Sixteenth and Seventeenth Century*, edited by Brian Pullan, 175–203. London: Methuen & Co, 1968.

Zannini, Andrea. 'Il "pregiudizio meccanico" a Venezia in Età moderna. Significato e trasformazioni di una frontiera sociale'. In *Le regole dei mestieri e delle professioni. Secoli XV-XIX*, edited by Maria Grazia Meriggi and Alessandro Pastore, 36–51. Milano: Franco Angeli, 2000.

1 Venetian Business Models

Family Business and Its Characteristics

'Venetian business enterprise, having been fathered by the State and mothered by the family, remained subordinated to these older and stronger institutions'.[1] It is with a parental metaphor that Frederic Lane describes Venetian family-style merchant companies, or more precisely, Venetian family capitalism. An idyllic situation, where the business partners, literally brothers, hence the name *fraterna*, and occasionally cousins, trade and act peacefully in the name of the family, both in Venice and on international markets. However, was it so? What were the advantages and disadvantages associated with the use of this business form?

The Fraterna Operational Dynamics

To address these issues, it is essential to first grasp the nature of a Venetian *fraterna*, its operational dynamics, and the participants involved. In medieval Venice, the family firm served as the foundational business unit, comprising primarily of close relatives (brothers and sons) who collectively owned merchandise, shared in the profits of trade, held real estate, and, at least initially, resided together. Diverging from practices elsewhere, where formalization of a family business required legal acknowledgement by a notary or court,[2] in Venice, the mere act of living together and managing business affairs collectively sufficed under Venetian law to recognize family members as full-fledged business partners, eliminating the need for a formal contract.[3]

The *fraterna* extended beyond mere commerce to encompass the management of all familial assets and properties within the inheritance framework. Consequently, Venetian accounting ledgers do not solely detail commercial transactions but also capture a broad spectrum of household expenditures, costs related to properties in the Mainland, their income, and operational expenses.[4] Expenses for food, property upkeep, and even gifts for family members are noted in these ledgers, right alongside transactions for spices and foreign textiles. Commercial accounts are typically marked by high precision, contrasting with the personal and familial expense entries, which are somewhat less detailed, often summarizing totals—in cash or expense accounts—from daily records or miscellaneous notebooks. The Michiel

DOI: 10.4324/9781032628103-2

ledger's treatment of food and beverage consumption is an example. In an entry from February 1474, the ledger specifies a disbursement of around 5 ducats for the monthly meat and fish needs of the entire household. This figure stands alone, as subsequent records of similar expenses are notably absent, implying their absorption into broader categories labelled as miscellaneous in the ledger's later pages. This pattern of record-keeping extends to the acquisition of vegetables and other groceries, which, lacking specific notations, are encapsulated under general household outlays. The ledger also records transactions for grain and wine, alongside detailing the personal and familial events of the period, giving insight on the family consumption and the role of Mainland properties for the household economy. For instance, it reveals the integration of 'agrestic' wine from Michiel's Peraga estate in the Padua region[5]—likely a staple for everyday family use but perhaps not chosen for guest hospitality—complemented by white and red wines sourced from other Venetian locales, such as Monselice (south of the Euganean Hills in Padua) or the Marca Trevigiana area, today celebrated for its prosecco production. Additionally, the Peraga estate contributed wheat and spelt to Venice's supply, provided by tenant farmers in a barter system, plus cash leasehold payments amounting to 1,600 ducats across the decade.[6]

The ledger transcends mere financial accounting; it illuminates the personal expenditures of the time, offering insight into consumption patterns, lifestyle choices, and the stark realities of mortality, thereby filling in the historical gaps where other records of daily life are missing. The case of Zilia Corner, wife of Alvise Michiel, is illustrative. Zilia's influence reached into the commercial realm, with her marriage to Alvise not only enhancing domestic life but also enriching their business through connections to notable ancestry, including Marco Corner, Doge of the Republic from 1365 to 1368, and her relation to Caterina Corner, queen of Cyprus, Jerusalem, and Armenia from 1474 to 1489.[7] The *fraterna*'s ledgers note Zilia's purchases of jewellery, like pearl rings and gold bracelets, and fine silk accessories, reflecting the family's affluent lifestyle from 1470 to 1477. Her passing in the winter of 1478 in Padua is marked by recorded funeral costs totalling around 65 ducats. Beyond Alvise and Zilia, the ledger also chronicles wider family expenses, such as the wages for nannies and tutors for the younger children, including Fantino and Zaneto, and tragically, the costs associated with their deaths. In April 1479, for instance, expenditures for candles for Zaneto's grave were noted, indicating his passing between 1478 and 1479. Zaneto was not the sole child of Alvise and Zilia's eleven to die before their parents. The eldest son, Silvestro, previously Alvise's chief agent, is recorded until at least 1470. Silvestro's travels took him across the Mediterranean to Syria, Egypt, and Barbary, and through Europe to Germany, dealing in spices, silver, and European textiles until 1472. Alvise accounts for Silvestro's journeys, opening accounts under his name for commissions on his trading activities. An entry from 24 September 1472 notes Alvise's expenditure to retrieve Silvestro's possessions and, most notably, his writings left in Rhodes, charged against Silvestro's inheritance.[8] Silvestro's death during his return journey from Alexandria to Venice in the summer of 1472 left unresolved accounts in the Middle East and a significant void in the *fraterna*s' business management. His activities and premature death reflect the broader narrative of the family's personal and business challenges captured within the pages of the ledger. The unique insight these ledgers provide into both the family and business aspects of the Michiel household is invaluable. This is especially significant given the rarity of finding such extensive family archives that include accounting records, letters, and memoirs, a feature more common in other Italian regions like Tuscany.[9]

A Business of Their Own

As observed, there was a seamless integration of business and personal capital within the family firm. Despite this integration of interests, individual members could still engage in independent ventures, occasionally leading to the establishment of what could be considered subsidiaries of the main family business. Although the personal wealth of family members could be distinguished from that of the family's collective assets through distinct accounting practices, it was uncommon for siblings not to share responsibility for the liabilities generated by these subsidiary ventures.[10] The concept of brothers serving as mutual spokesmen for a singular interest, specifically that of their family enterprise, and thereby one brother acting as an automatic delegate for the other, is a recurring theme in Venetian records, especially within commercial correspondence. For instance, in his communications with agents, Marco Bembo delineates his view of the Zivran siblings, Tomado and Francesco, engaged in the Greek market of Modon, as essentially interchangeable entities. He articulates that resolving a debt with Tomado could be seamlessly managed through Francesco, who acts as a complete surrogate. Nevertheless, it was imperative to maintain an accurate 'arrangement' or updating of the company's financial records to forestall any potential disputes. As delineated in Chapter 5, the practice of regularly updating the ledgers emerged as a pivotal management strategy for Venetian traders, effectively permitting family businesses to designate multiple legal representatives without inviting complications.[11]

Distinguishing between personal and familial matters was complex, even in instances of sudden death among members of the company or its patriarch. This complexity is highlighted in testamentary commissions, where appointed commissioners were responsible for administering the deceased's estate and safeguarding the heirs' interests.[12] This challenge was a recurrent theme for Venetian merchants, evidenced by the management of a *commissaria*, hereditary succession, in each of the three cases examined in this volume. Specifically, for Michiel, this pertained to his son Silvestro. The financial records concerning Silvestro's *commissaria* are detailed in the *fraterna*'s ledgers, largely in connection with his role as an agent. Notably, there is an instance where goods were explicitly listed under Silvestro's name alone, suggesting he possessed a small amount of personal capital (slightly less than 400 ducats).[13] The limited amount of personal capital implies that individual fortunes were primarily built through profits earned as commission agents. This finding reflects the Venetian practice of not limiting one's work solely to their family business. Indeed, representing other *fraterne*—often belonging to in-laws or friends—was a common practice, as explored further in Chapter 5.

For Giovanni Foscari as well, there exists a detailed ledger documenting the partnership between his son, Agostino Foscari, and his cousin, Francesco di Alvise Foscari. This ledger documents the financial activities related to Giovanni's estate management from 1486 to 1496, showing a capital fluctuating between 5,000 and 7,000 ducats, with a focus on investments in silver, pepper, and cotton.[14] Giovanni's inheritance, unlike Silvestro's, encountered challenges. It was brought before the Venetian Court of Petitions, which handled estate and guardianship matters,[15] due to allegations of mismanagement by Giovanni's brother, Alvise, made by the son, Marco. Appointed in Giovanni's 1478 will as the estate's commissioner,[16] Alvise faced accusations related to the mishandling of a coral trade agreement Giovanni had entered with Genoese merchants.[17] This controversy escalated to the point where, within a few years, the heirs started to go their separate ways: by 1486, the business led by Giovanni remained under the control of his son, Agostino, while Alvise's sons were involved as partners but not as integral members of the family enterprise. Property divisions followed suit, leading to the eventual partition of the San Simeon Piccolo household by the early 16th century. Ownership was equally divided between Giovanni's descendants (Marco and Giovanni, Agostino's son, after his passing) and those of Alvise (Francesco).[18]

The intertwining of inheritance, personal and familial wealth, and commercial records is also illustrated in Marco Bembo's correspondence. The Bembo family encountered significant turbulence from 1474 to 1485, witnessing the loss of three central figures in less than a decade: Girolamo, the patriarch, followed by Lorenzo, the elder brother, in 1480,[19] and finally, Marco himself, who tragically died on 6 September 1484, after falling from scaffolding at his new home's construction site in the San Salvador area.[20] Marco's letters frequently touch upon managing Lorenzo's estate, in which he was merely one executor among others, including Marco's sister, Maddalena Bembo. Maddalena, along with her children, would later play a crucial role in executing Marco's will and authored several letters on behalf of Marco Bembo's estate executors after his demise. A letter Marco wrote to Alberto Contarini in January 1483 is particularly revealing, highlighting ongoing disputes exacerbated by Bembo's departure from Flanders in 1478.[21] Mismanagement by Contarini, including the neglect of spices in Flemish warehouses and unresolved debts, soured their relationship. Marco was especially perturbed by Contarini's failure to distinguish between personal affairs and Lorenzo's estate, a differentiation clearly mandated by Venetian law and custom. Marco pointedly reminded Contarini 'the affairs from my late brother [Lorenzo]'s estate are completely distinct and separate from my own; I am merely one of five executors, which includes his wife [Andriana Vendramin], who has a 14-year-old son'.[22] This clarification highlights the need to protect the interests of heirs, including the widow and minor child, from being conflated with Marco's personal liabilities. This blurring of lines by Contarini between personal and estate finances was deemed unacceptable by Bembo. He remained vigilant over his brother's accounts to ensure the estate's proper administration and the protection of his nephew's interests. Bembo firmly instructed

Contarini to return any of Lorenzo Bembo's assets in his possession to Venice, directly to the estate's management, underlining the critical distinction between personal and estate matters in safeguarding familial and financial legacies.[23]

The inclusion of these transactions in the *fraternas*' records highlights the enduring connection between personal finances, business activities, and the family firm and is due to the very structure of Venetian family firms, deeply reliant on the integrity of the family unit and its assets.[24] It is crucial to note that the family firm operated within a hierarchical structure, led by either the father or the eldest brother. The leader typically resided in Venice, directing family members who conducted business abroad. This arrangement aimed to safeguard the family's wealth, while still allowing for individual entrepreneurial efforts.

Partnerships, Management, and Practices

The family business engaged in diverse economic arenas. Specifically, family capital was allocated between commercial ventures and real estate holdings. In commerce, the focus was on long-distance trade, aimed at importing Asian goods to European markets and exporting European goods to Asia. These investments, while offering returns over several years, were vital to the Venetian economy, establishing it as a fundamental intermediary between the West and the East. On the domestic front, the family firms were instrumental in providing Venetian producers with essential raw materials and supplying goods to retail markets. Furthermore, a significant portion of their capital was invested in real estate within Venice, including residential properties and warehouses, and in the Venetian mainland, encompassing estates and industrial operations such as silk and wool mills. Over the medieval period, these real estate investments became increasingly critical, reflecting the growing significance of Venetian manufacturing to the broader Mediterranean trade network.[25] Focusing on commerce, the maritime sector represented the essential investment domain for the family firms. The role of public navigation, understood as formal institutions, will be detailed in the second chapter while this section focuses on the organizational and structural approaches Venetian companies adopted for maritime trade investments, culminating in a comparative analysis with commercial enterprises from a distinct geographical and cultural context: the Armenians and the Indian diaspora.

Investing in Maritime Trade

The features of the Venetian navigation system, encompassing both public and private sectors, provided all Venetian merchants with secure and cost-effective entry into international trade markets.[26] Venetian firms had several strategies for investing in maritime ventures. Utilizing a galley or private ship solely as a transporter represented the financially least risky option: merchants could lease cargo space at a fixed rate. This approach required minimal capital investment, yielding two notable benefits: it enabled younger merchants or those with limited resources to engage in international trade and diminished the necessity of establishing investment partnerships involving multiple stakeholders. Merchants from family businesses who wished to allocate personal capital towards specific transactions typically undertook leasing space on galleys. Alternatively, temporary consortia, often created for a single transaction, pursued it. These consortia consisted of multiple merchants who agreed to jointly own the cargo, entrusting a single agent (usually one of the partners) with the sales task, who would later distribute profits among the participants.[27] In essence, Venetian traders could not only minimize their financial outlay but, crucially, also mitigate the risk associated with engaging in ventures that could easily spiral out of control.

For merchants prepared to allocate greater resources, an option existed to directly invest in a single voyage by chartering a ship from the state fleet to become its patron. In these scenarios, family businesses could either shoulder the full cost of the journey—encompassing the charter fee for the galley, contributions to the arsenal for the ship's refurbishment, and direct sailing expenses such as crew wages, provisions, and ship operational costs (including repairs and maintenance)[28]—or they could mitigate the investment risk. Mitigation strategies included inviting external financiers into the venture by establishing temporary consortia, known as 'galley companies', which lasted for the duration of the voyage. These consortia were structured into 24 shares (termed 'carats'), with investors known as *parcenevoli*.[29] Furthermore, the patron might also engage financiers, termed *plegi*, who underwrote the capital for the voyage's expenses borne by the patron. Although these financiers did not participate actively in the venture, they served as guarantors for the patron's financial obligations, particularly in covering crew salaries and various ship-related expenses.[30] To gain a deeper insight into the corporate arrangements related to public navigation, we turn to the accounting ledgers of Giovanni Foscari, who was the patron aboard a galley for the Flanders voyage during two periods (1463–64 and 1467–68).[31] These ledgers do not document the official accounting of the ship (which was recorded in a separate ledger termed *salariatto*[32]) but detail all transactions that directly pertained to Foscari in his capacities as patron, commission agent, and merchant. This includes the purchase and sale of merchandise—both his and that of others—expenses for provisions and the ship, and wages for the crew. These records offer a detailed account of the expenses the Foscari *fraterna* undertook to engage in this state-led venture, highlighting the involvement of various associated companies.

Fixed expenses for chartering a galley included operational costs, which spanned from ship maintenance to provisioning and required significant financial contributions from the patrons. Foscari, for instance, recorded outlays of 7,400 ducats for the 1463–64 voyage and 8,200 ducats for the 1467–68 journey, constituting 26% and 27%, respectively, of his managed business volume,[33] not factoring in the auction and arsenal fees (approximately 700 ducats per ship). To cover these financial demands, Foscari turned to financial allies, notably via galley companies.[34] Such companies were usually divided into 24 shares, a structure that facilitated risk distribution among investors. In exchange, investors were guaranteed space for their merchandise in the ship's hold—where they often had ownership interests—and the allocation of cargo in the safest sections to prevent water damage. Additionally,

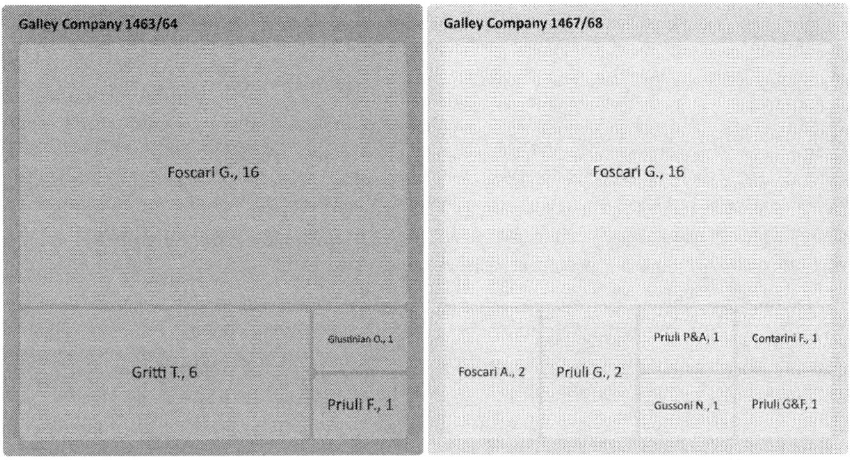

Figure 1.1 Comparative analysis of share distribution in the Foscara galley companies.
Source: ASVe, GrM, folder 250, reg. 2.

this setup allowed for the distribution of any investment returns, typically made alongside the investors of other ships, in the procurement of specific goods through partnerships known as *maone*. This strategic collaboration and investment framework shows the critical role of galley companies in managing and mitigating the financial and operational risks associated with maritime ventures.[35]

The decision to sell shares was not mandatory and hinged on two key factors. Firstly, it depended on the financial stability of the entity winning the ship's charter bid. The state required sufficient financial guarantees to accept a bid, demonstrating the bidder's company's solidity.[36] It follows that the intention to retain a greater number of shares in a galley company necessitated higher personal guarantees. Secondly, holding the majority of shares granted control over the company, similar to modern corporations, thereby offering a larger profit margin should the voyage prove successful. Furthermore, controlling the majority also allowed the shareholder to appoint individuals to the company's management, chosen either for personal trustworthiness or for the advantageous contacts they could bring.

The financial guarantees and their implications for the Foscari *fraterna* are elusive due to the absence of additional contemporary records on the family's economic ventures. Nonetheless, the Foscari family's standing among Venice's elite is undeniable, even if Giovanni's lineage did not occupy the most illustrious branch.[37] The existing accounts from the galley voyages provide insight into Foscari's financial strategies. In the formation of galley companies, only a fraction of shares were sold: in the first venture, Foscari sold a third (8 out of 24 shares, each valued at approximately 10 *lire di grossi*), and in the second, he sold slightly over half (see Figure 1.1). This approach was notably aggressive, with Foscari's investment being twice the usual amount as patrons typically acquired eight shares, entrusting the remainder to external investors.[38] The allocation of shares was particularly concentrated in the first venture, involving only four partners, and more dispersed in the second, with nine different entities. With Giovanni retaining a majority stake in both ventures, the question arises: who were the financial contributors? In the 1463 venture, three investors divided the shares: Orsatto Giustinian di Marco, Giacomo Francesco Priuli and brothers (with a share each), and Triadano Gritti's company (holding six shares). In 1467, ownership was more diversified, with investments mainly from the Priuli brothers-in-law totalling four shares, Alvise, Giovanni's brother, with two shares, Nicolò Gussoni, a brother-in-law, with one, and Nicolò Cocco, a nephew, also holding one share.[39]

Let us delve deeper into the profiles of these key figures. While direct documentary evidence linking Orsatto Giustinian to Giovanni Foscari remains elusive, Giustinian's significant influence and achievements in mid-15th-century Venice are undisputed. His diplomatic skill and prestigious political offices, including his role as Dogal elector for Doges Pasquale Malipiero in 1457 and Cristoforo Moro in 1462, and his 1459 Procurator of San Marco appointment, underscore his prominent status. The question arises: what led Giustinian to invest in the company of a relatively uninfluential merchant? The first clue may lie in the Giustinian family's well-established role as financial and commercial intermediaries in Northern Europe, notably in Flanders and England.[40] A second, more speculative link, involves the intertwining of familial and political interests: Orsato was a Dogal elector alongside Giovanni's father, Marco, in 1462.[41] Could it be that during this time, Marco promoted his son as a reliable merchant for investment? This, of course, remains a hypothesis to be proven. But it would explain his interest in Foscari's travels.

In the investment landscape of 1463, the remaining investors can be linked to the Foscari family through marital alliances. Focusing on the same year, Francesco Priuli acquired a share of the galley company. He was a member of a prominent Venetian noble family with historical marital ties to the Foscari. This connection began with the union between Doge Francesco Foscari and Maria Priuli in 1396 and was further cemented in 1450 when Antonio Priuli married Maria Foscari, who was none other than Giovanni's sister. Antonio, son of Lorenzo and brother to Francesco—who invested in the 1463–64 voyage—and Piero, Girolamo, and Zuan Francesco—who invested in the 1467–68 voyage—were deeply involved in the Foscari's business ventures. Beyond his investment in the galley company, Francesco Priuli loaded various goods on board, both in the name of his own family firm (which included his brother Antonio as a named partner, contributing 1,400 ducats) and in partnership with Alvise Foscari, the patron's brother (for 1,200 ducats).[42] The third investor was Triadano Gritti, who through his family firm, dispatched goods valued at 5,500 ducats, plus an additional 600 in the name of the Gritti-Foscari company. The reasons behind Gritti's participation in the galley company were multiple. The first was linked to his interests in Northern Europe, which he, as an heir to one of Venice's wealthiest families and with a robust political and commercial career, had cultivated—enabling him to invest in the galley company also of another Flanders-bound galley in the 1467 voyage, particularly that captained by Lorenzo Loredan.[43] The second reason was personal, related to his connection with the galley's patron; Triadano was the father-in-law of Giovanni Foscari, having married his daughter Paola Gritti. Triadano was not the only in-law to send goods northward; his sons, Omobuono and Luca, also invested in the galley, albeit with significantly lower amounts. It is noteworthy that while the father invested the family company's funds, the sons traded independently with their personal capital. As mentioned, despite being full members of the family firm, it was possible for the sons to trade on their own,[44] safeguarding the family's social capital and creating their own modest fortunes.[45] The accounts of the Gritti family are particularly revealing of the Venetian mindset with respect to attributing personal or business reasons. Luca Gritti's accounts, which included cargo on the ship (primarily spices and spice powders) and capitalized on favourable currency exchanges through bills of exchange between Venice and London, are settled within the Gritti family firm accounts, where his father Triadano was the named partner. This was particularly true for debts or expenses,[46] highlighting a lack of clear separation between the interests of the family firm's partners and the firm itself: it is evident that personal liabilities were expected to be settled by the family firm if necessary. This ambiguity and potential confusion are well-documented, as seen in Marco Bembo's letter to his correspondent in Bruges, and subsequently, in the Venetian judicial archives of the period. For Foscari, who maintained the majority share in the galley company, the first voyage was financed with family capital. In contrast, the second voyage saw individual investments by the brothers Giovanni and Alvise, who separately contributed to both the galley company and the ship's cargo.[47]

The venture companies, which demanded variable and minor investments from Venetian medieval merchants, were particularly advantageous for the younger entrepreneurs. These ventures allowed them to invest modest sums into trade, safeguarding their capital while concurrently building a reputable *buona fama*—an asset of significant value in the Venetian era. Furthermore, the use of temporary joint companies and commission agents exemplified here provided family businesses with the means to strategically diversify their investments. This approach mitigated excessive financial exposure, enabling these firms to remain agile and competitive in the international marketplace. Simultaneously, it postponed the necessity within the Venetian lagoon to transition towards more modern corporate structures, like joint-stock companies, highlighting a careful balance between tradition and innovation in Venetian commerce.[48] These temporary joint ventures were characterized by their diverse structures and modes of participation, focusing primarily on the transaction of a single type of merchandise. They divided ownership among participants, while delegating the tasks of purchasing and selling to a sole agent. One illustrative case involved the collaboration between Alvise Foscari and the Priuli brothers, formulated to dispatch spices, pharmaceuticals, and cotton to Northern Europe.[49] For an in-depth examination of this business model, attention is directed towards the family enterprise operated by Alvise Michiel from 1470 to 1481. In this timeframe, the enterprise was uniquely represented by Alvise, who orchestrated operations alongside his son Silvestro until Silvestro's demise in 1474 following a journey to Syria.[50] The

Table 1.1 Temporary joint ventures involving Alvise Michiel.

Year	*Merchandise*	*Partners and share distribution*	*Intermediary*	*Sum (ducats)*
1474	Alum powder	Alvise Michiel (1/3), Vittore Soranzo di Nicolò (1/3), Marco e Antonio Loredan (1/3)		468
1474	Myrrh	Alvise Michiel (1/2), Piero Malipiero q. Dario (1/2)	Nicolò Contarini, cousin	135
1474	San Matteo wool	Alvise Michiel (1/4), Unknown partners (3/4)	Alvise Loredan	78
1475	Silver bullion	Alvise Michiel (1/2), Nicolò Soranzo di Mafio (1/2)		145
1477	Scrap sugars	Alvise Michiel (1/3), Leonardo Contarini (1/3), Domenico Bembo, brother-in-law (1/3)	Domenico Bembo, brother-in-law	n.n.
1479	Silver bullion	Alvise Michiel (2/3), Nicolò Corner, brother-in-law (1/3)		210
1480	Pepper	Alvise Michiel (2/3), Marco Corner, brother-in-law (1/3)		241
1480	Clove barrels	Alvise Michiel (1/2), Nicolò Corner, brother-in-law (1/2)		169
1480	Pepper	Alvise Michiel (1/3), Andrea Corner, brother-in-law (1/3), Polo Colbbrauch from Vienna (1/3)	Andrea Corner, brother-in-law	336

Source: ASVe, MG, folder 15, reg. 2

primary source for this analysis is the enterprise's account ledger. As mentioned before, this document records, adhering to Venetian conventions, all financial activities encompassing household expenditures, business transactions, and real estate management both in Venice and on the Mainland. This alternative perspective seeks to illuminate the routine deployment of temporary joint ventures in daily commercial activities and their application to specific types of transactions. Over the course of approximately ten years, Alvise Michiel executed transactions worth tens of thousands of ducats. His capital was allocated across a diverse array of ventures, characterized by varying seasonal and annual intensities. Despite his extensive commercial operations and the absence of other named partners during this period, Michiel was involved in fewer than ten companies focused on the buying and selling of goods. The broader context of these companies' dealings remains largely unknown, as transaction details were typically recorded in a separate ledger (Table 1.1).

The composition of the companies reveals that they were not established to manage substantial investments. Only two of the companies engaged capital exceeding 300 ducats, with the rest allocating less than 250 ducats each,[51] suggesting that risk-sharing was not a primary motivation behind their formation for Michiel. Notably, an analysis of the members involved in these companies highlights a prevalent trend: six out of nine feature members from Michiel's extended family or close associates as partners or intermediaries. These include the Corner brothers, who served as Michiel's agents, Domenico Bembo, and Nicolò Contarini. Domenico Bembo[52] became a relative by marriage to Angela, the sister of the three Corner brothers, stressing the Corner *fraterna*'s significant role in Michiel's ventures. Nicolò Contarini, Michiel's cousin, though the precise familial connection remains unspecified, was closely associated with our merchant, acting as his representative in Syria.[53] This pattern emphasizes the influence of familial and close personal connections in the formation and operation of Michiel's business ventures.[54]

In the context of the remaining partners, the Soranzo family firm holds significant importance. For years, Nicolò Soranzo and his son Vittore were consistent business allies of Michiel, representing one of Venice's most affluent and distinguished households.[55] Nevertheless, the alliance with the Soranzos faced disruptions due to disputes in a venture established in the early 1470s for the procurement of alum powder. The conflict arose over disagreements concerning the precise allocation of shares, leading Alvise Michiel to present his case against Vittore and the other partners, Marco and Antonio Loredan, to the Court of Petitions.[56] Initiating legal action against a business associate was not undertaken lightly; it typically followed extensive negotiations, carried out directly and through written correspondence, and threats, proceeding to litigation only when compromise seemed unattainable. As will be explored in the next chapters, particularly through Marco Bembo's letters, initiating a lawsuit was indeed aimed at securing what was owed and rebalance power relations through the use of public institutions. However, it also represented a challenge to the accused's integrity, suggesting a breach of the traditional virtues of honour and word expected from a reputable merchant. This perspective is validated by the fact that Michiel's lawsuit against the Soranzos marked a significant rupture in their relationship, effectively ending any further business dealings between them. This action had indeed serious implications of undermining the traditional expectations of merchant behaviour, in an era where controlling international traders was challenging and word and honour were paramount. Temporary commercial partnerships were strategically employed for financing voyages, minimizing transactional exposure, accessing new markets or networks through partnerships, and reinforcing bonds with agents and partners by aligning interests.[57] The Michiel family firm's engagement in less than ten such partnerships over a decade, all of relatively minor economic value, points to their strategic use primarily for market access, notably the Syrian market, and for solidifying partnerships. The success of these ventures, typically established among Venice-resident merchants, emphasizes the central role of agents and factors in driving the success of family firms in the international trade arena.

Family, Agents, and International Trade

For the success of these companies, typically established among merchants residing in Venice, the crucial role of agents and factors for the international trade success of family firms is evident. To manage trade from Venice, Alvise Michiel, like most Venetian merchants, relied on a network of commission agents in the major trading ports of the time, as will be discussed in Chapter 5. The choice to compensate the agent with a commission on sales, rather than sharing profits, has been practised in Venice since the 14th century. As highlighted by Frederic Lane, there were essentially two reasons for this. First, profit sharing would effectively create a sort of stable partnership, which could act as a subsidiary of the family firm abroad, where one of the partners (the agent) had only limited responsibility. Second, this arrangement would add continuous negotiation to determine the actual value of the shipped goods, to then calculate the exact profit to be distributed, and the difficulty, for the resident merchant, to access the accounting of an agent who was also a 'passive' business partner.[58] In the Venetian business and familial context, it is important to remember that one of the primary objectives was the preservation of family wealth. Thus, all these mechanisms, from anonymous companies to commissioned agents, should be interpreted as attempts to keep the business and family wealth undivided. This is probably why *fraterne* chose members of other companies, those from their respective families, as their agents, thereby managing both their own activities and others' as an agent. Why venture into serving other merchants? In Venice, acting as an agent for others was the primary method for acquiring international market experience, building a solid reputation (beneficial upon returning to Venice), establishing trustworthy relationships, and beginning to amass personal wealth. The experiences of Giovanni Foscari and Alvise Michiel illuminate this practice.

During his voyages to Flanders, Giovanni Foscari served as an agent for several Venetian merchants. By charging 2% on sales and 3% on purchases, Foscari amassed 470 ducats in commissions in 1464 and 510 in 1468.[59] These commissions, along with his 300-ducat salary as the ship's patron and profits from his personal transactions, provided Foscari with a modest but solid financial base. These earnings enabled him to pursue additional investments, progressively building his personal capital.[60] The Michiel case offers a contrasting perspective: as the residing merchant and sole named partner of his family firm, Alvise was compelled to rely on commission agents from the outset. The selection of agents was primarily based on two factors: reputation and the ability to exercise oversight. In terms of reputation, only merchants who had spent time abroad and demonstrated their capabilities could establish a good name and become desirable agents. For instance, the Dandolo brothers, Marino and Francesco, exemplify this. The Foscari ledger entries reveal that the brothers had been active in the English and Flemish markets since the 1450s. Specializing in the textile trade, they served as key contacts for Venetian merchants operating in Flemish and British hubs for decades. And this expertise likely contributed to their role as Alvise Michiel's agents in Bruges between 1470 and 1476.[61]

However, reputation was not the sole factor influencing the choice of an agent. Equally, if not more critical, was the resident merchant's ability to influence the agent's actions. The most straightforward strategy to achieve this was to select an agent who was subject to the jurisdiction of Venetian courts. This way, any misconduct could be pursued legally. Yet, the Venetian commercial courts faced challenges in enforcing judgements, as evident from the records of the Judges of

Petition, which often required merchants to repeatedly appear before the judges to ensure compliance with the court's decisions. To circumvent this issue, an alternative was to choose agents who had a strong connection with the resident merchant, with the most significant and valued link in Venice being familial. While there were exceptions, it was generally safer to build one's network of agents on family ties. The Michiel case exemplifies this strategy, demonstrating how leveraging familial connections could effectively manage and control commercial operations. In the wake of his eldest son Silvestro's premature death, Alvise Michiel faced the challenge of identifying a commission agent from among less closely related family connections, given the youth of his remaining children. This led him to rely on his wife's brothers, particularly brother-in-law Andrea Corner, who took on a central role within the Michiel firm as both agent and trusted advisor. Following Silvestro's demise in 1472, Andrea emerged as the firm's primary agent. Although he did not serve exclusively—since Corner also managed his own business interests—his efforts for Michiel were concentrated on Southern Italy and Egypt. Andrea's strategic insight was instrumental during the initial stages of the Venetian-Ottoman war, helping the Michiel firm to pivot its investment from the spice and silk trades, which were hampered by the conflict, to olive oil and woollen cloth markets.[62] It is important to note that Michiel's approach to agency was dual-layered: the first layer was represented by dynamic individuals like Silvestro and later Andrea, who could navigate multiple trading hubs, showcasing a broad understanding of various markets. The second layer consisted of more stationary agents, often locals with deep knowledge of the region's commercial traditions, facilitating deeper integration of Venetian firms into these markets. This agency structure allowed the Michiel family firm to adapt during the turbulent wartime period of the first Venetian-Ottoman war, focusing on alternative trade goods that not only preserved existing commercial relationships but also ensured profitability amidst shifting market demands.[63]

The relationship between the resident merchant and the agent required meticulous attention. To strengthen this bond, various strategies could be employed. The first involved their participation in temporary commercial partnerships, effectively making the agent a stakeholder in the business. Another common approach among Venetian resident merchants was to manage some affairs in Venice on behalf of their agents, fostering a mutual dependency that made it more challenging to deviate from established rules and agreements. This practice is illustrated in the Michiel account books. In 1481, the Corner family faced a minor crisis: sisters Lucrezia and Bianca were to be married to Nicolò Pisani and Fantino Contarini, respectively, necessitating the payment of their dowries.[64] Brothers Marco and Nicolò, responsible for the sisters' dowries, were abroad and temporarily unable to liquidate the necessary funds, approximately 10,000 ducats. To circumvent issues with the families of their new brothers-in-law, the Corners turned to Alvise Michiel for assistance. The resident merchant then facilitated part of the payment in cash and partly through the commitment of real estate, a warehouse-home located in San Samuele. This reciprocal business care could be directly requested by agent-partners, as in Michiel's case,[65] or offered unilaterally by the resident merchant. In the latter scenario, creating a morally indebted situation could foster a favourable relationship between the two parties. The dynamics of agency relationships and control strategies will be detailed in Chapter 5.

Accounting Practices in Family Organizations: A Management Tool

The management of family businesses and the increasing complexities they faced in the growing Mediterranean economy of the medieval period, as well as the need to track economic trends and enhance capital control, historically drove the adoption of sophisticated accounting methods. The introduction of Indo-Arabic numerals in the 11th century, facilitated by Leonardo Fibonacci's seminal work 'Liber Abaci', marked a significant advancement in commercial calculation. This development, along with improvements in writing tools, not only simplified record-keeping procedures but also refined accounting techniques to ensure more effective performance and user-friendly practices. However, it was during the medieval period in Italy that the use of double-entry bookkeeping emerged as a revolutionary method of recording commercial and financial transactions.[66]

The evolution of company records has closely paralleled the changing needs of businesses, particularly in response to the expansion of trade and the growth of trading companies. Until the 13th century, the relatively modest scale of businesses and the local scope of their economic activities necessitated simple record-keeping systems appropriate for municipal or regional trading environments.[67] During this era, 'tabular' entries became widely adopted for recording and balancing a company's credits and debits. It's important to note that these entries did not represent legally enforceable obligations but were viewed as mature administrative practices within business accounting.[68] Tabular entries, widely recognized by historians as precursors to the double-entry system, featured a straightforward layout. Despite resembling the format of double-entry bookkeeping, with debits on the left and credits on the right, tabular entries had significant differences.[69] Firstly, these entries strictly recorded debits and credits without considering them binding obligations. Secondly, they typically included simple annotations of received credits or paid debits without detailed cross-references to corresponding offsets. This absence of precise cross-referencing has sparked considerable debate among accounting historians regarding the criteria for identifying the use of double-entry bookkeeping.[70]

The economic expansion in Italy during the 13th and 14th centuries, however, necessitated more advanced accounting techniques to monitor the increasingly complex and geographically dispersed activities of businesses. Prior to this period, the simpler recording methods were adequate for the scope of operations. These methods, which were akin to memoranda rather than detailed account entries, sufficed for the less complex trading practices of the time. They did not detail transactions meticulously—whether involving cash or barter—but rather made simple notations of claims related to business dealings. As commerce grew and the internal structures of companies became more intricate, these rudimentary systems proved inadequate for the demands of managing widespread economic interests. The need for a more systematic approach became apparent, especially for travelling merchants whose accounts until the 13th century were typically straightforward and lacked the comprehensive transactional details necessary for larger scale operations. This shift marked a crucial turning point in the development of accounting practices, steering towards methods that could provide a clearer and more accurate reflection of a company's financial activities across diverse markets.[71]

By the latter half of the 13th century, the limitations of simple debit and credit recordings became apparent as commerce expanded. Merchants required a more analytical approach to their accounting to comprehensively assess all economic and equity elements. This need led to the development of methods that could systematically account for all variations in assets and liabilities, reflecting the growing complexity and geographical spread of their business operations.

Double-entry bookkeeping emerged as a revolutionary system that enabled merchants to track their assets and liabilities with greater precision by recording each transaction in at least two accounts. This system hinged on the principle of duality, ensuring that every transaction was accounted for with corresponding debit and credit entries. The adoption of double-entry bookkeeping was a gradual evolution, largely driven by the need to oversee the activities of agents who acted like the company's extensions in foreign ports.[72] This practice was commonplace among Venetian family enterprises, where multiple members of the family engaged not only in Venice but also across global markets, advancing the operations of the family business. These agents managed the business remotely without the capability to instantly relay changes in the company's capital. Ensuring that accounts were meticulously up-to-date was a major priority.[73] Consequently, agents were required to regularly and promptly communicate updates, allowing to 'adjust the books' in Venice.[74] These updates were typically derived from the accounting books that agents maintained for their own use, which, in the Venetian context, have rarely survived.[75] These records could employ various accounting methods, ranging from simple bookkeeping to double-entry systems. Agents transmitted their financial accounts within letters to merchants based in Venice, who then integrated this information into their official ledgers. The agents' and intermediaries' books provide insights that are often absent from the ledgers of Venetian firms and have predominantly come to us through transcriptions of commercial correspondence sent by the agents to their Venice-based merchant partners. This correspondence includes details on operations conducted in foreign ports. For example, the accounts that Francesco Zisberto sent from Damascus to Marco Bembo include descriptions of legal actions initiated by Damascene merchants against Zisberto, who acted as Bembo's legal representative locally. These accounts also detail demands from these merchants for negotiations over merchandise pricing, involving the Qadi courts on one side, and the agents and Venetian community locally on the other.[76] The role of the consul in these disputes is of particular interest, as he often effectively facilitated negotiations that led to reduced merchandise prices.[77] The role of the consul will be explored in more detail in the next chapter. Additionally, the educational background and training of merchants and agents will be examined in Chapter 5.

This transition marked a significant advancement in financial management, providing merchants with a clearer understanding of their financial standing and aiding in the more effective management of their expansive trade networks. The system was based on the fundamental principle of duality, where every transaction had both a debit and credit component. The switch to double-entry bookkeeping, like all innovations, was a gradual process and mostly linked to the need to keep track of the work of the agents, which, as said, acted as the company's representatives in foreign ports.[78] While the genesis of accounting methods, particularly double-entry bookkeeping, is commonly attributed to Northern Italy, regional variations within Italy are noteworthy. Each area exhibited unique developments in accounting techniques, though they shared several fundamental similarities. The oldest and most numerous accounting records originate from Tuscany, leading some to believe that double-entry bookkeeping first emerged there before spreading to other regions.[79] However, it is more accurate to recognize that this advanced accounting system developed concurrently across several major Italian cities during the same period. These cities included Genoa, various Tuscan centres, and Venice. Each played a pivotal role in the evolution of these methods, influenced by their respective economic complexities and the need for more sophisticated financial oversight. This simultaneous development reinforces the widespread recognition among Italian merchants of the benefits that double-entry bookkeeping offered for managing their increasingly intricate business affairs.[80] In Tuscany, the approach to accounting during the Renaissance exhibited unique characteristics that set it apart from practices in other Northern Italian cities like Milan, Genoa, and Venice. One key difference is the extensive use of multiple accounting books by Tuscan companies, a practice not as prevalent in the other cities mentioned. Tuscan firms maintained a rich array of records, reflecting a more comprehensive and detailed method of documenting administrative events. This extensive use of multiple books allowed Tuscan businesses to capture a broader range of financial activities and provided a more granular view of their operations.[81]

As mentioned, double-entry bookkeeping involves recording each financial transaction in two separate accounts: one as a debit and the other as a credit. This system ensures that all economic activities affecting the company are mirrored in these entries. Essentially, each transaction leads to the creation of a balance, wherein entries are allocated to specific accounts reflecting the nature of the transaction. The accounts in this system compile records that monitor the initial state of a financial element and track its changes over time. This method enables the management of circular investments and complex supply chains, such as Marco Bembo's operations with wine barrels in Crete or the management of commodity chains that involve transferring goods to third-party companies, such as the Feltrian wool cloths. Such business operations were feasible due to the interconnected accounting systems, which enabled merchants to meticulously monitor each phase of the process. This ensured that the minimum selling prices covered the invested capital and facilitated the organic control of corporate capital, extending beyond isolated transactions. Such meticulous management facilitated the harmonization of investments, allowing a merchant like Alvise Michiel, for instance, to cyclically reinvest capital while avoiding excessive financial exposure (see, for instance, Figure 3.8).[82]

The key principle of double-entry bookkeeping is balance: every transaction is entered twice, in corresponding debit and credit sections, ensuring that the sum of all debits equals the sum of all credits. This method provides a comprehensive view of a company's financial health, allowing for accurate tracking of assets, liabilities, and equity changes through systematic record-keeping. In double-entry bookkeeping, each business transaction is recorded by specifying which accounts are affected and the nature of their impact, whether as a debit or a credit. This accounting method adheres to a systematic set of rules governing the format, sequence, and procedures for making entries into the accounts. Consequently, each transaction results in at least two simultaneous entries in separate accounts. These entries can be adjacent or opposing, ensuring that the totals in the Debit column exactly match those in the Credit column. This coordination across accounts helps maintain the fundamental accounting equation where assets equal liabilities plus equity. Thus, double-entry bookkeeping provides a clear, structured way to capture all dimensions of a company's financial transactions, enhancing the accuracy and reliability of financial reporting.[83]

During the 14th–16th centuries in Venice, the primary accounting records comprised two types of books: the journal and the ledger. The journal, known locally as the '*zornal*', served as a comprehensive daily record of managerial activities. Entries in the journal were documented in a sequential manner, reflecting the order of transactions as they occurred day by day. This method ensured a systematic and chronological compilation of all financial operations. The journal served as a comprehensive daily record of management activities, systematically cataloguing each transaction in chronological order to provide a clear sequence of financial events. This meticulous recording facilitated the orderly transfer of entries to the '*mastro*' or '*quaderno*'—the principal book where the entirety of the company's accounts was managed. In simpler organizational structures, transactions might be recorded directly in the ledger, omitting the journal altogether. Additionally, for preliminary notes, merchants often used a memoir, also known as a '*vacchetta*' or '*brogliaccio*' (translated as 'little book' due to its usual compact size), where brief entries were made before their detailed inclusion in the journal or ledger. This layered approach to record-keeping ensured thorough documentation and enhanced clarity in financial management.[84]

Registers such as the Michiel ledger embody the 'Venetian-style' accounting format. This style features accounts arranged in parallel on two adjacent pages, categorized under Debit and Credit across the two opposing sections of the notebook. Each entry is headed by a title that summarizes all economic activities related to a particular subject or various kinds of expenses and revenues. Each entry is cross-referenced with its counterpart, not directly across but indicated in the consignment on another page. In contrast, the Foscari ledgers, while similar in annotation style to the Michiel's, adopt a more streamlined approach described by Lane as 'venture-like'. This approach consolidates transactions related to a single deal or contact within individual accounts, aiming to centralize all pertinent information.

The closure of entries in these ledgers often coincides with the conclusion of the business transactions they record, necessitating swift and definitive account settlements. Unlike the extensive detail found in *fraterna* ledgers like Michiel's, where accounts include comprehensive records of transactions, payments, and deferred payments, the Foscari ledgers present more succinct accounts. These are organized under specific headings related to distinct transactions or items, with a clear focus on closing accounts quickly without the complexities of payment scheduling.[85]

To better understand the structure of the two ledgers, it is essential to describe both the overall structure of the ledger and the individual accounts within it. Each ledger starts with sections labelled '*per rason de chrededori*' (Credit) and '*rason de debittori*' (Debit) to summarize accounts still open from previous ledgers. Pages are dual-numbered, with Arabic numerals for Debit and Roman for Credit, ensuring each facing page pair corresponds. Dormant accounts are marked as concluded and crossed out. Each account begins by documenting related persons or goods, noting the date and location. Transactions typically involve at least two, often four entries (two in Debit and two in Credit), providing detailed transaction records. These descriptions include quantities, intermediaries, payment methods, and are followed by monetary amounts categorized into *lire*, *denari grossi*, *soldi*, and *piccoli*.[86] Roman numerals are used for listing quantities to reduce the risk of falsification, while Arabic numerals tally the sums to ensure accurate and secure record-keeping. To distinguish initial entries from their counterparts, terms like '*a l'inchonttro*' are used. The term '*tratto netto*' often appears at account closures, indicating the net trading result, which does not equate to profit as it excludes the cost of goods sold. Balanced accounts facilitate the quick identification of losses. If accounts are well maintained and expenses exceed revenue, losses are recorded as '*per danno seguito*'. If a transaction extends beyond the space available or continues into a new period, it can be transferred to a new account on a different page of the same ledger, typically indicated by '*per il resto porto avanti*'.[87]

The structure of accounting records, though not formalized by any treaty until the 15th century, displayed remarkable uniformity across central and northern Italy. This consistency likely arose from the protective and validating roles that meticulous bookkeeping, particularly double-entry accounting, fulfilled in the mercantile settings of the medieval and Renaissance periods. Furthermore, these records also possessed public credibility. In addition to their legal significance in judicial proceedings, accounting books served as a trusted medium that not only verified proper capital management but also demonstrated appropriate merchant conduct. Consequently, it was common practice to request updates from correspondents to correct any discovered errors or adjust for payment settlements conducted across different markets.[88]

In conclusion, the development and meticulous application of accounting systems, particularly double-entry bookkeeping, were central in the management and control of family firms, agents, and corporate capital throughout the medieval and Renaissance periods. These systems allowed merchants to efficiently oversee extensive trade networks and complex international transactions. By enabling precise tracking of assets and liabilities and facilitating a comprehensive view of the company's financial health, accounting practices played a critical role in the strategic planning and sustainability of businesses. This was especially crucial in managing the activities of agents across diverse markets, ensuring that family wealth remained intact and that corporate capital was optimized. These accounting advancements not only supported the operational needs of the firms but also provided the necessary legal documentation to protect their economic interests in court.[89] The evolution of these accounting methods reflects a response to the increasing complexity of business activities and the need for more sophisticated financial oversight.

Advantages, Disadvantages, and Comparisons

The enduring preference for family-based business forms in Venice, and the slow adoption of joint-stock companies that can be observed since the 16th century reflect not a lack of cultural progress but an advanced integration of economic and familial values. This approach propelled the Venetian state to develop innovative commercial support mechanisms, establishing Venice as a coveted trading partner. The primacy of the *fraterna*, or family firm, and its dominance over other business models yielded several clear benefits. Foremost among these was the complete control retained by the family over the company's decisions regarding trade investments and, alternatively, manufacturing ventures. This control extended to estate management, with inheritances typically staying within the family, thus pursued with vested interest by heirs and estate administrators, often overlapping roles within the familial circle.

Moreover, this system allowed all family members, including brothers and cousins, to actively contribute to and benefit from the company's successes, thus supporting the family's economic well-being through their efforts. It is noteworthy that not all family members were involved in the commercial enterprise, with many directed towards religious vocations or political careers.[90] The political sphere was particularly vital for Venetian family businesses, as it enabled control over State resources to be channelled towards merchant sector development, a topic explored in the forthcoming chapter. Public navigation, trade protections, monopoly or quasi-monopoly privileges, and diplomatic efforts were essential for Venetian firms, which, despite their modest size, leveraged political capital effectively. This blending of public and private interests, coupled with significant investments in the commercial sector, fostered a pervasive mercantile culture within Venice. This culture supported a multitude of small- and medium-sized enterprises, which, from the 14th century onwards, allowed Venice to maintain its significance in the Mediterranean. This was despite a shift in the *fraterne*' investment strategies towards land acquisitions since the 15th century, illustrating a strategic pivot that preserved Venice's status as a key Mediterranean player amidst evolving commercial dynamics.

The complexities of the *fraterne* manifest not only in their strengths but also in their vulnerabilities. Central to these challenges is the involvement of all eligible male family members in the operations of the family firm' where each served as a legal representative. This structure could introduce complications in the event of an unexpected death, affecting the delineation between personal and corporate affairs and the resolution of debts, credits, sales, purchases, and any disputes arising from independently managed foreign market activities. Consequently, as explored further in this book, merchants emphasized the importance of receiving both updates and accounting records from their partners to ensure their ledgers accurately reflected all transactions and to safeguard against potential disputes.

This centralized business model led to two significant outcomes. First, there was an inherent need for numerous commission agents to be deployed across strategic ports, necessitating sophisticated control and management strategies for their activities. These efforts were both time-consuming and not guaranteed to yield success. Hence, state intervention became fundamental, serving as a de facto merchants' guild for these enterprises that would otherwise struggle to assert their influence in both local and global markets.[91] The structure of the *fraterne*, characterized by a streamlined workforce, reliance on personal capital, and a strategic approach to financial exposure to preserve family assets, necessitated the adoption of venture companies, such as galley companies or temporary partnerships, as a means to navigate the intricacies of international trade.

These temporary companies, despite their finite lifespan, provided distinct advantages that aligned with the Venetian merchants' needs without necessitating long-term commitment or collaboration. Consider the case of the galley company, as seen for the Foscari case, as an illustrative example. Key among these advantages was the ability for patrons to distribute the significant expenses related to armament and navigation, as well as share the inherent risks of maritime ventures. Moreover, these arrangements fostered stronger bonds with business partners while enabling patrons to retain substantial control over the company by holding a majority of the shares. This strategic shareholding allowed for the reallocation of freed-up capital towards new ventures, enhancing the family firms' investment agility. The strategic employment of temporary commercial entities and familial agents (including extended family members) met the critical requirements of Renaissance commerce: minimizing business risk, ensuring control over assets and operations, and maintaining market adaptability. The relatively low commitment associated with these partnerships allowed Venetian merchants unparalleled flexibility in their investment strategies, enabling them to capitalize on emerging market opportunities swiftly.[92] The deployment of agents, whether itinerant or based in foreign markets, served to reduce overhead costs associated with direct market presence (thanks to their commission-based remuneration) and offered operational flexibility in both investment choices and task delegation. This approach made it feasible to rapidly adjust or revoke assignments, ensuring that the most competent individuals were always in charge of executing specific tasks, thereby safeguarding and promoting the interests of the Venetian mercantile ventures.

Global commerce and local ties: Venetian, Armenian, and Indian Family Firms

Venice was not the only entity to cultivate a strong commercial orientation alongside a comprehensive set of trade management tools, all the while prioritizing familial connections and wealth at the centre of its network. This has been detected by studies on the Armenian trade network of the 17th century as well as the Indian diaspora in Iran and Russia in the 18th century.[93] The economic systems of Venice and New Julfa in the 17th century, though geographically and culturally distinct, shared commonalities in their commercial strategies and family-centred organizational structures. Both operated from central urban hubs, with Venice and New Julfa acting as gravitational centres attracting business from across their respective regions. Their success hinged on the amphibious development of trade routes, leveraging both land and sea pathways to access key ports and cities globally. Unlike Venetians, who developed a state-controlled maritime system to manage trade flows, Armenians did not establish a similar state navigation system. However, both societies built their economies around family firms led by resident merchants utilizing networks of agents and factors for international operations. Despite focusing on a diaspora, a similar emphasis on family connections can be observed within the Indian 'firm' operating in Astrakhan. This setup demonstrates either that the vast majority of Indians arriving in the city had family ties there or, if acting as agents, represented the interests of their family of origin. Moreover, a significant portion of their merchandise was sourced from relatives in either Iran or India. This practice, which began in the 17th century, remained robust until the 19th century when the diaspora shifted further up the Volga River, reaching Moscow, highlighting the central role of familial networks in sustaining commercial operations across generations and geographies.[94]

In Venice, agents often belonged to family firms, blending their independent business endeavours with services for other merchants. In contrast, New Julfa's merchants typically engaged agents through exclusive *commenda* contracts,[95] fostering longer-term, more stable relationships. This difference in stability stems from the contractual framework, which awarded agents a share of profits, thereby requiring detailed accounting and consistent communication to accurately allocate earnings. Venetian traders in the 15th century preferred arrangements that did not involve sharing profits. Positioned between these practices were the Indian diaspora in Russia, notable for forming *commenda* partnerships, especially with Russian traders outside the diaspora willing to accompany goods along the Volga River. This approach was selective, typically reserving riskier ventures for those outside the familial network, presumably to safeguard family firm members from potential dangers. This methodology reflects a clear strategy to mitigate risks while engaging in expansive trade networks.[96]

This arrangement was predicated on the contract's design, which rewarded agents with a profit share, requiring adept accounting and robust communication for accurate profit tracking. Unlike 15th-century Venetian merchants, who preferred profit-sharing arrangements, the Indian diaspora in Russia offers a nuanced middle ground. They engaged in *commenda* partnerships, especially with non-diaspora traders like the Russians, who would carry goods down the Volga River. This selective approach was aimed at reducing exposure to risk, particularly protecting family business interests by assigning riskier ventures to external partners. Cultural norms and specialized training played a significant role in shaping these strategic choices, highlighting how commercial cultures navigated risk, familial ties, and business strategies. Both Venice and the Indian diaspora emphasized rigorous training for prospective agents and merchants. In Venice, family-led training was the norm, as seen when Michiel sent his son to Alexandria under his uncle's tutelage to grasp the trade's fundamentals, showcasing the blend of risk management, family responsibility, and strategic commercial operations in diverse trading environments. New Julfa, however, institutionalized agent training through centralized schools. All systems sought agents within their territories for trust-based reasons. In New Julfa, the choice was driven by the agents' mercantile education and the resident merchant's proximity to the agent's family, fostering a sense of moral obligation and loyalty. This practice was less prevalent in Venice, where familial relations with agents were less stable, and scholars have likened New Julfa's approach to using family members as moral leverage in maintaining faithful agent relationships.[97]

Despite the apparent similarities, the underlying reasons for opting between commission-based agency contracts and profit-sharing agreements differ significantly. The key distinction arises from varying institutional factors. In the Venetian context, even though companies operated with a high degree of autonomy, there was notable state intervention in the economy. The existence of specific institutions, such as public navigation systems and mercantile courts, provided family businesses—many of which had members in the Senate—with the infrastructure to continue their commercial activities without the need for establishing overly stable or long-term agency relationships. The strategic use of public navigation and the preference for employing Venetian agents, who were often closely related by blood or marriage and engaged in their own trade, allowed Venetian merchants to minimize their need for external collaborations. This approach preserved the essential operational flexibility for intermediary firms while leveraging state-supported mechanisms to sustain their commercial ventures.

In the forthcoming chapter, we will delve into the support mechanisms established by the Venetian State for Venetian family firms engaging in international trade. These mechanisms include public navigation and the establishment of a consular network along with international treaties. Public navigation, consistently operational for over two centuries, facilitated stable relations with key economic entities of the era and played a vital role in safeguarding convoys laden with precious goods. The consulate served as Venice's official diplomatic presence in foreign territories, ensuring ongoing relations with local rulers. It functioned as the primary collector of customs duties and provided the initial legal recourse for disputes involving Venetian merchants. Moreover, consuls offered indispensable support to merchants aboard state galleys, aiding with both commercial and financial transactions.

Notes

1 Frederic C. Lane, 'Family Partnerships and Joint Ventures in the Venetian Republic', *The Journal of Economic History* 4, no. 2 (1944): 178.

2 Thomas Max Safley, *Family Firms and Merchant Capitalism in Early Modern Europe: The Business, Bankruptcy and Resilience of the Hoechstetters of Augsburg* (Abingdon, Oxon, New York: Routledge, 2019), 32–65.

3 Lane, 'Family Partnerships and Joint Ventures in the Venetian Republic', 178–79; Giuseppe Trebbi, 'La società veneziana', in *Storia di Venezia, VI, Dal Rinascimento al*

Barocco, ed. Gaetano Cozzi and Paolo Prodi (Roma: Istituto della Enciclopedia Italiana, 1994), 129–213.

4 Lane, 'Family Partnerships and Joint Ventures in the Venetian Republic'; Stefania Montemezzo, 'Fra pubblico e privato: la *fraterna* veneziana nel commercio del secondo Quattrocento', *Ricerche di Storia Economica e Sociale* 3 (2017): 7–34.

5 The estate, known today as the Castello dei Da Peraga, is located in the Padua region, to the northeast of the main city. Like many summer villas of the Venetian nobility, it is strategically situated along a watercourse, the Tergola, enabling the use of small boats for transporting farm produce and goods to Venice. About the Venetian presence in the Padua area: Marco Bolzonella, *Oltre i confini del dogado: l'espansione patrimoniale degli enti ecclesiastici veneziani nel Padovano (secoli IX-XIV)* (Roma: Viella, 2022), 13–25, 36–42, 100–02.

6 ASVe, MG, folder 15, reg. 2, ff. 3 *avere*, 34 *avere* and 47 *avere*. It is important to highlight that for the nobility, spending on food and drinks represented just a minor fraction of their wealth. On the other hand, for the lower socio-economic classes, expenditures on essential goods accounted for a significantly larger proportion of the household income. Carole Shammas, 'Standard of Living, Consumption, and Political Economy over the Past 500 Years', in *The Oxford Handbook of the History of Consumption*, ed. Frank Trentmann (Oxford University Press, 2012), 211–26.

7 Alvise was not the only Michiel brother to marry into a highly prestigious family; his brother Girolamo also married Paola Foscari, the daughter from the second marriage of Doge Francesco Foscari, and cousin to Giovanni, one of the protagonists of this book. ASVe, *Notarile Testamenti*, 1186/129; Giuseppe Gullino, *La saga dei Foscari: storia di un enigma* (Verona: Cierre, 2005), 123. The importance of marriage in forming business networks is also evident in other communities, such as the Sephardic Jews: Francesca Trivellato, *The Familiarity of Strangers: The Sephardic Diaspora, Livorno, and Cross-Cultural Trade in the Early Modern Period* (New Haven, CT, London: Yale University Press, 2009), 132–39.

8 ASVe, MG, folder 15, reg. 2, f. 48 *dare*.

9 Francesca Trivellato, 'Renaissance Florence and the Origins of Capitalism: A Business History Perspective', *Business History Review* 94, no. 1 (2020): 231–32.

10 Lane, 'Family Partnerships and Joint Ventures in the Venetian Republic', 184.

11 ASVe, MdC, folder 29, reg. 2, letter to Toma Zivran in Modon, 16 September 1472.

12 Marco Ferro, 'Commissaria', in *Dizionario del diritto comune e veneto*, ed. Marco Ferro(Venezia: Andrea Santini, 1845), 439–41.

13 ASVe, MG, folder 15, reg. 2, ff. 6 and 107.

14 ASVe, GrM, folder 250, reg. 2, ff. 2, 11, 17, 54. For the purposes of accuracy, I have relied directly on the archival source rather than a published edition: Mario Bulgarelli, ed., *Agostino Foscari. Viaggi di Alessandria e di Londra 1486–1496* (Venezia: La Malcontenta, 2015).

15 On the Venetian court of petitions: Giovanni Italo Cassandro, 'La curia di petizion e il diritto processuale di Venezia', *Archivio Veneto*, V, 19 (1936): 72–144; Giovanni Italo Cassandro, 'La curia di petizion e il diritto processuale di Venezia', *Archivio Veneto*, V, 20 (1937): 1–210.

16 ASVe, GrM, folder 251, file 3.

17 ASVe, GrM, folder 246, file 5.

18 ASVe, *Dieci Savi alle Decime in Rialto, Filze, Redecima 1514*, 67, San Simeon Piccolo 7,https://asve.arianna4.cloud/patrimonio/efffe76c-2568-4170-9145-bf6019f2aa57/marco-foscari-quondam-giovanni-31-08-1514.

19 Alessio Sopracasa, 'Passage au Levant. Le «voyage» de Candie-Constantinople de la compagnia Bembo dans la seconde moitié du xve siècle: organisation et séjour', *Cahiers d'études italiennes* 25 (2017): 9–10, https://doi.org/10.4000/cei.3499.

20 ASVe, MdC, folder 29, reg. 2, cc. 79v and following. Freddy Thiriet, 'Les lettres commerciales des Bembo et le commerce venitien dans l'Empire Ottoman à la fin du XVe siecle', in *Studi in onore di Armando Sapori*, vol. II (Milan: Istituto Editoriale Cisalpino,

1957), 911–33; Alberto Sacerdoti, 'Bembo Marco', in *Dizionario Biografico Degli Italiani* (Rome: Istituto della Enciclopedia Italiana, 1966), 127–28.

21 ASVe, MdC, folder 29, reg. 2, letter to Alberto Contarini in Bruges, 13 January 1483.

22 '*Ett perche ditte venderette per ell chorso per servirve di quello io debo io prendo amirazione de tal vostro dire, che alltra che non ve abi a dar chossa alguna quando vi dovesse le chose di la chomisaria del quondam ditto mio fradello sono ttotalmentte destinte ett separatte dalle mie ett io son per la minima parte di IIIII chomesarii, fra i quall ne la dona con uno fioll di anni XIIII per ell tutto. E per nome de i ditti ve scrivo chome di sopra ve ho naratto, che quello traxerette de ditti inzensi con quello ve attrovatte del suo remettette de qui a ditta chomesaria*'. ASVe, MdC, folder 29, reg. 2, letter to Alberto Contarini in Bruges, 13 January 1483.

23 Conversely, situations could arise where the surviving heirs refused to acknowledge a debt incurred by a deceased family member. This was evident when Marco Bembo was approached by Giovanni Da Ponte to mediate with Lorenzo Barbarigo's brother and executor of his will. Barbarigo's brother contended that, although the accounts indicated a debt, the deceased's records showed it as paid. This instance highlights how familial and personal dynamics could complicate the settlement of debts. ASVe, MdC, folder 29, reg. 2, letter to Alberto Contarini in Bruges, 6 July 1482.

24 The preservation of commercial documents, especially from Venice, requires some context. Unlike Tuscany, where extensive merchant family archives have survived, Venice typically did not maintain such records. According to Ugo Tucci, Venice valued only current economic data, deeming the long-term storage of correspondence unnecessary. Additionally, letters and registers lacked official status, further diminishing their perceived importance. However, the most significant loss occurred due to the archival purges of the 19th century, severely limiting available accounting records in Venice. Ugo Tucci, 'Costi e ricavi di una galera veneziana ai primi del Cinquecento', in *Mercanti, navi e monete nel Cinquecento veneziano* (Bologna: Il Mulino, 1981), 110; Trivellato, 'Renaissance Florence and the Origins of Capitalism', 231.

25 Edoardo Demo, 'Wool and Silk. The Textile Urban Industry of the Venetian Mainland (15th-17th Centuries)', in *At the Centre of the Old World. Trade and Manufacturing in Venice and the Venetian Mainland, 1400–1800*, ed. Paola Lanaro (Toronto: Centre for Reformation and Renaissance Studies, 2006), 217–44; Andrea Mozzato, 'The Production of Woollens in Fifteenth- and Sixteenth-Century Venice', in *At the Centre of the Old World. Trade and Manufacturing in Venice and the Venetian Mainland, 1400 – 1800*, ed. Paola Lanaro (Toronto: CRRS, 2006), 73–107.

26 Sergio Tognetti, 'Galeras estatales y veleros privados en la República Florentina del Cuatrocientos: la praxis mercantil', in *Navegación institucional y navegación privada en el Mediterráneo medieval*, ed. Raoul González Arévalo (Granada: Grupo de Investigación Toponimia, Historia y Arqueología del Reino de Granada, 2016), 105–44.

27 Frederic C. Lane, 'Venetian Merchant Galleys, 1300–1334: Private and Communal Operation', *Speculum* 38, no. 2 (1963): 179–205; Stefania Montemezzo, 'Ships and Trade: The Role of Public Navigation in Renaissance Venice', in *Reti marittime come fattori dell'integrazione europea / Maritime Networks as a Factor in European Integration,* (Florence: Firenze University Press, 2019), 473–84.

28 Claire Judde de Larivière, *Naviguer, commercer, gouverner: économie maritime et pouvoirs à Venise (XVe-XVIe siècles)* (Leiden, Boston: Brill, 2008), 124 and 276.

29 Lane, 'Family Partnerships and Joint Ventures in the Venetian Republic', 187–91.

30 Judde de Larivière, *Naviguer, commercer, gouverner*, 124–25.

31 Stefania Montemezzo, 'Galley Routes and Merchant Networks between Venice and the North Sea in the Fifteenth Century', in *Commercial Networks and European Cities, 1400–1800*, ed. Andrea Caracausi and Christof Jeggle (London: Pickering & Chatto, 2014), 153–69; Stefania Montemezzo, *Giovanni Foscari. Viaggi di Fiandra 1463–1464 e 1467–1468* (Venice: La Malcontenta, 2012). Biographical information on the Foscari family in Giuseppe Gullino, *Marco Foscari (1477–1551): l'attività*

politica e diplomatica tra Venezia, Roma e Firenze, (Milano: F. Angeli, 2000); Gullino, *La saga dei Foscari*; Giuseppe Gullino, 'Il clan dei Foscari: politica matrimoniale e interessi familiari (secc. XIV–XV)', *Studi veneziani* 54 (2007), https://doi.org/10.1400/99775.

32 This type of ledger is comprehensively analyzed in Tucci, 'Costi e ricavi di una galera veneziana ai primi del Cinquecento'.

33 This amounted to 28,000 ducats for the first voyage and 30,000 for the second, after accounting for financial transactions. ASVe, GrM, folder 250, reg. 2.

34 In his ledger, Foscari lists these individuals as '*caratisti*', specifying the precise number of shares they purchased. Thus, they appear not to be *plegi* of which we have no mention in the records.

35 Judde de Larivière, *Naviguer, commercer, gouverner*, 249–52.

36 Frederic Chapin Lane, *Venice, a Maritime Republic* (Baltimore, MD: Johns Hopkins University Press, 1973), 124–31; Judde de Larivière, *Naviguer, commercer, gouverner*, 123–35.

37 Gullino, 'Il clan dei Foscari'.

38 Judde de Larivière, *Naviguer, commercer, gouverner*, 132–35.

39 Additionally, we have insights into the nephew's situation from another source: a letter by Alvise Foscari, dispatched from Tripoli in April 1473, detailing Cocco's demise in Syria. Foscari expressed profound sorrow over the swift nature of Cocco's passing, which unfolded over three nights. Nevertheless, the correspondence swiftly shifts focus to pragmatic concerns, as Foscari inquires about the timing of Cocco's most recent will. ASVe, GrM, folder 250, reg. 2, cc. 70 *dare* e *avere*; ASVe, GrM, folder 189, file 1, miscellaneous documents.

40 Giorgio Ravegnani, 'Giustinian Orsotto', in *Dizionario Biografico Degli Italiani* (Roma: Istituto della Enciclopedia Italiana, 2001), 274–77; Giorgia Nordio, 'La colonia mercantile veneziana nella Londra di metà Quattrocento: attività commerciale e movimento anti-alien', in *Atti del congresso internazionale "Politiche del credito. investimento, consumo e solidarietà"*, eds. Gemma Boschiero and Barbara Molina(Asti: Cassa di risparmio di Asti, 2004), 222–40; Montemezzo, 'Galley Routes and Merchant Networks between Venice and the North Sea in the Fifteenth Century'.

41 ASVe, *Maggior Consiglio, Regina*, reg. 23, f. 39r, 40v (9 and 11 May 1462) via Benjamin G. Kohl, Andrea Mozzato, and Monique O'Connell, 'Rulers of Venice (1332–1554)', accessed 10 February 2024, http://rulersofvenice.org.

42 ASVe, *Giudici di Petizion, Sentenze a Giustizia*, reg. 195, c. 146r. Little is known about Alvise's biography, partly due to the merchant's untimely demise. Giuseppe Gullino, 'Francesco Foscari (detto Franzi)', in *Dizionario biografico degli italiani* (Roma: Istituto della Enciclopedia Italiana, 1997), 304–06.

43 The Flemish and English interests appear to be confirmed by Gritti's career, which saw him in his younger years as the patron of the same shipping line. Giuseppe Gullino, 'Triadano Gritti', in *Dizionario biografico degli italiani* (Roma: Istituto della Enciclopedia Italiana, 2002), 753–56. ASVe, GrM, folder 250, reg. 2, f. 72 avere.

44 Family members could be held accountable for liabilities arising from individual business transactions if creditors successfully demonstrated the association with the family enterprise and the absence of distinct accounting practices. In these scenarios, the Venetian courts, particularly the Court of Petitions, were tasked with evaluating each case on its individual merits.

45 Sebouh David Aslanian, *From the Indian Ocean to the Mediterranean: The Global Trade Networks of Armenian Merchants from New Julfa*, (Berkeley: University of California Press, 2014), 121–65.

46 ASVe, GrM, folder 250, reg. 2, c. 97 *dare* and *avere*.

47 This could indicate some underlying issues between the brothers, although the partnership was only dissolved later, upon the death of both. ASVe, GrM, folder 246, file 5.

48 Lane, 'Family Partnerships and Joint Ventures in the Venetian Republic'.

49 This refers to both processed and raw turbit (a root with laxative properties), zedoary (turmeric root, used for various purposes), and long pepper. ASVe, GrM, folder 250, reg, 2m cc. 60.

50 Stefania Montemezzo, 'Strategie familiari e commercio internazionale: i Michiel da San Barnaba', *Studi storici Luigi Simeoni* 65 (2015): 29–40.

51 For the enterprise engaged in the trade of scrap sugars, no data is available. This venture was initiated towards the end of the timeframe documented in Michiel's ledger, potentially leading to the absence of finalized records for this particular company.

52 From the San Cancian lineage, which constitutes a separate branch of the family in contrast to Marco, who belonged to the Della Riva del Carbon one. ASVe, *Miscellanea codici, Storia veneta (Genealogie Barbaro, vol. I A-B)*, b. 17, c. 320. Angelo Ventura, 'Giovanni Bembo', in *Dizionario biografico degli italiani* (Roma: Istituto della Enciclopedia Italiana, 1966), 117–19.

53 Nicolò Contarini was also the nephew of Leonardo Contarini, who was Michiel's partner in the scrap sugar business. Franco Rossi, 'Contarini Leonardo', in *Dizionario biografico degli italiani* (Rome: Istituto della Enciclopedia Italiana, 1983), 229–31.

54 Medieval Venetian small- and medium-sized enterprises are a clear example of familial and origin-based endogamy. In contrast, other communities, such as the Sephardic Jews, illustrate how business strategy often guided decisions, leading to partnerships with individuals of diverse backgrounds. Trivellato, *The Familiarity of Strangers*, 153–67. For a different perspective, see Ana Sofia Ribeiro, *Early Modern Trading Networks in Europe: Cooperation and the Case of Simon Ruiz*, (Abingdon, Oxon, New York: Routledge, Taylor & Francis Group, 2016), 123–29.

55 Both held the prestigious position of Procurators of San Marco, a highly coveted role within the Venetian administrative hierarchy. This detail is sourced from the database Kohl, Mozzato, and O'Connell, 'Rulers of Venice (1332–1554)'.

56 Giuseppe Gullino, 'Loredan Marco', in *Dizionario biografico degli italiani* (Rome: Istituto della Enciclopedia Italiana, 2005), 754–58.

57 Lane, 'Family Partnerships and Joint Ventures in the Venetian Republic'.

58 Lane; Frederic C. Lane, *Andrea Barbarigo. Merchant of Venice* (Baltimore, MD: Johns Hopkins University Press, 1944), 85–100.

59 Foscari meticulously recorded his earnings from commissions, clearly delineating his roles as both an agent and the legal representative of his family business.

60 To provide a rough estimate of the value of these sums, consider that in the following decade, a cooper who moved from Venice to Crete to construct barrels for Marco Bembo earned 5 ducats per month. Assuming he worked the entire year without any additional income, this would total 60 ducats annually. ASVe. MdC, folder 29, reg. 2, letter to Francesco Giustinian in Candia, 29 July 1482.

61 ASVe, *Giudici di Petizion, Sentenze a giustizia*, reg. 150, cc. 20v and ss.

62 ASVe, MG, folder 15, reg. 2.

63 Montemezzo, 'Fra pubblico e privato: la fraterna veneziana nel commercio del secondo Quattrocento'.

64 ASVe, MG, folder 15, reg. 2, cc. 58 *dare.*

65 The documentation specifies that the operation was executed following direct instructions from the brothers-in-law. ASVe, MG, folder 15, reg. 2, c. 58 *dare* e *avere.*

66 Federigo Melis, Storia della ragioneria: contributo alla conoscenza e interpretazione delle fonti più significative della storia economica, illustrato con 54 tavole fuori testo e 55 figure (Bologna: C. Zuffi, 1950), 33–43; Basil S. Yamey, 'The Historical Significance of Double-Entry Bookkeeping: Some Non-Sombartian Claims', Accounting, Business & Financial History 15, no. 1 (1 March 2005): 77–88.

67 Melis, Storia della ragioneria, 25.

68 Tommaso Zerbi, *Le origini della partita doppia: gestioni aziendali e situazioni di marcato nei secoli XIV e XV* (Milano: C. Marzorati, 1952), 15; Carlo Antinori, 'La

contabilitità pratica prima di Luca Pacioli: origine della partita doppia', De Computis. Revista espanola de historia de la contabilidad 1, no. 1 (2004): 4–23.

69 Luca Pacioli, Trattato di partita doppia, Venezia 1494, ed. Annalisa Conterio (Venezia: Albrizzi, 1994), 106.

70 Zerbi, *Le origini della partita doppia*, 14–17, 43–53; B. S. Yamey, 'Notes on Double-Entry Bookkeeping and Economic Progress', *The Journal of European Economic History* 4, no. 3 (1975): 717–23; Frederic C. Lane, 'Double Entry Bookkeeping and Resident Merchants', *The Journal of European Economic History* 6, no. 1 (1977): 177–91.

71 Zerbi, *Le origini della partita doppia*; Lane, 'Double Entry Bookkeeping and Resident Merchants'; Raymond De Roover, 'Aux origines d'une technique intellectuelle: la formation et l'expansion de la comptabilité à partie double', *Annales d'Histoire Économique et Sociale* 9, no. 44 (1937): 171–93.

72 Vittorio Alfieri, *La partita doppia applicata alle scritture delle antiche aziende mercantili veneziane* (Torino: Paravia, 1891), 40–64; Raymond De Roover, *Money, Banking and Credit in Mediaeval Bruges. Italian Merchant-Bankers Lombards and Money-Changers: A Study in the Origins of Banking* (Cambridge, MA: The Mediaeval Academy of America, 1948), 12–13.

73 An interesting analysis of time in account books has been made in Maria Ryabova, 'The Time Factor in the Account Books of the Soranzo Fraterna (Venice 1406—1434)', *ISTORIYA* 14, no. 7 (129) (2023): 1-27.

74 *'aconziar i libri'*. ASVe, MdC, folder 29, reg. 2, letter to Zuan Confetto in Cyprus, 22 novembre 1482.

75 Frederic C. Lane, 'Venture Accounting in Medieval Business Management', *Bulletin of the Business Historical Society* 19, no. 5 (1945): 164–73, https://doi.org/10.2307/3111058.

76 Georg Christ, *Trading Conflicts: Venetian Merchants and Mamluk Officials in Late Medieval Alexandria* (Leiden, Boston: Brill, 2012), 91–94.

77 ASVe, MdC, folder 29, reg. 2, letter to Antonio Negro in Damascus, June 1482.

78 Zerbi, *Le origini della partita doppia*, 19–22; Raymond De Roover, 'The Development of Accounting Prior to Luca Pacioli According to the Account-Books of Medieval Merchants', in *Studies in the History of Accounting*, ed. AC Littleton and Basil S. Yamey (Homewood, IL: Irwin, 1956), 114–74.

79 Antinori, 'La contabilitità pratica prima di Luca Pacioli: origine della partita doppia', 11.

80 De Roover, 'The Development of Accounting Prior to Luca Pacioli According to the Account-Books of Medieval Merchants', 114–114, 123–31.

81 Zerbi, *Le origini della partita doppia*, 33–48; Edwin S. Hunt, *The Medieval Super-Companies. A Study of the Peruzzi Company of Florence* (Cambridge: Cambridge University Press, 1994), 101–23.

82 The business of barrels for Cretan wine and the commodity chain of Feltre woollens are discussed in Chapter 3.

83 Zerbi, *Le origini della partita doppia*, 48–53, 61–136.

84 Alfieri, *La partita doppia applicata alle scritture delle antiche aziende mercantili veneziane*, 40–44.

85 Lane, 'Double Entry Bookkeeping and Resident Merchants'.

86 Alfieri, *La partita doppia applicata alle scritture delle antiche aziende mercantili veneziane*, 45–46.

87 Many of these characteristics were described by Pacioli in his treatise: Pacioli, *Trattato di partita doppia, Venezia 1494*.

88 ASVe, MdC, folder 29, reg. 2, letter to Alberto Contarini in Bruges, 23 April 1483. On the legal standing of accounting books, see Alfieri, *La partita doppia applicata alle scritture delle antiche aziende mercantili veneziane*, 48; Zerbi, *Le origini della partita*

doppia, 281; Maura Fortunati, *Scrittura e prova: i libri di commercio nel diritto medievale e moderno* (Roma: Fondazione Sergio Mochi Onory per la storia del diritto italiano, 1996), 48–52, 56–82; Andrea Caracausi, 'Formazione mercantile, conoscenza del diritto e idiomi politici', in *Formazione alla politica, politica della formazione a Venezia in Età moderna*, ed. Andrea Caracausi and Antonio Conzato (Roma: Viella, 2013), 141–57; Maria Ryabova, 'The Account Books of the Soranzo Fraterna (Venice 1406–1434) and Their Place in the History of Bookkeeping', *The Accounting Historians Journal* 45, no. 1 (2018): 1–27.

89 Fortunati, *Scrittura e prova*.

90 Ugo Tucci, 'La psicologia del mercante veneziano', in *Mercanti, navi e monete nel Cinquecento veneziano* (Bologna: Edizioni Il Mulino, 1981), 43–94; Gullino, 'Il clan dei Foscari'.

91 For a European overview: Sheilagh Ogilvie, *Institutions and European Trade: Merchant Guilds, 1000–1800* (Cambridge: Cambridge University Press, 2011).

92 Lane, 'Family Partnerships and Joint Ventures in the Venetian Republic'.

93 Aslanian, *From the Indian Ocean to the Mediterranean*, 121–65; Sebouh Aslanian, 'The Circulation of Men and Credit: The Role of the Commenda and the Family Firm in Julfan Society', *Journal of the Economic and Social History of the Orient* 50, no. 2/3 (2007): 124–71; Ina Baghdiantz McCabe, *The Shah's Silk for Europe's Silver: The Eurasian Trade of the Julfa Armenians in Safavid Iran and India (1530–1750)* (Atlanta, GA: Scholars, 1999), 199–270; Stephen Frederic Dale, *Indian Merchants and Eurasian Trade, 1600–1750*, (Cambridge: Cambridge University Press, 1994).

94 Dale, *Indian Merchants and Eurasian Trade, 1600–1750*, 112–20.

95 The *commenda* partnership offered two primary configurations for financial collaboration: In one scenario, the travelling merchant contributed one-quarter of the necessary capital, with the resident merchant supplying the remaining three-quarters, leading to profits being equally divided between them. Alternatively, the entire venture could be financed by the resident merchant, who would then be entitled to receive three-quarters of the profits generated from sales. These arrangements provided a versatile framework for managing investments and sharing profits, tailored to the specific contributions and risk appetite of the participants.

96 Aslanian, 'The Circulation of Men and Credit'; Dale, *Indian Merchants and Eurasian Trade, 1600–1750*, 119–20.

97 Aslanian, *From the Indian Ocean to the Mediterranean*, 121–65, 166–201, 222–23.

Bibliography

Alfieri, Vittorio. *La partita doppia applicata alle scritture delle antiche aziende mercantili veneziane*. Torino: Paravia, 1891.

Antinori, Carlo. 'La contabilitità pratica prima di Luca Pacioli: origine della partita doppia'. *De Computis. Revista espanola de historia de la contabilidad*, no. 1 (2004): 4–23.

Aslanian, Sebouh. 'The Circulation of Men and Credit: The Role of the Commenda and the Family Firm in Julfan Society'. *Journal of the Economic and Social History of the Orient* 50, no. 2/3 (2007): 124–71.

Aslanian, Sebouh David. *From the Indian Ocean to the Mediterranean: The Global Trade Networks of Armenian Merchants from New Julfa*. The California World History Library 17. Berkeley: University of California Press, 2014.

Baghdiantz McCabe, Ina. *The Shah's Silk for Europe's Silver: The Eurasian Trade of the Julfa Armenians in Safavid Iran and India (1530–1750)*. Atlanta, GA: Scholars, 1999.

Bolzonella, Marco. *Oltre i confini del dogado: l'espansione patrimoniale degli enti ecclesiastici veneziani nel Padovano (secoli IX-XIV)*. Roma: Viella, 2022.

Bulgarelli, Mario, ed. *Agostino Foscari. Viaggi di Alessandria e di Londra 1486–1496*. Venezia: La Malcontenta, 2015.

Caracausi, Andrea. 'Formazione mercantile, conoscenza del diritto e idiomi politici'. In *Formazione alla politica, politica della formazione a Venezia in Età moderna*, edited by Andrea Caracausi and Antonio Conzato, 141–57. Roma: Viella, 2013.

Cassandro, Giovanni Italo. 'La curia di petizion e il diritto processuale di Venezia'. *Archivio Veneto*, V, 19 (1936): 72–144.

Cassandro, Giovanni Italo. 'La curia di petizion e il diritto processuale di Venezia'. *Archivio Veneto*, V, 20 (1937): 1–210.

Christ, Georg. *Trading Conflicts: Venetian Merchants and Mamluk Officials in Late Medieval Alexandria*. Leiden, Boston, MA: Brill, 2012.

Dale, Stephen Frederic. *Indian Merchants and Eurasian Trade, 1600–1750*. Cambridge Studies in Islamic Civilization. Cambridge: Cambridge University Press, 1994.

De Roover, Raymond. 'Aux origines d'une technique intellectuelle: la formation et l'expansion de la comptabilité à partie double'. *Annales d'Histoire Économique et Sociale* 9, no. 44 (1937): 171–93.

De Roover, Raymond. *Money, Banking and Credit in Mediaeval Bruges. Italian Merchant-Bankers Lombards and Money-Changers: A Study in the Origins of Banking*. Cambridge, MA: The Mediaeval Academy of America, 1948.

De Roover, Raymond. 'The Development of Accounting Prior to Luca Pacioli According to the Account-Books of Medieval Merchants'. In *Studies in the History of Accounting*, edited by AC Littleton and Basil S. Yamey, 114–74. Homewood, IL: Irwin, 1956.

Demo, Edoardo. 'Wool and Silk. The Textile Urban Industry of the Venetian Mainland (15th-17th Centuries)'. In *At the Centre of the Old World. Trade and Manufacturing in Venice and the Venetian Mainland, 1400–1800*, edited by Paola Lanaro, 217–44. Toronto: Centre for Reformation and Renaissance Studies, 2006.

Ferro, Marco. 'Commissaria'. In *Dizionario del diritto comune e veneto*, I:439–41. Venezia: Andrea Santini, 1845.

Fortunati, Maura. *Scrittura e prova: i libri di commercio nel diritto medievale e moderno*. Roma: Fondazione Sergio Mochi Onory per la storia del diritto italiano, 1996.

Gullino, Giuseppe. 'Francesco Foscari (Detto Franzi)'. In *Dizionario biografico degli italiani*, XLIX:304–06. Roma: Istituto della Enciclopedia Italiana, 1997.

Gullino, Giuseppe. 'Il clan dei Foscari: politica matrimoniale e interessi familiari (secc. XIV-XV)'. *Studi veneziani*, 54 (2007). https://doi.org/10.1400/99775.

Gullino, Giuseppe. *La saga dei Foscari: storia di un enigma*. Verona: Cierre, 2005.

Gullino, Giuseppe. 'Loredan Marco'. In *Dizionario biografico degli italiani*, LXV:754–58. Rome: Istituto della Enciclopedia Italiana, 2005.

Gullino, Giuseppe. *Marco Foscari (1477–1551): l'attività politica e diplomatica tra Venezia, Roma e Firenze*. Studi e ricerche storiche 260. Milano: F. Angeli, 2000.

Gullino, Giuseppe. 'Triadano Gritti'. In *Dizionario biografico degli italiani*, LIX:753–56. Roma: Istituto della Enciclopedia Italiana, 2002.

Hunt, Edwin S. *The Medieval Super-Companies. A Study of the Peruzzi Company of Florence*. Cambridge: Cambridge University Press, 1994.

Judde de Larivière, Claire. *Naviguer, commercer, gouverner: économie maritime et pouvoirs à Venise (XVe-XVIe siècles)*. Leiden, Boston: Brill, 2008.

Kohl, Benjamin G., Andrea Mozzato, and Monique O'Connell. 'Rulers of Venice (1332–1554)'. Accessed 10 February 2024. http://rulersofvenice.org.

Lane, Frederic C. *Andrea Barbarigo. Merchant of Venice*. Baltimore, MD: Johns Hopkins University Press, 1944.

Lane, Frederic C. 'Double Entry Bookkeeping and Resident Merchants'. *The Journal of European Economic History* 6, no. 1 (1977): 177–91.

Lane, Frederic C. 'Family Partnerships and Joint Ventures in the Venetian Republic'. *The Journal of Economic History* 4, no. 2 (1944): 178–96.

Lane, Frederic C. 'Venetian Merchant Galleys, 1300–1334: Private and Communal Operation'. *Speculum* 38, no. 2 (1963): 179–205.

Lane, Frederic C. 'Venture Accounting in Medieval Business Management'. *Bulletin of the Business Historical Society* 19, no. 5 (1945): 164–73. https://doi.org/10.2307/3111058.

Lane, Frederic Chapin. *Venice, a Maritime Republic*. Baltimore, MD: Johns Hopkins University Press, 1973.

Melis, Federigo. *Storia della ragioneria: contributo alla conoscenza e interpretazione delle fonti più significative della storia economica, illustrato con 54 tavole fuori testo e 55 figure*. Bologna: C. Zuffi, 1950.

Montemezzo, Stefania. 'Fra pubblico e privato: la fraterna veneziana nel commercio del secondo Quattrocento'. *Ricerche di Storia Economica e Sociale,* 3 (2017): 7–34.

Montemezzo, Stefania. 'Galley Routes and Merchant Networks between Venice and the North Sea in the Fifteenth Century'. In *Commercial Networks and European Cities, 1400–1800*, edited by Andrea Caracausi and Christof Jeggle, 153–69. London: Pickering & Chatto, 2014.

Montemezzo, Stefania. *Giovanni Foscari. Viaggi di Fiandra 1463–1464 e 1467–1468*. Venice: La Malcontenta, 2012.

Montemezzo, Stefania. 'Ships and Trade: The Role of Public Navigation in Renaissance Venice'. In *Reti marittime come fattori dell'integrazione europea / Maritime Networks as a Factor in European Integration*, 50:473–84. Florence: Firenze University Press, 2019.

Montemezzo, Stefania. 'Strategie familiari e commercio internazionale: i Michiel da San Barnaba'. *Studi storici Luigi Simeoni* 65 (2015): 29–40.

Mozzato, Andrea. 'The Production of Woollens in Fifteenth- and Sixteenth-Century Venice'. In *At the Centre of the Old World. Trade and Manufacturing in Venice and the Venetian Mainland, 1400–1800*, edited by Paola Lanaro, 73–107. Toronto: CRRS, 2006.

Nordio, Giorgia. 'La colonia mercantile veneziana nella Londra di metà Quattrocento: attività commerciale e movimento anti-alien'. In *Atti del congresso internazionale "Politiche del credito. investimento, consumo e solidarietà"*, eds. Gemma Boschiero and Barbara Molina, 222–40. Asti: Cassa di risparmio di Asti, 2004.

Ogilvie, Sheilagh. *Institutions and European Trade: Merchant Guilds, 1000–1800*. Cambridge: Cambridge University Press, 2011.

Pacioli, Luca. *Trattato di partita doppia, Venezia 1494*, edited by Annalisa Conterio. Venezia: Albrizzi, 1994.

Ravegnani, Giorgio. 'Giustinian Orsotto'. In *Dizionario biografico degli italiani*, 57:274–77. Roma: Istituto della Enciclopedia Italiana, 2001.

Ribeiro, Ana Sofia. *Early Modern Trading Networks in Europe: Cooperation and the Case of Simon Ruiz*. Abingdon, Oxon, New York: Routledge, Taylor & Francis Group, 2016.

Rossi, Franco. 'Contarini Leonardo'. In *Dizionario biografico degli italiani*, XXVIII:229–31. Rome: Istituto della Enciclopedia Italiana, 1983.

Ryabova, Maria. 'The Account Books of the Soranzo Fraterna (Venice 1406–1434) and Their Place in the History of Bookkeeping'. *The Accounting Historians Journal* 45, no. 1 (2018): 1–27.

Ryabova, Maria. 'The Time Factor in the Account Books of the Soranzo Fraterna (Venice 1406—1434)'. *ISTORIYA* 14, no. 7 (129) (2023). https://history.jes.su/s20798784 0026930-2-1/.

Sacerdoti, Alberto. 'Bembo Marco'. In *Dizionario biografico degli italiani*, VIII:127–28. Rome: Istituto della Enciclopedia Italiana, 1966.

Safley, Thomas Max. *Family Firms and Merchant Capitalism in Early Modern Europe: The Business, Bankruptcy and Resilience of the Hoechstetters of Augsburg*. Abingdon, Oxon, New York: Routledge, 2019.

Shammas, Carole. 'Standard of Living, Consumption, and Political Economy over the Past 500 Years'. In *The Oxford Handbook of the History of Consumption*, 211–26. ed. Frank Trentmann. Oxford University Press, 2012.

Sopracasa, Alessio. 'Passage au Levant. Le « voyage » de Candie-Constantinople de la compagnia Bembo dans la seconde moitié du xve siècle: organisation et séjour'. *Cahiers d'études italiennes* 25 (2017). https://doi.org/10.4000/cei.3499.

Thiriet, Freddy. 'Les lettres commerciales des Bembo et le commerce vénitien dans l'Empire Ottoman à la fin du XVe siècle'. In *Studi in onore di Armando Sapori*, II:911–33. Milan: Istituto Editoriale Cisalpino, 1957.

Tognetti, Sergio. 'Galeras estatales y veleros privados en la República Florentina del Cuatrocientos: la praxis mercantil'. In *Navegación institucional y navegación privada en el Mediterráneo Medieval*, edited by Raoul González Arévalo, 105–44. Granada: Grupo de Investigación Toponimia, Historia y Arqueología del Reino de Granada, 2016.

Trebbi, Giuseppe. 'La società veneziana'. In *Storia di Venezia, VI, Dal Rinascimento al Barocco*, edited by Gaetano Cozzi and Paolo Prodi, 129–213. Roma: Istituto della Enciclopedia Italiana, 1994.

Trivellato, Francesca. 'Renaissance Florence and the Origins of Capitalism: A Business History Perspective'. *Business History Review* 94, no. 1 (2020): 229–51.

Trivellato, Francesca. *The Familiarity of Strangers: The Sephardic Diaspora, Livorno, and Cross-Cultural Trade in the Early Modern Period*. New Haven, CT, London: Yale University Press, 2009.

Tucci, Ugo. 'Costi e ricavi di una galera veneziana ai primi del Cinquecento'. In *Mercanti, navi e monete nel Cinquecento Veneziano*, 109–175. Bologna: Il Mulino, 1981.

Tucci, Ugo. 'La psicologia del mercante veneziano'. In *Mercanti, navi e monete nel Cinquecento Veneziano*, 43–94. Bologna: Edizioni Il Mulino, 1981.

Ventura, Angelo. 'Giovanni Bembo'. In *Dizionario biografico degli italiani*, VIII:117–19. Roma: Istituto della Enciclopedia Italiana, 1966.

Yamey, B. S. 'Notes on Double-Entry Bookkeeping and Economic Progress'. *The Journal of European Economic History* 4, no. 3 (1975): 717.

Yamey, Basil S. 'The Historical Significance of Double-Entry Bookkeeping: Some Non-Sombartian Claims'. *Accounting, Business & Financial History* 15, no. 1 (1 March 2005): 77–88.

Zerbi, Tommaso. *Le origini della partita doppia: gestioni aziendali e situazioni di marcato nei secoli XIV e XV*. Milano: C. Marzorati, 1952.

2 Companies and Public Institutions

Public Institutions and the Merchant Class

To understand the operations of small- and medium-sized commercial enterprises in the Venetian Renaissance, it is essential to delineate the influence of public institutions on their activities. This analysis is critical because, although familial connections provided a significant support network in Venice,[1] mercantile documentation clearly demonstrates the profound impact of public institutions on merchants' decision-making and strategies.[2] This influence highlights that the Venetian State was neither neutral nor passive in its engagement with the economy. The State's direct involvement through the provision of public navigation routes, the appointment of consuls and ambassadors abroad, customs control and taxation, and the obligation for public appointees (from consuls to galley patrons) to report their activities to the Senate illustrate its proactive and interventionist approach in the economic and commercial domain. The examination of mercantile records demonstrates that state interventions significantly influenced merchant behaviour, leading to both compliance with and circumvention of regulations.[3] This was made possible through the Venetian State's instrumental role in supporting merchant activities by providing mechanisms to alleviate cooperation problems and resolve disputes, enforce contracts, protect the interests of city merchants, and bestow privileges upon its citizens, thereby ensuring the smooth operation and success of Venice's mercantile efforts.[4] These interventions were vital in a context where the business landscape primarily comprised nuclear family structure. Such considerations hold particular significance within historiographical debates, where Italian Republics, Venice included, are often likened to guilds due to these distinct features.[5]

The first way the Venetian State had an instrumental role in shaping the commercial landscape was to control and limit access to trade, regional and international. This control was a powerful tool for the preindustrial states as commerce was not a right but a privilege, and merchants could participate in trade only with the explicit consent of public authorities.[6] In Venice, the commercial class itself constituted these authorities thereby intertwining the state's regulatory mechanisms with the mercantile aristocracy's commercial interests.[7] This restriction meant that foreigners and a considerable segment of Venice's inhabitants were precluded from playing an active and independent part in the city's international

DOI: 10.4324/9781032628103-3

trade.[8] This exclusion was linked to the type of citizenship one possessed, highlighting the intersection of civic status and economic participation within the Venetian Republic.[9] So, who could define themselves as merchants in Venice? The attitude of the Venetian authorities in this regard and the laws governing the access to Venetian citizenship changed over the centuries. However, during the 15th century, three ways permitted access to trade under a Venetian flag. The first was to belong to the patriciate and therefore is the case of Bembo, Foscari, and Michiel. This class was at the heart of long-distance Venetian trade: it included the noble families of the city, which had capitals to invest in trade, especially international, and occupied the most important posts in public offices. Patricians had even further privileges, such as being able to participate in tenders for state maritime travels, giving the young scions of noble families the chance to take a sort of apprenticeship on the galleys (with a guaranteed wage, since wealth and nobility didn't always coincide) and to have access to the offices that managed the organization of commercial traffic and customs.[10]

Besides nobility, the Venetian population was classified into various tiers that granted different levels of access and privileges. The first element to possess to become a citizen was to be an active contributor in economic terms, which meant being a resident and taxpayer in Venice for 25 years. In Venice, there were two kinds of citizenships, the first being *de intus et de extra*, that offered the most comprehensive commercial privileges, including engaging in international trade, protection as merchants and travellers, access to public galley convoys, customs and financial benefits, and jurisdictional privileges abroad. In contrast, *De intus* and *De intus tantum* citizenships limited holders to local trade and minor government roles, without access to international commerce.[11] The consequence of this control over the access to trading activities made Venice's mercantile class quite cohesive. One of the most evident demonstrations of such internal support was the ban imposed on those who revealed Venetian commercial secrets or on whoever deceived a citizen of the Republic.[12]

The Interplay of Personal Interests and Information Creation

The prevention of fraud or deceit by an agent, partner, or merchant was a key reason for the replication of incentive structures at the state level, similar to those found within family and business settings.[13] This was largely due to the exclusive trading rights granted to a select group of individuals typically organized into familial businesses. This exclusivity necessitated involvement in political life for Venetian family firms, allowing them to influence Venetian State actions to favour the broader commercial system or even specific trade goods (such as salt and wheat).[14] To elucidate the dynamics between private interests and public positions, as well as the expectations businesses had regarding the performance of institutions, an illustrative episode recounted by Marco Bembo in his letters merits examination. This narrative involves Marco Bembo, the Genoese merchant Battista Spinola (addressed as the traitor in the correspondence[15]), and Francesco Marcello di Antonio, the Venetian consul in Damascus, appointed in August 1482.[16] The incident likely initiated the previous year when Bembo entered into a partnership with Spinola for the acquisition of potash, a key ingredient in the production of glass and soap.[17] The venture soured, not due to a lack of market demand for potash but because Spinola, burdened with debt, failed to settle his share of approximately 1,700 ducats, and hastily fled Turkey to evade his creditors.[18]

Recognizing the potential misjudgement in selecting Spinola as a business partner, Bembo took proactive steps involving both his network of agents and leveraging institutional avenues. He directed his agents and correspondents spread between Syria and Constantinople—Vielmo Anzelieri, Antonio Negro, and Francesco Zisberto—to exchange the entire stock of potash for spices under his name alone, given Spinola's delinquency in fulfilling his financial obligations. This initiative encountered more than one challenge. The attempt to barter the potash with Syrian merchants culminated in a dispute adjudicated by the qadi of Damascus,[19] where Zisberto was compelled to accept a reduced valuation for the potash. This was due to the Syrian merchants' demand for the potash to be sifted, a quality assurance measure to confirm the merchandise's standard.[20]

Marco Bembo, determined to secure an upper hand over his business partner, whom he aimed to have held in Venice due to debts, took further action. He sent bills of exchange issued by Spinola in Pera to Consul Francesco Marcello, seeking authorization to auction Spinola's portion of potash to be acquired by Bembo with the bills of exchange that he sent, to recover his investment. To persuade Marcello to grant this request, Marco hinted to Antonio Negro that the consul himself had outstanding credits with Spinola, suggesting this connection could work to their advantage.[21] Contrary to Bembo's expectations, Marcello declined the request, insisting that the sale could only proceed following a legal trial and judgement. Bembo expressed his astonishment at this refusal, arguing

> He seems a novice for such words since, as a merchant, he should understand the power of bills of exchange, which act as judgments and are always accepted in the consul's office without the need for further adjudication, and executed immediately due to their credit strength.[22]

In response to Marcello's refusal, Bembo took two significant steps: he asked Marcello to provide a written explanation for his decision, allowing Bembo to challenge it with Venice's *Auditori nuovi* (an appellate court) and consult the Consuls of Merchants. Subsequently, he conveyed the Auditors' decision to Marcello in a pointed letter, emphasizing that 'friends should be prioritized over strangers'.[23] This incident sheds light on the nuanced relationship between public roles and private interests among Venetian merchants. From one side, merchants expected their political representatives, who were also merchants and part of the same social circle, to have an inherent understanding of commercial practices and possibly a preferential treatment or at least more lenient consideration compared to his Genoese peer. It was also conceivable that public officials, elected from the ranks of the Venetian merchant nobility, might exploit their position to advance their own interests, thereby impinging upon the needs of other traders. In this regard,

Marcello's hesitation to accelerate Bembo's petition invites speculation about his motives, notably in light of his financial ties to Spinola. The expeditious issuance of a favourable injunction by the *Auditori Novi* to Bembo indicates that his appeal was not an exceptional case. This course of action gives rise to the possibility of a conflict of interest on the part of Marcello. However, it ultimately serves to illustrate the complex interrelationship between the Venice merchant elite and the public officials who are drawn from their ranks.[24]

Bembo's approaches and his subsequent communication with the consul highlight a crucial aspect of the Venetian public institutions' role: the generation and management of information. The Republic's various judicial bodies served as platforms where continuous streams of data were produced to meet merchants' needs, significantly reducing the risks associated with international trade by clarifying trustworthiness and potentially enhancing profits. If Bembo had been aware of Spinola's reputation for leaving debts, it is unlikely he would have risked a partnership, thereby avoiding the entanglement of capital and the cumbersome process of legal recourse to reclaim it. Information about the reliability of partners, sellers, and buyers was crucial in Venice's commercial strategy, leading to the development of a singular institution known as '*abatelazion*'. This hybrid institution was designed to merge data from Venetian merchants about foreign markets with the formal information processes provided by public institutions.[25] The procedure initiated with a '*garbuio*', a legal proceeding started by a foreign merchant, frequently from Egypt or Syria, against a Venetian counterpart, often in a local court. When feeling wronged, the Venetian would appeal to Venetian authorities for a commercial embargo against the offenders to protect Venetian interests. Bembo explains this process: following disputes on foreign markets, in his case multiple court appearances, the agents would compile and send all pertinent documentation to their Venetian principal. This Venice-based merchant would then formally request the issuance of a decree to suspend business transactions with the disputing parties. This decree was subsequently sent to agents, who would pass it to the appropriate Venetian authorities in the area. In the Bembo's case, the decree targeted individuals who had complicated the trade of potash mentioned before, leading to a case in the court of the Mamluk judge: Zotto di Sagor, Ben Ezume, Sabadin Misaben, Ali Pecuvit, and Azi Mar, a sultan's official.[26]

Controls and Incentives

The vital role of Venice's public institutions in mitigating information asymmetry within mercantile groups and companies significantly eased the challenges merchants encountered daily in international markets. This effectiveness stemmed from integrating information streams from private enterprises with those generated by public entities, particularly their judicial branches.[27] The intricacy of Venetian governance and the diverse perspectives within the public sector helped navigate issues that arose when members of the mercantile class occupied government roles—the same class the State aimed to protect—potentially leading to conflicts of interest.

Venice's sophisticated institutional framework enabled it to assert influence well beyond its borders, managing market dynamics and bolstering the city-state's international standing. The incident involving the potash trade serves as a prime example of this capability. Through its public institutions, Venice not only oversaw domestic trade, especially regulating exchanges and managing flows during trade fairs, but also made its presence felt in foreign markets.[28] In the potash dispute, local merchants who were eventually subjected to a commercial embargo by Bembo sought to sieve Bembo's potash at the Qadi's court to check its quality. This insistence on checking the merchandise, common in Mamluk and Ottoman legal practices, was likely less about quality control and more a strategy for price negotiation.[29] The involvement of Francesco Zisberto, as detailed in communications to Bembo (which Bembo then relayed to Negro to update him on the potash issue), illustrates how the Qadi's court functioned as a venue for negotiating peaceful settlements.[30] Judgements were passed only when negotiations failed, with Bembo's case seeing the court fully siding with the demands of the local buyer in only one instance.[31]

The intervention to check the quality of the merchandise, while ostensibly reasonable since in his letter the agent indicated that yielding to such demands would significantly diminish profits, placed agent Francesco Zisberto in a difficult situation. Encountering a Qadi who was not inclined to favour his case, Zisberto sought permission from the Venetian consul to negotiate a compromise without conceding any fault, in pursuit of an amicable resolution. This step prompts the question: why did Zisberto involve the consul in what was essentially a private dispute in a local court?

The Consulate and the Resolution of Mercantile Conflicts

Initiating this discussion requires a brief exploration of the consul's responsibilities in foreign ports, their connection to Venice's central governance, and the underlying need for Venetian commercial representation overseas. Let us delve into the latter aspect first.

The revival of international trade came along with the merchants' increasing demands to be able to travel and stay in foreign ports. Since the Middle Ages, Italian maritime cities had shared the tendency to create mercantile communities in foreign cities and to nominate a community leader under the direct control of Venice's government.[32] The evolution of Venetian representation abroad has undergone significant changes over the centuries linked to the city's unique approach to consular law, distinct from the broader *ius commune*, that led to the development of specialized aspects within its consular institution, setting a precedent for modern consular practices.[33] Venetian government representation abroad evolved significantly throughout the Middle Ages, including changes in terminology, duties, and rights. Initially, representatives were known as *vicedomini* or *baili*, with the former mainly handling administrative duties in nearby ports and the latter representing Venice in more distant, especially Near Eastern, markets with broader responsibilities, including diplomatic roles. The title 'bailus' possibly originated from Islamic tradition, implying a high-ranking position similar to a *visir*.[34] From the 15th century, ambassadors took over foreign representation, especially in major courts like Rome, except in Constantinople where the *bailo* role combined consular and ambassadorial functions.[35] This layered structure highlights the adaptability and hierarchical organization of Venetian overseas governance.

Since the 15th century, the title of consul became commonly used to denote government officials representing Venice in foreign lands, endowed with judicial powers. The term initially described magistracies tied to commerce, such as the merchants' consuls, and later evolved to denote officials who regulated the affairs of Venetian communities abroad and administered justice within them. By 1443, consuls could be either nobles or citizens of Venice, although key consulates remained predominantly patrician roles for at least another century. It was not until 1575 that citizens predominantly assumed consul positions. On the contrary, vice-consuls always enjoyed broader eligibility criteria, with the role being accessible even to non-Venetian individuals, reflecting the adaptable nature of Venice's diplomatic network and its consular system's evolution over time.[36]

Venetian consulates were categorized into three geographical regions: the Levant, the West, and the Gulf, with Gulf consulates in the Adriatic's Balkan cities and coastal Dalmatia directly managed by Venice. The complex Italian political scene led to a widespread network of consulates across major economic areas, particularly in Marche and Apulia, due to their active olive oil and fabric trades.[37] Venice's international diplomatic presence, initiated during the Crusades, included early consular offices in strategically vital locations like Tunis and Alexandria, showing their importance in Venice's international trade and diplomatic endeavours.[38] In certain areas, especially within the eastern Mediterranean, capital-based consuls handled relations with local rulers, although this practice varied and was subject to the *Maggior Consiglio*'s, the Great Council, discretion. This council also managed the election of consuls (apart from those under the *bailo* of Constantinople) and supervised their operations. The consul's term of office was never determined very precisely, at least until the end of the 17th century, and different locations adopted different customs (two years in office in Egypt and Syria, a lifelong assignment in Smirne or the assignment to a specific family, as in Palermo and Apulia).[39]

The duties and responsibilities of Venetian consuls varied by location, yet their primary objective was always to uphold and protect the interests of Venice and its merchants. This context is essential to comprehend the involvement of consuls in the private commercial disputes of Venetian merchants, exemplified by Consul Marcello's role in Damascus. Seeking a consul's permission (*licentia*)[40] to resolve a dispute in a specific manner within foreign courts should not be perceived as an intrusion by the state into private commerce. Rather, it represents a strategy to safeguard the Venetian community at large. Firstly, it ensured that Venetian commercial enterprises were backed by the political support of the Venetian State. Secondly, conceding to a buyer's demands by allowing goods inspection, and eventually admitting fault, could have led to reduced prices for certain Venetian goods in the local market. This market often relied on barter, which was only advantageous if one's goods were appraised at the highest quality and value. Additionally, granting concessions risked setting a precedent that price negotiations could be simplified by appealing to a local court, potentially predisposed in favour of local merchants who, by familiarity, held a procedural advantage in such settings. This could significantly impede capital circulation and investment returns, impacting the broader Venetian commercial interests. Price fluctuations were a significant concern for merchants, influencing their decisions on where to sell their goods. An increase in market prices could prompt them to reroute merchandise back to their homeland or another market for higher profits.[41] Conversely, changes in prices due to factors like civil wars, governmental incentives, or crop yields played a critical role in shaping their commercial strategies and investment choices over the short and medium term.[42]

In this commercial environment, the consul's participation and sanctioning of the settlement were strategically designed to dispel any rumours of Venetians trading in substandard goods, thereby protecting market prices and potential profits. This rationale underpins the consul's dual role as both mediator and judge, with the latter function performed alongside a council of Venetian residents in the city, ensuring the community's interests were safeguarded and upheld.[43] The consul adjudicated both civil and criminal cases involving at least one Venetian party. From a commercial standpoint, the availability of legal assistance from a Venetian judge in foreign ports was crucial. This support was especially significant for Venetian citizens travelling on state or private vessels through major foreign ports, as it facilitated the swift resolution of disputes and ensured the smooth continuation of business activities.

Price stability was of utmost importance to Venice, a State heavily reliant on commerce and finance, as was the flow of information back to the homeland.[44] Consequently, consuls regularly corresponded with the Senate regarding the circumstances impacting Venetian merchants abroad. They proposed actions that would benefit their commercial pursuits or suggested negotiating or revising the relationships between the central government and local communities. One such instance is evidenced in an October 1483 communication from the consul of Damascus, Francesco Marcello, to the Senate.[45] Marcello discusses several matters, including the operation of the Venetian *fondaco*. Specifically, he addresses the *cottimo*, a tax levied by the local consulate on Venetian goods used for the upkeep of the *fondaco*. Marcello refers to two letters from the Senate demanding the consulate pay 4,000 ducats (both capital and interest) to Andrea Zorzi, following the annulment of a previous consul's decision by the *Auditori nuovi*. Marcello's defence of the Venetian community in Damascus centres on two main arguments: whether admitted or not (as Marcello states) that Zorzi is unrelated to the *cottimo*, the decision's severity is significant both due to the external nature of the adjudicators and because the motherland's institutions should not interfere with the affairs of overseas communities, given they are equipped with all procedures and institutions to make decisions. The first claim hinges on Marcello's assertion that no member of the Venetian community in Damascus was consulted by the homeland authorities, whereas several resident Venetian merchants, including the former consul who was no longer part of the community, were. He then used his appointment document against the central institutions to defend and clarify jurisdictional issues: the *cottimo* belongs to the Venetian community in Damascus, which alone can decide on its use.[46] This defence of the community's independence from central organs is intriguing, as it sheds light on how the consul and the Damascus community might have reacted when Bembo from Venice appealed against the consul's decision to auction Spinola's potash. The consul had requested indeed a legal judgement from a trial to proceed with the sale, which would absolve the consul of any liability in case Spinola appealed. This jurisdictional conflict, arising from undefined hierarchies within the Venetian courts of justice, was commonplace throughout the 15th and early 16th centuries until around the 1540s when the Venetian magistrates underwent internal restructuring to rationalize duties and avoid jurisdictional conflicts and court shopping by involved parties.[47]

In his communication with the Senate, Marcello also addressed the challenges associated with commercial navigation, emphasizing the critical role of consuls in the organization and success of Venice's public navigation routes. His concerns centred on punctuality, communication, and safety. He noted the galleys' premature and unannounced arrival, which unexpectedly prompted the Mamluks to begin trade negotiations earlier than planned, to the detriment of all involved, as the Eastern commodities had not yet arrived. Additionally, Marcello commented on the preparation of cargo, which left the Syrian Venetian community ill prepared for the imminent spice trade. He urged the Senate to maintain a consistent schedule for state voyages towards the East, highlighting the importance of such measures in mitigating piracy threats and safeguarding Venice's commercial interests. Marcello's insights highlight the indispensable role of consular support in facilitating smooth operations and ensuring the well-being of Venetian traders abroad.[48]

As previously discussed, a comprehensive network of consulates throughout Europe and the Mediterranean provided substantial support to Venetian merchants navigating aboard state galleys or private ships. Consuls and vice-consuls fulfilled many different roles, but they were all fundamental for the trading business. The consul's first concern was to ensure the safety of Venetian citizens, achieved through the guarantees offered by agreements with local authorities. Consuls also had the role of guarding the property of Venetians who died abroad,[49] managing the nation, intended as the merchant diaspora in foreign ports,[50] and, above all, collecting the taxes on Venetian goods passing through the *fondaco*.[51] However, the role of consuls also had informal connotations that were crucial for the smooth running of trade. They acted as intermediaries for merchants travelling on state galleys and spending only limited time in foreign ports. One example of this activity is given by Giovanni Foscari's ledgers, which show how the local consul Bartolomeo Zorzi was actively involved in favouring the Venetian merchants who arrived in Bruges on the state galleys. The activities Zorzi was directly involved in went beyond his official duties of tax collection, assisting Venetian merchants and facilitating their integration into the city. His role extended to personal and commercial support for Foscari, including arranging accommodation, an office space, and warehouse rentals. Even after the departure of the convoy, Zorzi continued managing outstanding payments for future settlements. Notably, he served as Foscari's intermediary, handling the sales of goods left under his care in Bruges. His involvement in financial operations was significant, acting as an intermediary in transactions, especially with London, involving a total of 1,686 ducats. Additionally, Zorzi was named the beneficiary in a bill of exchange by Giovanni Foscari, covering various advances made by the consul. Despite the legal restriction against trading for personal gain and acting as an agent for others—aimed at maintaining neutrality essential for his role—Zorzi's engagement in commercial activities is evident. For instance, in Foscari's first ledger, Zorzi, alongside Girolamo Michiel, is listed as a intermediator in transactions for the Dandolos, Venetian residents in London, without directly being identified as their agent. He even became a member of the exclusive commercial company, known as a '*maona*' in Venetian, for the purchase of dates, further illustrating the blurred and often indistinct line between his private endeavours and public duties.[52]

The Public Navigation System

The Venetian institution that most blended corporate interests and public support was likely the public navigation system. Since the 15th century, the nature of Venice's mercantile activities underwent significant transformation. Merchants adopted a more sedentary approach to business. This change was driven by developments in trading practices, notably the adoption of advanced accounting techniques. These innovations allowed Venetian merchants to oversee their enterprises directly from the city, utilizing third-party agents to carry out transactions.[53] This transition was further supported by the establishment of regular trading routes between the Serenissima and markets in Europe and the Orient, maintained by the state-operated galley convoys.[54]

The intensification of mercantile exchanges during the 13th century encouraged the State's intervention in the commercial sector. There were multiple reasons for such intervention, most of which were connected to the economic development that required a gradual intensification of mercantile exchanges, and the consequent need to favour the Venetian market.[55] The main goal was to ensure the consistency of navigation flows by improving the smooth running of city fairs, which represented continuous work for the arsenal, even in times of peace,[56] and increasingly safer ships. Navigation in convoys and the requirement to arm the ships[57] proved to be essential for the competitiveness of Venetian merchants. The cost of transport was lower, in proportion to the value of the goods load, and there was a guaranteed level of protection from organized violence at sea. Market galleys were the most suitable ships for the voyages' needs, despite an inferior load capacity compared to tall ships and a more frequent need of supplies during navigation. Another important feature of these ships was the agility of their movements, provided by the ability to manoeuvre the ships with oars: this aspect turned out to be extremely useful during navigation in the lagoon, in the Adriatic Sea, approaching river ports and during battles.[58]

The development of maritime trade in Venice in the 13th century had been supported by the free enterprise of private ship-owners. Only in 1294, the State, for the first time, took part in the management of mercantile galleys. The actions to regulate commercial flows, which by the end of the 13th century were only occasional, became more consistent during the first decades of the following century. From 1329, galleys started to be put up for auction and managed according to public instructions. Venice's government felt the need to control and regulate certain commercial routes that were particularly important for its economic dominion and in order to maintain the diplomatic relationships necessary for the proper administration of commercial exchanges. Consequently, from the 14th century, Venice's merchant navy consisted of two complementary sectors: public and private. The public sector was the armament of the State that used the market galleys, built in the arsenal and contracted through tenders to Venice's patricians, to guarantee the trade in products with high added value (such as spices, fine fabrics, and precious materials).[59] The private sector was dominated by independent ship-owners who operated round ships or smaller vessels. These private fleets primarily facilitated the trade of less valuable and bulkier commodities—such as wheat, salt, textiles, and timber—to nearby markets. Their trading networks spanned the Adriatic coasts and North Africa, reaching as far as Spanish cities and occasionally venturing into the Atlantic.[60] A notable instance was the Cocca Querina, which, en route to Flanders in 1431-32, found itself stranded on the coast of Norway due to a storm.[61] Private navigation played a crucial role in sustaining Venetian commerce, especially in provisioning the lagoon city with essential food supplies.[62] In contrast, public navigation was instrumental in regulating financial markets and the cost of capital on the Rialto, while also serving as a guarantor for international trading endeavours. The zenith of state-sponsored voyages occurred in the latter half of the 15th century, marked by the expansion of mercantile galley expeditions to more remote ports and venturing into the ocean to reach destinations like Flanders, as exemplified by the Foscari's ventures.[63]

The Venetian government identified several crucial maritime routes for its strategic interests, establishing convoy systems known as *mude* to secure these vital trade channels. Venice's maritime trade network, established in the early 14th century, was strategically oriented towards both the East and West, leveraging key maritime routes to bolster its commercial dominance. To the East, the essential lines included Romania–Black Sea,[64] Syria–Beirut, and Alexandria, facilitating trade towards the Orient. The Romania *muda*, operational since 1318 and extended to Trebizond following a treaty, capitalized on the Black Sea's access to Oriental flows and its rich markets. Despite Constantinople's declining importance due to Northern Romania's economic downturn, it remained a fundamental Black Sea access point, where Venice countered Genoa's influence with Byzantine support.[65] By the 1460s and 70s, Venice's confrontation with the Ottomans suspended the Romania route, redirecting focus towards the Middle East through arrangements with the Mamluks.[66] On the other side of the Mediterranean Basin, to counter Tuscan and Genoese competition, Venice established the Aigues Mortes, to France and Spain, and Barberìa lines, for the Berber territories.[67] The unique Flanders convoy, managed exclusively by the State since 1322, facilitated direct imports from Northern Europe, bypassing intermediaries for critical commodities like English tin and wool, and exporting oriental goods, marking Venice's ambitious reach beyond the Mediterranean.[68] In the 1460s, facing challenges with the consistency of exchanges in the western Mediterranean, particularly along the Northern Coast of Africa, an additional convoy, *Trafego*, was initiated to address these issues, thereby reinforcing Venice's comprehensive network of maritime trade routes essential for its economic dominance and strategic interests.[69] The primary objective of the Serenissima was to create commercial flows that would cover the whole Mediterranean basin, thereby allowing the regular exchange of products, quick turnovers, and the fast reinvestment of capitals. The mercantile network built by Venice, by directly managing the voyages towards the major Oriental, African and Northern European markets, as well as the rules imposed by Venice, were intended to consolidate Venice's strategic position and its role as a commercial fulcrum, once again affirming its hegemony and ensuring the largest possible market for its goods. This system even allowed it to 'confront customs, techniques and behaviour to form a kind of maritime ecumenism'.[70]

The organization of *mude* (convoy voyages) was meticulously regulated by the Venetian State, with all voyage parameters detailed in a document known as the *incanto*, outlining the engagement rules established by the *Cinque Savi agli Ordini* (senior magistrates who supervised all maritime matters).[71] This document required Senate approval, which could suggest modifications. The process, from the text's confirmation to the contractor's assumption of galley responsibility, was clearly defined. Following approval, the tendering process for the galleys, an auction exclusive to the Venetian patriciate, commenced at Rialto, where nobles bid for ships within the convoy.[72] A successful auction necessitated buyers for all ships. Winning bidders had eight days to present themselves before the *Avogadori de Comun*, Public Prosecutors, to submit proof of nobility, age over 30, financial capacity for the voyage, and details on all company members. Upon verification, the Senate confirmed the tender as valid.[73] This procedure was likely followed in 1463 when Giovanni Foscari secured a patronage role for the Flanders-bound galleys, paying a mere 7 ducats for the ship lease, while other charterers contributed a nominal 1 ducat, marking the willingness of the Venetian State to invest in this institution.[74] The *Incanto* document issued by the Senate in 1463 adheres to a traditional format, detailing the obligations and incentives for the *patrono*. It specified a payment of 500 ducats to the Arsenal for ship outfitting, with delivery scheduled for April. Each patron was granted a *donum* of 4,000 ducats by the State, a measure to encourage investment in maritime ventures despite the looming threat of war with the Ottomans and the associated risk of ships being commandeered for military use. This increased incentive, manifesting as a higher *donum* of 5,500 ducats for Giovanni Foscari's subsequent northern voyage, likely elucidates the State's strategy to encourage merchant participation in these ventures.[75] The document also outlined the loading procedure and included other operational specifics, such as designated stopovers, crew treatment, and the process for electing officials.[76]

The vessel was leased unrigged, making it the charterer's responsibility to prepare it for the voyage. Consequently, the State mandated the *patrono* to demonstrate financial solvency to the Public prosecutors, which typically involved forming a temporary management company for the journey's duration. This entity, explored in Chapter 1, known as the *compagnia di galera*, was established specifically to ensure adequate financial backing and operational readiness of the ship for travel.[77] Once the necessary capital had been raised, the debts paid to the Arsenal, and his financial position had been certified by the State, Foscari moved on to taking care of the crew and loading the cargo. The months before departure would have been chaotic for the traders involved, since they were embarking on more than a year-long commercial trip.

Venetian and Oriental products, including low-quality cloth, berets, wine, pepper, silks, and wax, were dispatched to Bruges and London. State-imposed restrictions prioritized high-value items like silk and spices for loading onto ships, with other goods such as Italian cloth considered only after these prime commodities were accommodated. This strategic loading policy aimed at maximizing profits and sustaining Venice's market presence in the North. The Foscari account books affirm adherence to these guidelines: during their second voyage, Oriental products—spices, fabrics, and cotton—accounted for approximately 16,000 of the 18,813 ducats earned from sales, predominantly in Bruges, a major consumer of spices and textiles, and to a lesser extent in London, where cotton and a smaller variety of spices were traded for woollen fabrics and raw wool. Bruges consistently served as the primary entry point for Venetian merchants. Despite the emerging significance of English markets, notably Southampton, Bruges retained its status as one of Venice's crucial commercial allies until the century's close.[78]

The Foscari family's reliance on Venice's public navigation system was profound, as demonstrated by Giovanni Foscari's role as the patron of two galleys destined for Flanders, marking the era's most challenging sea route, and his later engagement in the Beirut galley tender.[79] This commitment raises the question: how did other merchant firms interact with the state-operated maritime lines? The Michiel enterprise offers further insight. While Michiel's utilization of the state galleys between 1470 and 1481 was not as extensive as the Foscaris', it displayed a consistent pattern. During this period, Michiel transported merchandise worth around 7,000 ducats via the state navy, predominantly in pepper, which was arguably the most profitable commodity at the time, totalling nearly 3,000 ducats. This pepper was often exchanged for Italian cloth dyed to meet the preferences of the Egyptian market, a strategy informed by their Alexandria agent, although cash payments were more typical. Significant amounts of ginger, valued at close to 1,000 ducats, were shipped to Flanders, whereas copper and tin found their way to Egypt and the Barbary Coast. The Venetian enterprise utilized state galleys for its shipments, ranging from a minimum of twice to a maximum of four times annually, targeting three primary destinations: Flanders and England, the Berber territories, and the Mamluk domain, predominantly Alexandria. As mentioned, the merchandise transported on these state galleys was valued at approximately 7,000 ducats, excluding freight and additional costs, against a backdrop of 75,000 ducats invested in acquisitions (covering both land and maritime routes) throughout the period. This data suggests a modest engagement with public navigation.[80] However, the contemporary context has to be considered. During Venice's initial conflict with the Ottomans, not only did commercial networks face disruptions, but the availability of ships for Mediterranean trade also declined. Galleys headed towards the East risked being commandeered for military efforts, heightening the danger of cargo loss due to enemy actions. Consequently, Michiel's investments in state galleys predominantly favoured regions distant from the conflict zones, such as Egypt's Alexandria, the Berber lands, and Flanders. This strategic choice reflects the broader challenges of the era: the ongoing war acted as a significant deterrent to investing in the public navy, given that the potential benefits were overshadowed by the risks of maritime engagements, confiscation, and repurposing of ships for military needs. In Michiel's case, whether due to the ongoing war or a preference for trading on private ships—which offered easier means to evade duties, as we'll explore in upcoming chapters—the significance of public navigation was somewhat limited. It could even be argued that Michiel's business endeavours could have persisted without this institution. Yet, why did many, including Consul Marcello, advocate for keeping the State's lines active?

Public navigation served multiple economic and social purposes, benefiting the public interest.[81] Firstly, maintaining a public commercial fleet was a safety measure. Vessels could be repurposed for military needs also aligned with the public interest, offering strategic flexibility in times of conflict, while keeping the arsenal active and functioning.[82] Secondly, public navigation enforced a rigorous schedule for departures and returns, establishing a steady flow of merchant activity that bolstered the consistency of the city's market dynamics.[83] Venice saw the rhythm and intensity of its commercial exchanges significantly influenced by the convoy's scheduling. The busiest period for trade, particularly noticeable in rate increases, spanned from May to June, coinciding with the departures towards Barberìa and Aigues Mortes, Flanders, Romania, and Syria.[84] A quieter period followed, marked by the departure of two additional convoys to Beirut and Alexandria. From September to December, the city witnessed the return of convoys that had departed in the spring or summer, though this did not substantially affect exchange rates. The Venetian year wound down between January and February, with minimal activity due to preparations for the ships set to depart mid-February to Syria (for the cotton *muda*) and the *Trafego* galleys leaving in early March.[85] The strategic coordination of these departures and returns, to which traffic linked to private lines should be added, facilitated rapid investment turnovers. Advancements in navigation allowed the convoys to adhere to the Senate's schedule, enabling the state to control fleet movements efficiently, reinvest swiftly in new ventures, and supply the market with goods essential for sustaining the commercial ecosystem.[86] Although the buying, selling, and pricing of goods were left to the private sector, the Venetian State effectively functioned as a corporate board, with the Senate predicting supply and demand rather than the market itself.[87]

Thirdly, as highlighted by Consul Marcello in his correspondence with the Senate, the management of fully operational public lines, with cargo at capacity, offered considerable benefits to the state. This arrangement not only generated significant revenue through freight charges, trade taxes, and duties but also aligned with the public interest by keeping a commercial fleet that could be swiftly repurposed for military use. Freight served as a secondary income source, with the primary financial gains stemming from taxes and duties. Mandating all goods to pass through Venetian customs afforded the city a twofold benefit: it cemented Venice's position as the Mediterranean's trading hub and, through strict control over ship cargoes, ensured a consistent flow of tax revenue to the state treasury.[88] The dual-use capability of the commercial fleet for military purposes emphasizes the public navigation system's integral role in Venice's economic and defensive strategy.

Lastly, public navigation served as a means of reinforcing Venetian social cohesion, as it brought together all strata of Venetian society aboard the market galleys. These voyages, protected under the State's auspices, conferred distinct benefits across the social spectrum. For the nobility, these journeys acted as a formative apprenticeship for the youth, offering them first-hand experience in the nuances of mercantile trade. Meanwhile, young cadets from less affluent patrician families found opportunities as arbalesters, gaining valuable experience alongside a wage. Commoners, employed in roles ranging from rowers and trumpeters to fishermen and canteen staff, not only received compensation but were also permitted to engage in limited trade. The arsenal's dedication to constructing market galleys provided substantial employment for commoners, particularly benefiting many families in the Castello district through various facets of public navigation. Furthermore, onboard 'there was a strong bond between men of the crew, merchants and nobles after sailing together for several months'.[89]

Considering these elements, we can agree with Hocquet when he states that the state's intervention in the commercial sector was more political than economic; it did not purchase goods directly but established a framework of regulations, procedures, and incentives that supported Venetian merchant enterprises.[90] This system depended on businesses complying with state oversight, including undergoing inspections, paying customs duties, and adhering to restrictions on galley cargo for public navigation. In exchange, public institutions offered benefits such as a legal system that worked as a third party in disputes, protection in international markets through consular presence, and the opportunity to sail under the Venetian flag, benefiting from conditions guaranteed to Serenissima's merchants through international treaties. The prominent role of public institutions in commerce—in terms of both oversight and the potential for benefits and access to Republic-provided services like public navigation—made compliance with regulations, avoiding deceitful practices and maintaining a good reputation advantageous for merchants.[91] In Venice, contrary to what is often seen in reputation-based systems where public institutions play a minimal role, we find a unique interplay between personal reputation and a robust legal framework. Personal reputation continued to be crucial for ensuring compliance with agreements. Yet, Venice's comprehensive legal system also enabled the pursuit of defaulters, melding the advantages of both informal and formal institutional benefits. This approach stresses Venice's refined strategy to maintain commercial integrity and cultivate trust within its trading network, emphasizing the potential for oversight and control to ensure adherence to established standards.[92] These strategies not only mitigated the costs and risks of international commerce but also allowed small- and medium-sized enterprises to engage in profitable ventures.[93]

Notes

1 Isabella Cecchini and Luciano Pezzolo, 'Merchants and Institutions in Early-Modern Venice', *The Journal of European Economic History* 41, no. 2 (2012): 89–114; Luciano Pezzolo, 'The via Italiana to Capitalism', in *The Cambridge History of Capitalism, I, The Rise of Capitalism: From Ancient Origins to 1848*, ed. Larry Neal and Jeffrey G. Williamson (Cambridge: Cambridge University Press, 2014), 266–313.

2 Research into the dispositions of merchants, the influence of public institutions on international commerce, and the movement of goods has significantly contributed to discussions surrounding the emergence of commercial capitalism, European expansion, and entrepreneurial activity, particularly in the Tuscan region. This focus is partly attributable to the extensive availability of data. For detailed examinations on this topic, refer to the following key studies: Armando Sapori, *Una compagnia di Calimala ai primi del Trecento*, (Firenze: Leo S. Olschki, 1932); Armando Sapori, *Studi di storia economica medievale*, Biblioteca storica Sansoni. N. S (Firenze: Sansoni, 1940); Raymond De Roover, *Money, Banking and Credit in Mediaeval Bruges. Italian Merchant-Bankers Lombards and Money-Changers: A Study in the Origins of Banking* (Cambridge, MA: The Mediaeval Academy of America, 1948); Federigo Melis, *Aspetti della vita economica medievale* (Firenze: Olschki, 1962).

3 Michael N. Pearson, 'Merchants and States', in *The Political Economy of Merchant Empires. State, Power and World Trade, 1350-1750*, ed. James D. Tracy (Cambridge: Cambridge University Press, 1991), 41–116; Frederic C. Lane, 'The Role of Governments in Economic Growth in Early Modern Times', *The Journal of Economic History* 35, no. 1 (1975): 8–17.

4 Numerous scholars have emphasized the state's central role in the economy, considering it a key player in shaping a new societal framework: Douglass C. North, John Joseph Wallis, and Barry R. Weingast, *Violence and Social Orders: A Conceptual Framework for Interpreting Recorded Human History* (Cambridge, New York: Cambridge University Press, 2009); Daron Acemoglu, *Why Nations Fail: The Origins of Power, Prosperity, and Poverty*, (New York: Crown Publishers, 2012). Conversely, in a pointed critique, some argue that transformative change lies in the rise of a new social group, the bourgeoisie, grounded more in knowledge and ideas than in capital and institutions: Deirdre N. McCloskey, *The Bourgeois Virtues: Ethics for an Age of Commerce* (Chicago, IL: University of Chicago Press, 2006); Deirdre N. McCloskey, *Bourgeois Dignity: Why Economics Can't Explain the Modern World* (Chicago, IL: University of Chicago Press, 2010); Deirdre N. McCloskey, *Bourgeois Equality: How Ideas, Not Capital or Institutions, Enriched the World* (Chicago, IL, London: University of Chicago Press, 2016); Joel Mokyr, *The Lever of Riches:Technological Creativity and Economic Progress* (New York, Oxford: Oxford University Press, 1990); Joel Mokyr, *The Gifts of Athena: Historical Origins of the Knowledge Economy* (Princeton, NJ: Princeton University Press, 2011); Joel Mokyr, *A Culture of Growth: The Origins of the Modern Economy* (Princeton, NJ: Princeton University Press, 2016).

5 Avner Greif, Paul Milgrom, and Barry R. Weingast, 'Coordination, Commitment, and Enforcement: The Case of the Merchant Guild', *Journal of Political Economy* 102, no. 4 (1994): 745–76; Avner Greif, 'Family Structure, Institutions, and Growth: The Origins and Implications of Western Corporations', *American Economic Review* 96, no. 2 (2006): 308–12.

6 Anna Bellavitis, '«Per cittadini metterete...»: la stratificazione della società veneziana cinquecentesca tra norma giuridica e riconoscimento sociale', *Quaderni Storici* 89 (1995): 359–83; Sheilagh Ogilvie, *Institutions and European Trade: Merchant Guilds, 1000-1800* (Cambridge: Cambridge University Press, 2011), 164; Andrea Caracausi, Giovanni Favero, and Paola Lanaro, 'A Political Economy? Some Preliminary Thoughts on Economic Privileges in Early Modern Venice', in *Die ökonomie des privilegs, Westeuropa 16.-19. Jh./L'économie du privilege, Europe Occidentale XVIe-XIX siecles*, ed. Guillaume Garner (Frankfurt am Mainz: Vittorio Klostermann, 2016), 365–95.

7 Frederic C. Lane, *Andrea Barbarigo. Merchant of Venice* (Baltimore, MD: Johns Hopkins University Press, 1944), 11–15; Reinhold C. Mueller, *Immigrazione e cittadinanza nella Venezia medievale* (Roma: Viella, 2010), 18–32.

8 Mohamed Tahar Mansouri, 'Foreign and Mediterranean: Integration and Rejection', *Imago temporis. Medium Aevum 1,* (2007): 13–23; Mueller, *Immigrazione e cittadinanza nella Venezia medievale*, 32–49; Maartje van Gelder, *Trading Places: The Netherlandish Merchants in Early Modern Venice* (Leiden, Boston, MA: Brill, 2009); Maria Fusaro, 'Politics of Justice/Politics of Trade: Foreign Merchants and the Administration of Justice from the Records of Venice's Giudici del Forestier', *Mélanges de l'École française de Rome - Italie et Méditerranée modernes et contemporaines*, no. 126-1 (2014), https://doi.org/10.4000/mefrim.1665; Tamsin Prideaux, 'Navigating Family Welfare and Dwelling Space for Mercantile Migrants in Venice, 1550-1700', *Cultural and Social History* 19, no. 4 (2022): 371–87.

9 Anna Bellavitis, *Identité, mariage, mobilité sociale: citoyennes et citoyens à Venise au XVIe siècle*, (Rome: Ecole française de Rome, 2001), 19–41; Mueller, *Immigrazione e cittadinanza nella Venezia medievale*, 17–63.

10 Ugo Tucci, *Mercanti, Navi e Monete Nel Cinquecento Veneziano* (Bologna: Edizioni Il Mulino, 1981), 18–19.

11 Bellavitis, *Identité, mariage, mobilité sociale*, 19–41; Mueller, *Immigrazione e cittadinanza nella Venezia medievale*, 17–63; Maria Pia Pedani, 'Consoli Veneziani Nei Porti Del Mediterraneo in Età Moderna', in *Mediterraneo in Armi (Secc. XV-XVIII)*, ed. Rossella Cancila, vol. 1 (Palermo: Mediterranea, 2007), 180.

12 Tucci, *Mercanti, Navi e Monete Nel Cinquecento Veneziano*, 21–22.

13 Avner Greif, 'Reputation and Coalitions in Medieval Trade: Evidence on the Maghribi Traders', *The Journal of Economic History* 49, no. 4 (1989): 857–82; Greif, 'Family Structure, Institutions, and Growth'; Yadira González de Lara, 'The Secret of Venetian Success: A Public-Order, Reputation-Based Institution', *European Review of Economic History* 12 (2008): 247–85.

14 Jean-Claude Hocquet, *Le sel et la fortune de Venise. II. Voiliers et commerce en Mediterranée* (Villeneuve-d'Ascq: Publications de l'Université de Lille III, 1978); Sofia Gullino, 'Northern Grain and the Flemish Nation in Genoa: The Structural Consequences of a Famine (1585-1616)', *Business History*, Advance online publication (2021), https://doi.org/10.1080/00076791.2021.1979518; Marina Romani and Rachele Scuro, 'Grain Trade in Early Modern Mantua and Venice: The Role of Ashkenazi and Italian Jews', *Business History*, Advance online publication (2022), https://doi.org/10.1080/00076791.2022.2103543.

15 ASVe, MdC, folder 29, reg. 2, letters to Antonio Negro in Damascus, June 1482.

16 ASVe, *Segretario alle voci*, reg. 6, f. 96r, August 1482.

17 ASVe, MdC, folder 29, reg. 2, letters to Antonio Negro in Damascus, June 1482 and, 22 November 1482; Francesco Marcello, Consul in Damascus, 22 November 1482; Vielmo Anzelieri in Damascus, 20 August 1483.

18 ASVe, MdC, folder 29, reg. 2, letter to Antonio Negro in Damascus, 22 November 1482.

19 Muhammad Khalid Masud, Rudolph Peters, and David Stephan Powers, *Dispensing Justice in Islam: Qadis and Their Judgements*, (Leiden, Boston, MA: Brill,

2006); Gad G. Gilbar, 'The Qadi, the Big Merchant and Forbidden Interest (Ribā)', *British Journal of Middle Eastern Studies* 39, no. 1 (2012): 115–36.

20 ASVe, MdC, folder 29, reg. 2, letter to Antonio Negro, June 1482. Complaints regarding the treatment of their merchants were frequent, as evidenced by the letter sent by Doge Niccolò Tron in 1473 to the Sultan of Egypt, Qāytbāy. John Wansbrough, 'A Mamluk Letter of 877/1473', *Bulletin of the School of Oriental and African Studies* 24, no. 2 (1961): 200–213. On the Mamluk strategies to keep control of the East-West trade passing through Egypt: John L. Meloy, 'Imperial Strategy and Political Exigency: The Red Sea Spice Trade and the Mamluk Sultanate in the Fifteenth Century', *Journal of the American Oriental Society* 123, no. 1 (2003): 1–19.

21 ASVe, MdC, folder 29, reg. 2, letter to Antonio Negro in Damascus, 22 November 1482.

22 '*Parmi da novo di ttal suo parolle perché esendo marchadante doveria inttender quall forza à le lettere di chambio, che sono senttenzie paratte e senpre che lle sia aprezenttade all'ofizio di consolli e fuora ad ogni iudize inmediatte è mandà a segizion ell vigor del credito'*. ASVe, MdC, folder 29, reg. 2, letter to Vielmo Anzelieri in Damascus, 20 August 1483.

23 '*perché li amizi se die anteponer alli stranii*'. ASVe, MdC, folder 29, reg. 2, letter to Francesco Marcello, Consul in Damascus, 20 August 1483.

24 Georg Christ, *Trading Conflicts: Venetian Merchants and Mamluk Officials in Late Medieval Alexandria* (Leiden, Boston, MA: Brill, 2012), 204. The consul was not usually allowed to trade independently unless in exceptional circumstances and was normally only allowed to sell a limited number of products. Pedani, 'Consoli veneziani nei porti del Mediterraneo in Età moderna'. The blending of public and private interests and the 'hunt' for public offices and positions is also described for the Netherlands. See Julia Adams, *The Familial State: Ruling Families and Merchant Capitalism in Early Modern Europe* (Ithaca, NY: Cornell University Press, 2005), chaps 3 and 4.

25 Ugo Tucci, 'Mercanti veneziani e usi di piazza ad Alessandria alla fine del Quattrocento', in *Relazioni economiche tra Europa e mondo islamico, secc. XIII-XVIII: Atti della 'Trentottesima Settimana di Studi' 1-5 Maggio 2006*, ed. Simonetta Cavaciocchi (Firenze: Le Monnier, Istituto internazionale di storia economica 'F. Datini', 2007), 365–73; Francisco Javier Apellániz Ruiz de Galarreta, *Pouvoir et finance en Méditerranée pré-moderne: le deuxième état mamelouk et le commerce des épices (1382-1517)* (Barcelona: Consejo superior de investigaciones científicas, Institución Milá y Fontanals, Departemento de estudios medievales, 2009), 202; Alessio Sopracasa, *Venezia e l'Egitto alla fine del Medioevo: le tariffe di Alessandria* (Alexandrie: Centre d'études alexandrines, 2013), 329, 350.

26 ASVe, MdC, folder 29, reg. 2, letter to Antonio Negro in Damascus, June 1482.

27 Travis Bruce, 'Commercial Conflict Resolution across the Religious Divide in the Thirteenth-Century Mediterranean', *Mediterranean Historical Review* 30, no. 1 (2015): 19–38.

28 Frederic C. Lane, 'Fleets and Fairs: The Functions of the Venetian Muda', in *Studi in Onore Di Armando Sapori*, vol. I (Milan: Istituto Editoriale Cisalpino, 1957), 649–64.

29 Benjamin Arbel, 'The Last Decades If Venice's Trade with the Mamluks: Importations into Egypt and Syria', *Mamluk Studies Review* 8, no. 2 (2004): 37–86; Christ, *Trading Conflicts*, 19–54.

30 Apellániz Ruiz de Galarreta, *Pouvoir et finance en Méditerranée pré-moderne*, 13–46; Christ, *Trading Conflicts*, 91–93.

31 ASVe, MdC, folder 29, reg. 2, letter to Antonio Negro in Damascus, June 1482.

32 Pedani, 'Consoli veneziani nei porti del Mediterraneo in Età moderna'.

33 Antonio Trampus, 'La formazione del diritto consolare moderno a Venezia e NElle Province Unite tra Seicento e Settecento', *Rivista di storia del diritto italiano* 67 (1994): 283–319.

34 Giorgio Zordan, *I Visdomini di Venezia nel sec. XIII: ricerche su un'antica magistratura finanziaria*, (Padova: CEDAM, 1971), 1–18; Maria Pia Pedani, 'Venetian Consuls in

Egypt and Syria in the Ottoman Age', *Mediterranean World* 18 (2006): 7–21; Georg Christ, 'The Venetian Consul and the Cosmopolitan Mercantile Community of Alexandria at the Beginning of the Ninth/Fifteenth Century', *Al-Masaq* 26, no. 1 (2014): 62–77.

35 Pedani, 'Consoli veneziani nei porti del Mediterraneo in Età moderna ', 176.

36 Pedani, 180–81; Christ, *Trading Conflicts*, 67–87; Christ, 'The Venetian Consul and the Cosmopolitan Mercantile Community of Alexandria at the Beginning of the Ninth/ Fifteenth Century'.

37 Corrado Marciani, 'Consolati veneti in Abruzzo', *Studi Veneziani, n.s.* 9 (1967): 625–41; Mario Infelise, 'Consoli e mercanti veneti a Monopoli', in *Monopoli nell'età del Rinascimento*, ed. Domenico Cofano, vol. 2 (Monopoli: Grafischena, 1988), 767–75; Umberto Signori, 'I consoli veneziani nel Regno di Napoli: appunti e riflessioni su un'istituzione consolare durante la prima età moderna', *Annali dell'Istituto Italiano di Studi Storici* 32 (2019): 109–42.

38 Maria Pia Pedani Fabris, 'The Oath of a Venetian Consul in Egypt (1284)', *Quaderni Di Studi Arabi* 14 (1996): 216; Alberto Sacerdoti, 'Il consolato veneziano del Regno Hafsida di Tunisi (1274 – 1578)', *Studi Veneziani, n.s.* 11 (1969): 531–35; Eric Vallet, *Pour l'honneur et Le Profit. Marchands Vénitiens En Syrie à La Fin Du XVe Siècle* (Paris: ADHE, 1999), 195–205.

39 Umberto Signori, 'Supplier pour le consulat. Entre défense des intérêts personnels et service fidèle des consuls vénitiens dans le Levant ottoman (1670-1703)', *Cahiers de la Méditerranée 98*, (2019): 29–44; Umberto Signori, 'Between Misery and Reward: The Culture of Vigilance in the Experience of a Venetian Consul during the Early Modern Period', *Società e Storia 177*, (2022): 526–45.

40 ASVe, MdC, folder 29, reg. 2, letter to Antonio Negro in Damascus, June 1482.

41 ASVe, MdC, folder 29, reg. 2, letters to Francesco Giustinian in Crete (*addendum*), 16 July 1482; Giacomo Van Chlei, in Bruges, 16 November 1482; Alvise Malipiero, in Constantinople, 22 November 1482; Andrea Alberga, in Candia (*addendum*), 21 November 1482; Alvise Malipiero in Constantinople, 11 December 1482.

42 ASVe, MdC, folder 29, reg. 2, letters to Antonio Negro in Damascus, June 1482; Antonio Negro, in Damascus, 10 August 1482; Alvise Malipiero, in Constantinople, 17 February 1483.

43 A similar council, known as the Council of Twelve, was also formed on all Venetian ships to manage the most urgent issues. Pedani, 'Consoli veneziani nei porti del Mediterraneo in Età moderna', 189.

44 Gino Luzzatto, 'Vi furono fiere a Venezia?', in *Studi di storia economica veneziana* (Padova: CEDAM, 1954).

45 ASVe, *Senato, Dispacci antichi rettori ed altre cariche al Senato*, folder 1, file 1, c. 1, letter from Francesco Marcello, consul in Damascus, to the Venetian Senate, 28 October 1483.

46 The case lingered until at least 1485, by which time Marcello, in a letter to the Doge, even accused Zorzi of circumventing the Doge himself, driven solely by the desire to enrich himself at the expense of those who work and take risks in genuine trade. These serious words convey the extent of the potential harm Zorzi's actions could have inflicted on Damascus's cottimo through his lawsuit. ASVe, *Senato, Dispacci antichi rettori ed altre cariche al Senato*, folder 1, file 1 and 2, letter from Francesco Marcello to the Doge, 31 May 1485. For the functioning of merchant communities abroad: Benjamin Arbel, 'Colonie d'oltremare', in *Storia di Venezia. Dalle origini alla caduta della Serenissima, V, Il Rinascimento. Società Ed Economia*, ed. Alberto Tenenti and Ugo Tucci (Roma: Istituto della Enciclopedia Italiana, 1996), 947–85. For the interplay between private and public interest and power management: Reinhold C. Mueller, 'Pubblico e privato nel dominio veneziano delle isole greche a metà Quattrocento. Il caso dei Giustinian', in *Venezia e le Isole Ionie*, ed. Chryssa Maltezou and Gherardo Ortalli (Venezia: Istituto Veneto di Scienze, Lettere ed Arti, 2005), 71–100.

47 Giovanni Italo Cassandro, 'La curia di petizion e il diritto processuale di Venezia', *Archivio Veneto* V, no. 19 (1936): 72–144; Giovanni Italo Cassandro, 'La curia di petizion e il diritto processuale di Venezia', *Archivio Veneto* V, no. 20 (1937): 1–210; Fusaro, 'Politics of Justice/Politics of Trade'; Claudia Passarella, *Interessi Di Parte e Logiche Del Processo. La Giustizia Civile a Venezia in Età Moderna* (Torino: G. Giappichelli Editore, 2018). On legal pluralism: Paolo Prodi, *Una storia della giustizia: Dal pluralismo dei fori al moderno dualismo tra coscienza e diritto* (Bologna: Il Mulino, 2015); Guillaume Calafat, 'Jurisdictional Pluralism in a Litigious Sea (1590–1630): Hard Cases, Multi-Sited Trials and Legal Enforcement between North Africa and Italy', *Past & Present* 242, no. Supplement 14 (2019): 142–78; Niels Fieremans, 'Forum-Shopping Pirates? Litigation Strategies to Address Maritime Plunder in Late-Medieval Flanders', *International Journal of Maritime History* 35, no. 1 (2023): 3–23.

48 ASVe, *Senato, Dispacci antichi rettori ed altre cariche al Senato*, folder 1, file 1, c. 1, letter from Francesco Marcello, consul in Damascus, to the Venetian Senate.

49 Deborah Howard and Francesco Bianchi, 'Life and Death in Damascus: The Material Culture of Venetians in the Syrian Capital in the Mid-Fifteenth Century', *Studi Veneziani*, n.s., 46 (2003): 233–300.

50 David Abulafia, 'Cittadino e denizen: mercanti mediterranei a Southampton e a Londra', in *Sistema di rapporti ed élites economiche in Europa (secoli XII - XVII)*, ed. Mario Del Treppo (Napoli: Liguori, 1994), 288–90; Giovanna Petti Balbi, *Comunità forestiere e 'nationes' nell'Europa dei secoli XIII-XVI*, (Napoli: Liguori, 2001); Giovanna Petti Balbi, 'Le nationes italiane all'estero', in *Il Rinascimento Italiano e l'Europa.* IV. *Commercio e cultura mercantile*, ed. Franco Franceschi, Richard Goldthwaite, and Reinhold Mueller, (Vicenza: Colla Editore, 2007), 397–424; Giorgia Nordio, 'La colonia mercantile veneziana nella Londra di metà Quattrocento: attività commerciale e movimento anti-alien', in *Atti del congresso internazionale "Politiche Del credito. investimento, consumo e solidarietà"*, eds. Gemma Boschiero and Barbara Molina (Asti: Cassa di risparmio di Asti, 2004), 222–40.

51 Christ, *Trading Conflicts*; Christ, 'The Venetian Consul and the Cosmopolitan Mercantile Community of Alexandria at the Beginning of the Ninth/Fifteenth Century'.

52 ASVe, GrM, folder 250, reg. 2, cc. 9, 15, 16, 17, 18, 25, 26, 38, 44, 47.

53 Frederic C. Lane, 'Double Entry Bookkeeping and Resident Merchants', *The Journal of European Economic History* 6, no. 1 (1977): 177–91.

54 For insights into the coexistence of public and private maritime commerce in the 15th-century Mediterranean, see Raoul González Arévalo, ed., *Navegación institucional y navegación privada en el Mediterráneo medieval* (Granada: Alhulia, 2015).

55 The cultural foundations of the Venetian leadership, within which certain historians discern a distinct ethos of cooperation and mutual assistance, offer insightful explanations for the initiation of the State convoy system. Fernando Fagiani, 'Schizzo storico-antropologico di un gruppo dirigente: il patriziato veneziano (secoli XII-XV)', *Studi Veneziani, n.s.* XV (1988): 32–33.

56 Frederic Chapin Lane, *Venice, a Maritime Republic* (Baltimore, MD: Johns Hopkins University Press, 1973), 124–31.

57 Before the introduction of cannons, an armed ship referred to a vessel that carried a large crew, including marines or crossbowmen, and was capable of navigation both by oars and sails. Lane, 48–54.

58 Lane, 119–24.

59 Ships equipped with a large crew, about 200 men, who could travel both rowing and sailing. It was called a 'long ship' as its length was about eight times the width. Fast and easy to manoeuvre, in the mid-15th century they came to have a capacity of over 250 tons. Alberto Sacerdoti, 'Note sulle galere da mercato veneziane nel XV secolo', *Bollettino dell'Istituto di storia della società e dello stato* IV (1962): 80–105; Frederic C. Lane, 'Venetian Merchant Galleys, 1300-1334: Private and Communal Operation', *Speculum* 38, no. 2 (1963): 179–205.

60 Bernard Doumerc, 'Il dominio del mare', in *Storia di Venezia*. IV, *Il Rinascimento. Politica e cultura*, ed. Alberto Tenenti and Ugo Tucci, (Roma: Istituto della Enciclopedia Italiana, 1996), 118; Gino Luzzatto, 'Navigazione di linea e navigazione libera nelle grandi città marinare del Medio Evo', in *Studi di storia economica veneziana* (Padova: Cedam, 1954), 55.
61 Cristofalo Fioravante and Pietro Querini, *'Infeliçe e sventuratta coca Querina': i racconti originali del naufragio dei Veneziani nei mari del Nord*, ed. Angela Pluda (Roma: Viella, 2019).
62 Freddy Thiriet, 'Quelques observations sur le traffic des galeres venitiennes d'apres le chiffres des incanti (XIVe – XVe siecles)', in *Studi in onore di Amintore Fanfani*, ed. M.R. Caroselli, vol. III (Milano: Giuffrè, 1962), 495–522.
63 Lane, 'Double Entry Bookkeeping and Resident Merchants'. For the interrelation between public and private navigation in the Mediterranean, see Raoul González Arévalo, 'Navegación institucional y navegación privada en el Mediteráneo Medieval', in *Navegación institucional y navegación privada en el Mediterráneo Medieval*, ed. Raoul González Arévalo (Granada: Alhulia, 2015), 5–10.
64 Persia engaged in direct competition with the Mamluks, who controlled Egypt and Syria, maintaining the Trebizond route as an alternative to the Red Sea pathway. Lane, *Venice, a Maritime Republic*, 79–82.
65 Luzzatto, 'Navigazione di linea e navigazione libera nelle grandi città marinare del Medio Evo'.
66 Lane, *Venice, a Maritime Republic*, pp. 144–146.
67 The shipping line had become particularly useful for Venice's commercial partners, who, indeed, did not accept the idea of suspending the galleys' transit: the sheikhs reacted with confiscations of Venetian goods, for example, at every interruption of the navigation lines. Doumerc, 'Il dominio del mare', 138.
68 Doumerc, 119–22.
69 Sacerdoti, 'Note sulle galere da mercato veneziane nel XV secolo', 80.
70 David Igual Luis, 'Las galeras mercantiles venecianas y el puerto de Valencia (1391 – 1534)', *Anuarios de Estudios Medievales* 24 (1994): 180.
71 Alberto Tenenti and Corrado Vivanti, 'Le film d'un grand systeme de navigation: les galeres marchandes venitiennes XIVe-XVIe siècles', *Annales. Histoire, Sciences Sociales* 16, no. 1 (1961): 84.
72 Sacerdoti, 'Note sulle galere da mercato veneziane nel XV secolo', 88.
73 Doris Stöckly, *Le système de l'incanto des galées du marché à Venise: fin XIIIe-milieu XVe siècle* (Leiden, New York, Köln: Brill, 1995), 49–52.
74 ASVe, *Senato Mar*, reg. 7, c. 112r. Four years later, in 1467, despite the war, the price paid by Foscari for the *Incanto* increased to 180 ducats. ASV, Senato Mar, reg. 8, c. 119v.
75 ASVe, *Senato Mar*, reg. 8, cc. 116v–119v.
76 ASVe, *Senato Mar*, reg. 7, cc. 109r–112r.
77 Claire Judde de Larivière, *Naviguer, commercer, gouverner: économie maritime et pouvoirs à Venise (XVe-XVIe siècles)* (Leiden, Boston: Brill, 2008), 200–04.
78 J. L. Bolton and Francesco Guidi Bruscoli, 'When Did Antwerp Replace Bruges as the Commercial and Financial Centre of North-Western Europe? The Evidence of the Borromei Ledger for 1438', *The Economic History Review* 61, no. 2 (2008): 360–79.
79 ASVe, *Senato, Deliberazioni, Incanti di galere*, reg. 1 (1469–1489), ff. 49v–50r.
80 ASVe, MG, folder 15, reg. 2, ff. 1, 4-8, 11, 14, 15, 18, 19, 28, 35, 46, 62, 71, 75, 80, 87, 118, 129, 131.
81 Judde de Larivière, *Naviguer, commercer, gouverner*, 44–48. The comparison, made by François Gipoloux, between the Italian maritime republics, the Hansa League, and the system of monopoly and tributary trade in Medieval China underlines the crucial role of public institutions in regulating the expanding trade sector. This parallel illuminates the diverse strategies employed across cultures to manage and foster trade, highlighting the universal necessity for structured oversight in flourishing trade environments.

François Gipouloux, *La Méditerranée asiatique: villes portuaires et réseaux marchands en Chine, au Japon et en Asie au Sud-Est, 16.-21. siècle* (Paris: CNRS, 2018), 89–99.

82 Lane, 'Venetian Merchant Galleys, 1300-1334'; Lane, *Venice, a Maritime Republic*, 124–32; Jean Claude Hocquet, 'I meccanismi dei traffici', in *Storia di Venezia. Dalle origini alla caduta della Serenissima, III, La formazione dello stato patrizio*, ed. Girolamo Arnaldi, Giorgio Cracco, and Alberto Tenenti (Roma: Istituto della Enciclopedia Italiana, 1997), 529–616.

83 To maintain its primacy, Venice implemented measures designed to support its merchants. This included prohibiting the use of the lagoon city as a mere transit port. A foreign merchant wishing to send goods to the Levant via Venice was required to do so by selling these products to a Venetian merchant. Fagiani, 'Schizzo storico-antropologico di un gruppo dirigente: il patriziato veneziano (secoli XII-XV)', 35–35.

84 Sacerdoti, 'Note sulle galere da mercato veneziane nel XV secolo'; Lane, 'Venetian Merchant Galleys, 1300-1334'; Jean Claude Hocquet, 'Les routes maritimes du commerce vénitien au XVe et XVIe siècles', in *Atti del V convegno internazionale di studi colombiani, navi e navigazione nei sec. XV e XVI*, ed. Graziella Galliano and Ausilia Roccatagliata (Genova: Civico Istituto Colombiano, 1990), 581–605.

85 Luzzatto, 'Vi furono fiere a Venezia?'; Judde de Larivière, *Naviguer, commercer, gouverner*, 17–25.

86 Lane, *Andrea Barbarigo. Merchant of Venice*, 45–51.

87 Lane, 48.

88 Roberto Cessi, 'Le relazioni commerciali tra Venezia e le Fiandre nel secolo XIV', *Nuovo Archivio Veneto* 27 (1914): 9; Judde de Larivière, *Naviguer, commercer, gouverner*, 45–46.

89 Ennio Concina, *L'Arsenale della Repubblica di Venezia: tecniche e istituzioni dal medioevo all'età moderna* (Milano: Electa, 1988); Robert C. Davis, *Shipbuilders of the Venetian Arsenal Workers and Workplace in the Preindustrial City* (Baltimore, MD: Johns Hopkins University Press, 1991); Judde de Larivière, *Naviguer, commercer, gouverner*, 44–48.

90 Hocquet, *Le sel et la fortune de Venise. II. Voiliers et commerce en Mediterranée*, 217.

91 For the role of public institutions: González de Lara, 'The Secret of Venetian Success: A Public-Order, Reputation-Based Institution'.

92 Avner Greif, 'On the Political Foundations of the Late Medieval Commercial Revolution: Genoa during the Twelfth and Thirteenth Centuries', *The Journal of Economic History* 54, no. 2 (1994): 271–87; González de Lara, 'The Secret of Venetian Success: A Public-Order, Reputation-Based Institution'; Jeremy Edwards and Sheilagh Ogilvie, 'Contract Enforcement, Institutions, and Social Capital: The Maghribi Traders Reappraised', *The Economic History Review* 65, no. 2 (2012): 421–44.

93 Lane, *Venice, a Maritime Republic*, 67–73.

References

Abulafia, David. 'Cittadino e denizen: mercanti mediterranei a Southampton e a Londra'. In *Sistema di rapporti ed élites economiche in Europa (secoli XII - XVII)*, edited by Mario Del Treppo, 288–90. Napoli: Liguori, 1994.

Acemoglu, Daron. *Why Nations Fail: The Origins of Power, Prosperity, and Poverty*. 1st edition. New York: Crown Publishers, 2012.

Adams, Julia. *The Familial State: Ruling Families and Merchant Capitalism in Early Modern Europe*. Ithaca, NY: Cornell University Press, 2005.

Apellániz Ruiz de Galarreta, Francisco Javier. *Pouvoir et finance en Méditerranée prémoderne: le deuxième état mamelouk et le commerce des épices (1382-1517)*. Barcelona: Consejo superior de investigaciones científicas, Institución Milá y Fontanals, Departemento de estudios medievales, 2009.

Arbel, Benjamin. 'Colonie d'oltremare'. In *Storia di Venezia. Dalle origini alla caduta della Serenissima, V, Il Rinascimento. Società ed economia*, edited by Alberto Tenenti and Ugo Tucci, 947–85. Roma: Istituto della Enciclopedia Italiana, 1996.

Arbel, Benjamin. 'The Last Decades of Venice's Trade with the Mamluks: Importations into Egypt and Syria'. *Mamluk Studies Review* 8, no. 2 (2004): 37–86.

Bellavitis, Anna. *Identité, mariage, mobilité sociale: citoyennes et citoyens à Venise au XVIe siècle*. Rome: Ecole française de Rome, 2001.

Bellavitis, Anna. '«Per cittadini metterete...»: la stratificazione della società veneziana cinquecentesca tra norma giuridica e riconoscimento sociale'. *Quaderni Storici* 89 (1995): 359–83.

Bolton, J. L., and Francesco Guidi Bruscoli. 'When Did Antwerp Replace Bruges as the Commercial and Financial Centre of North-Western Europe? The Evidence of the Borromei Ledger for 1438'. *The Economic History Review* 61, no. 2 (2008): 360–79.

Bruce, Travis. 'Commercial Conflict Resolution across the Religious Divide in the Thirteenth-Century Mediterranean'. *Mediterranean Historical Review* 30, no. 1 (2015): 19–38.

Calafat, Guillaume. 'Jurisdictional Pluralism in a Litigious Sea (1590–1630): Hard Cases, Multi-Sited Trials and Legal Enforcement between North Africa and Italy'. *Past & Present* 242, no. Supplement 14 (2019): 142–78.

Caracausi, Andrea, Giovanni Favero, and Paola Lanaro. 'A Political Economy? Some Preliminary Thoughts on Economic Privileges in Early Modern Venice'. In *Die Ökonomie des Privilegs, Westeuropa 16.-19. Jh./L'économie du privilège, Europe Occidentale XVIe-XIX siècles.*, edited by Guillaume Garner, 365–95. Frankfurt am Mainz: Vittorio Klostermann, 2016.

Cassandro, Giovanni Italo. 'La curia di petizion e il diritto processuale di Venezia'. *Archivio veneto* V, no. 19 (1936): 72–144.

Cassandro, Giovanni Italo. 'La curia di petizion e il diritto processuale di Venezia'. *Archivio veneto* V, no. 20 (1937): 1–210.

Cecchini, Isabella, and Luciano Pezzolo. 'Merchants and Institutions in Early-Modern Venice'. *The Journal of European Economic History* 41, no. 2 (2012): 89–114.

Cessi, Roberto. 'Le relazioni commerciali tra Venezia e le Fiandre nel secolo XIV'. *Nuovo archivio veneto* 27 (1914): 5–116.

Christ, Georg. 'The Venetian Consul and the Cosmopolitan Mercantile Community of Alexandria at the Beginning of the Ninth/Fifteenth Century'. *Al-Masaq* 26, no. 1 (2014): 62–77.

Christ, Georg. *Trading Conflicts: Venetian Merchants and Mamluk Officials in Late Medieval Alexandria*. Leiden, Boston, MA: Brill, 2012.

Concina, Ennio. *L'Arsenale della Repubblica di Venezia: tecniche e istituzioni dal medioevo all'età moderna*. Milano: Electa, 1988.

Davis, Robert C. *Shipbuilders of the Venetian Arsenal Workers and Workplace in the Preindustrial City*. Baltimore, MD: Johns Hopkins University Press, 1991.

De Roover, Raymond. *Money, Banking and Credit in Mediaeval Bruges. Italian Merchant-Bankers Lombards and Money-Changers: A Study in the Origins of Banking*. Cambridge, MA: The Mediaeval Academy of America, 1948.

Doumerc, Bernard. 'Il dominio del mare'. In *Storia di Venezia*. IV, *Il Rinascimento. Politica e cultura*, edited by Alberto Tenenti and Ugo Tucci, 113–80. Roma: Istituto della Enciclopedia Italiana, 1996.

Edwards, Jeremy, and Sheilagh Ogilvie. 'Contract Enforcement, Institutions, and Social Capital: The Maghribi Traders Reappraised'. *The Economic History Review* 65, no. 2 (2012): 421–44.

Fabris, Maria Pia Pedani. 'The Oath of a Venetian Consul in Egypt (1284)'. *Quaderni di studi arabi* 14 (1996): 215–22.

Fagiani, Fernando. 'Schizzo storico-antropologico di un gruppo dirigente: il patriziato veneziano (secoli XII-XV)'. *Studi Veneziani, n.s.* XV (1988): 15–69.

Fieremans, Niels. 'Forum-Shopping Pirates? Litigation Strategies to Address Maritime Plunder in Late-Medieval Flanders'. *International Journal of Maritime History* 35, no. 1 (2023): 3–23.

Fioravante, Cristofalo, and Pietro Querini. *'Infeliçe e sventuratta coca Querina': i racconti originali del naufragio dei Veneziani nei mari del Nord*, edited by Angela Pluda. Roma: Viella, 2019.

Fusaro, Maria. 'Politics of Justice/Politics of Trade: Foreign Merchants and the Administration of Justice from the Records of Venice's Giudici del Forestier'. *Mélanges de l'École française de Rome - Italie et Méditerranée modernes et contemporaines*, no. 126-1 (2014). https://doi.org/10.4000/mefrim.1665.

Gelder, Maartje van. *Trading Places: The Netherlandish Merchants in Early Modern Venice*. Leiden, Boston, MA: Brill, 2009.

Gilbar, Gad G. 'The Qadi, the Big Merchant and Forbidden Interest (Ribā)'. *British Journal of Middle Eastern Studies* 39, no. 1 (2012): 115–36.

Gipouloux, François. *La Méditerranée asiatique: villes portuaires et réseaux marchands en Chine, au Japon et en Asie au Sud-Est, 16.-21. siècle*. Paris: CNRS, 2018.

González Arévalo, Raoul. 'Navegación institucional y navegación privada en el Mediteráneo medieval'. In *Navegación institucional y navegación privada en el Mediterráneo medieval*, edited by Raoul González Arévalo, 5–10. Granada: Alhulia, 2015.

González de Lara, Yadira. 'The Secret of Venetian Success: A Public-Order, Reputation-Based Institution'. *European Review of Economic History* 12 (2008): 247–85.

Greif, Avner. 'Family Structure, Institutions, and Growth: The Origins and Implications of Western Corporations'. *American Economic Review* 96, no. 2 (2006): 308–12.

Greif, Avner. 'On the Political Foundations of the Late Medieval Commercial Revolution: Genoa during the Twelfth and Thirteenth Centuries'. *The Journal of Economic History* 54, no. 2 (1994): 271–87.

Greif, Avner. 'Reputation and Coalitions in Medieval Trade: Evidence on the Maghribi Traders'. *The Journal of Economic History* 49, no. 4 (1989): 857–82.

Greif, Avner, Paul Milgrom, and Barry R. Weingast. 'Coordination, Commitment, and Enforcement: The Case of the Merchant Guild'. *Journal of Political Economy* 102, no. 4 (1994): 745–76.

Gullino, Sofia. 'Northern Grain and the Flemish Nation in Genoa: The Structural Consequences of a Famine (1585-1616)'. *Business History*, Advance online publication (2021). https://doi.org/10.1080/00076791.2021.1979518.

Hocquet, Jean Claude. 'I meccanismi dei traffici'. In *Storia di Venezia. Dalle origini alla caduta della serenissima, III, La formazione dello stato patrizio*, edited by Girolamo Arnaldi, Giorgio Cracco, and Alberto Tenenti, 529–616. Roma: Istituto della Enciclopedia Italiana, 1997.

Hocquet, Jean Claude. 'Les routes maritimes du commerce vénitien au XVe et XVIe siècles'. In *Atti del V Convegno internazionale di studi colombiani, navi e navigazione nei sec. XV e XVI*, edited by Graziella Galliano and Ausilia Roccatagliata, 581–605. Genova: Civico Istituto Colombiano, 1990.

Hocquet, Jean-Claude. *Le sel et la fortune de Venise. II. Voiliers et commerce en Mediterranée*. Villeneuve-d'Ascq: Publications de l'Université de Lille III, 1978.

Howard, Deborah, and Francesco Bianchi. 'Life and Death in Damascus: The Material Culture of Venetians in the Syrian Capital in the Mid-Fifteenth Century'. *Studi Veneziani, n.s.*, 46 (2003): 233–300.

Igual Luis, David. 'Las galeras mercantiles venecianas y el puerto de Valencia (1391 – 1534)'. *Anuarios de Estudios Medievales* 24 (1994): 179–200.

Infelise, Mario. 'Consoli e mercanti veneti a Monopoli'. In *Monopoli nell'età del Rinascimento*, edited by Domenico Cofano, 2:767–75. Monopoli: Grafischena, 1988.

Judde de Larivière, Claire. *Naviguer, commercer, gouverner: économie maritime et pouvoirs à Venise (XVe-XVIe siècles)*. Leiden, Boston: Brill, 2008.

Lane, Frederic C. *Andrea Barbarigo. Merchant of Venice*. Baltimore, MD: Johns Hopkins University Press, 1944.

Lane, Frederic C. 'Double Entry Bookkeeping and Resident Merchants'. *The Journal of European Economic History* 6, no. 1 (1977): 177–91.

Lane, Frederic C. 'Fleets and Fairs: The Functions of the Venetian Muda'. In *Studi in onore di Armando Sapori*, I:649–64. Milan: Istituto Editoriale Cisalpino, 1957.

Lane, Frederic C. 'The Role of Governments in Economic Growth in Early Modern Times'. *The Journal of Economic History* 35, no. 1 (1975): 8–17.

Lane, Frederic C. 'Venetian Merchant Galleys, 1300-1334: Private and Communal Operation'. *Speculum* 38, no. 2 (1963): 179–205.

Lane, Frederic Chapin. *Venice, a Maritime Republic*. Baltimore, MD: Johns Hopkins University Press, 1973.

Luzzatto, Gino. 'Navigazione di linea e navigazione libera nelle grandi città marinare del Medio Evo'. In *Studi di storia economica veneziana*, 53-58. Padova: Cedam, 1954.

Luzzatto, Gino. 'Vi furono fiere a Venezia?' In *Studi di storia economica veneziana*, 201-209. Padova: CEDAM, 1954.

Marciani, Corrado. 'Consolati Veneti in Abruzzo'. *Studi Veneziani, n.s.* 9 (1967): 625–41.

Masud, Muhammad Khalid, Rudolph Peters, and David Stephan Powers. *Dispensing Justice in Islam: Qadis and Their Judgements*. Studies in Islamic Law and Society 22. Leiden, Boston, MA: Brill, 2006.

McCloskey, Deirdre N. *Bourgeois Dignity: Why Economics Can't Explain the Modern World*. Chicago, IL: University of Chicago Press, 2010.

McCloskey, Deirdre N. *Bourgeois Equality: How Ideas, Not Capital or Institutions, Enriched the World*. Chicago, IL, London: University of Chicago Press, 2016.

McCloskey, Deirdre N. *The Bourgeois Virtues: Ethics for an Age of Commerce*. Chicago, IL: University of Chicago Press, 2006.

Melis, Federigo. *Aspetti della vita economica medievale*. Firenze: Olschki, 1962.

Meloy, John L. 'Imperial Strategy and Political Exigency: The Red Sea Spice Trade and the Mamluk Sultanate in the Fifteenth Century'. *Journal of the American Oriental Society* 123, no. 1 (2003): 1–19.

Mokyr, Joel. *A Culture of Growth: The Origins of the Modern Economy*. Princeton, NJ: Princeton University Press, 2016.

Mokyr, Joel. *The Gifts of Athena: Historical Origins of the Knowledge Economy*. Princeton, NJ: Princeton University Press, 2011.

Mokyr, Joel. *The Lever of Riches:Technological Creativity and Economic Progress*. New York, Oxford: Oxford University Press, 1990.

Mueller, Reinhold C. *Immigrazione e cittadinanza nella Venezia medievale*. Roma: Viella, 2010.

Mueller, Reinhold C. 'Pubblico e privato nel dominio veneziano delle isole greche a metà Quattrocento. Il caso dei Giustinian'. In *Venezia e le Isole Ionie*, edited by Chryssa Maltezou and Gherardo Ortalli, 71–100. Venezia: Istituto Veneto di Scienze, Lettere ed Arti, 2005.

Nordio, Giorgia. 'La colonia mercantile veneziana nella Londra di metà Quattrocento: attività commerciale e movimento anti-alien'. In *Atti del congresso internazionale "Politiche del credito. investimento, consumo e solidarietà"*, edited by Gemma Boschiero and Barbara Molina, 222–40. Asti: Cassa di risparmio di Asti, 2004.

North, Douglass C., John Joseph Wallis, and Barry R. Weingast. *Violence and Social Orders: A Conceptual Framework for Interpreting Recorded Human History*. Cambridge, New York: Cambridge University Press, 2009.

Ogilvie, Sheilagh. *Institutions and European Trade: Merchant Guilds, 1000-1800*. Cambridge: Cambridge University Press, 2011.

Passarella, Claudia. *Interessi di parte e logiche del processo. la giustizia civile a Venezia in Età moderna*. Torino: G. Giappichelli Editore, 2018.

Pearson, Michael N. 'Merchants and States'. In *The Political Economy of Merchant Empires. State, Power and World Trade, 1350-1750*, edited by James D. Tracy, 41–116. Cambridge: Cambridge University Press, 1991.

Pedani, Maria Pia. 'Consoli veneziani nei porti del Mediterraneo in Età moderna'. In *Mediterraneo in armi (secc. XV-XVIII)*, edited by Rossella Cancila, 1:175–205. Palermo: Mediterranea, 2007.

Petti Balbi, Giovanna. *Comunità forestiere e 'nationes' nell'Europa dei secoli XIII-XVI*. Napoli: Liguori, 2001.

Petti Balbi, Giovanna. 'Le nationes italiane all'estero'. In *Il Rinascimento italiano e l'Europa* IV, *Commercio e cultura mercantile*, edited by Franco Franceschi, Richard Goldthwaite, and Reinhold Mueller, 397–424. Vicenza: Colla Editore, 2007.

Pezzolo, Luciano. 'The via Italiana to Capitalism'. In *The Cambridge History of Capitalism, I, The Rise of Capitalism: From Ancient Origins to 1848*, edited by Larry Neal and Jeffrey G. Williamson, 266–313. Cambridge: Cambridge University Press, 2014.

Pia Pedani, Maria. 'Venetian Consuls in Egypt and Syria in the Ottoman Age'. *Mediterranean World* 18 (2006): 7–21.

Prideaux, Tamsin. 'Navigating Family Welfare and Dwelling Space for Mercantile Migrants in Venice, 1550-1700'. *Cultural and Social History* 19, no. 4 (2022): 371–87.

Prodi, Paolo. *Una storia della giustizia: Dal pluralismo dei fori al moderno dualismo tra coscienza e diritto*. Bologna: Il Mulino, 2015.

Romani, Marina, and Rachele Scuro. 'Grain Trade in Early Modern Mantua and Venice: The Role of Ashkenazi and Italian Jews'. *Business History*, Advance online publication (2022). https://doi.org/10.1080/00076791.2022.2103543.

Sacerdoti, Alberto. 'Il consolato veneziano del regno hafsida di Tunisi (1274 – 1578)'. *Studi Veneziani, n.s.* 11 (1969): 531–35.

Sacerdoti, Alberto. 'Note sulle galere da mercato veneziane nel XV secolo'. *Bollettino dell'istituto di storia della società e dello stato* IV (1962): 80–105.

Sapori, Armando. *Studi di storia economica medievale*. Firenze: Sansoni, 1940.

Sapori, Armando. *Una compagnia di Calimala ai primi del Trecento*. Firenze: Leo S. Olschki, 1932.

Signori, Umberto. 'Between Misery and Reward: The Culture of Vigilance in the Experience of a Venetian Consul during the Early Modern Period'. *Società e Storia*, 177 (2022): 526–45.

Signori, Umberto. 'I consoli veneziani nel Regno di Napoli: appunti e riflessioni su un' istituzione consolare durante la prima età moderna'. *Annali dell'Istituto Italiano di Studi Storici* 32 (2019): 109–42.

Signori, Umberto. 'Supplier pour le consulat. Entre défense des intérêts personnels et service fidèle des consuls vénitiens dans le Levant ottoman (1670-1703)'. *Cahiers de la Méditerranée* 98 (2019): 29–44.

Sopracasa, Alessio. *Venezia e l'Egitto alla fine del Medioevo: le tariffe di Alessandria*. Alexandrie: Centre d'études alexandrines, 2013.

Stöckly, Doris. *Le système de l'incanto des galées du marché à Venise: fin XIIIe-milieu XVe siècle*. Leiden, New York, Köln: Brill, 1995.

Tahar Mansouri, Mohamed. 'Foreign and Mediterranean: Integration and Rejection'. *Imago temporis. Medium Aevum* 1 (2007): 13–23.

Tenenti, Alberto, and Corrado Vivanti. 'Le film d'un grand système de navigation: les galères marchandes vénitiennes XIVe-XVIe siècles'. *Annales. Histoire, Sciences Sociales* 16, no. 1 (1961): 83–86.

Thiriet, Freddy. 'Quelques observations sur le traffic des galères vénitiennes d'après le chiffres des incanti (XIVe – XVe siècles)'. In *Studi in onore di Amintore Fanfani*, III:495–522. Milano: Giuffrè, 1962.

Trampus, Antonio. 'La formazione del diritto consolare moderno a Venezia e nelle Province Unite tra Seicento e Settecento'. *Rivista di storia del diritto italiano* 67 (1994): 283–319.

Tucci, Ugo. *Mercanti, navi e monete nel Cinquecento veneziano*. Bologna: Edizioni Il Mulino, 1981.

Tucci, Ugo. 'Mercanti veneziani e usi di piazza ad Alessandria alla fine del Quattrocento'. In *Relazioni economiche tra Europa e mondo islamico, secc. XIII-XVIII: Atti della 'Trentottesima settimana di studi' 1-5 Maggio 2006*, edited by Simonetta Cavaciocchi, 365–73. Firenze: Le Monnier, Istituto internazionale di storia economica 'F. Datini', 2007.

Vallet, Eric. *Pour l'honneur et le Profit. Marchands vénitiens en Syrie à la fin du XVe siècle*. Paris: ADHE, 1999.

Wansbrough, John. 'A Mamluk Letter of 877/1473'. *Bulletin of the School of Oriental and African Studies* 24, no. 2 (1961): 200–13.

Zordan, Giorgio. *I Visdomini di Venezia nel sec. XIII: ricerche su un'antica magistratura finanziaria*. Padova: CEDAM, 1971.

3 Commercial Strategies

How did family firms operate when trading luxury goods and what strategies were they able to devise when war destabilized international markets? This chapter examines the market dynamics and the challenges posed by international trade to Venetian mercantile firms, analysing these challenges from the *fraterne*'s own perspectives and the strategic adaptations they employed to face these obstacles. The initial focus is on Venice's intermediary role between the East and West, with an aim to elucidate why phenomena such as wars or pandemics significantly impeded those whose profits predominantly derived from international import and export rather than from production. Subsequent analysis explores the variability across markets in terms of commodities, interactive engagements, and financial transactions, shedding light on the manner in which Venetian firms manoeuvred through these challenges. The discourse progresses to the dilemma of markets rendered inaccessible, particularly due to the impacts of warfare and health crises, and the dependence on commercial networks trading in consistently demanded commodities, such as oils and metals, which found markets in both their raw and processed forms. Furthermore, this chapter delves into the strategy of constructing commodity chains by leveraging local resources and labour to facilitate and sustain international commerce.

Bridging Continents

The role that Venice wanted to play, and indeed played for many centuries, in international trade was that of a distribution hub for the flow of goods that were to supply European markets, on the one hand, and Eastern markets, on the other, capitalizing on its strategic position. Since the late 13th century, an expansion in contacts between Europe and Asia built upon earlier interactions, which, despite their decline following the collapse of the Roman and Chinese empires, were revitalized from the 11th century onwards. Despite challenges like language barriers and political differences, this era paved the way for a robust exchange system.[1] The Middle East emerged as a crucial connector between the Mediterranean and the Indian Ocean, facilitating trade and cultural exchanges.[2]

However, the Mongol Empire's disintegration in the late 14th century led to increased instability and danger on traditional trade routes through the Black Sea,

DOI: 10.4324/9781032628103-4

Armenia, and Persia.[3] The vital trading post of Tana was severely impacted by Tamerlane's raid in 1395, shifting significant trade flows towards safer routes through Syria and Egypt, under Mamluk control.[4] This re-routing aimed to enhance trade safety and establish the Egyptian route as the primary path for spices and goods between Europe and the Indies, managed efficiently by the Jewish Kârim merchants.[5]

Trade between Venice and the Near East, notably through key cities like Damascus, Beirut, Alexandria, and Cairo, surged in the early 15th century, making these locations crucial for importing goods such as pepper, silk, and spices, and exporting Venetian manufactured artefacts.[6] Alexandria served as the foremost portal from the West to the East, facilitated by Venetian merchants operating from their local *fondaco*. Similar to the Germans in Venice, the allocation of spaces by local authorities for storing goods, conducting trade, as well as living and practising religion, was generally tied not only to community control but also to the recognition of their dominant position.[7] Despite strict oversight, Venetians enjoyed a privileged status due to a protective consular system, and the reliable organization of state galleys ensuring safe voyages, as seen in the previous chapter, and ample silver and copper supplies from Germany, besides effective bartering practices.

The trade routes, spanning maritime, caravan, or a mix, originated from the Indian Malabar coast and the China and Malacca Straits. Three main pathways connected to European markets: one through Persia to Constantinople, potentially extending to Novgorod and Northern Europe; a route from the Orient to the Mediterranean via Hormuz, Mesopotamia, and Aleppo; and a primarily maritime path along the Indian coast through Hormuz and Aden, culminating in the Red Sea towards Cairo and Alexandria's markets.[8] Trade with the East faced challenges due to political instability, notably from fluctuating Mamluk policies that imposed variable duties and taxes on Western merchants. Despite these challenges, Venetian merchants remained a constant presence, thriving in the region.[9] However, the rise of the Ottomans in the mid-15th century destabilized trade, especially after their conquest of Syria and Egypt in 1517. This led to disrupted trade flows until Venetian diplomacy secured new trade agreements with the Ottomans.[10] These agreements maintained many of the previous conditions but slightly favoured Venice's rivals, the Genoese. Nonetheless, the opening of the spice trade and Western artefacts under Ottoman rule helped to minimize the disparities between Venetian and Genoese merchants, leading to a period of cooperation and distinct spheres of influence.[11]

The Ottoman conquests in Syria shifted the silk and spice trade routes northward towards Tripoli, Aleppo, and the ports of Iskenderun and Latakia. This shift, facilitated by political unity in the region, led Western merchants to migrate from Damascus and Beirut to Aleppo, becoming the new hub of international trade. Venice's early establishment of a vice-consul in Aleppo during the late 15th century was crucial for maintaining and even enhancing the dominance of Venetian merchants in Eastern trade. This move, which initially disadvantaged European rivals, facilitated the expansion of the Venetian community in the region.[12] By the 1470s, the Michiel family firm anticipated shifts in trade routes, leveraging these changes to their advantage, had not only positioned its agents in traditional markets such as Alexandria and Beirut, where they stationed two agents each but also explored emerging markets like Aleppo.[13] These cities became central for importing raw cotton, a commodity for which the Venetians managed to secure a monopoly.[14] In the 15th century, the trade in cotton alone was worth on average between 200,000 and 250,000 ducats yearly, with peaks (as in 1442) of 400,000 ducats.[15] Since spices and silk also began to be present on the market in Aleppo, Venetian interests revolved more and more intensively around the city: 'as affairs had been initially been conducted between Damascus, Aleppo, Tripoli and Beirut, in these times they are all reduced to Aleppo'.[16]

The development of trade routes connecting Asian goods to European ports based its success primarily on two factors. Firstly, the establishment of a land route facilitated the transport of goods from China and India through Central Asia and Persia to the Mediterranean, bypassing the control of Russian populations and falling under the easier management of the Byzantine Empire. This shift allowed Italian merchants to establish permanent settlements in major trading hubs, securing their dominance in the Asian goods trade. Concurrently, a significant development within Europe further benefited Italian traders: the traditional overland routes that carried European goods to Italy increasingly fell under Italian control. Italian merchants expanded their reach into the European hinterland, exchanging European for Levantine products. Historians often cite the rise and flourishing of the Champagne fairs as evidence of Italian commercial prowess in Europe and their dominance over continental trade routes.[17]

Markets and Commercial Integration

The goods that arrived in Western markets from the East were of various kinds and nature—ranging from artefacts to precious fabrics, from spices to soap. During the years considered in this book, Syrian markets, such as Damascus, and Beirut, as well as Egyptian markets such as Alexandria, were the main supply hubs for goods from Asia.

Markets and Products

For many centuries, one of the most important products for the Venetian trade network, and most requested by European markets, was pepper. Native to southern India, from Malabar, this spice had various applications over the centuries: in cooking and meat preservation, to improve the taste of foods, it was also used in medicine, as a cough suppressant and to improve digestion. Since ancient times, pepper had become a hallmark of the upper class consumption[18] and was one of the key products for Europe's economic development.[19] The quantities of pepper supplying the European markets varied considerably, depending on war events in the Mediterranean or possible drops in supplies from Asia.[20] As for the supply of pepper to Europe by the Venetians, there is a lack of reliable quantitative data. Considering the data provided by the Michiel ledger, covering the decade of war from 1470 to 1480, more than 145,000 pounds *sottili*[21] of black pepper arrived in Venice, mainly by means of state galleys, from the ports of Alexandria and Beirut. This number is notably significant given that pepper purchases were focused primarily between 1470 and 1472 and then again from 1477 onwards, experiencing a total cessation of imports during the mid-century because of the first Venetian-Ottoman War moving to the Adriatic.[22]

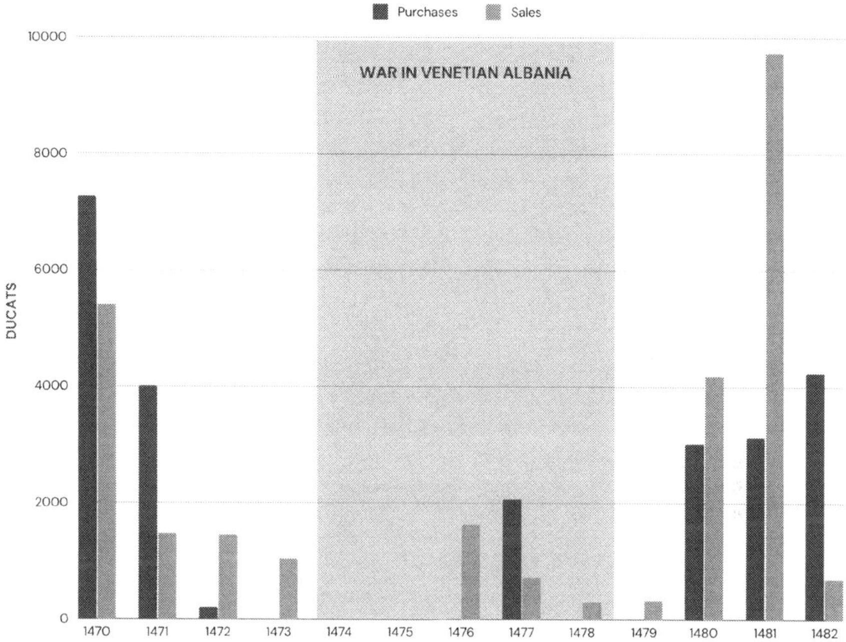

Figure 3.1 The pepper trade trends of Alvise Michiel's fraterna between 1470 and 1482.
Source: ASVe, MG, folder 15, reg. 2.

The war notably affected also the Euro-Asian trade of pepper, causing a significant reduction in its supply. Michiel's entire imports were absorbed by the local market, primarily sold to merchants from other Italian regions, such as Rome and Milan, and to German merchants within the Rialto market. Notably, in specific years like 1472, 1473, and 1475, there was a complete absence of pepper purchases, reflecting the war's severe impact on this trade segment (Figure 3.1). However, the cessation of hostilities between Venice and the Ottoman Empire marked a resurgence in the pepper trade. The years 1480 and 1481 alone saw a dramatic increase in pepper imports, totalling 55,367 pounds. This surge accounted for a staggering 63% of the decade's pepper purchases from 1471 to 1481, and this proportion is even more significant considering that the data for 1481 are incomplete, illustrating the revitalizing effect of peace on the spice trade's dynamics.

Pepper is probably the prime example of the fluctuations that trade the Mediterranean and continental Europe in quantity and price depending on both international and local circumstances. Given that a significant portion of the pepper was exported to Northern Europe, it is noteworthy to examine the quantities of this spice carried by Foscari on two voyages to Flanders. The export data reveal a substantial increase in the amount of pepper transported: from 2,890 pounds on their initial voyage before the war to 14,967 pounds on a subsequent journey four years later. It is crucial to underline that the data from the Foscari ledger exclusively represents goods directly associated with or under the stewardship of the

Table 3.1 Minimum, maximum, and average prices of pepper in Alexandria, Venice and Bruges between 1464–68 and 1470–79.

Market	*Price minimum*	*Price maximum*	*Average*
Alexandria	48.5	50	50.24
Venice	53	70	58.8
Bruges	97	106	100

patron, not encompassing the ship's full cargo. Hence, these figures should be regarded as the minimum quantities.[23] Shipments during peacetime were probably considerably larger, as indicated by the Michiel ledger. After the cessation of the Venetian-Turkish war, Alvise Michiel recorded receiving a significant pepper shipment from Alexandria, coordinated by his local agent. This shipment comprised 25,928 pounds *sottili*, sent to Venice in just one delivery.[24]

The insatiable European appetite for pepper[25] saw Venetian merchants poised to capitalize on this relentless demand, as reflected in historical pricing data (Table 3.1). By examining the account books of Alvise Michiel and Giovanni Foscari, we can trace an approximate price trajectory of pepper across various markets from purchase to sale. The markets analysed span Alexandria from 1470 to 1480, Venice during the same period, and Bruges in 1468. Despite the different years considered for the final sale market of Bruges and the increase in pepper prices during the 1470s due to the scarcity of Venetian imports, the disparity between the supply markets and the intermediary Venetian market was not substantial. Moreover, even though Foscari's purchase price was lower than Michiel's—a detail corroborated by the stable prices Foscari paid before the war compared to those in 1467—it's evident that the selling price in European markets was on average double what Venetians paid in Egypt, marking up nearly 100%. Indeed, the significant mark-up on pepper prices was driven purely by transportation and brokerage costs. Importantly, this mark-up did not involve any transformation or refinement of the pepper itself; it was sold in the same unaltered state as it was purchased. This highlights the role of logistics and intermediary handling in the value chain of trade goods during the Renaissance, where simple raw commodities could accrue substantial added value en route to their final markets without undergoing any alteration.

Pepper was just one of many spices that routinely reached the Venetian port. Ginger, cinnamon, cloves, holy seeds, malagueta pepper, mace, and nutmeg were also commonly transported to Venice aboard its galleys. Similar to pepper, these spices served both medicinal and culinary purposes and were sold in various forms: whole, powdered, or 'garbled'. The powdered spice trade was particularly profitable, not only facilitating the recovery of investments but also generating additional revenue. While garbled spices were somewhat cheaper than their whole counterparts were, the price difference was marginal. For example, in the 1460s, ginger sold for ten Flemish *grootes* per pound on the Northern markets (equating to an average cargo value of just over 85 ducats), whereas powdered ginger fetched around seven *grootes* per pound (totalling 58 ducats for the cargo).[26]

In addition to spices, expensive dyeing substances such as *grana*, and luxurious textile materials like silk and cotton, were imported from Asia. These items were not just commodities but symbols of status among Europe's elite, who vied for the most exquisite textiles to demonstrate their wealth and status. The personal expenditure records in Venetian ledgers illustrate this trend; for instance, Michiel allocated approximately one-third of his apparel budget to purchasing silk fabrics and garments. The assortment ranged from decorated belts and premium textiles like damask and velvet to more affordable silks such as *zendado*, all dyed with kermes.[27] Conversely, the Michiel ledger lacks entries for domestic expenses on cotton textiles, despite them being significantly cheaper than silk. In the mid-1470s, silk prices hovered around 2.5 ducats per pound, compared to cotton's mere 0.08 ducats. Instead, the entire cotton supply was sold to merchants from Milan, Germany (particularly from the Ulm area), and Northern Europe. Notably, a significant transaction involved the sale in Venice of 523 pounds *grosse* of cotton to Bulfardo Scraver of Edinburgh.[28] This highlights the practice of trading Syrian cotton in its raw, unprocessed state, primarily to Northern European merchants and Northern Italian textile manufacturers.[29] For these reasons, this raw material became a staple of the cargoes destined for Flanders and England. For instance, the Foscara, en route to Northern Europe, carried 46,126 pounds of cotton in 1463 and an impressive 152,116 in 1467, with none of this cargo owned by the patron.[30]

Markets and Networks

Selling cotton in Northern Europe, although facilitated by its high local demand, required establishing local contacts, achievable through either mandated local intermediaries, as in Bruges where foreign merchants could only trade if accompanied by a local intermediary, or through fellow countrymen residing locally, as seen in London.[31] These two capitals provide an intriguing contrast in their approaches towards Italian merchants, particularly Venetians. Bruges served not just as a trading hub for Eastern, Mediterranean, and Northern goods but also as a central point for banking and financial transfers. The city's role in stimulating financial flows, chiefly through the use of promissory notes, allowed for significant movement of capital between Northern Europe and Mediterranean economic centres. The influence of Italian trading and financial strategies was so profound that Raymond de Roover emphasized it was the Italians, rather than the local merchants, who were instrumental in transforming Bruges into a hub of international finance.[32] Nevertheless, Flemish traders played a crucial role in establishing and maintaining the local market that underpinned the financial network devised by the Italians.[33]

Across the English Channel, the dynamics shifted. The solid ties with England led Italian merchants to bolster their presence in London, a city that was also gaining prominence in the spice trade. By the 16th century, London had surpassed Bruges as the primary spice market, partly due to Antwerp's rising competition with the Flemish city.[34] The Italian population in England dates back to the 13th century. Most of it consisted of merchants of Tuscan and Genoese origin and, until 1319, there had been no Venetians in the area. Until the middle of the 14th century, the main activities of the Italian merchants were banking, mostly for loans to the Crown, and the export of fine English wool to Flanders and the Mediterranean.[35] The Italians' significant presence in England sparked local resentment, with accusations of usury

Table 3.2 Foscari's Commercial transactions in 1463/64

Location	*Contacts*	*Purchases (ducats)*	*Sales (ducats)*	*Total*
Tunis	4	4,110	4,385	8,495
London	4	2,381	4,797	7,178
Bruges	24	1,052	4,232	5,284
Southampton	3	3,397	43	3,440
Malaga	2	897	1,012	1,909
Syracuse	1	213	808	1,021
Cadiz	–	27	787	814
Honaine	–	–	474	474
Almeria	1	143	143	286
Majorca	–	–	101	101
Palermo	–	–	82	82
Messina	–	71	10	81
Oran	1	38	32	70
Muros	–	–	24	24

Source: ASVe, GrM, folder 250, reg. 2, cc. 1–50.

Table 3.3 Foscari's Commercial transactions in 1467/68

Location	*Contacts*	*Purchases (ducats)*	*Sales (ducats)*	*Total*
Bruges	40	1,555	13,141	14,696
Tunis	3	2,845	2,247	5,092
Southampton	8	3,870	631	4,501
London	8	2,085	1,207	3,292
Poreč	1	386	171	557
Syracuse	1	104	313	417
Cadiz		255	139	394
Sandwich		5	379	384
Oran	1	123	53	176
Pula	1		100	100
Malaga			23	23
Capo San Vincenzo		3		3
Majorca		4		4
Palermo		4		4
Sluis		2		2

Source: ASVe, GrM, folder 250, reg. 2, cc. 51–132.

against them. This led to tensions and attempts to undermine Italian financial and commercial activities, culminating in an anti-alien movement in the 1450s. The resulting disruptions in the London area, along with restrictive policies towards the Lombards, severely affected the merchants. Consequently, many were compelled to relocate their operations temporarily from London to Winchester. The root of the issue appeared to be the superior efficacy of Italian financial and commercial practices, particularly credit, provoking the ire of local merchants. Nevertheless, the uprising was short-lived, preventing the mass displacement of Italian merchants to Winchester that had been anticipated if the unrest persisted.[36]

The Foscari ledgers highlight strategic consistency and shifts in investment focus across two journeys, particularly noting the distinct market dynamics of Bruges and London. Bruges emerges primarily as a sales market for Venetians, especially for spices and wine, while England serves as a key export market, notably for raw wool. This distinction holds true across both voyages, despite variations in the nature of transactions conducted by Foscari on each occasion. In the voyage of 1464, Bruges experienced a notable decrease in transaction value compared to 1468, when it surged to 45% of the total transactions (14,696 ducats), up from a mere 18% previously. This shift away from Bruges in 1464 saw increased activity in Tunis, capturing 30% of the trade value, and the English markets (London and Southampton), which together accounted for 35%. Additional trading occurred in Malaga and Syracuse during the return voyage of 1464. By 1467/68, Bruges reasserted itself as the primary market, overshadowing the English markets, which held 27% of trade value, and Tunis at 20%. London's share in goods sold saw a drastic reduction, dropping from 4,797 ducats in the first voyage to 1,207 ducats in the second, a decline of nearly 75%. This decrease appears unrelated to political factors, as the 1460s did not witness significant political events affecting Bruges. The city was under the rule of Philip the Good, Duke of Burgundy, for 48 years until 1467 when his eldest son, Charles the Bold, succeeded him. The transition did not alter the policies towards trade and Italian merchants, nor were there significant price fluctuations. Indeed, the Venetian nation was granted new commercial privileges by Charles in 1468 (Tables 3.2 and 3.3).[37] Therefore, the reasons for the change in trade volumes likely pertain to Foscari's operations and may stem from either adjustments in Venetian contacts in London or a notable (310%) surge in transactions in Bruges. It is speculated that the war with the Ottomans may have hindered the flow of Eastern goods to Flanders, enabling the market to absorb more merchandise than in previous years. This theory is supported by Marco Bembo's correspondence with his agent in Bruges, indicating that the non-arrival of goods like incense in Venice and delays in spring navigation could be exploited for profit using aged warehouse stock, which, due to these disruptions, could now be sold at favourable prices.[38]

In the second journey, other Mediterranean markets appear less emphasized, with no substantial transactions reported. The 1460s underscored a stark distinction between the Northern European and Tunisian markets compared to others, with the former seeing substantially higher trade volumes. Notably, the North African markets received attention not only from the Flanders convoy but also from the *Trafego* one, focused on North African ports, and numerous private vessels. Apart from expenditures related to galley operations (such as provisions, water, and harbour fees) and minor transactions in Messina (1463) and Pula (1467), no merchandise exchanges occurred on the voyage towards Flanders. Commerce commenced exclusively in Bruges, underlining a customary and contractual obligation to transport all goods directly to Northern Europe. This directive aimed to maintain a steady influx of Eastern commodities into Bruges and London, curbing potential price manipulation.[39]

Table 3.4 Foscari's main commercial partners in 1463/64.

Location	*Merchant or company*	*Origin*	*Sum in ducats*
Bruges	Andrea and Francesco Bragadin	Venetian	381
	Colart	Flemish	242
	Filippo Donde Clocon	Flemish	435
	Francesco Zorzi	Venetian	723
	Gervaso Corner	Venetian	218
	Iacopo Bules	Flemish	483
	Iacopo Devett	Flemish	673
	Ruzier	Flemish	225
London	Rizardo drapier	English	298
	Tommaso Belleter	English	786
	Tommaso Stalbruc	English	2,051
Southampton	Marco da Pesaro	Venetian	1,104
	Tommaso Stalbruc	English	569
Malaga	Amet el Brentillo	Arab-Iberian	1,794
Almeria	Baco Moro	Arab-Iberian	286
Tunis	Chierico Cattaneo and Benedetto Imperiale	Genoese	1,863
	Chierico Cattaneo, Benedetto Imperiale and Giovanni Pinello	Genoese	1,785
	Piero Contarini (Dandolo's agent)	Venetian	400
	Lionello Spinola	Genoese	287

ASVe, GrM, folder 250, reg. 2, cc. 1–50

Giovanni Foscari's voyages to Flanders are particularly noteworthy for providing insight into both the value of individual markets and the support networks of these travelling merchants. The records document a significant number of contacts across both journeys. Specifically, in 1463/64, Foscari interacted with 148 distinct entities by name, a figure that increased to 255 in 1467/68.[40] The nature and volume of relationships and transactions differed significantly by location, with a notable differentiation between Mediterranean ports, Bruges, and English cities. Local contacts significantly influenced the number and size of transactions in various ports, serving as a crucial resource for travelling merchants with limited time in foreign markets. Giovanni Foscari's network in different locations reveals a pronounced contrast between Northern European cities and the Mediterranean. This distinction is notably pronounced, given Foscari's focus on the Northern European venture, particularly the Flanders journey. In the Northern capitals, the composition of Foscari's network presents intriguing variations. In Bruges, Foscari leveraged a broad network, including Flemish merchants, bankers, and brokers (54 contacts in 1463/64 and 114 in 1467/68, of which 26 and 61 were Flemish, respectively). Meanwhile, the London scene presented a contrast: in 1464, Foscari engaged with 'only' 15 individuals (including five English), but by 1467/68, this number increased to 22, plus an additional seven contacts in Southampton, totalling 13 local connections (see Tables 3.4 and 3.5; for a network visualization, see Figures 3.2 and 3.3).

Table 3.5 Foscari's main commercial partners in 1467/68.

Location	*Merchant or company*	*Origin*	*Sum in ducats*
Bruges	Ambrogio Rubuis	Flemish	726
	Antonio Ruzier	Flemish	842
	Donazio de Mor	Flemish	6,189
	Giovanni Dunt Gross	Flemish	495
	Giovanni Loscardo	Flemish	576
	Giovanni Stanbi	Flemish	305
	Iacopo Rat	Flemish	355
	Marco Vandeveler	Flemish	294
	Michiel Hottino	Flemish	498
	Nicolao Labie	Flemish	250
	Paolo Rubin from Antwerp	Flemish	420
	Piero Soranzo	Venetian	382
	Rigo Bus	Flemish	493
London	Antonio Licanelli	English	220
	Filippo Pini	English	240
	Giovanni Stanbi	English	305
	Giovanni Vand	English	346
	Rizardo Lalton	English	851
	Tommaso Mocenigo e Bernardo Giustinian	Venetian	739
Southampton	Donazio de Mor	Flemish	450
	Filippo Lomellin	English	1,326
	Marco da Pesaro	Venetian	960
	Piero Vattazi	English	340
Tunis	Giovanni Battista Grimaldi, Ilario Grimaldi and Benedetto Giovanni Pinello	Genoese	3.47

ASVe, GrM, folder 250, reg. 2, cc. 51–132

Mediterranean markets, by comparison, featured significantly fewer partners, with trade activities being more geographically and commercially concentrated. Despite Tunis emerging as a key market in 1464, Foscari had merely four contacts there, including two firms with identical partners.[41] This trend of limited interaction extended across other Mediterranean ports, albeit with a notable distinction in capital engagement. Commercially, the Berber and Spanish markets were relatively specialized, engaging with a few merchants for a specific range of goods (wax, leather, and gold in exchange for English and Dutch cloth), reflecting a more focused trading strategy.

The breadth and dynamism of a merchant's contacts, in both quantity and type, offer a compelling insight into their capacity to select partners, negotiate agreements, and seize market opportunities. Such contacts are crucial for accessing essential market intelligence, thereby enhancing the efficiency and effectiveness of their commercial endeavours. This factor was particularly vital for 'seasonal' merchants or those with short-term stays in ports, who did not have the advantage of time to build extensive networks. Operating within narrow time frames—often mere months—these merchants relied on a select group of familiar contacts, often fellow countrymen, and the networks they had established. Their objective was to

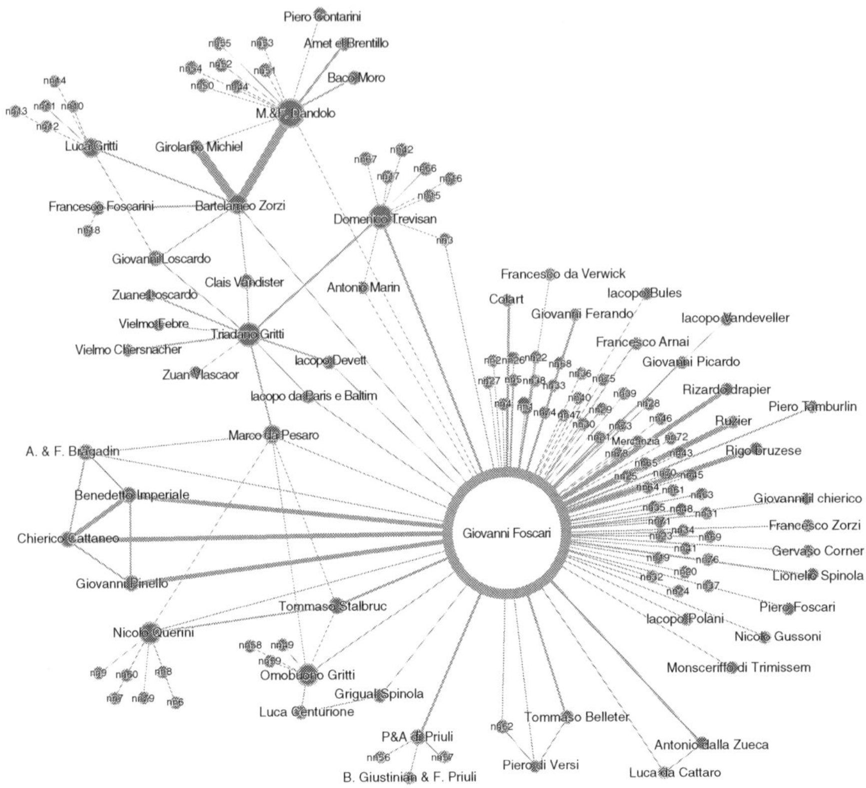

Figure 3.2 Giovanni Foscari's social network in 1463/64.

Source: ASVe, GrM, folder 250, reg. 2.

swiftly integrate into existing trade networks, broaden their connections, gather as much information as possible, and execute transactions that maximized profits during their time in locales like Flanders and England. This is precisely what Foscari managed to accomplish, as evidenced by comparing the networks from his two journeys: the first shows a strong clustering around key figures who introduced Foscari to the local market. In contrast, by the second voyage, four years later, the network appears more centralized, indicating the development of personal connections that the merchant could rely on, leading to a significant increase in the number of transactions.

Scarcity and Strategic Merchandises

Since the medieval period, Venice has prospered through its extensive trade networks with the Levant, capitalizing on its strategic position to mediate between Asia and Northern Europe. In peaceful times, Italy was the gateway for importing coveted goods like spices, silk, cotton, ash, and sugar for redistribution across

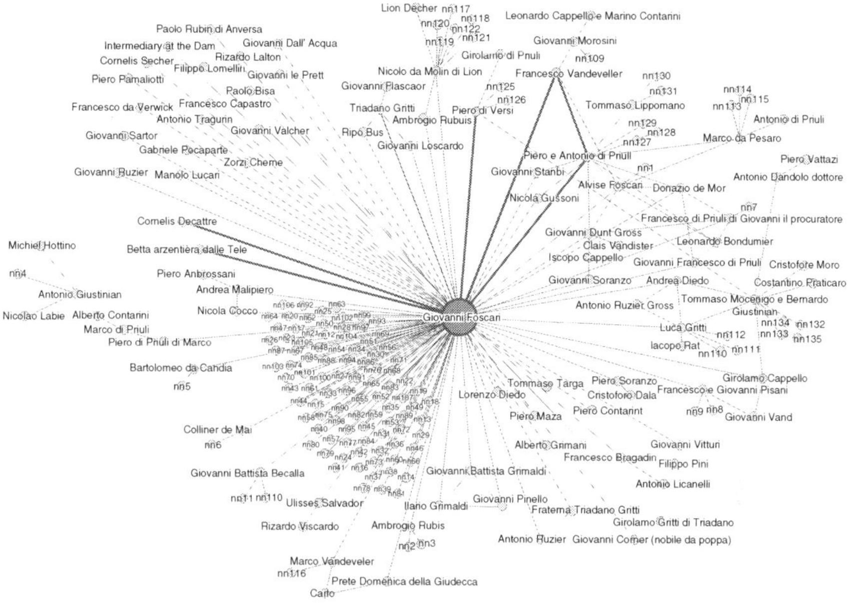

Figure 3.3 Giovanni Foscari's social network in 1467/68.

Source: ASVe, GrM, folder 250, reg. 2.

Europe. Conversely, Europe exported woollen textiles, precious metals (gold and silver), furs, and amber to the Middle East. This vibrant trade bolstered economic activity across the Mediterranean and spurred production within the Venetian mainland, an area Venice expanded into during the 15th century.[42] These extensive trade networks often encountered challenges, such as market closures or disruptions in trade routes, raising questions about how merchant enterprises responded to conflicts-related issues.

To understand how Venetian family firms navigated the challenges and limitations imposed by external factors such as wars, we examine the strategies of specific enterprises. This discussion focuses on Alvise Michiel's business operations during the First Ottoman-Venetian War, between 1463 and 1479, a conflict that signifies the fluctuating dynamics between the Ottoman Empire and European powers.[43] This period was part of a longer era of hostility that stretched from 1463 to 1573, punctuated by four out of seven wars that characterized the Renaissance and early modern periods, leading to Venice's gradual loss of territories in the Eastern Mediterranean and the Balkans. The threat to the Venetian empire predated the Ottoman conquest of Constantinople, as shown by events like the Battle of Gallipoli in the early 15th century.[44] However, direct conflict only ignited in the late 15th century, sparked by the escape and conversion of an Albanian slave under Venetian protection. The war spanned the Aegean and Adriatic Seas, even touching Venetian mainland regions like Friuli, from Istria to Bergamo, until 1479 when

Venice was forced to cede parts of its maritime state, including Euboea, Morea, and Venetian Albania. The First Ottoman-Venetian War was more than a military engagement; it significantly impacted the socio-economic and political framework of the Eastern Mediterranean, heralding the rise of Ottoman naval dominance and marking a decline in Venetian influence in the region.[45]

Woollen Cloths: A Commodity Chain Attempt for Export

In response to the vagaries of war, the Michiel firm broadened its trading strategy to focus on vital goods. This adaptation involved olive oil, necessitating barrel production and repair, minerals (tin, copper, iron), and wool textiles. Despite continuing to trade in iconic Venetian luxury items—silk, spices, jewels, wax, and premium textiles—the firm invested significantly in goods of lesser value or quality, particularly olive oil and wool textiles, setting them apart from high-demand minerals. This tactical shift enabled the Michiel firm to sustain its market presence during challenging wartime, effectively balancing trade in both essential and luxury items to navigate economic turbulence. In exchange for spices, fine fabrics, dyes, and cotton from the East, strongly hampered by the Veneto Ottoman War, Europe could export various goods to the southern and eastern Mediterranean coasts. Mineral materials such as tin, iron, copper, and silver were imported to Venice from Northern and Central Europe. Tin and silver in particular were often processed in Venice and then exported to Northern Africa and Egypt as manufactured goods.[46] There, these materials were used to fund trade with local goods through barter. Silver was indeed on average more valuable in the Middle East than in Europe and thus was extensively used by the Venetians to acquire precious and expensive Oriental goods.[47] Even during the war with the Ottomans, this practice persisted: from German merchants, both within and outside the *fondaco*, Michiel continued to secure tin, iron, lead, pewter, and copper for export primarily to Alexandria and North Africa.

During the Veneto-Ottoman war, merchants had to navigate through the challenges of warfare with innovative commercial strategies. Among them, Alvise Michiel's method was notably sophisticated, incorporating comprehensive intelligence, an extensive network of agents, collaborations with local producers, and the strategic use of locally sourced materials to maintain trade operations under difficult circumstances. Michiel meticulously established a network of agents responsible for overseeing business activities in various ports and staying abreast of market developments (Figure 3.4).

His ledgers reveal the strategic dispatch of a variety of goods—including lower-quality woollen cloths, olive oil, almonds, and metals—according to precise instructions. A key figure in this network was his principal agent in Alexandria, Andrea Corner, who played a crucial role in the multitude of transactions recorded. The Feltre woollen cloths trade between 1474 and 1476, orchestrated by Michiel and his main agent, Andrea, serves as a prime example of Michiel's ability to establish a temporary commodity chain, leveraging their deep understanding of international market dynamics. This operation involved sourcing inexpensive woollen

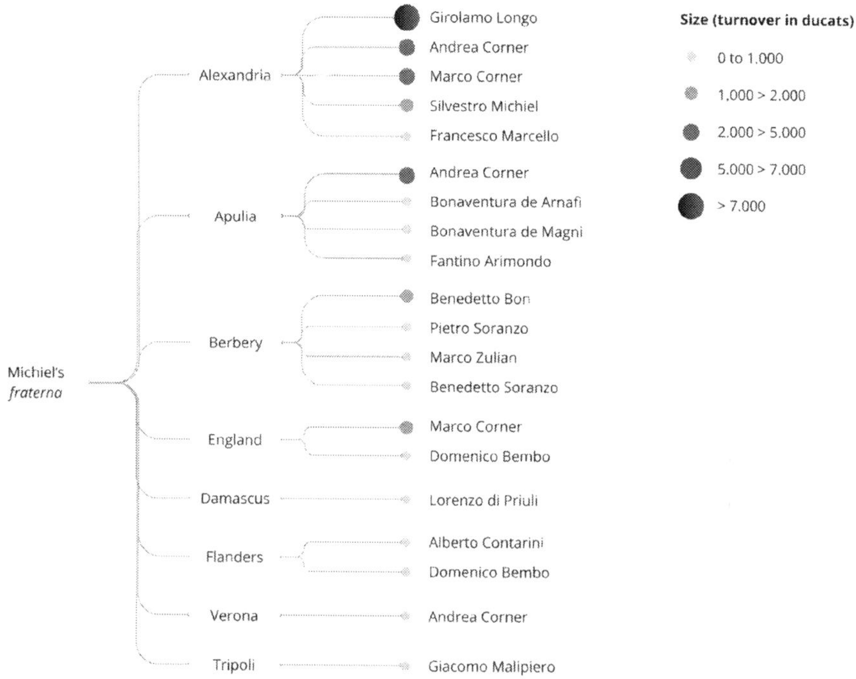

Figure 3.4 The agent network of Alvise Michiel spanning from 1470 to 1482.
Source: ASVe, MG, folder 15, reg. 2.

cloths from Feltre, a pre-alpine region, finishing them in Venice, and then exporting them to Apulia[48] and the Mamluk area. Michiel's strategic focus on these lower-cost woollens was influenced by the international textile market dynamics. Specifically, the increase in European cloth production and export to Alexandria and Syria was partly due to the decline in Mamluk textile manufacturing. The Mamluk industry, faced with a prolonged crisis and stagnation in technological innovation, struggled to produce affordable cloths for its lower-income population segments, creating an opportunity that Michiel capitalized on, thanks to his and Corner's insights into market trends and demands. In this way, European cloths, and in particular those of the emerging Venetian manufacture, found an unexpected market in Islamic lands.[49]

This trend is evidenced by the trafficking of Alvise Michiel who, in the two-year period 1474–76, managed to send to Egypt and North Africa 10,800 six-foot lengths[50] of cloth produced in Feltre. Over a decade, our analysis revealed 19 acquisitions for 1,500 ducats, primarily sourced from the pre-alpine Feltre region. These cloths were procured in two ways: either through intermediation by Venetian merchants, which tended to raise the acquisition cost, or by directly engaging with local merchants who brought their goods to Venice. Michiel showed a preference for the latter method (indeed, only one purchase was made from a Venetian merchant).[51] The production and customization of woollen cloths by Alvise Michiel

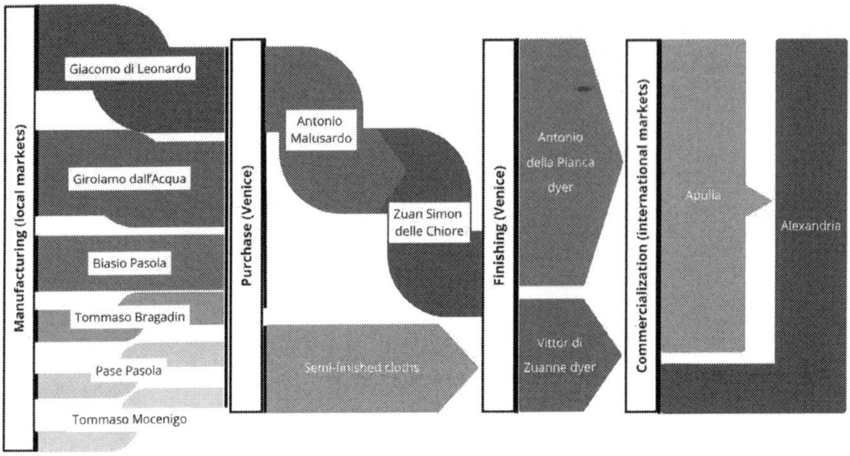

Figure 3.5 Diagram of the Feltre Woollen Cloth Commodity Chain.

Source: ASVe, MG, folder 15, reg. 2.

highlight the complex nature of the textile industry. Starting with raw materials, Michiel navigated through a complex process primarily focused on the critical stages of finishing and dyeing to prepare the textiles for the market, particularly tailoring them for the demands in Alexandria under Andrea Corner. This customization involved specific dyeing, stretching, and shearing steps, all carefully overseen by Michiel and carried out by skilled Venetian artisans (Figure 3.5).[52]

The economic landscape is illuminated by the stark contrast in pricing between raw textiles, approximately nine to ten *soldi* per piece, and the much higher valued cotton fabrics from Syria and Germany, priced between two and four ducats. Michiel's commitment to quality dyeing is demonstrated in his collaborations with artisans such as Vittor di Zuanne and Antonio della Pianca, preferring the latter's services despite higher costs, suggesting a focus on quality or specific services over mere cost savings.[53] The records reveal extensive dyeing operations, with thousands of *braza* of cloth dyed in various colours, showcasing the operational complexity and scale of Michiel's efforts. The handling and sale of dyes, especially the sought-after *grana* for its rich hues, and *verzino*, a more affordable alternative, highlight the strategic financial and operational planning involved in the textile production process.[54]

After dyeing, the cloths underwent crucial finishing steps like brushing and stretching, crucial for enhancing their quality and market appeal. Key artisans, including Antonio Malusardo dalla Volta and Zuan Simon Dalle Chiore, processed a significant volume of Feltre cloths, specifically 4,800 *braccia*, preparing them for Apulia as directed by Andrea Corner.[55] This stage significantly increased the cloth's value through cost-effective methods that required less expense than dyeing.[56] The finished cloths, alongside metals from Germany, were shipped to Apulia and Egypt between 1474 and 1475. Notably, a large portion of the merchandise, particularly the Feltre cloths, found a market in Egypt, fetching an average price of 7 ducats per 100 *braza*. However, the exact cost structure for these cloths remains unclear due to Michiel's accounting methods, which amalgamated duties and freight costs, and potentially more detailed records are lost.[57] Moreover, numerous shipments of textiles from the Mainland, as the cloths from Brescia, and German cloth, often dyed in Venice at the merchant's cost, were dispatched to Apulia and Alexandria. Fustian cloth from Milan, though in lesser amounts, served as another export. This fabric, particularly the *cordellate* used for curtains, was acquired through barter with ginger from Alexandria and distributed to North African and Spanish markets via the Barberia convoy. Michiel's strategic diversification of exports towards Mamluk territories and Apulia aimed to counterbalance the significant value of merchandise imported from these regions. Regions like Egypt and Apulia functioned predominantly as import markets for Venetian traders, including spices and oil. Consequently, it was vital to balance the flow of payments, which in Apulia were conducted mainly via bills of exchange, and in Alexandria through the export of metals like silver and copper, themselves imported into Venice. This strategy forged a trade loop where Venice's production of manufactured goods was minimal, necessitating a compensation of payments, particularly with markets averse to non-physical forms of payment, such as bills of exchange, notably within the Islamic world.[58]

A Strategic Import: Olive Oil

Shipments of Feltre textiles played a crucial role in balancing the import of large quantities of commodities into Venice, including significant volumes of olive oil from Apulia, Marche, and Verona. This oil was essential not only for household use but also in the textile industry, particularly during the initial wool processing stages for unravelling wool staples.[59] Only in 1472, Alvise Michiel imported over 330 barrels of Apulian oil (exceeding 68,600 litres) into Venice, primarily selling it to Alpine and German merchants, with a smaller portion exported to Egypt.

The consumption of olive oil, a staple of Mediterranean and ancient Italian diets, experienced a notable decline in the Middle Ages due to the Barbarian invasions disrupting trade, leading to a shift towards animal fats. However, as trade resumed and textile-related production activities grew in the late Middle Ages, there was a resurgence in the use of olive oil, particularly for industrial purposes such as soap manufacturing and wool processing.[60] During the modern age, there was an overall decline in oil consumption for food not due to changing tastes but rather due to limited oil supply that required constant importation. And this was a challenge for Venice's oil trade, as this product became essential for the economy.[61] To highlight the significance of olive oil in Venice, it's important to note that olive oil made up one-third of the weight of soap, a product monopolized by the city since 1489.[62] This soap was highly valued for its purity and hardness, and its price was closely tied to the olive oil trade. Any disruptions in the import of olive oil quickly led to an increase in the price of soap, emphasizing the importance of olive oil in Venice's economy.[63]

Since the late 13th century, the central role of oil in Venice's economy prompted the State to regulate its import, measurement, and retail sale. This responsibility was entrusted to a new magistracy, the *Visdomini della Ternaria*, established specifically to oversee the rationing and regulation of fats entering and leaving Venice. While initially overseeing a broader range of commodities including iron, leather, hides, yarn, meat, and cheese, from 1248, after the office was segmented into three distinct magistracies, their focus narrowed primarily to oil and fats, with the position held by four officials.[64] The consistent issue of oil supply from the beginning led to regulated commercial freedom, closely tied to the city's oil needs. By 1302, Venetian merchants were required to deposit 50% of their oil imports in the Venetian *Ternaria*'s warehouses. However, perhaps due to increased imports, this mandate was reduced to a third and eventually to a quarter or a fifth by the 15th century. The oils, categorized as new or old within the *Ternaria*, supported both food consumption and manufacturing needs within the city. According to the records of Michiel's ledger, sales conducted through the magistracy were at a regulated, generally lower price than private transactions. For example, in 1474, oil prices at the *Ternaria* varied between 15 and 29 ducats per *mier*,[65] lower than the 30–36 ducats charged in private dealings and significantly beneath the retail prices of 40 ducats per *mier*. That year, Alvise Michiel delivered approximately 59.92 hectolitres of mostly Apulian oil to the *Ternaria*, with 22% of his annual purchase of 264.52 hectolitres stored there for direct sales within Venetian territory. Merchants then collected the profits from these sales, minus any duties, through their agents or intermediaries. Oil not allocated to the *Ternaria*, thus not for Venice's internal consumption, was freely sold to foreign merchants, who constituted the majority of Michiel's clientele.

The preference for Apulian olive oil in meeting Venice's needs was deliberate. The 15th century saw a surge in imports from the Adriatic, driven by strong domestic demand and the oil's export to regions like Friuli, Trieste, and Austria.[66] Renowned for its superior quality and longevity, Apulian oil was highly sought after on international markets, overshadowing oil from the Marche region and significantly impacting Mainland production, particularly in the Garda area.[67]

Michiel's agents in Apulia, who sequentially included Andrea Corner, Bonaventura de Magni, Fantino Arimondo, and Leonze de Bitone, oversaw the purchase of oil. This oil was then transported to Venice via private ships.[68] Upon arrival, the oil not earmarked for the *Ternaria* was processed through customs and stored in warehouses leased annually by the Michiel family. In the years 1474/75, the storage was leased from Marino and Girolamo Morosini at a cost of 12 ducats and 6 grossi[69]; in 1473, 1478, and 1479, Domenico Morosini provided storage for 5 ducats annually; and between 1473 and 1475, Giovanni Alvise Bondumier offered his warehouse for 15 ducats per year.[70]

Oil trading by the firm exhibited seasonality, concentrating transactions in May, June, and July, and significantly increasing its engagement in the oil market since 1472. Before this, the only oil transaction was from Barbary, directly shipped to Alexandria to finance purchases of camel hides, carpets, leather, and spices, including saffron and pepper.[71] In 1472, the firm initiated substantial investments in oil, importing at least 817.5 hectolitres across nine transactions, focusing on Apulia in 1472 and 1473. Starting in 1474, Michiel broadened his supply sources, incorporating oils from Lake Garda and, notably, the Marche region. This diversification

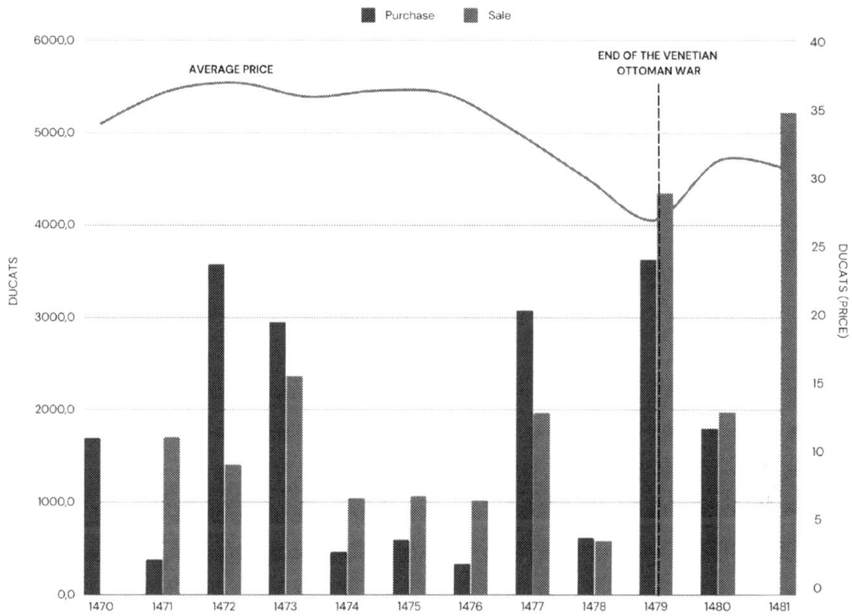

Figure 3.6 Olive oil purchases and sales by Alvise Michiel, including the average selling price.

Source: ASVe, MG, folder 15, reg. 2.

likely stemmed from disruptions in the supply line from the lower Adriatic, which may have been related to warfare or harvest issues. While purchases from the Garda area were limited, accounting for only 5% (184.3 hectolitres) of Michiel's ten-year oil purchases, what is important is the attempt to establish a new supply channel through the contacts of the ever-present Andrea Corner in Verona. The procurement and transportation of these barrels via waterways, leveraging the extensive network of navigable canals and rivers, highlight the firm's strategic approach to broadening and diversifying its sources.[72] Despite Corner's expertise in quality assessment and negotiations, Garda oil did not fare well in Venice, indicated by its one-off purchase and slow market sales. Between 1475 and 1476, only three sales of Garda oil occurred, with the bulk sold in 1477, three years post-purchase, suggesting challenges in integrating Garda oil into the Venetian market.

The fluctuation in the Venetian oil market, as depicted in Michiel's records, might also reflect the periodic nature of production. The years 1472, 1477, and 1479 experienced pronounced activity (see Figure 3.6), interspersed with intervals of significant trade reduction, notably in 1476, following two years of decreased oil transactions, and, to a lesser extent, in 1478. The variation in oil acquisitions could be attributed to the storage capability of oil, allowing it to be marketable several years post-purchase. Conversely, the sudden shifts in sales volume, such as the −58% decrease from 1477 to 1478 and the +261% increase from 1478 to 1479, remain somewhat perplexing, especially since these fluctuations did not coincide with notable changes in pricing, which typically occurred in years of high trade

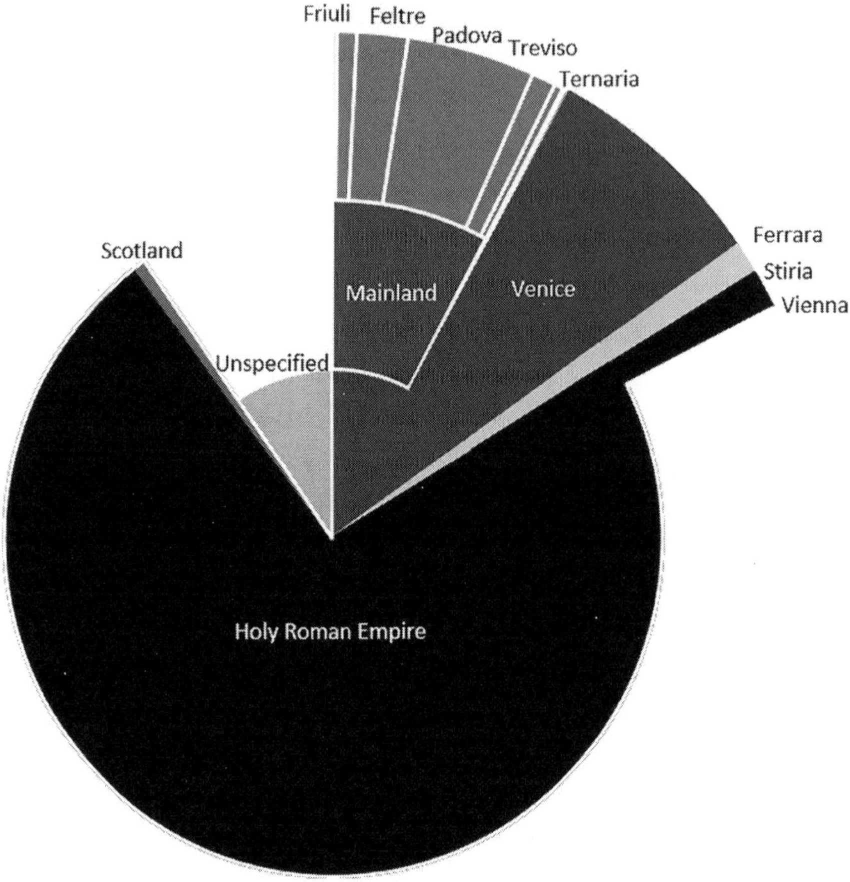

Figure 3.7 Destination of Michiel's olive oil sales.

Source: ASVe, GM, folder 15, reg. 2.

volumes.[73] The year 1477 stood out as the peak period for oil trade, with Michiel's purchases exceeding 1,213.7 hectolitres, accounting for 32% of the *fraterna*'s imports for the decade 1470–80 and 2.33% of Venice's total annual oil imports.[74]

The imported Apulian oil was chiefly allocated to international merchants in wholesale volumes, with retail distribution remaining rare. Alvise Michiel took a hands-on approach in the transactions, recording comprehensive details of the purchasers, including their nationalities and accommodation, notably the Germanic merchants resident at the *Fondaco dei Tedeschi*. Roughly 10% of the oil was sold within Venice, particularly to Murano's local merchants and the soap and wool industries, while the Mainland markets, such as Padua and Feltre, received supplies likely intended for their textile manufacturers. As mentioned, a substantial segment, however, found its way to Germanic buyers from regions like Germany, Austria, and Tyrol. The years 1473 and 1474 saw the majority of these interactions, accounting for 93% of sales to Central European merchants, with a few additional transactions occurring during the winter of 1477–78 (Figure 3.7).

Prices for oil, denominated in ducats per Venetian *mier*, were subject to variation based on quality and sale type. Generally, the lower price range was associated with lower-quality oil, referred to as '*grosso*'—essentially the sediment-heavy dregs at the bottom of barrels. Conversely, the higher end of the pricing spectrum was often linked to retail sales, which could push the average price up by 4 or 5 ducats per *mier*.[75] Slightly lower prices, usually 2 or 3 ducats lower than the others, around 30 ducats per *mier* or less, were accorded to the merchants from the Mainland: this was the case with Piero dalla Fontana, Daniel di Nicolò da Treviso, and Daniel di Canti da Bassano. Between 30 and 33 ducats per *mier* were charged to Tadio da Quinto, Marco Antonio Badoer, Zuan Piero Stan Polen, Ianus di Tolmezzo and Giacomo di Leonardo di Feltre, Francescotto da Cividale and again to Daniel di Canti.

Transactions with German merchants were predominantly focused on oil sales, yet three exchanges in 1474 with Lorenzo Roscafain, Vanzilao Amer Smit, and Zuan Vazer stand out due to their broader commercial engagements with Michiel. Not only were these merchants oil buyers, but they also engaged in deals for copper and iron and acquired spices, including a notable purchase of pepper and cloves worth 883 ducats. Despite their varied dealings with Michiel, these merchants were not afforded preferential pricing; they were charged 37 ducats per *mier* by the first two and 33 by the third. Price determinations for these trades seemed to lack a clear rationale, except for a pre-established relationship with Zuan Vazer, who had previously made a significant spice acquisition in 1472 and was charged the least among them.[76] In 1479, Bernardin Conto's purchase of 133 hectolitres of oil at a notably reduced price of 18 ducats per *mier* stands out due to the bartering nature of the transaction, with the oil being exchanged for soap manufactured by Conto and his sons in Venice. The competitive pricing was associated with Michiel's acquisition of export-ready soap, highlighting the impact of bartering on reducing the prices of commodities. The year 1479 also saw Michiel clearing accumulated stock by selling mixed oil reserves, following a period of extensive purchases in 1477. Significant direct shipments of oil to Alexandria, bypassing Venice, marked this year as well, although records of these sales in Alexandria are not detailed in the available documentation.[77]

Factors such as the oil's origin, the type of transaction, and the buyers' background were significant influencers of price fluctuation. However, another consistent pattern emerges across all recorded years: the virtual cessation of oil sales beginning in the spring and continuing through the summer months. This pause in sales likely stemmed from the seasonal window that permitted the transit of oil across the Alps, incentivizing German merchants to finalize their acquisitions before the onset of spring. Summer marked a period of heightened activity as ships laden with European, Venetian, and Eastern goods converged, redirecting the firm's focus.[78] Moreover, oil's sensitivity to high temperatures and exposure to light posed risks to its preservation, deterring its trade during the hotter months and likely contributing to the summertime slowdown in the Venetian oil market.

Sustaining the Circular Commerce

In order to balance the large investment in oil purchases, and to maintain the circularity of goods that guaranteed the Venetians a large share of the Mediterranean trade, Michiel imported mineral materials, and metals in particular, from Central Europe and England.[79] Thanks to the merchants residing in the *Fondaco dei Tedeschi*, two minerals that were particularly in demand on the Rialto market arrived from Central and Alpine Europe: iron and copper. With regard to iron, there were no particularly significant transactions in the ten years under observation. There was effectively only one transaction concerning this material: a barter for the payment of a purchase of oil made by the merchant Vanzilao (Wenceslas) Amer Smit (worth 40.5 ducats).[80] By order of Andrea Corner, in 1475, the iron was then sent and sold in Apulia, making a net profit of 15.5 ducats. However, the quantities of copper that Michiel dealt with were more substantial: between 1476 and 1479, there were eight different purchases, totalling 52,288 pounds *grosse*. The most important purchase was made in 1476 and involved 13,267 pounds and 3 ounces of Hungarian copper (for 669 ducats), from a Dubrovnik merchant, Francesco da Sorgo.[81] In that year, Michiel purchased 10,955 pounds of hard copper from Vienna through Leopold of Lorenz Roscafain; the latter is a familiar name, as his father, Lorenz, was involved in transactions with Michiel for Apulian oil in 1474. Additionally, a purchase of 11,024 pounds of Viennese copper was made from Zorzi (Georg) Pronstatter, who had previously acquired over 12 hectolitres of oil from Alvise in 1475. A significant portion of this copper was crafted into saucers and bowls in Treviso, at Michiel's expense. This strategy appears to mirror the approach taken with Feltre textiles: leveraging local manufacturing to refine the materials, thereby potentially increasing their market value. This is evidenced by the pattern that unrefined copper was typically sold within Venice, primarily to local merchants, whereas finished goods fetched higher prices in Alexandria (about 4 or 5 ducats more per *mier* than the same grade of copper sold in Venice).

What's intriguing is the yearly comparison between oil and metal transactions is that there's an inverse relationship between the two. In years marked by low oil trading, an increase in metal trading is observed, and the reverse is also true. This cyclical trend, evident on an annual basis, likely relates to the companies' resource allocation and the recovery of invested capital in these ventures. For instance, if in a given year, an investment ranging from 3,000 to 4,000 ducats was made in oil, Michiel would restrain from heavily investing in another commodity, choosing to wait for the returns from oil sales before committing to metal purchases (Figure 3.8).

The effort to rebalance imports from the Mediterranean basin did not end with the Feltre textiles, as seen in the previous section, or with Central European metals. The trade basket comprised other goods that found a market in the East. Among these were woollen cloths from Northern Europe, such as those acquired from Flanders (*bastardi* and *fini*) and London (*scossi*), totalling 414.4 ducats.[82] Additionally, 800 fathoms of *canevaze*, low-quality cloths, from Vercelli were obtained through bartering with ginger, the surplus of which was then dispatched

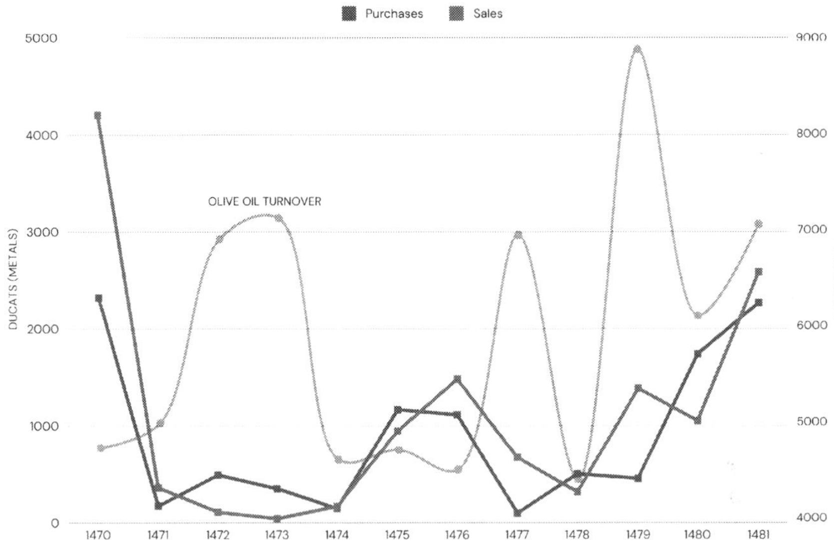

Figure 3.8 Comparative analysis of metal trade dynamics and investment patterns in the oil market.

Source: ASVe, GM, folder 15, reg. 2.

to Flanders and London. A notable focus was on the distribution of these textiles, with nearly all directed towards Apulia. This region played a dual role in Michiel's commerce, serving either as the final market for the cloths, offsetting oil purchases within the region, or as a transitional point to other markets like Egypt or Syria. This strategy appears to have been implemented not solely by Michiel but also by his agent and nephew, Andrea Corner. Specifically, Corner was responsible for directly sending the goods, managing sales within Apulia, and exporting the surplus to Alexandria. During the May 1479 shipment to Alexandria from Apulia (following the conclusion of the Turkish-Venetian War), 5,000 Feltre and 800 German cloths were loaded, culminating in a net profit of 393 ducats.[83]

Michiel's adeptness in managing a diversified trading portfolio across a wide array of key commodities and markets, adhering to strategic trading principles, is showcased in the variety of merchandises he sent to the Apulian and Egyptian ports. To supplement the goods exported to Egypt, indeed, Michiel's shipments included oil and almonds from Apulia. Specifically, 48 *mieri* and 71 *staia* of oil led to a net gain of 1,471 ducats, while 32 sacks of common almonds, equating to 96 Apulian *cantari*, netted a profit of 484 ducats. The assortment also featured a piece of silver, generating a 145 ducats profit, tin yielding 56 ducats, and substantial quantities of copper sheets (2,667 pounds), which contributed 159 ducats to the profits. Additionally, a smaller batch of textiles, dispatched directly from Venice to Syria, consisted of cloth from Brescia (11 bolts) shipped on Lorenzo Cadena's boat in 1478, resulting in sales revenue of 82.5 ducats and marking a 68% increase over the purchase cost.[84] Tin procurement was a noteworthy aspect of Michiel's operations, obtained in England for transport to Venice on state galleys or bought locally at the *Fondaco dei Tedeschi* (totalling nearly eight tonnes from 1470 to 1475). This tin was subsequently marketed not only in Venice but also in Apulia, Egypt, and Barbary.[85]

The trade of Oriental commodities, including drugs, dyes, and spices, experienced considerable disruption due to the Turkish-Venetian War from 1470 to 1479. During this period, the commerce of these goods persisted, albeit in limited quantities. Santonica, a vermifuge drug, saw a total movement of 600 pounds from Aleppo, all of which was dispatched to Bruges and London. The red dye *verzi* accounted for 7,697 pounds, part of which was purchased in Venice and then either resold locally or in Northern Europe. Ginger, weighing in at 3,469 pounds, was acquired from both Alexandria and Venice and distributed among German merchants in the city, across Northern Europe, and employed in various exchanges for textiles from Vercelli and Milan. While data on other spices, such as saffron and rhubarb, transactions is scant, owing to acquisitions predating 1470, cloves trade was more substantial. A total of 12,238 pounds *sottili* of cloves were procured, with over 10,000 pounds bought directly in Venice by the Michiel *fraterna* to be predominantly resold in the city to merchants residing in the *Fondaco*. The purchase and resale of goods within the same market, Venice in this case, indicate that Michiel maintained a particularly close relationship with the German merchants present in Venice, positioning him as a favoured intermediary. This connection allowed for an intricate trade network, enabling Michiel to effectively navigate and exploit the local market dynamics, especially during the challenging period of the Turkish-Venetian War.[86]

As particularly shown by the case of the Michiel company, in times of war, merchants managed to replace the products they usually traded with equally profitable alternatives in order to maintain the trade cycle that was vital to Venetian centrality. However, the traditional trade flows, particularly for what concerns spices and precious oriental materials, were back even stronger than before as the exogenous factor that halted it ends. It is clear that the elasticity and strategic diversions put in place by the Venetian traders were indicative of their capability to devise strategies concerning alternative commercial routes. That, however, were only temporary, as they did not grant the same turnover and profit as the import of oriental products.

The considerable worth of goods from Asia and the Middle East required Venetian traders to exert extensive efforts to identify commodities that could be marketed in Middle Eastern domains, thereby financing, at least partially, the importation of silks and spices.

As we have seen thanks to the activity of the Michiel family firm, during periods of war the trade in fabrics from Northern Europe, but especially from the Venetian mainland, was crucial for Venice in an attempt to remedy the negative balance of payments situation with the East. In order to maintain the trade system active and Venice's central role therein, it was necessary to rebalance the flow of high-value goods arriving from Asia and the inland areas of the North African coast through the Syrian, Berber, and especially Egyptian ports. The high value of Asiatic and Middle Eastern goods necessitated Venetian merchants putting considerable effort into finding goods that could be sold to Middle Eastern markets and finance, at least in part, the import of silks and spices.[87] The simplest method chosen by the Venetian merchants was to supply the Levantine ports with goods that were not available locally but were essential for the local production of goods and for export to Asia: tin, copper, iron, furs, amber, and wool were thus purchased from Central and Northern Europe. Nevertheless, these exports were, on the one hand, insufficient to cover the value of imports from the Middle East and, on the other, made Venice a mere port of passage, an emporium. To overcome this problem, and to boost the development not only of the Venetian economy, but also that of the Veneto mainland, Venetian merchants adopted a different strategy. As demonstrated by the Michiel case, one of the methods used by the Venetian merchants was to adapt the unprocessed goods bought on the European markets, especially in the case of cloth and copper, to the demand from the Eastern markets. The customisation of unfinished goods, such as medium-quality white woollen cloths (such as those from Feltre) and copper (supplied by the German regions in large sheets or rods), was crucial for the acquisition of new market segments in the Islamic regions and resisting competition. In fact, the supply of 'tailor-made' goods that met demand (or in some cases created it) in the target markets was crucial to keeping the trade circuit active and, at the same time, stimulating local production and processing activities in Venice or the Mainland (copper processing was effectively carried out in Treviso). On the other hand, the direct management of some product transformation processes could lead to advantages in terms of both cost and flexibility of supply. This point is central to a deeper understanding of how part of the Venetian economy functioned in the late Middle Ages. The city was not merely a commercial emporium, nor was it just a manufacturer.[88] If considering it in terms of a network, it was possible in Venice—which was the network's focal point—to gather the necessary information to complete the production of those manufactured goods, such as woollen cloths, that were not available in the other hubs (such as Feltre, but also Padua and Treviso). This was a production configuration that would recur to an even greater extent during the 16th and 17th centuries, but which was already present at the end of the Middle Ages.[89] Two textile sectors became particularly successful during the Renaissance: wool and silk. The woollen mill expanded in Venice during the first half of the 16th century, because of the difficulties encountered inland damaged by wars, and due to the successful imitation of English cloths. The contribution that Venice gave to wool production on the Mainland—which was already quite advanced in the areas of Vicenza, Verona, Brescia and Padova—shows how extremely advanced Venice's production organization systems were, as well as its ability to adapt to periods of crisis.[90] Silk had been another fundamental sector in the Venetian economy, also because of its support of the trading business. This sector involved multiple figures, including many merchants at an international level, who introduced silk products from the Veneto and Lombardy within long-haul trading circuits.[91] The silk factory, along with the wool sector, developed secondary productions that were able to tackle the new requests from local and international markets, and to adjust to changes in economic situations and in taste. The textile industries, in order to maintain a highly competitive standard, was repositioning itself following demand, diversifying products and showing a certain amount of flexibility in the matter of organizational models.

This aspect is more evident when looking at it from another angle of the network. The 'tailoring' of goods according to demand seemed to be less common in Northern Europe. As demonstrated by the Foscari case, the goods exported to Flanders and England already had a high added value in themselves (like spices and fine fabrics, to which cotton and precious stones were added) and did not require any special intervention by Venetian manufactures, with the exception of some gold threads sold in Palermo in 1463 and gold and precious stone jewellery exported to Northern Europe in 1468. This was due to the fact that the high value of the goods and, above all, the insatiable demand for spices and fine textiles in Northern Europe gave Venetian, and Italian, merchants important leverage to do good business in Northern Europe. Moreover, the ability, shared with other Italian communities, to make a profit not only on trade, but also on fluctuations in local currencies, made their work particularly effective (to the extent that it triggered the English *anti-alien* rebellion carried out by London merchants).[92]

Within this scenario, the role of the agent in foreign markets becomes particularly relevant. If, as the comparative analyses of the Foscari and Michiel ledgers suggest, the markets of London and Bruges were integrated and open to the work of the agents alone, the ports of Alexandria, Syria, and Barbary had, on the other hand, to be entrusted to different agents who, in coordination, managed the trade of products from Venice and the other regions of the Italian peninsula. As demonstrated by the Michiel case, the presence of a leading agent (in order Silvestro Michiel and, after his death, Marco Corner) at the ports of greatest importance in the *fraterna's* trade network (the ports of Apulia and Alexandria in Egypt) ensured a supply, and demand, of goods that matched the demand of the Rialto market and the ports of Apulia and Levant. Michiel's records show how shipments were made by order (*a ordene*) of the *fraterna's* main agents and intermediaries, tailored to the sales market and thus following a precise distribution strategy. The role of agents/managers was then crucial to the success of the family firms' commercial operations, all the more so in an unstable and complicated period such as the first Turkish-Venetian War.

The combined action of merchants and agents was crucial for the management of the flow of goods and capital between markets. This was even truer in times of crisis, when some of the supply and sales ports were completely or partially inaccessible to Venetians. The first Venetian-Ottoman conflict complicated, or made impossible, the supply of spices from the Aegean cities and Constantinople, as well as the export of European products and materials that supported purchases in precious Asian goods. To solve this problem, Venetian merchant companies had to change strategy and relocate their investments, creating different flows of goods to support the circulation of capital while waiting for the imbalance caused by the armed conflict to end. From this point of view, the case of the Michiels is exemplary. As it turned out, the *fraterna*'s a big share of the firm's capital was directed to the purchase of oil. Although this product could not ensure the same high profits obtained in the spice trade, it did manage to trigger a commercial circuit that, together with cloth (Flemish, felt and German), copper and tin, allowed the Michiel *fraterna* to carry out lucrative transactions and to specialize in the supply of oil and other Apulian products for the German market.

Notes

1 Jacques Bottin, 'La pratique des langues dans l'espace commercial de l'Europe de l'Ouest au début de l'époque moderne', in *Langues et langages du commerce en Méditerranée et en Europe à l'époque moderne*, ed. Gilbert Buti, Michèle Janin-Thivos, and Olivier Raveux (Aix-en-Provence: Presses Universitaires de Provence, 2013), 83–97.
2 Janet L. Abu-Lughod, *Before European Hegemony: The World System A.D. 1250–1350* (New York, Oxford: Oxford University Press, 1989), 3–42.
3 A. H. Lybyer, 'The Ottoman Turks and the Routes of Oriental Trade', *The English Historical Review* XXX, no. CXX (1915): 579, 581; Eliyahu Ashtor, *Levant Trade in the Later Middle Ages* (Princeton, NJ: Princeton University Press, 1983), 105–06.
4 Ashtor, *Levant Trade in the Later Middle Ages*, 105–06; Georg Christ, *Trading Conflicts: Venetian Merchants and Mamluk Officials in Late Medieval Alexandria* (Leiden, Boston, MA: Brill, 2012), 21–22.
5 Philip D. Curtin, *Cross-Cultural Trade in World History* (Cambridge: Cambridge University Press, 1984), 97–100; Christ, *Trading Conflicts*, 22–27.
6 Benjamin Arbel, 'The Last Decades of Venice's Trade with the Mamluks: Importations into Egypt and Syria', *Mamluk Studies Review* 8, no. 2 (2004): 62, 71.
7 Christ, *Trading Conflicts*, 72–77.
8 Paul Freedman, *Out of the East: Spices and the Medieval Imagination* (New Haven, CT: Yale University Press, 2008), 38; Curtin, *Cross-Cultural Trade in World History*, 96–101, 120–23; Ashtor, *Levant Trade in the Later Middle Ages*, 103–05.
9 Arbel, 'The Last Decades of Venice's Trade', 37–38.
10 The instability was partly due to the embargo imposed by the Ottomans on the importation of Iranian silk. John H. Munro, 'South German Silver, European Textiles, and Venetian Trade with the Levant and Ottoman Empire, c. 1370 to c. 1720: A Non – Mercantilist Approach to the Balance of Payments Problem', in *Relazioni economiche tra Europa e mondo islamico, secc. XIII – XVIII*, ed. Simonetta Cavaciocchi (Firenze: Le Monnier, 2006), 939.
11 P. Malanima, 'Pisa and the Trade Routes to the Near East in the Late Middle Ages', *The Journal of European Economic History* 16, no. 2 (1987): 336.
12 Patrick Chorley, 'Rascie and Florentine Cloth Industry during the Sixteenth Century', *The Journal of European Economic History* 32, no. 3 (2003): 491–92.
13 ASVe, MG, folder 15, reg. 2, cc. 5, 9, 10, 30, 42, 74, 75, 124.
14 Jong-Kuk Nam, *Le commerce du coton en Méditerranée a la fin du moyen age* (Leiden: Brill, 2007), 107–36.
15 Eliyahu Ashtor, 'Le Proche-Orient au bas moyen-age: une région sous-développée', in *Sviluppo e sottosviluppo in Europa e fuori Europa dal secolo XIII alla rivoluzione industriale. Atti della decima Settimana di studio dell'Istituto Internazionale di Storia economica F. Datini*, ed. Annalisa Guarducci (Firenze: Le Monnier, Istituto internazionale di storia economica 'F. Datini', 1983), 400–01.
16 '*... siccome per avanti le faccende erano partite tra Damasco, Aleppo, Tripoli e Barutto, così a questi tempi sono tutte ridotte ad Aleppo*'. Emanuele Antonio Cicogna, *Relazioni dei consolati di Alessandria e di Soria per la Repubblica veneta tenuti da Lorenzo Tiepolo negli anni 1552–1560* (Venezia: G. Antonelli, 1857), 39.
17 Herman Van der Wee, 'Structural Changes in European Long – Distance Trade, and Particularly in the Re-Export Trade from South to North, 1350 – 1750', in *The Rise Od*

Merchant Empires. Long Distance Trade in the Early Modern World, 1350 – 1750, ed. James D. Tracy (Cambridge: Cambridge University Press, 1990), 14–17.

18 James Innes Miller, *The Spice Trade of the Roman Empire, 29 B.C. to A.D. 641* (Oxford: Clarendon Press, 1969), 1–26.

19 Andrew Dalby, *Dangerous Tastes: The Story of Spices* (Berkeley: University of California Press, 2000), 90–94.

20 For the interplay of pepper imports, finance, and war, see Benedetta Crivelli, *Commercio e finanza in un impero globale: mercanti milanesi nella Penisola Iberica (1570–1610)*, (Roma: Edizioni di storia e letteratura, 2017), 83–88, 146–78.

21 The *libbra* serves as a weight measurement specific to Venetian commerce, equivalent to 12 ounces. This measurement was categorised into '*grossa*' and '*sottile*', differentiated by the nature of the goods being weighed. In the case of spices, the *libbra sottile* was normally used. Stefania Montemezzo, *Giovanni Foscari. Viaggi di Fiandra 1463–1464 e 1467–1468* (Venice: La Malcontenta, 2012), 18. For additional details regarding the trade conditions between Venice and Alexandria in Egypt, a principal harbour for acquiring pepper, please refer to Alessio Sopracasa, *Venezia e l'Egitto alla fine del Medioevo: le tariffe di Alessandria* (Alexandrie: Centre d'études alexandrines, 2013).

22 Halil Inalcik, 'An Outline of Ottoman-Venetian Relations', in *Venezia centro di mediazione tra Oriente e Occidente (secoli XV-XVI): aspetti e problemi*, ed. Hans Georg Beck, Manoussos Manoussacas, and Agostino Pertusi, vol. 1 (Florence: Olschki editore, 1977), 83–90; Marie F. Viallon, *Venise et la porte Ottomane (1453–1566): un siècle de relations vénéto-ottomanes de la prise de Constantinople à la mort de Soliman*, (Paris: Economica, 1995).

23 ASVe, GrM, folder 250, reg. 2, cc. 1, 16, 52, 55, 60, 62.

24 ASVe, MG, folder 15, reg. 2, cc. 5, 6, 9, 10 e 28 *dare*, 75 *avere*, 9, 126, 134, 141, 144 e 154 *dare*.

25 C. H. Wake, 'The Changing Pattern of Europe's Pepper and Spice Imports, ca 1400–1700', *The Journal of European Economic History* 8, no. 2 (1979): 361–403; Paul Freedman, 'Spices and Late-Medieval European Ideas of Scarcity and Value', *Speculum* 80, no. 4 (2005): 1209–27.

26 ASVe, GrM, folder 250, reg. 2, cc. 6, 11, 13, 53, 59, 61, 75, 93.

27 ASVe, MG, folder 15, reg. 2, cc. 7, 22, 27, 34, 45, 71, 101, 127. Kermes was highly valued in international markets for its ability to produce the prestigious scarlet colour. Franco Franceschi, 'Il ruolo dell'allume nella manifattura tessile toscana dei secoli XIV-XV', *Mélanges de l'École Française de Rome - Moyen Âge [En Ligne]* 126, no. 1 (2014), http://journals.openedition.org/mefrm/1582.

28 ASVe, MG, folder 15, reg. 2, cc. 17, 39, 40, 78, 80, 84–86, 134

29 Eliyahu Ashtor, 'The Venetian Cotton Trade in Syria in the Later Middle Ages', *Studi Medievali* 17, no. 2 (1976): 675–715.

30 ASVe, GrM, folder 250, reg. 2, cc. 6, 16, 57, 58, 59.

31 Michael E. Bratchel, 'Italian Merchants Organization and Business Relationships in Early Tudor London', in *Merchant Networks in the Early Modern World*, ed. Sanjay Subrahmanyam (Aldershot, Brookfield, WI: Variorum, 1996), 1–28; Giorgia Nordio, 'La colonia mercantile veneziana nella Londra di metà Quattrocento: attività commerciale e movimento anti-alien', in *Atti del congresso internazionale "Politiche del credito. investimento, consumo e solidarietà"*, ed. Gemma Boschiero and Barbara Molina (Asti: Cassa di risparmio di Asti, 2004), 222–40; Giovanna Petti Balbi, 'Bruges, port des italiens', in *Les marchands de la Hanse et la banque des Medicis. Bruges, marché d'échanges culturels en Europe*, ed. Andre Vandewalle (Oostkamp: Stichting Kunstboek, 2002), 58–62; J. L. Bolton and Francesco Guidi Bruscoli, 'When Did Antwerp Replace Bruges as the Commercial and Financial Centre of North-Western Europe? The Evidence of the Borromei Ledger for 1438', *The Economic History Review* 61,

no. 2 (2008): 360–79; Jan Dumolyn and Bert Lambert, 'Cities of Commerce, Cities of Constraints. International Trade, Government Institutions and the Law of Commerce in Later Medieval Bruges and the Burgundian State', *Tijdschrift Voor Sociale En Economische Geschiedenis* 11, 4 (2014): 89–102.

32 Raymond De Roover, *The Bruges Money Market around 1400* (Brussels: Paleis der Academiën, 1968), 15.

33 James M. Murray, *Bruges, Cradle of Capitalism, 1280–1390* (Cambridge, New York: Cambridge University Press, 2005), 248–58.

34 J.-A. Van Houtte, 'Bruges et Anvers, marchés « nationaux » ou « internationaux », du XIVe au XVIe siècle', *Revue du Nord* 34, no. 134 (1952): 89–108.

35 Francesco Guidi Bruscoli, 'I rapporti con il Nord-Europa', in *Francesco di Marco Datini: l'uomo, il mercante*, ed. Giampiero Nigro (Firenze, Prato: Firenze University Press, Fondazione Istituto internazionale di storia economica "F. Datini", 2010), 410.

36 Alwyn A. Ruddock, 'Alien Hosting in Southampton in the Fifteenth Century', *The Economic History Review* 16, no. 1 (1946): 30–37; Edmund Fryde, 'Italian Maritime Trade with Medieval England (c. 1270–c. 1530)', in *Studies in Medieval Trade and Finance*, ed. Edmund Fryde (London: Bloomsbury Publishing UK, 1983), 291–338, https://doi.org/10.5040/9781472599155.ch-014.; Ian W. Archer, 'Responses to alien immigrants in London c. 1400 – 1650', in *Le migrazioni in Europa: secc. XIII-XVIII*, ed. Simonetta Cavaciocchi (Firenze: Le Monnier, 1994), 755–74; Jim L. Bolton, 'La répartition spatiale de la population étrangère à Londres au XVe siècle', in *Les étrangers dans la ville: minorités et espace urbain du bas Moyen âge à l'époque moderne*, ed. Jacques Bottin and Donatella Calabi (Paris: Editions de la Maison des sciences de l'homme, 1999), 425–37; Nordio, 'La colonia mercantile veneziana nella Londra di metà Quattrocento: attività commerciale e movimento anti-alien'.

37 Peter Stabel, 'Venezia e i Paesi Bassi: contatti commerciali e stimoli intellettuali', in *Il Rinascimento a Venezia: e la pittura del Nord ai tempi di Bellini, Durer, Tiziano*, ed. Bernard Aikema, Beverly Louise Brown, and Giovanna Nepi Scirè (Milano: Bompiani, 1999), 31–33.

38 ASVe, MdC, folder 29, reg. 2, letter to Alberto Contarini in Bruges, 6 July 1482; letter to Girolamo Tiepolo in London, 8 January 1483.

39 Doris Stöckly, *Le système de l'incanto des galées du marché à Venise: fin XIIIe-milieu XVe siècle* (Leiden, New York, Köln: Brill, 1995), 32–36; Francesco Balducci Pegolotti, *La pratica della mercatura*, ed. Allan Evans (Cambridge, MA: Mediaeval Academy of America, 1936), 142.

40 The count of contacts would increase substantially if it included unnamed individuals involved solely in merchandise transactions rather than capital. The challenge of accurately identifying these individuals and differentiating between multiple instances of engagement with the same entity without identification, precludes their inclusion in the analysis of Foscari's trade network. The omission of their names suggests Foscari either did not anticipate future interactions or did not deem them significant for his network's development.

41 The two companies consist of one formed by Chierico Cattaneo and Benedetto Imperiale, and the other by Chierico Cattaneo, Benedetto Imperiale, and Giovanni Pinello. All Genoese.

42 Franco Franceschi and Luca Molà, 'L'economia del Rinascimento: dalle teorie della crisi alla 'preistoria del consumismo', in *Il Rinascimento italiano e l'Europa, v. I, Storia e storiografia*, ed. Marcello Fantoni (Treviso: Colla Editore, 2005), 185–246; Paolo Malanima, *The Economy of Renaissance Italy* (Abingdon, Oxon, New York: Routledge, 2022).

43 As shown by Eric Dursteler, *Venetians in Constantinople: Nation, Identity, and Coexistence in the Early Modern Mediterranean*, (Baltimore, MD: Johns Hopkins University

Press, 2006); E. Natalie Rothman, *Brokering Empire: Trans-Imperial Subjects between Venice and Istanbul* (Ithaca, NY: Cornell University Press, 2012).

44 Viallon, *Venise et la porte Ottomane (1453–1566)*, 139–245.

45 Paolo Preto, *Venezia e i turchi* (Firenze: G. C. Sansoni, 1975); Inalcik, 'An Outline of Ottoman-Venetian Relations'; Maria Pia Pedani, *The Ottoman-Venetian Border (15th-18th Centuries)* (Venice: Edizioni Ca' Foscari, 2017).

46 ASVe, MG, folder 15, reg. 2, cc. 86, 88, 96, 113, 128, 129, 131.

47 Ina Baghdiantz McCabe, *The Shah's Silk for Europe's Silver: The Eurasian Trade of the Julfa Armenians in Safavid Iran and India (1530–1750)* (Atlanta, GA: Scholars, 1999); Munro, 'South German Silver, European Textiles, and Venetian Trade with the Levant and Ottoman Empire, c. 1370 to c. 1720: A Non – Mercantilist Approach to the Balance of Payments Problem'.

48 The Feltre cloths were well known in Apulia, where they were defined as *terzaroli*. Bartholomeo Di Pasi, *Tariffa de pexi e mesure. Qui comincia la utilissima opera chiamata taripha la qual tracta de ogni sorte de pexi e misure conrispondenti per tuto il mondo* (Venice: Albertin da Lisona Vercellese, 1503), 109r.

49 Eliyahu Ashtor, 'Les lainages dans l'Orient medieval. Emploi, production, commerce', in *Produzione, commercio e consumo dei panni lana (nei secoli XII-XVIII), Atti della seconda settimana di studio (10–16 Aprile 1970)*, ed. Marco Spallanzani (Firenze: Leo S. Olschki, 1976), 657–86; Eliyauh Ashtor, 'L'exportation de textiles occidentaux dans le Proche Orient musulman au bas moyen âge (1370–1517)', in *Studi in memoria di Federigo Melis* (Napoli: Giannini editore, 1978), 303–77. The trade of woollen cloths produces in Northern Italy increased in the following centuries: Andrea Caracausi, 'The Wool Trade, Venice and the Mediterranean Cities at the End of the Sixteenth Century', in *Commercial Networks and European Cities, 1400–1800*, ed. Andrea Caracausi and Christof Jeggle (London: Pickering & Chatto, 2014), 201–22.

50 In medieval and early modern Venice, 1 *braccio* of wool corresponds to 0.68 centimetres.

51 ASVe, MG, folder 15, reg. 2, cc. 72.

52 Andrea Caracausi, 'Mesurer et controler. Les temps de l'organisation du travail dans les manufactures de laine de Padoue (XVIe-XVIIe siècles)', *Genèses* 85 (2011): 6–26.

53 ASVe, MG, folder 15, reg. 2, cc. 72, 83.

54 ASVe, MG, folder 15, reg. 2, cc. 15, 18, 39. For the use of dyes in the textile industry: Dominique Cardon, 'Du "verme cremexe" au "veluto chremesino": un filière vénitienne du cramoisi au XVe siècle', in *La seta in Italia dal Medioevo al Seicento*, ed. Reinhold C. Mueller, Claudio Zanier, and Luca Molà (Venezia: Cini, 2000), 63–73; Dominique Cardon, 'La Garrigue, Monde de l'écarlate', *Études Rurales* 151–152 (1999): 33–42; Franceschi, 'Il Ruolo Dell'allume Nella Manifattura Tessile Toscana Dei Secoli XIV-XV'.

55 Marco Bembo refers to the instructions received from agents, containing information on market demands, forecasts, and subsequent requests for the dispatch of goods, as '*rezette*'. ASVe, MdC, folder 29, reg. 2, letter to Francesco Giustinian in Crete, 16 July 1482.

56 ASVe, MG, folder 15, reg. 2, cc. 72.

57 ASVe, MG, folder 15, reg. 2, cc. 72, 81.

58 In his correspondence with Consul Marcello in Damascus, Bembo points out Marcello's lack of expertise with bills of exchange, noting his specialization in Egyptian trade where such payment methods are uncommon. Marcello's proficiency in Egyptian commerce is indeed corroborated by Alvise Michiel's ledger from the 1470s, which lists him as Michiel's agent in Alexandria. ASVe, MdC, folder 29, reg. 2, letter to Francesco Marcello, consul in Damascus, 20 August 1483.

59 Information on the trade of Apulian, Marche, and Venetian oil can be found in various contemporary works. For the emporiums under Islamic dominion, Pegolotti notes the necessity of sending new barrels for oil transportation to those places. Islamic law, in fact, prohibits the consumption of pork, which was often transported in the same barrels.

The high number of new barrels in Apulia (for the oil to be taken to Alexandria) proves the truthfulness of this statement. Balducci Pegolotti, *La pratica della mercatura*, 39, 46, 49, 51, 130–32, 135, 139, 142, 146, 156, 162–64; Di Pasi, *Tariffa de pexi e mesure*, 4, 61, 62. For the use of oil in the wool manufacture: Edoardo Demo, *L'anima della città: l'industria tessile a Verona e Vicenza, 1400–1550* (Milano: UNICOPLI, 2001), 90–110.

60 For an overview of the use of both vegetable and animal fats in European culinary practices, refer to Massimo Montanari, 'Condimento, fondamento. Le materie grasse nella tradizione alimentare europea', in *Alimentazione e nutrizione, secc. XIII – XVIII*, ed. Simonetta Cavaciocchi (Florence: Le Monnier, 1997), 27–51.

61 Salvatore Ciriacono, 'L'olio a Venezia in Età moderna: i consumi alimentari e gli altri usi', in *Alimentazione e nutrizione secc. 13.-18.: atti della ventottesima Settimana di studi, 22–27 aprile 1996*, ed. Simonetta Cavaciocchi (Firenze: Le Monnier, 1997), 302–12; Salvatore Ciriacono, *Olio Ed Ebrei Nella Repubblica Veneta Del Settecento* (Venezia: Deputazione di Storia patria, 1975), 10–11.

62 Domenico Sella, *Commerci e industrie a Venezia nel secolo 17.* (Venezia: Istituto per la collaborazione culturale, 1961), 132–34.

63 ASVe, MdG, b. 29, reg. 2, letter to Toma Zivran in Modon, 20 November 1483.

64 Ciriacono, *Olio ed ebrei nella repubblica veneta del Settecento*, 9.

65 The Venetian '*mier*' or '*miaro*' equated to 1.210 pounds *grosse*, a measure also used in Apulia.

66 Gian Maria Varanini, 'L'olivicoltura e l'olio gardesano nel medioevo. Aspetti della produzione e della commercializzazione', in *Un lago, una civiltà: il Garda*, ed. Giorgio Borelli (Verona: Banca popolare di Verona, 1983), 117–56.

67 Ciriacono, 'L'olio a Venezia in Età moderna: i consumi alimentari e gli altri usi', 306–08.

68 Up until 1473, the task of handling cargoes was consistently assigned to a core group of individuals: Nicolò di Frigi, Alvise de Pase, Nicolò de Zivitan, and Donato di Bernardo. After this period, new names emerge (Andrea Darbe, Giovanni di Pase, Cola d'Agnolo, Matteo da Candia, Zuanne de Nicolò, and Bartolomeo Carisato), who were given responsibilities for single journeys, unlike the sustained partnerships established with the initial group. The captains of these ships were professional navigators, notably Bartolomeo Carisato, who is frequently mentioned in Bembo's letters as the captain of a 2,000-barrel capacity ship and a 'safe ride' for transporting wine between the Adriatic and the Aegean. ASVe, MdC, folder 29, reg. 2, letter to Francesco Giustinian draper in Candia, 19 November 1483.

69 ASVe, MG, folder 15, reg. 2, c. 89 *dare*

70 ASVe, MG, folder 15, reg. 2, c. 52 *dare*.

71 ASVe, MG, folder 15, reg. 2, c. 10. For the import and export from Apulia: Di Pasi, *Tariffa de pexi e mesure*, 48–51; Balducci Pegolotti, *La pratica della mercatura*, 161–76.

72 ASVe, MG, folder 15, reg. 2, cc. 67, 70.

73 Price fluctuations were especially noticeable in 1477. It is important to note that these evaluations include retail sales, typically priced above 40 ducats per *mier*, as well as bulk transactions of oil in *Ternaria*, which generally fetch less than 20 ducats per *mier*.

74 According to Venetian estimates, the annual production of Apulian olive oil was approximately 20,000 miera at the outset of the 16th century, with half of this quantity exported to the territories of the Serenissima. This demand spurred a significant agricultural transformation in Apulia, notably the intercropping of other fruit-bearing trees, such as almond trees. Saverio Russo, 'Il paesaggio agrario', in *Storia della Puglia, 1, Dalle Origini al Seicento*, ed. Angelo Massafra and Biagio Salvemini (Rome, Bari: Laterza, 2005), 208–10; Mario Del Treppo, 'Il regno aragonese', in *Storia del Mezzogiorno, 4, Il Regno dagli Angioini ai Borboni*, ed. Giuseppe Galasso and Rosario Romeo (Roma: Edizioni del sole, 1986), 88–201.

75 ASVe, MG, folder 15, reg. 2, folder 15, reg. 2, cc. 67, 69, 89.

76 ASVe, MG, folder 15, reg. 2, cc. 28 avere, 50 dare e avere, 67 dare, 85 dare, 98 avere, 112 dare.

77 For the exports from the Kingdom of Naples to Alexandria: Di Pasi, *Tariffa de pexi e mesure*, 151.

78 Paola Lanaro, 'Venezia e le grandi arterie del commercio internazionale: strade, flusso di merci, organizzazione dei trasporti tra '500 e '700', in *Mercanti e vita economica nella Repubblica veneta (secoli XIII-XVIII)*, ed. Giorgio Borelli (Verona: Banca Mutua Popolare, 1985), 271–351.

79 For commodities traded among Venice, the Low Countries, and London, please refer to Di Pasi, *Tariffa de pexi e mesure*, 185–87, 189–91.

80 In Michiel's ledger, two types of iron are recorded: *moleta* and *verzela*, both sold in bundles. The duty imposed on goods at the fondaco amounted to 2.5 ducats per *mier*. ASVe, MG, folder 15, reg. 2, cc. 68 dare e avere.

81 ASVe, MG, folder 15, reg. 2, cc. 94 dare e avere. Francesco da Sorgo is a well-recognized figure in the Venetian commercial landscape, noted for his acquisition of woollen cloths from Verona. Demo, *L'anima della città*, 335.

82 ASVe, MG, folder 15, reg. 2, cc. 16 dare, 30 avere, 34 dare, 101 dare.

83 ASVe, MG, folder 15, reg. 2, cc. 81 dare e avere, 101 avere, 133 dare.

84 ASVe, MG, folder 15, reg. 2, cc. 124 avere.

85 Factoring in the acquisition cost of tin in Venice at 78 ducats per mier, alongside the net proceeds from selling 3,747 pounds of tin in Barbary, we can deduce that the potential profit margin relative to the purchase price approximately amounted to 104%. ASVe, MG, folder 15, reg. 2, c. 27 dare, 96 avere. For the trade of metals in the Mediterranean: Di Pasi, *Tariffa de pexi e mesure*, 48–51, 59.

86 Frederic Chapin Lane, *Venice, a Maritime Republic* (Baltimore, MD: Johns Hopkins University Press, 1973), 234–37.

87 John Day, 'The Levant Trade in the Middle Ages', in *The Economic History of Byzantium: From the Seventh to the Fifteenth Century*, ed. Angeliki E. Laiou (Washington, DC: Dumbarton Oaks, 2002), 791–98. For Venetian policies in the Quattrocento supporting the export of cloth, refer to Andrea Mozzato, 'I drappieri di Venezia incontrano i lanaioli di Terraferma. Per una storia del lanificio veneto nel Quattrocento (Prima Parte)', *Studi Storici Luigi Simeoni* LX (2010): 47–60; Andrea Mozzato, 'I drappieri di Venezia incontrano i lanaioli di Terraferma. Per una storia del lanificio veneto nel Quattrocento (Seconda Parte)', *Studi Storici Luigi Simeoni* LXI (2011): 25–42.

88 On these aspects, with reference to the diamond trade in the early modern age, refer to Karin Hofmeester, 'Working for Diamonds from the 16th to the 20th Century', in *Working on Labor. Essays in Honor of Jan Lucassen*, ed. Marcel Van der Linden and Leo Lucassen (Leiden: BRILL, 2012), 19–46. These strategies are also present in many contemporary industries. See for instance Giovanni Favero, *Benetton: i colori del successo*, (Milano: EGEA, 2005), 187–233.

89 For the production of textiles in the Venetian Mainland: Walter Panciera, *L'arte matrice: i lanifici della Repubblica di Venezia nei secoli XVII e XVIII* (Treviso: Fondazione Benetton studi ricerche: Canova, 1996); Demo, *L'anima della città*; Paola Lanaro, 'Reinterpreting Venetian Economic History', in *At the Centre of the Old World. Trade and Manufacturing in Venice and the Venetian Mainland, 1400–1800*, ed. Paola Lanaro (Toronto: CRRS, 2006), 19–69; Andrea Mozzato, 'The Production of Woollens in Fifteenth- and Sixteenth-Century Venice', in *At the Centre of the Old World. Trade and Manufacturing in Venice and the Venetian Mainland, 1400 – 1800*, ed. Paola Lanaro (Toronto: CRRS, 2006), 73–107; Andrea Caracausi, *Dentro la bottega. Culture del lavoro in una città d'età moderna*, Saggi Marsilio (Venezia: Marsilio, 2008).

90 Edoardo Demo, 'Le manifatture tra Medioevo ed Età moderna', in *L'industria vicentina dal Medioevo a oggi*, ed. Giovanni Luigi Fontana, vol. 2, (Padova: CLEUP, 2004), 21–126; Andrea Caracausi, 'Mercanti e manifatture tessili fra Padova e Venezia: reti di scambio e specializzazioni produttive in Età moderna', *Mercanti e manifatture tessili fra*

Padova e Venezia: reti di scambio e specializzazioni produttive in Età moderna, 2008, 19–30, https://doi.org/10.1400/168210; Mozzato, 'I drappieri di Venezia incontrano i lanaioli di Terraferma. Per una storia del lanificio veneto nel Quattrocento (prima parte)'; Mozzato, 'I drappieri di Venezia incontrano i lanaioli di Terraferma. Per una storia del lanificio veneto nel Quattrocento (seconda parte)'.

91 Luca Molà, *The Silk Industry of Renaissance Venice* (Baltimore, MD: The Johns Hopkins University Press, 2000); Edoardo Demo, 'Wool and Silk. The Textile Urban Industry of the Venetian Mainland (15th-17th Centuries)', in *At the Centre of the Old World. Trade and Manufacturing in Venice and the Venetian Mainland, 1400–1800*, ed. Paola Lanaro (Toronto: Centre for Reformation and Renaissance Studies, 2006), 217–44.

92 Fryde, 'Italian Maritime Trade with Medieval England (c. 1270–c. 1530)'; Richard Britnell, 'Commerce and Capitalism in Late Medieval England: Problems of Description and Theory', *Journal of Historical Sociology* 6, no. 4 (1993): 359–76; Nordio, 'La colonia mercantile veneziana nella Londra di metà Quattrocento: attività commerciale e movimento anti-alien'.

References

Abu-Lughod, Janet L. *Before European Hegemony: The World System A.D. 1250–1350*. New York, Oxford: Oxford University Press, 1989.

Arbel, Benjamin. 'The Last Decades of Venice's Trade with the Mamluks: Importations into Egypt and Syria'. *Mamluk Studies Review* 8, no. 2 (2004): 37–86.

Archer, Ian W. 'Responses to Alien Immigrants in London c. 1400–1650'. In *Le Migrazioni in Europa: Secc. XIII-XVIII*, edited by Simonetta Cavaciocchi, 755–74. Firenze: Le Monnier, 1994.

Ashtor, Eliyahu. 'Le Proche-Orient au bas moyen-age: une région sous-développée'. In *Sviluppo e sottosviluppo in Europa e fuori Europa dal secolo XIII alla rivoluzione industriale. Atti della decima Settimana di studio dell'Istituto Internazionale di Storia economica F. Datini*, edited by Annalisa Guarducci, 375–434. Firenze: Le Monnier, Istituto internazionale di storia economica 'F. Datini', 1983.

Ashtor, Eliyahu. 'Les lainages dans l'Orient Médiéval. Emploi, production, commerce'. In *Produzione, commercio e consumo dei panni lana (nei secoli XII-XVIII), Atti della seconda settimana di studio (10–16 Aprile 1970)*, edited by Marco Spallanzani, 657–86. Fireze: Leo S. Olschki, 1976.

Ashtor, Eliyahu. *Levant Trade in the Later Middle Ages*. Princeton, NJ: Princeton University Press, 1983.

Ashtor, Eliyahu. 'The Venetian Cotton Trade in Syria in the Later Middle Ages'. *Studi Medievali* 17, no. 2 (1976): 675–715.

Ashtor, Eliyauh. 'L'exportation de textiles occidentaux dans le Proche Orient musulman au bas moyen âge (1370–1517)'. In *Studi in memoria di Federigo Melis*, 303–77. Napoli: Giannini editore, 1978.

Baghdiantz McCabe, Ina. *The Shah's Silk for Europe's Silver: The Eurasian Trade of the Julfa Armenians in Safavid Iran and India (1530–1750)*. Atlanta, GA: Scholars, 1999.

Balducci Pegolotti, Francesco. *La pratica della mercatura*, edited by Allan Evans. Cambridge, MA: Mediaeval Academy of America, 1936.

Bolton, Jim L. 'La répartition spatiale de la population étrangère à Londres au XVe siècle'. In *Les étrangers dans la ville: minorités et espace urbain du bas Moyen âge à l'époque moderne*, edited by Jacques Bottin and Donatella Calabi, 425–37. Paris: Editions de la Maison des sciences de l'homme, 1999.

Bolton, J. L., and Francesco Guidi Bruscoli. 'When Did Antwerp Replace Bruges as the Commercial and Financial Centre of North-Western Europe? The Evidence of the Borromei Ledger for 1438'. *The Economic History Review* 61, no. 2 (2008): 360–79.

Bottin, Jacques. 'La pratique des langues dans l'espace commercial de l'Europe de l'Ouest au début de l'époque moderne'. In *Langues et langages du commerce en Méditerranée et en Europe à l'époque moderne*, edited by Gilbert Buti, Michèle Janin-Thivos, and Olivier Raveux, 83–97. Aix-en-Provence: Presses Universitaires de Provence, 2013.

Bratchel, Michael E. 'Italian Merchants Organization and Business Relationships in Early Tudor London'. In *Merchant Networks in the Early Modern World*, edited by Sanjay Subrahmanyam, 1–28. Aldershot, Brookfield, WI: Variorum, 1996.

Britnell, Richard. 'Commerce and Capitalism in Late Medieval England: Problems of Description and Theory'. *Journal of Historical Sociology* 6, no. 4 (1993): 359–76.

Caracausi, Andrea. *Dentro la bottega. Culture del lavoro in una città d'età moderna*. Venezia: Marsilio, 2008.

Caracausi, Andrea. 'Mercanti e manifatture tessili fra Padova e Venezia: reti di scambio e specializzazioni produttive in Età moderna'. *Mercanti e manifatture tessili fra Padova e Venezia: reti di scambio e specializzazioni produttive in Età moderna*, 2008, 19–30. https://doi.org/10.1400/168210.

Caracausi, Andrea. 'Mesurer et contrôler. Les temps de l'organisation du travail dans les manufactures de laine de Padoue (XVIe-XVIIe siècles)'. *Genèses* 85 (2011): 6–26.

Caracausi, Andrea. 'The Wool Trade, Venice and the Mediterranean Cities at the End of the Sixteenth Century'. In *Commercial Networks and European Cities, 1400–1800*, edited by Andrea Caracausi and Christof Jeggle, 201–22. London: Pickering & Chatto, 2014.

Cardon, Dominique. 'Du "verme cremexe" au "veluto chremesino": un filière vénitienne du cramoisi au XVe siècle'. In *La seta in Italia dal medioevo al Seicento*, edited by Reinhold C. Mueller, Claudio Zanier, and Luca Molà, 63–73. Venezia: Cini, 2000.

Cardon, Dominique. 'La garrigue, monde de l'écarlate'. *Études Rurales* 151–152 (1999): 33–42.

Chorley, Patrick. 'Rascie and Florentine Cloth Industry during the Sixteenth Century'. *The Journal of European Economic History* 32, no. 3 (2003): 487–526.

Christ, Georg. *Trading Conflicts: Venetian Merchants and Mamluk Officials in Late Medieval Alexandria*. Leiden, Boston, MA: Brill, 2012.

Cicogna, Emanuele Antonio. *Relazioni dei consolati di Alessandria e di Soria per la Repubblica Veneta tenuti da Lorenzo Tiepolo negli anni 1552–1560*. Venezia: G. Antonelli, 1857.

Ciriacono, Salvatore. 'L'olio a Venezia in Età moderna: i consumi alimentari e gli altri usi'. In *Alimentazione e nutrizione secc. 13.-18.: atti della ventottesima Settimana di studi, 22–27 aprile 1996*, edited by Simonetta Cavaciocchi, 302–12. Firenze: Le Monnier, 1997.

Ciriacono, Salvatore. *Olio ed ebrei nella Repubblica Veneta del Settecento*. Venezia: Deputazione di Storia patria, 1975.

Crivelli, Benedetta. *Commercio e finanza in un impero globale: mercanti milanesi nella Penisola Iberica (1570–1610)*. Roma: Edizioni di storia e letteratura, 2017.

Curtin, Philip D. *Cross-Cultural Trade in World History*. Cambridge: Cambridge University Press, 1984.

Dalby, Andrew. *Dangerous Tastes: The Story of Spices*. Berkeley: University of California Press, 2000.

Day, John. 'The Levant Trade in the Middle Ages'. In *The Economic History of Byzantium: From the Seventh to the Fifteenth Century*, edited by Angeliki E. Laiou, 791–98. Washington, DC: Dumbarton Oaks, 2002.

De Roover, Raymond. *The Bruges Money Market around 1400*. Brussels: Paleis der Academiën, 1968.

Del Treppo, Mario. 'Il Regno aragonese'. In *Storia del Mezzogiorno, 4, Il Regno dagli Angioini ai Borboni*, edited by Giuseppe Galasso and Rosario Romeo, 88–201. Roma: Edizioni del sole, 1986.

Demo, Edoardo. *L'anima della città: l'industria tessile a Verona e Vicenza, 1400–1550*. Milano: UNICOPLI, 2001.

Demo, Edoardo. 'Le manifatture tra Medioevo ed Età moderna'. In *L'industria vicentina dal Medioevo a oggi*, edited by Giovanni Luigi Fontana, 2:21–126. History, Economy and Society. Padova: CLEUP, 2004.

Demo, Edoardo. 'Wool and Silk. The Textile Urban Industry of the Venetian Mainland (15th-17th Centuries)'. In *At the Centre of the Old World. Trade and Manufacturing in Venice and the Venetian Mainland, 1400–1800*, edited by Paola Lanaro, 217–44. Toronto: Centre for Reformation and Renaissance Studies, 2006.

Di Pasi, Bartholomeo. *Tariffa de pexi e mesure. Qui comincia la utilissima opera chiamata taripha la qual tracta de ogni sorte de pexi e misure conrispondenti per tuto il mondo*. Venice: Albertin da Lisona Vercellese, 1503.

Dumolyn, Jan, and Bert Lambert. 'Cities of Commerce, Cities of Constraints. International Trade, Government Institutions and the Law of Commerce in Later Medieval Bruges and the Burgundian State'. *Tijdschrift Voor Sociale En Economische Geschiedenis* 11, 4 (2014): 89–102.

Dursteler, Eric. *Venetians in Constantinople: Nation, Identity, and Coexistence in the Early Modern Mediterranean*. Baltimore, MD: Johns Hopkins University Press, 2006.

Favero, Giovanni. *Benetton: i colori del successo*. Milano: EGEA, 2005.

Franceschi, Franco. 'Il ruolo dell'allume nella manifattura tessile toscana dei secoli XIV-XV'. *Mélanges de l'École Française de Rome - Moyen Âge [En Ligne]* 126, no. 1 (2014) . http://journals.openedition.org/mefrm/1582.

Franceschi, Franco, and Luca Molà. 'L'economia del Rinascimento: dalle teorie della crisi alla 'preistoria del consumismo'. In *Il Rinascimento Italiano e l'Europa, v. I, Storia e Storiografia*, edited by Marcello Fantoni, 185–246. Treviso: Colla Editore, 2005.

Freedman, Paul. *Out of the East: Spices and the Medieval Imagination*. New Haven, CT: Yale University Press, 2008.

Freedman, Paul. 'Spices and Late-Medieval European Ideas of Scarcity and Value'. *Speculum* 80, no. 4 (2005): 1209–27.

Fryde, Edmund. 'Italian Maritime Trade with Medieval England (c. 1270–c. 1530)'. In *Studies in Medieval Trade and Finance*, edited by Edmund Fryde, 291–338. London: Bloomsbury Publishing, 1983. https://doi.org/10.5040/9781472599155.ch-014.

Guidi Bruscoli, Francesco. 'I rapporti con il Nord-Europa'. In *Francesco di Marco Datini: l'uomo, il mercante*, edited by Giampiero Nigro, 407–28. Firenze, Prato: Firenze University Press, Fondazione Istituto internazionale di storia economica "F. Datini", 2010.

Hofmeester, Karin. 'Working for Diamonds from the 16th to the 20th Century'. In *Working on Labor. Essays in Honor of Jan Lucassen*, edited by Marcel Van der Linden and Leo Lucassen, 19–46. Leiden, Boston: Brill, 2012.

Inalcik, Halil. 'An Outline of Ottoman-Venetian Relations'. In *Venezia centro di mediazione tra Oriente e Occidente (secoli XV-XVI): Aspetti e problemi*, edited by Hans Georg Beck, Manoussos Manoussacas, and Agostino Pertusi, 83–90. Florence: Olschki editore, 1977.

Lanaro, Paola. 'Reinterpreting Venetian Economic History'. In *At the Centre of the Old World. Trade and Manufacturing in Venice and the Venetian Mainland, 1400–1800*, edited by Paola Lanaro, 19–69. Toronto: CRRS, 2006.

Lanaro, Paola. 'Venezia e le grandi arterie del commercio internazionale: strade, flusso di merci, organizzazione dei trasporti tra '500 e '700'. In *Mercanti e vita economica nella Repubblica veneta (secoli XIII-XVIII)*, edited by Giorgio Borelli, 271–351. Verona: Banca Mutua Popolare, 1985.

Lane, Frederic Chapin. *Venice, a Maritime Republic*. Baltimore, MD: Johns Hopkins University Press, 1973.

Lybyer, A. H. 'The Ottoman Turks and the Routes of Oriental Trade'. *The English Historical Review* XXX, no. CXX (1915): 577–88.

Malanima, P. 'Pisa and the Trade Routes to the Near East in the Late Middle Ages'. *The Journal of European Economic History* 16, no. 2 (1987): 335.

Malanima, Paolo. *The Economy of Renaissance Italy*. Abingdon, Oxon, New York: Routledge, 2022.

Miller, James Innes. *The Spice Trade of the Roman Empire, 29 B.C. to A.D. 641*. Oxford: Clarendon Press, 1969.

Molà, Luca. *The Silk Industry of Renaissance Venice*. Baltimore, MD: The Johns Hopkins University Press, 2000.

Montanari, Massimo. 'Condimento, fondamento. Le materie grasse nella tradizione alimentare europea'. In *Alimentazione e nutrizione, secc. XIII – XVIII,* edited by Simonetta Cavaciocchi, 27–51. Florence: Le Monnier, 1997.

Montemezzo, Stefania. *Giovanni Foscari. Viaggi di Fiandra 1463–1464 e 1467–1468*. Venice: La Malcontenta, 2012.

Mozzato, Andrea. 'I drappieri di Venezia incontrano i lanaioli di Terraferma. Per una storia del lanificio veneto nel Quattrocento (Prima Parte)'. *Studi Storici Luigi Simeoni* LX (2010): 47–60.

Mozzato, Andrea. 'I drappieri di Venezia incontrano i lanaioli di Terraferma. Per una storia del lanificio veneto nel Quattrocento (Seconda Parte)'. *Studi Storici Luigi Simeoni* LXI (2011): 25–42.

Mozzato, Andrea. 'The Production of Woollens in Fifteenth- and Sixteenth-Century Venice'. In *At the Centre of the Old World. Trade and Manufacturing in Venice and the Venetian Mainland, 1400–1800*, edited by Paola Lanaro, 73–107. Toronto: CRRS, 2006.

Munro, John H. 'South German Silver, European Textiles, and Venetian Trade with the Levant and Ottoman Empire, c. 1370 to c. 1720: A Non – Mercantilist Approach to the Balance of Payments Problem'. In *Relazioni economiche tra Europa e mondo islamico, secc. XIII – XVIII*, edited by Simonetta Cavaciocchi, 905–60. Firenze: Le Monnier, 2006.

Murray, James M. *Bruges, Cradle of Capitalism, 1280–1390*. Cambridge, New York: Cambridge University Press, 2005.

Nam, Jong-Kuk. *Le commerce du coton en Méditerranée à la fin du moyen age*. Leiden: Brill, 2007.

Nordio, 'La colonia mercantile veneziana nella Londra di metà Quattrocento: attività commerciale e movimento anti-alien', in *Atti del congresso internazionale "Politiche del credito. investimento, consumo e solidarietà"*, edited by Gemma Boschiero and Barbara Molina (Asti: Cassa di risparmio di Asti, 2004), 222–40.

Panciera, Walter. *L'arte matrice: i lanifici della Repubblica di Venezia nei secoli XVII e XVIII*. Treviso: Fondazione Benetton studi ricerche: Canova, 1996.

Pedani, Maria Pia. *The Ottoman-Venetian Border (15th-18th Centuries)*. Venice: Edizioni Ca' Foscari, 2017.

Petti Balbi, Giovanna. 'Bruges, port des italiens'. In *Les marchands de la Hanse et la banque des Medicis. Bruges, marché d'échanges culturels en Europe*, edited by Andre Vandewalle, 58–62. Oostkamp: Stichting Kunstboek, 2002.

Preto, Paolo. *Venezia e i turchi*. Firenze: G. C. Sansoni, 1975.

Rothman, E. Natalie. *Brokering Empire: Trans-Imperial Subjects between Venice and Istanbul*. Ithaca, NY: Cornell University Press, 2012.

Ruddock, Alwyn A. 'Alien Hosting in Southampton in the Fifteenth Century'. *The Economic History Review* 16, no. 1 (1946): 30–37.

Russo, Saverio. 'Il paesaggio agrario'. In *Storia della Puglia, 1, Dalle origini al Seicento*, edited by Angelo Massafra and Biagio Salvemini, 204–13. Rome, Bari: Laterza, 2005.

Sella, Domenico. *Commerci e industrie a Venezia nel secolo 17*. Civiltà veneziana. Studi. Venezia: Istituto per la collaborazione culturale, 1961.

Sopracasa, Alessio. *Venezia e l'Egitto alla fine del Medioevo: le tariffe di Alessandria*. Alexandrie: Centre d'études alexandrines, 2013.

Stabel, Peter. 'Venezia e i Paesi Bassi: contatti commerciali e stimoli intellettuali'. In *Il Rinascimento a Venezia: e la pittura del Nord ai tempi di Bellini, Durer, Tiziano*, edited by Bernard Aikema, Beverly Louise Brown, and Giovanna Nepi Scirè, 30–43. Milano: Bompiani, 1999.

Stöckly, Doris. *Le système de l'incanto des galées du marché à Venise: fin XIIIe-milieu XVe siècle*. Leiden, New York, Köln: Brill, 1995.

Van der Wee, Herman. 'Structural Changes in European Long – Distance Trade, and Particularly in the Re-Export Trade from South to North, 1350–1750'. In *The Rise Od Merchant Empires. Long Distance Trade in the Early Modern World, 1350–1750*, edited by James D. Tracy, 14–33. Cambridge: Cambridge University Press, 1990.

Van Houtte, J.-A. 'Bruges et Anvers, marchés « nationaux » ou « internationaux », du XIVe au XVIe siècle'. *Revue du Nord* 34, no. 134 (1952): 89–108.

Varanini, Gian Maria. 'L'olivicoltura e l'olio gardesano nel medioevo. Aspetti della produzione e della commercializzazione'. In *Un lago, una civiltà: il Garda*, edited by Giorgio Borelli, 117–56. Verona: Banca popolare di Verona, 1983.

Viallon, Marie F. *Venise et la porte Ottomane (1453–1566): un siècle de relations vénéto-ottomanes de la prise de Constantinople à la mort de Soliman*. Collection Campagnes & stratégies. Grandes batailles 16. Paris: Economica, 1995.

Wake, C. H. 'The Changing Pattern of Europe's Pepper and Spice Imports, ca 1400–1700'. *The Journal of European Economic History* 8, no. 2 (1979): 361–403.

4 Capital

Tools, Turnover, and Investments

In pre-industrial Europe, the commercial sector, particularly international trade, represented the zenith of profitability. This domain leveraged the consumption dynamics of the feudal system, focusing on the exchange of high-value commodities, including spices, silks, and other goods from the Orient, as well as essential staples.[1] Despite a general trend towards decline of feudalism, there remained sufficient wealth within this system to sustain a stable demand for these luxurious products. Furthermore, the era extending from the late Middle Ages to the early modern period witnessed a notable surge in the consumption patterns of the urban middle classes, who increasingly chose to allocate their savings towards luxury consumables.[2]

In the specific context of Venice (a phenomenon paralleled to an extent in the Netherlands),[3] the nexus between commerce and political patronage, as elucidated in Chapter 2, played a central role. This symbiotic relationship afforded Venetian commercial entities a degree of market control, occasionally culminating in the establishment of semi-monopolistic dominions. This development occurred within a framework that was, in its essence, not yet capitalist and remained rooted in the feudal and manorial structures prevalent until the 15th century. Nonetheless, it was within the ambit of commerce that the seeds of capitalist practices were sown, facilitating a process of capital accumulation among the mercantile group. This evolution illustrates a gradual yet definitive shift towards modern economic paradigms, highlighting the transformative power of trade in the pre-modern economy.

Capital and Capitalism

Before we embark on a discussion regarding the utilization and investment of capital by medieval merchants, it is imperative to elucidate the concept of capital by succinctly exploring its definitions and interpretations. The notion of capital has been a focal point of historiographical discourse since the 19th century, sparking considerable debate among scholars. Its application spans across diverse fields, including economics, sociology, and history, where it is ascribed to multiple dimensions, thereby rendering its definition somewhat fluid and dynamic. Capital is understood in several ways: it can represent the monetary value assigned to

DOI: 10.4324/9781032628103-5

assets, the assets themselves that comprise the capital investment, or more broadly, the aggregate of resources designated for productive use with the aim of fostering additional output.[4] This term adapts its meaning according to the context of its investment.[5] Analysing capital from an economic and monetary perspective reveals its dual nature: fixed, or constant capital, refers to investments in tangible assets such as infrastructure, machinery, and raw materials. These components are incapable of enhancing the product's value beyond their inherent worth. Conversely, variable capital is invested in human labour, a dynamic resource not only capable of reproducing its value but also of creating surplus value, a fundamental element for generating profit.[6]

As the discussion around capital and capitalism evolved, particularly in viewing capital as an intrinsic value, the term has been broadened to encompass notions of power, particularly the purchasing power associated with investments in production.[7] This concept extends to the potential for utilization, encompassing both fixed capital, which is invested in durable goods capable of enduring multiple usage cycles, and circulating capital, allocated to goods that deplete their utility after a single use.[8] Irrespective of the specific interpretation, over the past two centuries, capital has given rise to a socio-economic system intricately linked to its existence, functionality, and flow. Capitalism, as an economic framework, inherently entails various critical issues, including economic inequality, resource concentration in the hands of a few, and exploitation of the economically disadvantaged, often exacerbated by inadequate economic policies. This perspective of capital, shaped through the modern and contemporary eras and refined through the process of industrialization advancing into the realm of finance, has assimilated into and profoundly affected global economic systems. It has also ignited debates concerning its essence, the development of capitalist economies, and its dominant influence on global economic structures.[9]

Prior to the emergence of capitalism, what was the prevailing economic structure? How was capital defined, and at what point did capitalism begin to take shape? The roots of capitalist systems can generally be traced to the 14th and 15th centuries, a period marked by the gradual disintegration of feudalism, catalysed by the devastating plague epidemics of the 14th century.[10] These epidemics, which decimated over 25% of Europe's population, significantly disrupted feudal relationships. This disruption paved the way for the formation of a new societal structure, initially centred around city-states and later evolving in the Italian Peninsula into regional states.[11] In this evolving society, city merchants emerged as central figures, fundamentally transforming the economic landscape. They amassed wealth through privileges afforded by public authorities and through monopolistic strategies. This wealth accumulation facilitated their subsequent investment in productive ventures from the 16th century onwards.[12] While some scholars argue that the full maturation of the capitalist system awaited the global expansion of the economy and the widespread availability of abundant free labour through the creation of colonial empires, others contend that it had already emerged earlier, with many of its essential elements present since the Renaissance period.[13]

Renaissance Capital

The 14th and 15th centuries represented the embryonic stages of capitalism, manifesting in limited forms within a largely non-capitalistic economic system.[14] During this period, 'capital' held specific significance for the early proponents of capitalism, the medieval merchants. This era witnessed merchants routinely invoking the term 'capital', imbuing it with meanings that reflected the nascent capitalist ethos of their time. The most prevalent were investment (usually in merchandises), monetary value, value reserve, and personal net worth.

The notion of personal net worth, in particular, may seem out of place in a predominantly family-driven economy like Venice's. A merchant's wealth was determined by deducting their financial obligations such as debts and loans from their total assets. This involved subtracting not only the business interests of siblings or other family members, which weren't always stated in the family firm ledgers, but also factoring in any joint investments or partnerships. While wealth was measured at a specific point in time, it served as an essential indicator of a merchant's financial stability and success within the competitive marketplace.[15] Venetian merchants, as well as other Italian merchants, employed double-entry bookkeeping, a technique famously explained by Luca Pacioli, among others, in his seminal work 'Summa de arithmetica et geometria' in 1494.[16] A case in point is Alvise Michiel, who, during the financial closure of 1473, recorded his personal capital, '*Cavedall de io Alvise Michiel*', at roughly 10,500 ducats.[17] Regrettably, Michiel does not delve into the origins or evolution of this sum, as it is not referenced again in subsequent discussions. Nonetheless, it is remarkable that he chose to record this figure in the family's financial books as an asset, deliberately keeping it separate from other financial engagements (the account is devoid of links to any internal ledger counterparts and probably refers to a Profit and Loss account held elsewhere).

Typically, the term capital was predominantly used within the context of trade transactions. Its most common interpretation aligned with the concept of investment, typically directed towards merchandise. Whether involving pearls or Ponentine fabrics, the goods traversing the Mediterranean and Europe were themselves considered capital. This capital was inherently dynamic, transitioning from a monetary form to a tangible state of goods (which, in the realm of commercial capitalism, often matches the wholesale purchase price of these items). Such capital could then accrue additional value or surplus value, through a production process encompassing both further labour and enhancement. A prime illustration of this is the finishing process for Feltre cloths described in the previous chapter. Raw cloths bought by a capitalist undergo a labour and enhancement process that elevates their market value (carried out by independent artisans with their own means of production), allowing them to capture and subsequently generate surplus value.

Surplus value can also emerge without the necessity for further processing of goods—simply through the act of transporting products across diverse markets to capitalize on variations in their use value, or market price.[18] Pepper serves as a prime illustration of this phenomenon. Aside from transaction costs and the logistical aspects of moving from one market to another, pepper did not undergo any

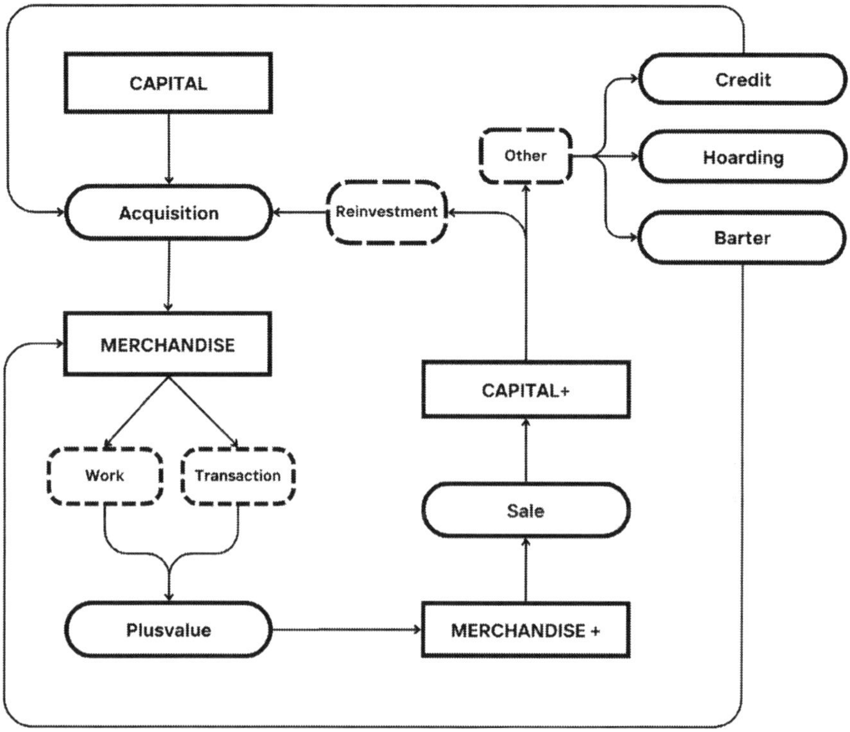

Figure 4.1 Schematic representation of capital circulation and multiplication in Renaissance commerce.

additional processing. Here, the surplus was generated through intermediation costs incurred by agents and Venetian merchants, as well as by shifting the goods from a market where it had a lower value (often due to local abundance) to one where it commanded a higher price (where there were buyers willing to pay a premium for a product scarce in that market and whose consumption was tied to status symbol). Upon a successful sale, the capital transforms yet again, morphing into other goods, credit, or cash, thereby completing its cycle of transformation (See Figure 4.1).[19]

Consider the scenario where Marco Bembo sent several Ponentine cloths to Greece. In his correspondence with the agent, Bembo delineates that each white piece of cloth carries a capital value of 18 ducats, with dyeing costs to be added on top.[20] This initial capital, essentially the purchase price, is poised for augmentation through production-related expenses (work and transaction: 'merchandise+'), aiming to generate a surplus that will be reflected in the final selling price. However, prior to this stage, this amount is not yet classified as capital, since it could readily morph into a loss due to potential damages or unsold inventory.[21] Upon a successful sale, the capital not only multiplies ('capital+') but also embarks on a transformative journey that could lead to exchanges of goods, credits, and money, sparking a new cycle of multiplication, or to the hoarding of capital, where it ceases to be reinvested and is instead accumulated by the capitalist. The Venetian merchants were proponents of reinvesting this capital into a diverse array of new commodities, including grains, wines, cheeses, and spices. These goods, mirroring the path of the cloths, were then redirected towards Venice, experiencing further transformation. This process initiated a continuous cycle of capital evolution, growth, and reinvestment, potentially without end.[22]

Lastly, the term capital could also be related to monetary value. Discussing the monetary system of the Renaissance era does not solely concern coined currency but, particularly in the commercial sector, extends to account money, crucial in the realms of finance and business management.[23] This account money played a critical role in enabling international trade. It was based on imperial units like the *libra*, *solidus*, and *denarius*, encompassing a series of abstract units used across Europe. This system, which changed across the centuries, ensured a stable exchange rate with locally minted currencies, facilitating seamless economic transactions across borders. Despite the fluctuating value of base metal coinage (often referred to as black money) and the relative stability of silver and gold coin currencies during the Renaissance, account currencies offered a reliable and international benchmark for appraising diverse local currencies. These units functioned in tandem with tangible coinage, serving as an indispensable instrument for managing substantial sums and establishing a universally recognized value against local currencies, thereby streamlining transactions. As the primary currency recorded in accounting ledgers, they also introduced a level of transparency into commercial documentation, enabling comprehensive scrutiny of accounts and transaction values by virtually any observer.[24]

Metal alloys such as gold, silver, and copper, imbuing currency with intrinsic value, underpinned the early capitalist monetary system. This framework ensured that a coin's worth was a direct reflection of the material it contained. If currency itself represented a form of capital, then what was its nature? In Renaissance society, money served multiple functions. Primarily, it acted as a medium of exchange, establishing itself as the standard measure for the value of goods. This role was pivotal for facilitating trade beyond simple barter, serving as both a baseline for every transaction and a means for transferring value between individuals or across markets. Moreover, currency also played a crucial role as a store of value, maintaining its worth over the medium term. This stability enabled deferred payments, thereby transforming trade and exchange methodologies. Although the role of money remained consistent across different contexts, each regional monetary system had its unique coinage, prone to fluctuations in value.[25] Such variability led to instability in exchange rates and market prices, compelling merchants to either recommend or advise against the use of certain currencies during specific periods.[26] These risks were mitigated by increasing the amount of information at their disposal. This was primarily achievable through the efforts of factors and correspondents in foreign markets, who provided up-to-date information on the exchange rates between currencies (as well as weights) from various markets, thereby facilitating the operations of resident merchants.[27]

The Limits of Capital

The concept of capital is varied, with medieval merchants applying the term in different contexts. In the day-to-day operations of businesses, the most significant challenges arose when there were issues in the circulation of capital, particularly in its monetary form. Currency fulfilled the crucial role of enabling the quantification of capital, assigning it an absolute value, even when its form diverged from that of physical money. Consequently, the availability of a standardized currency was essential for this purpose. The Venetian example highlights the use of state-minted currency, specifically the gold ducat, which was established by law to have a fixed value. Its stability and recognized worth made it a preferred medium of exchange not just locally but on international markets as well. The gold ducat was among several gold coins circulating in the Mediterranean, but it was far from unique. Similar currencies, such as the Florentine florin or the Genoese *genoino*, also held equivalent value and, since the 13th century, had been internationally recognized and accepted as valid currencies.[28] The Venetian monetary system was complex and evolved significantly over the centuries. By the second half of the 15th century, it included not only the ducat, which served as the benchmark currency in accounting ledgers and commercial correspondence, and had a comparable value to florin, genoino, and other international golden coins, but also silver coins such as the *grosso*, along with copper and other metal alloys.[29]

The variety in coinage was a reflection of each coin's intrinsic value and the specific purposes it served. Different denominations were essential to cater to the needs of local markets, distinguishing them from the currency denominations preferred for bulk transactions on the international stage.[30] The requirement to mint coins containing a fixed percentage of precious metals inevitably had its repercussions. First and foremost, it necessitated a metal market that could ensure a steady supply of gold, silver, and copper to the Venetian state. This was crucial for minting a sufficient volume of coins to sustain the exchange system and to keep the amount of precious metal within the coins stable. Linked to this was the need to establish and, when necessary, reform the system through the minting of new coins and the withdrawal of those no longer in circulation or worn out.[31] The risk associated with any shortfall in these areas was closely tied to price fluctuations, with potential for inflation or deflation, and the availability of enough currency in the Venetian market to support both retail and wholesale trade.[32]

The scarcity of currency, however, could also stem from political factors beyond the control of materials and mint operations, such as wars. These circumstances not only introduced risks and delays in the flow of capital but also markedly diminished the availability of money in the Venetian market, chiefly allocated for military expenditures.[33] This predicament is highlighted in Marco Bembo's correspondence with agents stationed in Levantine markets. He shared the challenges he faced in acquiring merchandise for export due to a severe shortage of funds in Venice, as money was primarily diverted to finance the troops involved in the War of Ferrara, which at the time was largely concentrated along the banks of the Po River.[34] To secure the funds required for military expenses, the Most Serene

Republic enforced the collection of taxes, including duties and tithes, strictly in cash, disallowing any extensions or the employment of financial instruments.[35] It is for this reason Bembo implored his agents to demonstrate exceptional foresight and agility, beyond the usual demands, to discern which commodities could potentially thrive in the challenging market conditions of Venice and thus facilitate the acquisition of the much-needed cash. He specifically highlighted the value of foodstuffs, asserting that 'Every merchandise sleeps and no coin is to be found, save for victuals and drink'.[36] For instance, while Cretan cheese is affordably priced on the island of Crete, it fetches considerable sums in Venice, with buyers readily paying in cash.[37]

Cash collection strategies were not limited to domestic markets but extended to international ones as well. In the winter of 1483, during a severe currency scarcity in Venice, Bembo managed to dispatch local commodities, such as soap, alongside German imports, including iron, linen, and hemp fabrics. These were sent with the clear objective of selling them for cash, aiming to mitigate the financial strain faced by his company in Venice.[38] The situation had deteriorated throughout 1482: although the initial months had seen a promising flow of newly minted silver from Florence—enabling Bembo to even pledge the dispatch of silver to Levantine markets by year's end—by late in the year, this vital influx of currency had ceased. The company was left in a dire state, with transactions at a standstill and virtual payment methods, like account transfers or bills of exchange, being rejected.[39] Indeed, by November 1483, Bembo was engaged in correspondence with his nephew, Zuan Malipiero, then serving as his agent in Candia (Crete), discussing strategies to generate cash independently from the Venice headquarters. Zuanne's proposal to ship soaps to Candia for cash sales caught Bembo off guard. He was surprised not just by his nephew's lack of insight into the high market value of soap and olive oil but also concerned that selling these commodities in Candia would incur losses due to the significantly higher prices back in Venice.[40] Bembo's reluctance to dispatch more goods to Crete was not without merit. With textiles, caviar, and metals already in Candia, Bembo's agents had approximately 5,000 ducats of capital at their disposal. This could be converted into cash to fund further investments, eliminating the need for Bembo to incur debts to supply his agents in Crete.[41]

The scarcity of liquidity represented a severe instance of a broader challenge affecting all forms of commercial capital: inertia. For merchants, the primary concern was the difficulty in mobilizing capital, be it in moving goods from one harbour to another or transferring funds from one individual to another. At the heart of this challenge lay a fundamental truth: capital that remains idle fails to generate profit. Marco Bembo underlines this concept repeatedly, highlighting it in discussions about both bills of exchange (monetary capital) and physical goods. The ability to maintain fluid capital distinguishes a skilled merchant from an ineffective one. As Marco clearly advises his agent and nephew in Constantinople: 'I caution you that merchants desire a rapid return of their capital, preferring an immediate loss to a profit delayed for a long time, as time consumes everything'.[42] Bills of exchange and commodities that have languished for years pose a significant challenge to reintegrate into the trading cycle, resulting in two distinct setbacks:

the depreciation of assets and the lost opportunity for a well-informed investor to enhance the value of the investment and realize its potential returns.[43] This line of reasoning extended to credits and debts as well: short-term credits or debts owed by individuals known to have a good reputation, thus deemed highly collectible, represented what Marco Bembo described as 'perfect' capital. Conversely, long-standing, stagnant debts not collected over time were not only viewed as challenging but were considered capital that could be almost regarded as lost.[44]

Circulating capital, even for marginal gains, to foster its growth is a principle also observed in the commodity chain of the Feltre cloths by Alvise Michiel, highlighted in the preceding chapter. Even minimal investments, such as purchasing low-grade woollen fabrics, become strategic when their value is augmented through further production stages, ultimately producing a surplus upon sale in international markets. This strategy ensures the continuous movement and viability of capital, simultaneously forging new commercial relationships and opportunities that will be advantageous during prosperous times. Moreover, the act of transferring capital—as merchandise—from the site of production to the consumption market inherently generates a surplus, attributed solely to the logistics of movement and brokerage. This not only maintains the momentum of capital but also amplifies the scope for commercial expansion and the realization of profits.

Furthermore, the circulation of capital enabled the circumvention of limitations inherent in cash-only transactions or bartering in specific markets, particularly those governed by Islamic law. This is evidenced by correspondence between Marco Bembo and the Damascus consul Marcello, wherein Bembo remarks on Marcello's unfamiliarity with using bills of exchange as a form of collateral. In contrast, this practice was prevalent in the West.[45]

The challenge of settling payments for the myriad valuable commodities imported from Egypt and Syria without financial tools significantly impacted Venice. This situation necessitated the export of large volumes of silver to the Middle East, diverting a precious resource that could have been employed in coinage.[46] The critical role of financial instruments in managing purchases in foreign markets becomes evident in the context of Alvise Michiel's olive oil trade with Apulia. Of the 19,000 ducats invested in olive oil during the 1470–80 decade, a significant portion, 8,600 ducats, was transacted through bills of exchange. This mechanism facilitated the procurement of goods without the physical transfer of cash between markets, simultaneously promoting the development of financial techniques in regions previously unfamiliar with such transactions, such as England, as we will explore further in the following section. Moreover, the issue of cash scarcity, exacerbated by the partial shutdown of local markets, compelled merchants to focus on investing in essential goods like grain, cheese, and wine. These commodities played a crucial role in mobilizing capital within an economy grappling with financial limitations.

Capital Circulation and Growth

Renaissance Venetian merchants possessed a positive ethos of capitalism, which involved long-term planning and strategic investments.[47] While not self-identifying as capitalists, they exemplified the principles of capital ownership, whether through personal net worth, as in the case of Alvise Michiel,[48] or by managing familial capital within their enterprises.[49] Bembo elucidates this to his agents, detailing the complexities of managing company capital, especially when the death of a partner necessitates tough decisions. Regardless, the paramount goal was always the multiplication of capital and exploring various avenues to achieve this. As observed, the essential strategy, whether the capital was monetary or tied up in goods, was to keep it in motion. There were two primary methods for ensuring the continuous circulation of assets and investments. Initially, in times of economic adversity, the emphasis pivoted towards commodities regarded as either stable or of high value within the Venetian marketplace. Subsequently, they engaged financial mechanisms like bills of exchange to navigate and benefit from fluctuations in exchange rates, facilitating loans and discreetly incorporating interest charges.

Safe Investments

Regarding investments in goods, the letters of Marco Bembo provide an insight into what we have partially observed with Alvise Michiel: Bembo articulates the challenges within the Venetian market, which extended well beyond the mere scarcity of cash. During the War of Ferrara, indeed, one of the challenges in marketing Oriental goods, such as silks, was compounded by the absence of foreigners in the city, a crucial market for these luxury items. By 'foreigners', Bembo refers not only to Central European or Flemish merchants but also to the array of Italian traders who relied on the Venetian market for luxury goods, notably those from Milan and Emilia. The war along the Po River effectively severed Venice from its customary trade and information networks, crucial for the direct sale of Oriental products.[50] Confronted with the prevailing conditions and the impediments brought about by wars, merchants such as Bembo and Michiel strategically channelled their capital into commodities with assured marketability. Despite existing constraints, these selected goods held the capacity to mobilize capital effectively. Emphasis was particularly placed on essential staples—grain, wine, and cheese—recognizing that, even amidst tumultuous periods, these commodities sustained a consistent demand, thereby ensuring a continuous flow of capital. This section will examine two commodities instrumental in these strategies: wine, for its reliable market in Europe and as a commodity allowing for deferred payments and generating enough revenue to cover significantly increased duties, and wheat, for the profitability of importing a scarce product, encouraged by the Venetian State, which facilitates the recoupment of cash.[51]

Wine

Wine held a pivotal role in Venetian commerce, serving both as a staple for everyday consumption and as a luxury good for the affluent.[52] The bulk of the wine exported by Venice originated from the Island of Crete, under Venetian dominion, where viticulture profoundly shaped the local economy. Beginning in the late 13th century, a significant portion of Crete's agricultural expansion was devoted to vineyards, suggesting a shift from mere subsistence farming prevalent in Byzantine times to a focus on wine production for export. Venetian ships facilitated a direct and efficient transport link from Crete's vineyards to Venice, establishing the city as a vital nexus for wine consumption and distribution across Europe. A notable decree issued on 25 January 1318, allowed Cretan wine, once dutied in Venice, to be freely exported, underlining the integral role wine played within Venetian trade strategies. This legislative move and the subsequent integration of Cretan wine into Venetian commercial networks underscored a period of transformative change, encompassing both viticulture advancements and maritime innovations. As will be demonstrated through Marco Bembo's wine trade, these changes were less about revolutionary techniques and more about evolving investment and organizational practices that facilitated the global reach of Venetian commerce. Moreover, the timber trade for barrel making emerged as an essential ancillary activity, driven by the need for quality barrels essential for wine transport. Despite Crete's lush forests, the specific types of trees ideal for barrel construction were often sourced from Venice and the broader Greek mainland, reflecting the intricate supply chains that underpinned the Venetian trading empire. This dynamic illustrates not only the economic interdependence within the Venetian territories but also the strategic importance of wine in fostering trade links, securing resources, and advancing Venetian maritime prowess[53] (Figure 4.2).

Harvested from the fertile lands of the Venetian Empire,[54] including Crete and the Greek Islands, wine emerged as a coveted product across Europe. Mediterranean sweet wines, in particular, enjoyed a robust demand in the northern European markets of England and Flanders. This demand provided Venetian merchants like Marco Bembo with lucrative trade opportunities, especially during wartime, by ensuring consistent exports and a reliable income stream. Unlike spices or silks, Venetian merchants could involve themselves in almost every aspect of wine production. This involvement ranged from supplying new barrels—thereby establishing a supply chain that ensured a surplus of barrels for sale to other merchants—to blending the wine itself.

For barrel production, Marco Bembo took an active role in sourcing the necessary materials, including timber and metal hoops. Timber was transported from the Adriatic basin or Greece, while metal components were supplied from Venice on leased ships. These ships not only transported raw materials but also served as floating workshops where master coopers, paid five ducats a month, commenced the barrel-making process en route to Candia. They continued this work ashore using materials already available in Crete.[55] Employing new, high-quality barrels was essential to maintaining the wine's subtle flavours, as using old barrels risked degrading the taste of the sweet wines, although these were deemed suitable for tart wines or could be sold to recover some costs. While Bembo directly managed this initial phase of the production chain, the responsibility of overseeing wine purchases fell to his agents. Bembo did not own vineyards himself, making it crucial to cultivate strong relationships with landowners and their managers to secure the best supplies. Determining which suppliers were the best involved a trial and error process that could occasionally result in suboptimal outcomes.[56]

In 1482, Bembo assigned his agent, Francesco Giustinian, with the task of finding new suppliers for his wine business. This may have involved discreetly reviewing competitors' sources and possibly establishing a partnership with Querini—known for producing the finest wines in Crete.[57] The arrangement would include providing direct capital for production and essential barrels for storage and transport.[58] Bembo emphasized acquiring all barrels from Querini to thwart competitors, underlining the strategic importance he placed on this relationship. When Giustinian declined to lend 200 ducats to Querini—a move that resulted in Querini seeking funds from a rival, Foscarini—Bembo was infuriated. He instructed Giustinian not only to ensure that Querini returned the borrowed money but also to offer an additional 400 ducats if needed.[59] Bembo favoured sourcing almost exclusively from Querini; however, he did acquire some barrels of sweet wine from local landlords like Sterigi and Barbarigo even if he believed that Querini's aged vineyards produced the highest quality sweet wine which 'are marketable and fetch a good price'.[60] According to him, this type of sweet wine was particularly well-suited for sale at places like *Fondaco dei Tedeschi*.[61]

The involvement in the initial production phase goes beyond just supplying barrels and financing the producers; it extends into the formulation of wine-blending recipes. Convinced of the need to avoid losses on '*garbi*', tart, wines—wines that had arrived in Venice the previous year but had no market in Western Europe while being preferred in the Mediterranean[62]—Bembo instructs his agent Giustinian on how to improve the taste of these wines. He advises that for each barrel of must, which typically contains 48 *mistatti*, an additional two *mistatti* of cooked wine and two of aged tart wines should be blended in.[63] This strategy aimed not only to enhance the flavour but also to utilize wines that lacked a market in the West, thereby preventing potential losses. The rationale is clear: 'it is better to renew and gain multiple times rather than just once',[64] effectively managing surplus stock by blending to preserve the wine's desirable characteristics.

Following the financing, production, and storage stages, transportation, distribution, and sale ensued. These operations, complex under normal circumstances, became exceedingly difficult during wartime when the availability of Venetian ships was scarce and the risk of capture was high. In this context, what was Bembo's approach? He opted for a secure strategy by forming a commercial partnership to mitigate these risks. This partnership was established in the spring of 1483 with the Tiepolo brothers, Girolamo and Paolo, who were actively engaged in Western markets, particularly in London and Flanders. Bembo shared a strong bond with the brothers, particularly Paolo; they had attended the joust in Padua together during the feast of Saint Anthony on 13 June the previous year, even enjoying some downtime in the city.[65] While the Tiepolo brothers provided Bembo with direct access to Northern European markets, he reciprocated by sharing his expertise in the Eastern Mediterranean. He granted them access to his extensive network of agents and contacts, and importantly, to his reserves of Malvasia wine in Crete.

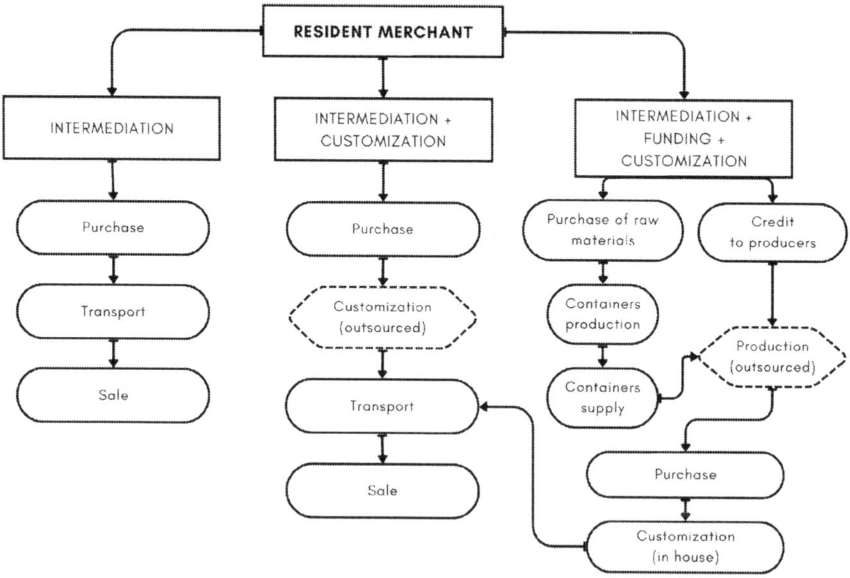

Figure 4.2 Diagram of the involvement of medieval resident merchants in commercial and production chains based on the activities of Marco Bembo and Alvise Michiel.

Marco instructed his agent to prepare 600 barrels of wine—200 from Rethymno and 400 from Candia—while considering his agent's insights about the higher cost of Rethymno wine despite the minimal price difference between the two in Western markets. Of these barrels, 300 would be registered under Bembo's name and 300 under the Tiepolo family's name. These were to be loaded onto the 'Ingillesca', a vessel flying under an English flag so that it could bypass Venice on its way directly to British markets such as Sandwich and Southampton before continuing upriver via Thames.[66] Bembo instructed his agent to wait for Paolo Tiepolo at Candia. Returning from Phocaea, Tiepolo's expertise in English markets would be crucial to assess whether the Cretan barrels were suitable for transport, or if they should switch to smaller Venetian *botticelle* or *carratelli*. This arrangement was particularly notable for two reasons: it underlines Bembo's keen awareness of price differentials across different markets and his readiness to utilize foreign ships for trade. This potentially bypassed Venice as an intermediary market. This arrangement allowed Bembo to multiply his capital by directly accessing lucrative markets and avoiding the fees and regulations imposed by Venice, going against a law established in 1451 aimed at securing Venetian commercial dominance over Cretan products through limitations placed upon their use aboard foreign ships. This adjustment would optimize both transportation efficiency and tax obligations, since customs duties were calculated based on container size rather than weight.[67] Amidst these preparations, Bembo stressed the importance of reserving some barrels of cooked wine and '*moroa*' wine to adjust the new wines expected by the end of summer. Another important tactic involved broadening the range of suppliers in order to lessen the impact of potential problems during the harvest or with a particular supplier, besides maintaining robust partnerships with other wine producers, particularly the dependable supplier Querini and the Patriarch of Constantinople, who had agreed to supply wines from the San Miro estate.[68] The meticulous oversight Venetian merchants exerted on wine production are illustrated by the example of Bembo and Tiepolo, with Tiepolo insisting on having his clerk, Piero da Ponte, present during the wine decanting.

Bembo's significant dedication to the wine trade is understandable when considering that the central role of wine in the pre-modern economy extended beyond its value as a commodity; it served as a vital catalyst for trade and cultural exchange, facilitating connections between distant regions and shaping social norms. Its robust demand in northern markets led Venetian merchants to utilize it as a medium of exchange on ships for various services, including renting houses and warehouses, as gifts for customs officials in various ports, and to facilitate broader trade exchanges. This practice is well-documented in the account books of Giovanni Foscari. On his first voyage, the entire cargo of wine was designated for various uses: 23 *caratelli* for consumption on the galley, 94 *caratelli* to facilitate the purchase of textiles, and 8 *caratelli* as gifts for customs officials. The consumption of wine during navigation was generally reserved for the officers' table on the galley and for paying guests on board. During Foscari's initial trip to Flanders in 1463–64, he actively managed the officers' needs, loading Malvasia wine in Venice and consuming 23 *caratelli* during the journey, incurring ship expenses of about 2 ducats per *caratello*. This approach changed markedly on his second voyage four years later, where only 3 *caratelli* of Foscari's wine were consumed on board as wine supplies were acquired directly in various ports. Additionally, another 5 *caratelli* were used as gifts for customs and clerical officials at Sluis or Dame, which were mandatory stops before entering Bruges. Revisiting his first voyage, the majority of the wine was bartered with Flemish merchants for Holland cloth, linens, mantles, and velvets, fetching a price of 3 ducats per *caratello*.[69] Conversely, the second voyage saw a different strategy, with 264 *caratelli* of wine being sold between Bruges and London at an average price of 3.5 ducats per *caratello*, this time without any bartering for other goods.[70]

Marco Bembo's deep engagement in the wine trade and its strategic use by Giovanni Foscari highlight the central role of wine in the Renaissance economy. Beyond its commodity value, wine facilitated extensive trade networks across Europe for Venetian merchants, serving as a versatile currency in complex trade negotiations and social exchanges. This dual role is illustrated in Foscari's account logs, which detail the use of wine for various strategic purposes—ranging from consumption on galleys to facilitating textile trades and as gifts in diplomatic contexts. These practices highlight wine's utility in smoothing commercial operations and building relationships with customs officials and local traders. Moreover, Foscari's evolving strategies—from bartering wine for essential goods to focusing on direct sales in his subsequent voyages—reflect an adaptation to the dynamic conditions of international trade, optimizing the use of wine to meet the high demand in northern markets.

Wheat

While wine secured steady income and maintained the flow of capital along with relationships with Western markets, wheat addressed different necessities. It too represented a reliable return on investment and an avenue to acquire cash during periods of scarcity, yet it satisfied a fundamental demand as a staple in Mediterranean diets, classifying it as a necessity rather than the luxury product that sweet wine typically represented. Given its importance, Italian states often subsidized its importation both to maintain adequate reserves for the future and to stabilize market prices.[71] This was exemplified in 1482 when the Republic of Venice authorized a subsidy of 10 shillings per *staio* for wheat imports to be completed by the end of the following March. Responding to this opportunity, Bembo, like many Venetian merchants, urgently directed his agents, particularly his nephew Alvise Malipiero in Constantinople, to suspend all other transactions and concentrate all available capital on purchasing Turkish and Greek wheat. To aid in these efforts, he employed a servant, Andrea Alberga, who was fluent in the local language, ensuring smooth communications and transactions.[72]

The drive to purchase Turkish and Greek wheat was influenced not only by the subsidy from the Republic, which was relatively modest (approximately 1/10 of the market price of wheat in Venice), but also by rising prices in the Paduan and Ravennan markets—from 100 shillings per *staio* to 124, equivalent to 1 ducat. Despite the expected increase in prices in Constantinople due to the heightened Venetian demand, high profits were still anticipated.[73] A few months later, Bembo updated his nephew in Constantinople: ships laden with wheat were beginning to arrive in Venice in such volumes that they were causing a gradual price decrease. However, this decline would not affect the profits from the shipment his nephew was to send from Constantinople, since 'this land is a cauldron of great consumption'.[74] What Bembo did not know at the time was that his nephew had delayed the shipment of the ship by 20 days, causing it not to arrive in time and resulting in a loss of at least 1,000 ducats for the merchant, as prices remained stable despite the large influx. Bembo's anger towards his nephew, who was responsible for causing such substantial financial damage, began to subside in June of the same year when the Venetian government introduced additional incentives for the importation of the new wheat harvest by the end of January 1484. The incentives offered were significantly higher than before: 25 *shillings* per *staio* for Black Sea wheat (beyond Gallipoli in Turkey, now Gelibolu); 20 *shillings* for wheat from the Aegean Sea (between Gallipoli and Nauplia); 10 *shillings* for wheat from Morea and Albania, thus between Nauplia and the Adriatic; and finally, no subsidy for wheat from Calabria and Apulia, as a retaliatory measure against King Ferdinand of Naples, who was severely disrupting Venetian navigation during that phase of the war.[75]

Stung by his nephew's mistake in delaying the wheat shipment in previous months, Bembo did not stand still. He began inquiring with Sicilian correspondents about the cost of importing Sicilian wheat. In this case, he asked not only about prices but also about the cost of transport on Sicilian ships, which would have faced much lower risks of an unfortunate encounter with the galleys of King

Ferdinand of Naples.[76] This strategy was not unique to Bembo: the incentives introduced by the Venetian government did not specifically favour Venetian navigation but offered a subsidy also to foreign ships rented by Venetians who imported grain into Venice.[77] This tactic is not new to the Venetian state; a similar approach was adopted as early as the 13th century in the salt trade, highlighting that in the case of essential goods, Venice did not strictly promote Venetian navigation per se but rather maritime trade (whether Venetian or not).[78] This consideration is particularly interesting because it displays Venice's nuanced approach to navigation: on one hand, it financed Venetian galleys with public funds, while, on the other, it did not hesitate to provide incentives for Mediterranean maritime trade if it was deemed more effective in achieving its objectives.

While for a merchant the circulation of capital in the form of goods was the most natural course of action, over the course of the Middle Ages, other tools were also developed—financial instruments—that enabled the capital to yield profits through favourable currency exchanges and the monetization of time.

Financial Tools

The employment of financial instruments significantly augmented the capacity of Renaissance Venetian merchants to multiply their capital. These merchants astutely leveraged tools such as bills of exchange and bank deposits, which were instrumental in enhancing the fluidity of capital and facilitating expansive trade networks. The bill of exchange, in particular, became an indispensable tool for conducting transactions within medieval markets. A persistent issue during this period was the shortage of liquidity, often exacerbated by the intermittent scarcity of precious metals across Europe.[79] This scarcity posed a substantial threat to trade continuity. Additionally, the challenges associated with the physical transport of money and the verification of coins' intrinsic value at the point of transaction frequently disrupted trade activities. Although banking systems for facilitating payments were still rudimentary until the late Middle Ages, the situation began to shift with the internationalization of banking in the 15th century. However, credit availability remained relatively limited in comparison to the scale of commercial and local transactions. The introduction of the bill of exchange marked a fundamental development, offering a solution for making payments in various currencies, transferring funds, and extending credit across long distances, thereby revolutionizing commerce practices during the late 14th and 15th centuries.

The need to manage mercantile transactions effectively without the physical transfer of coined money spurred merchant-bankers to innovate 'virtual' financial instruments for payment and fund transfer. One of the earliest mechanisms devised was the credit transfer system. This method required both parties involved to approach the bank. The payer would instruct the banker to transfer a specified sum, which the banker would then record in his ledger and shift the funds from one account to another. This instrument was predominantly utilized for local payments within the same marketplace.[80] For managing capital over long distances, which was essential both for financing trade deals and capitalizing on exchange rate fluctuations, merchants relied on the bill of exchange. This financial tool was critical for enabling the seamless flow of capital across regions and borders. Before delving into the usage of this tool by Venetian Renaissance traders, it's important to understand its basic operation and underlying principles.

The bill of exchange was developed to remit money in different places and also became widely used for credit financing. The practice of remitting money using a paper instrument instead of currency began in the late 12th century. The invention of the bill of exchange was essentially due to the reorganization of long-distance trade. In effect, since the end of the 13th century, merchants had become increasingly sedentary and preferred opening branches abroad or sending agents instead of travelling incessantly. Trade was therefore managed directly from the city of origin, thus favouring the development of methods and instruments to help coordinate the flow of goods and capital. As a consequence, they sought methods for sending money in local currency to their agents, or vice versa, in order to be able to finance trade, on the one hand, and, on the other, to obtain payments from abroad when necessary.[81] The bill of exchange combined three features that made it particularly useful to the medieval merchant operating over long distances. Firstly, it limited the costs and the risks of transporting large amounts of cash on long voyages; at the same time, it provided a useful instrument for international credit and currency exchange, as well as solving the problem of the Catholic prohibition against usury. There was an additional benefit: using bills of exchange facilitated 'one-way' trade, in situations where the flow of specific goods could not be balanced with exports but required monetary payments. The Michiel case provides a compelling illustration of this dynamic in relation to the acquisition of Apulian oil. Frequently, agricultural raw material markets encountered significant difficulties in accommodating the expensive Venetian products and needed alternative financing solutions. In essence, the bill of exchange enabled the transfer of money in a different currency on a specified date and to a different location for purchasing goods, providing short-term financing and generating liquidity at foreign ports; it also allowed for the redemption of the bill (in cases involving forward outright). This financial instrument expanded opportunities for cross-border trade and transactions by offering flexible payment options.[82]

The bill of exchange functioned not merely as a promise to pay but as a direct order to the banker to make a specified sum available to the beneficiary at a determined place, in a specific currency, and by a set date. The transaction's structure involved four key parties: the merchant, known as the giver, who initiated the process; the bank, or drawer, where the giver placed the order; the beneficiary, who would receive the funds; and the drawee, typically a branch of the initiating bank or a partnering institution in the target market such as Bruges or London. Here is how the process unfolded: the giver approached the drawer to send money to a designated market in the local currency of that market. The drawer then issued one or more coupons to the beneficiary. These coupons certified the beneficiary's right to collect the specified amount. Concurrently, the drawer notified the drawee bank about the required payment. Upon presentation of the coupon, the drawee would release funds to the payee in the local currency and the

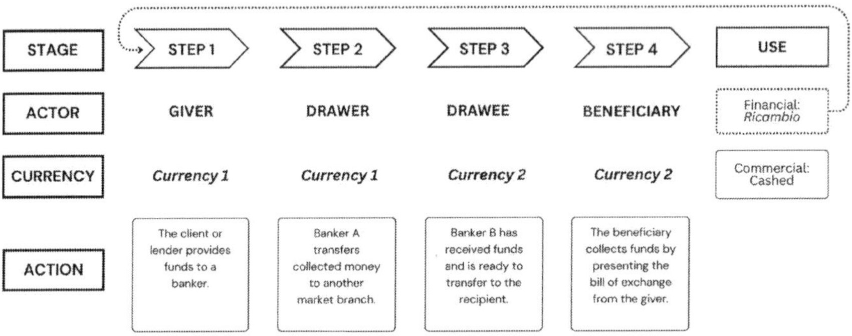

Figure 4.3 Schematic representation of bill of exchange process.

agreed amount. Each bill of exchange came with a payment deadline, known as the '*usanza*', which could be specifically stated on the bill or set according to a predetermined date relative to the transaction's destination.[83] (Refer to Figure 4.3 for further illustration.)

Bills of exchange served multiple functions: facilitating payment for goods, profiting from currency exchange, and extending credit. The process for profiting from foreign exchange involved the same mechanism that bankers utilized to finance their operations. This mechanism entailed overvaluing the currency provided to the drawer while paying the beneficiary in the actual exchange rate currency, thus securing a profit from the exchange rate discrepancy for the banker. The procedure was similar with forward outright exchanges: once the bill of exchange was received and the *usanza* expired, a reversal of the process occurred—from the beneficiary back to the drawer. In this phase, the foreign currency was again overvalued, creating a favourable exchange rate difference with respect to the ducat. This arrangement allowed the lender (acting as the giver) and the beneficiary to effectively lend money by systematically overestimating the currency given out (*pecunia presens*) and underestimating the currency received (*pecunia absens*). An additional manoeuvre involved issuing another draft in Venice, following the same route as the initial transaction. This tactic, known as '*stare sui cambi*' (staying on exchanges), could extend the loan terms for several months. By mutual consent, bills could be voluntarily protested, meaning the drawee refused to pay the beneficiary. This protest would return the bill to Venice, saving the cost of issuing the return leg but incurring notary fees to register the protest.[84]

As we have seen, the system of bills of exchange was complex, requiring the agreement of multiple parties including the payer, the beneficiary, and intermediaries, as well as acceptance and understanding of the system by all involved. Additionally, this system was recognized and sanctioned by the Venetian public authorities, so much so that merchants found it outrageous when the value and efficacy of bills of exchange were not fully acknowledged. An example of this is the bills of exchange related to the purchase of alkaline ashes by Bembo in partnership with Spinola, which we discussed in previous chapters. Writing to Vielmo

Anzelieri, a correspondent in Damascus, Bembo expressed his bewilderment over the consul's failure to recognize the power of the bills:

> I am astonished by such statements, as being a merchant, he should understand the authority of bills of exchange, which are akin to court judgments and, when presented to the office of the consuls and any other judge, are always executed. This should especially be the case for me, since I present them as collateral.[85]

In Northern Europe during the late 15th century, banking and financial services were highly developed and widely utilized. Notably, Venice itself hosted several prominent banks known as '*ponentini*'—including Giustinian, Contarini, Pesaro, and Tiepolo.[86] This banking infrastructure supported Venetian merchants like Giovanni Foscari, who also leveraged local banks during his travels to Northern Europe. His network prominently featured bankers who played crucial roles, especially in Bruges where banking services were extensively employed. The volume of transactions for payments and currency exchanges notably increased from Foscari's first to his second voyage. In 1464, the bankers in Bruges utilized by Foscari were Zuan Grisel, Zuan Rolando, and Girardo Febre; by 1467/68, Zuan Rolando continued his services alongside Collinet de Mai, a distinguished banker involved in wide-ranging transactions with merchants and financiers from across Europe during the 1460s and 1470s.[87] Despite the widespread use of these banking services and the significant investments managed through these banks, no records indicate their operation in any other ports visited by the convoy. In England, where the convoy also frequented, banking activities were managed by Venetian or other Italian firms, notably by Ambrogio and Giorgio Spinola, who executed a currency exchange of 1,413 ducats in 1468.[88] Bankers Antonio di Rebatta and Bernardo Cambi, well-regarded and engaged by Foscari in 1468, predominantly managed transactions between Bruges and Venice. They are also referenced in the voyage of 1463/64 in partnership with the Salviatis, although there is no specific mention of their activities in England where they were active during the same years (refer to Table 4.1).[89]

Bills of exchange were the financial transactions for which bankers' services were most widely used. These could be issued either for the payment of goods and

Table 4.1 Flemish bankers employed by Giovanni Foscari on his journeys to Flanders (1460s)

Name	*Year*	*City*	*Types of transaction*	*Sum in ducats*
Zuan Grisel	1463/64	Bruges	Bill of exchange; deposit	1412
Zuan Rolando	1463/64	Bruges	Bill of exchange; withdrawal	994
Girardo Febre	1463/64	Bruges	Bill of exchange; withdrawal	1638
Collinet de Mai	1467/68	Bruges	Bill of exchange	465
Zuan Rolando	1467/68	Bruges	Bill of exchange; deposit	9997

Source: ASVe, GrM, folder 250, reg. 2.

services (such as brokerage) or for the remittance, or transfer, of funds to other cities in different currencies, in order to profit from the convenient exchange of currency. In Foscari's case, the currencies used for speculation were Flemish and English. Once again, the term *differentiation* seems crucial. In 1464, the majority of drafts were issued for payment purposes, for goods and services (3,612 and 137 ducats, respectively), while only one-third of the money invested in bills was used for currency speculation purposes. In 1467/68, the situation was very different. First of all, from a quantitative point of view, the amount of money committed in bills of exchange was much greater and differently structured. More than half of the drafts were issued for currency exchange, totalling 9,595 ducats. Payments for goods and services also saw an increase in the use of drafts (although there was a decrease in the percentage), reaching 5,293 ducats for goods and 4,046 for services. Therefore, the increase in mercantile transactions was followed by an increase of capital investments in financial transactions. For the most part, these were made with Venetian merchants, or with other Italian (Genoese and Tuscan) and Flemish merchants. English merchants are conspicuously absent from the currency exchange drafts. Their exclusion can be attributed to multiple factors. Primarily, the hostile business environment towards Italian merchants and their approaches to financing and management played a central role, as the capitalistic methods employed by Italians for making investments significantly contributed to the anti-alien sentiment. This movement was a major disruptive force in the London market throughout the 15th century, repeatedly challenging the established trading norms and leading to a pushback against foreign merchant practices.[90]

Financial transactions involving bills of exchange or the engagement of bankers and financial brokers were typically not used in trade with Muslim merchants at Mediterranean ports. However, these financial practices remained prevalent within the Italian merchant communities. In an explanation to the consul in Damascus, the merchant emphasized the need for Venetian authorities in the East to adopt the same payment methods that were standard in their homeland, ensuring consistency across their trading empire:

> Your Magnificence is accustomed to the voyage to Alexandria and is not well-versed in the use of bills of exchange because they are not employed there. However, in the journey to the West, the situation is exactly the opposite, and I am well aware of this to the extent that a debt towards me, certified by a bill of exchange, is as binding as a final judgement. Here, sales are commonly settled upon the arrival of ships and galleys, and at that moment, it is within the creditor's right, without the need for further judgement but with the endorsement of the consuls, to claim the debtor's goods. I could present countless examples to Your Magnificence that attest to this practice, but I am confident that you will do as requested.[91]

As Bembo explained, in regions like North Africa and the Middle East, modern payment methods such as bill of exchange were not in use. Instead, transactions were predominantly conducted through cash or barter. Bartering, while still a viable means of circulating capital, posed significant challenges.[92] Firstly, it required finding a trading partner who was specifically interested in the goods the Venetians offered. Secondly, the barter process often resulted in acquiring goods of lesser value or in a devaluation of the merchandise offered for trade. Bembo advises his agent in Candia that accepting cash payments is preferable and most advantageous, while bartering should be a secondary option: 'buying with cash affords a better deal, whereas bartering is more about making do'.[93] Moreover, bartering significantly delays the return on capital. Unlike immediate transfers possible with cash or bills of exchange, trading goods necessitates waiting for suitable shipping conditions, such as the availability of armed galleys for valuable items or sufficient space on ships.[94] This could delay the return of capital by up to a year, not including the additional time needed to sell these goods in Venice. During periods of stagnant trade in Venice, engaging in barter was even riskier as it could mean tying up capital in commodities that might not find a market in the short term. This was especially true when the company required enhanced liquidity to maintain operations and meet financial obligations.[95]

Despite certain limitations, the value of the African markets was in the connections they established with merchants from various regions and the access they provided to essential goods. For Giovanni Foscari, regions like North Africa and Spanish ports were crucial for maintaining relationships with Genoese merchants active in the coral trade—a significant aspect of his business, given that his partnership had secured part of the Genoese contract for trading coral.[96] In Spain, Africa, and Sicily, Foscari's trading activities mainly involved exchanging English and Flemish goods for commodities such as exotic animals, gold, skins, slaves, waxes. While transactions with Genoese merchants were typically settled in cash, bartering was more prevalent with local traders, who are largely unrecorded in accounts. In Foscari's first voyage, barter transactions occurred 19 times across various ports, accumulating an exchange value of 2,560 ducats. These exchanges took place nearly everywhere the galleys docked, from Bruges to Tunis, and from Palermo to Malaga. In Bruges, Candia wine was commonly traded for local fabrics and tapestries. In London and Southampton, however, it was luxury fabrics like silks and gold cloths that were exchanged for multi-coloured woollen cloths. In the Mediterranean, silk was typically traded for grain cloths, except in Tunis where English cloths were bartered for Berber waxes and animal skins. During Foscari's first voyage to Flanders, bartering accounted for 8.6% of the total business turnover. The second voyage saw a significant reduction in bartering, which facilitated only six transactions involving the exchange of wine, cinnamon, and caps for English and Flemish cloth, amounting to 433 ducats—just 1.33% of the total value of transactions. It must be noted, however, that in North African ports the layover lasted no more than a week, restricting then trade to a few products, making it difficult to fully comprehend the dynamics of those markets.[97]

The data provided underlines the strong differentiation in the circulation of capital, in all respects, of the Mediterranean markets from the Northern European. Despite the increasing number of partners, Bruges and London had a fairly similar trading pattern. For a 'seasonal' merchant, both markets were well-organized, had a significant presence of institutions, and relied on the presence of compatriots who were experts, particularly in local markets and the mechanics of trade. In Bruges, some local merchants, mainly bankers, were a fundamental support for merchants transiting through the city. For them, the role of the consul or resident merchants was crucial for carrying out business, as seen in Chapter 2. However, it was also common practice in Bruges to entrust foreign merchants to a mediator appointed by the city council: this was undoubtedly a method by means of which the city controlled the actions of foreign merchants. Nonetheless, it was also a way of providing assistance to those who would only be staying for a short time, for those who arrived in the Flemish market without any established major connections and were completely unaware of local customs. These parties allowed the merchants temporarily present in the cities to create, or become part of, a commercial (even transitory) network that allowed them to circulate capital in its commercial and financial forms.[98] In London, however, the situation was different. Italian merchants faced much stricter control and rules compared to other players in purely financial transactions which might explain the lack of Anglo-Saxon representation in this aspect.

In the Mediterranean markets, traditional financial instruments such as bills of exchange were generally not utilized in dealings with local merchants; transactions were primarily conducted through barter or cash settlements. However, within the Venetian community and among partners from other Italian merchant communities, the circulation of bills of exchange was commonplace. In this setting, these documents could also serve as collateral in joint ventures, providing a means to collect owed amounts in the event of a partner's insolvency. Such capital flows required meticulous record-keeping in ledger books and the exchange of information through commercial correspondence, one of the features of the Italian firms of the period.

Notes

1 Alain Bihr, *Le premier âge du capitalisme (1415–1763)*, vol. 2 (Lausanne, Paris: Éditions Page 2-Syllepse, 2019), 25–31.
2 Maurice Dobb, *Studies in the Development of Capitalism* (New York: International Publishers, 1946), 77, 120n.
3 Julia Adams, *The Familial State: Ruling Families and Merchant Capitalism in Early Modern Europe* (Ithaca, NY: Cornell University Press, 2005), 22–28, 38–74.
4 See also Neal Harris and Gerard Delanty, 'What Is Capitalism? Toward a Working Definition', *Social Science Information* 62, no. 3 (2023): 323–44.
5 Adam Smith, *An Inquiry into the Nature and Causes of the Wealth of Nations*, vol. 2 (London: Strahan and Cadell, 1776), chap. 5; John Stuart Mill, *Principles of Political Economy: With Some of Their Applications to Social Philosophy*, vol. 1 (London: J. W. Parker and Son, 1848), chaps 4 and 5.
6 Karl Marx, *Capital. A Critical Analysis of Capitalist Production*, vol. 3 (London: Swan Sonnenschein, Lowrey Co., 1889), chaps 1–7.
7 Carl Menger, *Principles of Economics, I, General Part* (Glencoe: Free Press, 1950), 15.
8 Joseph A. Schumpeter, *The Theory of Economic Development* (Oxford: Oxford University Press, 1949), 115–23.
9 Dobb, *Studies in the Development of Capitalism*; Thomas Piketty, *Capital in the Twenty-First Century* (Cambridge, MA: The Belknap Press of Harvard University Press, 2014).

10 Stephan R. Epstein, 'The Late Medieval Crisis as an "Integration Crisis"', in *Early Modern Capitalism. Economic and Social Change in Europe*, ed. Maarten Prak (London, New York: Routledge, 2001), 25–50.
11 Dobb, *Studies in the Development of Capitalism*, 33–82.
12 Dobb, 33–82.
13 Immanuel Maurice Wallerstein, *The Modern World-System. I, Capitalist Agriculture and the Origins of the European World-Economy in the Sixteenth Century* (New York: Academic Press, 1974), chaps 1–2. The presence of capitalism before the birth of colonial empires is mainly argued in: Larry Neal and Jeffrey G. Williamson, eds., *The Cambridge History of Capitalism. Volume 1, The Rise of Capitalism: From Ancient Origins to 1848* (Cambridge: University Press, 2014). For an overview on the debate, see: Ian Blanchard, 'International Capital Markets and Their Users, 1450–1750', in *Early Modern Capitalism. Economic and Social Change in Europe, 1400–1800*, ed. Maarten Prak (Abingdon, Oxon, New York: Routledge, 2001), 107–24.
14 See the *Business History Review* 94, no. 1 (2020) issue on 'Italy and the Origins of Capitalism', and in particular: Robert Fredona and Sophus A. Reinert, 'Italy and the Origins of Capitalism', *Business History Review* 94, no. 1 (2020): 5–38; Maria Fusaro, 'The Burden of Risk: Early Modern Maritime Enterprise and Varieties of Capitalism', *Business History Review* 94, no. 1 (April 2020): 179–200; Corey Tazzara, 'Port of Trade or Commodity Market? Livorno and Cross-Cultural Trade in the Early Modern Mediterranean', *Business History Review* 94, no. 1 (2020): 201–28; Francesca Trivellato, 'Renaissance Florence and the Origins of Capitalism: A Business History Perspective', *Business History Review* 94, no. 1 (2020): 229–51.
15 Frederic C. Lane, *Andrea Barbarigo. Merchant of Venice* (Baltimore, MD: Johns Hopkins University Press, 1944), 182–86.
16 Luca Pacioli, *Summa de arithmetica, geometria, proportioni et proportionalita* (Florence: Paganino de Paganini, 1523). For an English translation: Luca Pacioli, *Summa de arithmetica, geometria, proportioni et proportionalita*, ed. Jeremy Cripps (Seattle, WA: Pacioli Society, 1994). For additional literature and detailed discussion on this subject, please refer to Chapter 1.
17 ASVe, MG, folder 15, reg. 2, c. 59.
18 André-Émile Sayous, 'Observations d'écrivains du XVIe siècle sur les changes et notamment sur l'influence de la disparité du pouvoir d'achat des monnaies', *Revue économique internationale* IV (1928): 289–320.
19 This perspective on commercial capital is inspired by the theories presented in Bihr, *Le premier âge du capitalisme (1415–1763)*, 2:21–23.
20 ASVe, MdC, folder 29, reg. 2, letter to Tommaso Zivran in Modon, February 1483.
21 ASVe, MdC, folder 29, reg. 2, letter to Francesco Giustinian in Candia, 22 November 1482; Zuan Confetto in Cyprus, 22 November 1482.
22 ASVe, MdC, folder 29, reg. 2, letter to Martino Malipiero a Tripoli, 10 August 1482; to Francesco Giustinian in Candia, 10 August 1482.
23 Reinhold C. Mueller, 'The Role of Bank Money in Venice 1300–1500', *Studi Veneziani, n.s.*, 3 (1979): 47–96; Frederic C. Lane and Reinhold C. Mueller, *Money and Banking in Medieval and Renaissance Venice*, vol. 1. Coins and Moneys of Account (Baltimore, MD: The Johns Hopkins University Press, 1985), 3–15, 333–40.
24 Peter Spufford, *Money and Its Use in Medieval Europe* (Cambridge: Cambridge University Press, 1988), 411–14; Luca Fantacci, 'The Dual Currency System of Renaissance Europe', *Financial History Review* 15, no. 1 (2008): 55–72.
25 Luciano Palermo, 'Sulla teoria e sulla funzione della moneta nel XIV secolo', *Mélanges de l'École française de Rome - Moyen Âge* 128, 32 (2016), https://doi.org/10.4000/mefrm.3390; Bihr, *Le premier âge du capitalisme (1415–1763)*, 2:69–72.
26 As when Marco Bembo discourages sales in Bruges due to the local currency being so devalued that achieving a profit would require excessively high pricing. ASVe, MdC, folder 29, reg. 2, letter to Andrea Magno, 15 February 1483.

27 ASVe, MdC, folder 29, reg. 2, letter to Donato Zivran in Modon, 22 November 1482.

28 Carlo M. Cipolla, *Le avventure della lira* (Milano: Edizioni de comunità, 1958); Lane and Mueller, *Money and Banking*, 1. Coins and Moneys of Account: 257–332.

29 Alan Sangster, *De Raphaeli: Venetian Double Entry Bookkeeping in 1475* (Stirling: Lomax Press, 2018), 124–28.

30 Tommaso Zerbi, *Moneta effettiva e moneta di conto nelle fonti contabili di storia economica* (Milano: C. Marzorati, 1955); Lane and Mueller, *Money and Banking*, 1. Coins and Moneys of Account: 8–9.

31 Alan M. Stahl, *Zecca: The Mint of Venice in the Middle Ages* (Baltimore, MD: The Johns Hopkins University Press in association with the American Numismatic Society, 2000), 103–9, 224–51, 359–61.

32 Lane and Mueller, *Money and Banking*, 1. Coins and Moneys of Account: 16–43; Bihr, *Le premier âge du capitalisme (1415–1763)*, 2:72–77.

33 Michael Edward Mallett, *The Military Organization of a Renaissance State: Venice, c. 1400 to 1617* (Cambridge: Cambridge University Press, 1984); William P. Caferro, 'Warfare and Economy in Renaissance Italy, 1350–1450', *The Journal of Interdisciplinary History* 39, no. 2 (2008): 167–209.

34 ASVe, MdC, folder 29, reg. 2, letter to 22 November 1482, a Francesco Giustinian in Candia

35 ASVe, MdC, folder 29, reg. 2, letter to Tommaso Zivran in Modon, 31 January 1483; Francesco Giustinian in Candia, 23 January 1483 and 9 April 1483; Girolamo Tiepolo in London, 19 March 1483. For the role of the state for capital circulation through taxation and forced loans, see Edwin S. Hunt and James M. Murray, *A History of Business in Medieval Europe, 1200–1550* (Cambridge, New York: Cambridge University Press, 1999), 204–12, 216–18.

36 '*ogni marcadantia dorme et non si trova contanti, salvo che di robe da manzar et da bever*'. ASVe, MdC, folder 29, reg. 2, letter to Francesco Giustinian in Candia, 23 January 1483.

37 ASVe, MdC, folder 29, reg. 2, letter to (addendum) Francesco Giustinian in Candia, 22 November 1482.

38 ASVe, MdC, folder 29, reg. 2, letter to Francesco Giustinian in Candia, 23 January 1483.

39 ASVe, MdC, folder 29, reg. 2, letter to Girolamo Tiepolo in London, 6 July 1482.

40 ASVe, MdC, folder 29, reg. 2, letter to (addendum) a Zuan Malipiero in Candia, 20 November 1483.

41 ASVe, MdC, folder 29, reg. 2, letter to Francesco Giustinian in Candia, 4 August 1483.

42 ASVe, MdC, folder 29, reg. 2, letter to Alvise Malipiero in Constantinople, 17 June 1483.

43 ASVe, MdC, folder 29, reg. 2, letter to Antonio Aiatta in Palermo, 7 October 1482, Andrea Magno in Palermo, June 1483.

44 ASVe, MdC, folder 29, reg. 2, letter to Francesco Giustinian in Candia, 4 August 1483; (addendum) Zuan Malipiero in Candia, 20 November 1483.

45 '*La vostra Magnificienzia è consuetta al viazo de Allesandria e non molto pratícha a lettere di chanbio perché de li non se adopera e del viazo di Ponente serva el contratio perho ne ho qualque chognizion che tanto è a mi aver da uno mio debittor una lettera de chanbio quantto una sentenzia fatta*'. ASVe, MdC, folder 29, reg. 2, letter to Francesco Marcello, consul in Damascus, 20 August 1483.

46 ASVe, MdC, folder 29, reg. 2, letter to Antonio Negro in Damascus, 9 August 1482; Vielmo Anzelieri in Damascus, 15 February 1483 and 20 August 1483. John H. Munro, 'South German Silver, European Textiles, and Venetian Trade with the Levant and Ottoman Empire, c. 1370 to c. 1720: A Non-Mercantilist Approach to the Balance of Payments Problem', in *Relazione economiche tra Europa e mondo islamico, secoli XIII - XVIII*, ed. Simonetta Cavaciocchi (Florence: Le Monnier, 2006), 905–60.

47 Frederic C. Lane, 'Recent Studies on the Economic History of Venice', *The Journal of Economic History* 23, no. 3 (1963): 312–34.
48 ASVe, MG, folder 15, reg. 2, c. 59.
49 '*perche le ochupazion mie sono grandisime, che la mortte dell quondam mio fradello voll chusi che m'é uno grandisimo dano, perche come ben sapette che chi à gran chapitalle ett fazi delle chose asai, intravegnando mortte che ttira in qua ett chi in la, io ho dellibera non lasar andar niuna delle nostre chose a malle*'. ASVe, MdC, folder 29, reg. 2, letter to Francesco Giustinian in Candia, 3 June 1483.
50 ASVe, MdC, folder 29, reg. 2, letter to Tommaso Zivran in Modon, 20 November 1483; Alberto Contarini in Bruges, 13 January 1483.
51 ASVe, MdC, folder 29, reg. 2, letter to Zuan Malipiero in Candia, November 1483.
52 Margery Kirkbribe James, *Studies in the Medieval Wine Trade*, ed. Elspeth M. Veale (Oxford: Clarendon Press, 1971); Gian Maria Varanini, 'Le strade del vino. Note sul commercio vinicolo nel tardo Medioevo (con parti-colare riferimento all'Italia settentrionale)', in *La civiltà del vino: fonti, temi e produzioni vitivinicole dal Medioevo al Novecento: atti del convegno, Monticelli Brusati - Antica Fratta, 5–6 ottobre 2001*, ed. Gabriele Archetti (Brescia: Centro culturale artistico di Franciacorta e del Sebino, 2003), 635–63; Susan Rose, *The Wine Trade in Medieval Europe 1000–1500* (London: Bloomsbury, 2011).
53 Gabriele Archetti, *Tempus vindemie: per la storia delle vigne e del vino nell'Europa medievale* (Brescia: Fondazione civiltà bresciana, 1998); Ugo Tucci, 'Il commercio del vino nell'economia cretese', in *Venezia e Creta. Atti del convegno internazionale di studi, Iraklion-Chanià, 30 Settembre-5 Ottobre 1997*, ed. Gherardo Ortalli (Venice: Istituto Veneto di Scienze, Lettere ed Arti, 1998), 183–206.
54 On the functioning of Venetian Crete: Monique O'Connell, 'Venice Outside the Lagoon: Politics and Local Administration in Fifteenth Century Venetian Crete' (Ph.D. Thesis, Evanston, IL, Northwestern University, 2002); M. O'Connell, 'Sinews of Rule: The Politics of Officeholding in Fifteenth-Century Venetian Crete', *Renaissance Studies* 15, no. 3 (2001): 256–71, https://doi.org/10.4000/1718.5818; Monique O'Connell, 'The Venetian Patriciate in the Mediterranean: Legal Identity and Lineage in Fifteenth-Century Venetian Crete', *Renaissance Quarterly* 57, no. 2 (2004): 466–93.
55 ASVe, MdC, folder 29, reg. 2, letter to Francesco Giustinian in Candia, 29 July1483.
56 For the relationship between resident merchants and intermediaries, producers, and capitalists see Pierre Gervais, 'Capitalism and (or) Age of Commerce: The Peculiarities of Market Exchange in the Early Modern Era', *Revue de La Société d'études Anglo-Américaines Des XVIIe et XVIIIe Siècles* 77 (2020): Online. https://journals.openedition.org/1718/5818
57 It is about Colonna's ship that came to Venice with better wines than Bembo's, pushing him out of the market. Bembo's nephew in Candia has been asked to look into this. ASVe, MdC, folder 29, reg. 2, letter to Zuan Malipiero, 19 November 1483.
58 ASVe, MdC, folder 29, reg. 2, letter to Francesco Giustinian in Candia, 23 January 1483.
59 ASVe, MdC, folder 29, reg. 2, letter to Francesco Giustinian in Candia, 16 July 1482, 3 June 1483; 22 November 1483; Zuan Malipiero in Candia, 19 November 1483.
60 '*I vini dolzi sono vendareschi e ano bon prexio*'. ASVe, MdC, folder 29, reg. 2, letter to Francesco Giustinian in Candia, 23 January 1483.
61 To secure a place in the market, it was essential to supply a product that met expectations, especially in terms of flavour, and sweetness in particular. The wines Bembo marketed in the Cretan and Greek markets were Malvasia and Moscatel, both sweet white wines. ASVe, MdC, folder 29, reg. 2, letter to Francesco Giustinian in Candia, 3 June 1483.
62 ASVe, MdC, folder 29, reg. 2, letter to Francesco Giustinian in Candia, 9 April 1483.

63 Cretan measurement for wines. The '*mistatto*' is a sub-measurement of the barrel, containing 48 of them. Its relation to Venetian measures is 100 *mistatti* to 6 *bigonci*. Bartholomeo Di Pasi, *Tariffa de pexi e mesure. Qui comincia la utilissima opera chiamata taripha la qual tracta de ogni sorte de pexi e misure conrispondenti per tuto il mondo* (Venice: Albertin da Lisona Vercellese, 1503), 4v.

64 '*l'è megglio renovar e pllui vollte avadagnar che una volta solla*'. ASVe, MdC, folder 29, reg. 2, letter to Francesco Giustinian in Candia, 11 July 1483.

65 ASVe, MdC, folder 29, reg. 2, letter to Francesco Giustinian in Candia, 3 June 1483.

66 Tucci, 'Il commercio del vino nell'economia cretese'.

67 Hannelore Zug Tucci, 'Un aspetto trascurato del commercio medievale del vino', in *Studi in memoria di Federigo Melis*, vol. 3 (Napoli: Giannini editore, 1978), 311–48.

68 ASVe, MdC, folder 29, reg. 2, letter to Francesco Giustinian in Candia, 9 April 1483.

69 Alain Derville, *Villes de Flandre et d'Artois: (900–1500)*, *Villes de Flandre et d'Artois: (900–1500)*, (Villeneuve d'Ascq: Presses universitaires du Septentrion, 2002), 149–56; Jan Dumolyn and Bert Lambert, 'Cities of Commerce, Cities of Constraints. International Trade, Government Institutions and the Law of Commerce in Later Medieval Bruges and the Burgundian State', *Tijdschrift Voor Sociale En Economische Geschiedenis* 11, 4 (2014): 89–102.

70 ASVe, GrM, folder 250, reg. 2, cc. 20 *dare*, 54 *avere*, 64 *dare*.

71 Riccardo Rosolino, 'Justice in the Marketplace. The Politics of Grain Supply in Early Modern Sicily', *Social History* 37, no. 2 (2012): 187–203; Amedeo Feniello, 'Un capitalismo mediterraneo. I Medici e il commercio del grano in Puglia nel tardo Quattrocento', *Archivio Storico Italiano* 172, no. 3 (641) (2014): 435–512; George Dameron, 'Feeding the Medieval Italian City-State: Grain, War, and Political Legitimacy in Tuscany, c. 1150–c. 1350', *Speculum* 92, no. 4 (2017): 976–1019; Sofia Gullino, 'Northern Grain and the Flemish Nation in Genoa: The Structural Consequences of a Famine (1585–1616)', *Business History*, Advance online publication (2021), https://doi.org/10.1080/00076791.2021.1979518; Marina Romani and Rachele Scuro, 'Grain Trade in Early Modern Mantua and Venice: The Role of Ashkenazi and Italian Jews', *Business History*, Advance online publication (2022), https://doi.org/10.1080/00076791.2022.2103543; Luca Andreoni et al., 'The Grain Trade and Minorities in the Early Modern Italian Peninsula and Beyond: An Introduction', *Business History*, Advance online publication (2023), https://doi.org/10.1080/00076791.2022.2159383.

72 ASVe, MdC, folder 29, reg. 2, letter to Alvise Malipiero in Constantinople, 22 November 1482.

73 ASVe, MdC, folder 29, reg. 2, letter to Alvise Malipiero in Constantinople, 22 November 1482 and 11 December 1482.

74 '*perché questa tera è uno caiero di gran consumamento*'. ASVe, MdC, folder 29, reg. 2, letter to Alvise Malipiero in Constantinople, 17 February 1483.

75 ASVe, MdC, folder 29, reg. 2, letter to Piero Anbrosani in Thessaloniki, 18 August 1483

76 ASVe, MdC, folder 29, reg. 2, letter to Zuan Corsino in Palermo, 23 August 1483.

77 ASVe, MdC, folder 29, reg. 2, letter to Alvise Malipiero in Constantinople, 11 December 1482, 29 April 1483 and 30 luglio 1483.

78 Jean-Claude Hocquet, *Le sel et la fortune de Venise. II. Voiliers et commerce en Mediterranée* (Villeneuve-d'Ascq: Publications de l'Université de Lille III, 1978), 200–01.

79 Munro, 'South German Silver, European Textiles, and Venetian Trade with the Levant and Ottoman Empire, c. 1370 to c. 1720: A Non-Mercantilist Approach to the Balance of Payments Problem'.

80 Mueller, 'The Role of Bank Money in Venice 1300–1500'; Reinhold C. Mueller, *Money and Banking in Medieval and Renaissance Venice, 2. The Venetian Money Market: Banks, Panics, and the Public Debt, 1200–1500* (Baltimore, MD: The Johns Hopkins University Press, 1997), 293–303; Francesco Guidi Bruscoli, 'Le tecniche bancarie', in *Rinascimento italiano e l'Europa. Commercio e cultura mercantile*, ed. Franco

Franceschi, Richard A. Goldthwaite, and Reinhold C. Mueller (Treviso: A. Colla, 2007), 543–66.

81 Raymond De Roover, *Money, Banking and Credit in Mediaeval Bruges. Italian Merchant-Bankers Lombards and Money-Changers: A Study in the Origins of Banking* (Cambridge, MA: The Mediaeval Academy of America, 1948), 12–13; Raymond De Roover, 'Cambium Ad Venetias: Contribution to the History of Foreing Exchange', in *Studi in onore di Armando Sapori*, vol. I (Milan: Istituto Editoriale Cisalpino, 1957), 629–48. For the use of the bill of exchange in relation to settlements associated with fairs, refer to: Claudio Marsilio, *Dove il denaro fa denaro: gli operatori finanziari genovesi nelle fiere di cambio del 17. secolo* (Novi Ligure: Città del silenzio, 2008), 32–38.

82 Mueller, *Money and Banking in Medieval and Renaissance Venice, 2. The Venetian Money Market: Banks, Panics, and the Public Debt, 1200–1500*, 293–303; Mueller, 'The Role of Bank Money in Venice 1300–1500'.

83 Mueller, *Money and Banking in Medieval and Renaissance Venice, 2. The Venetian Money Market: Banks, Panics, and the Public Debt, 1200–1500*, 295; De Roover, *Money, Banking and Credit in Mediaeval Bruges*, 48–56; John H. Munro, 'Il bullionismo e la cambiale in Inghilterra, 1272 – 1663: politica monetaria e pregiudizio popolare', in *L'alba della banca: le origini del sistema bancario tra medioevo ed Età moderna*, ed. Roberto Sabatino Lopez, (or. ed. Los Angeles, 1979) (Bari: Edizioni Dedalo, 1982), 193–270; David Abulafia, 'The Impact of Italian Banking in the Late Middle Ages and the Renaissance, 1300 - 1500', in *Banking, Trade and Industry: Europe and Asia from the Thirteenth o the Twentieth Century*, ed. Alice Teichova, Ginette Kurgan-van Hentenryk, and Dieter Ziegler (Cambridge: Cambridge University Press, 1997), 17–34.

84 Mueller, *Money and Banking in Medieval and Renaissance Venice, 2. The Venetian Money Market: Banks, Panics, and the Public Debt, 1200–1500*, 293–303; Sergio Tognetti, 'I mercanti-banchieri fiorentini e il ruolo di Venezia come piazza finanziaria europea nel tardo Medioevo. In margine al lavoro di R. C. Mueller', *Archivio storico italiano* 157, no. 2 (580) (1999): 351–56.

85 '*Parmi da novo di ttal suo parolle perché esendo marchadante doveria inttender quall forza à le lettere di chambio, che sono senttenzie paratte e senpre che lle sia aprezenttade all'ofizio di consolli e fuora ad ogni iudize inmediatte è mandà a segizion ell vigor del credito et tanto plui questo die eser fatto a mi che io prexentto ell pegno mio*'. ASVe, MdC, folder 29, reg. 2, letter to Vielmo Anzelieri in Damascus, 20 agosto 1483.

86 ASVe, MdC, folder 29, reg. 2, letter to Alberto Contarini in Bruges, 13 January 1483.

87 As an example, in the early 1970s, De Mai (or de May) was involved in settling some debts contracted by Luís Martins, a Portuguese merchant who died in Flanders without having time to close his affairs. During the same period, he was also implicated, along with the Portuguese merchant João de Santarém, in a legal process regarding the appropriation of some assets belonging to the deceased Flemish merchant Hector de Backere. Jacques Paviot, 'Les portugais à Bruges au XVe siècle', *Arquivos do centro cultural Calouste Gulbenkian* 38 (1999): 106, 108, 123, 125. Grateful acknowledgement to Flávio Miranda for bringing this to my attention.

88 Currency exchanges in the case of Foscari always refer to speculations made on the exchange rate of the Flemish pound (especially on the value of the *groote*) with the English pound. For details, please refer to the note Coinage, weights and measures.

89 ASVe, *Giudici di Petizion, Sentenze a giustizia*, reg. 150, cc. 20 and following.

90 Alwyn A. Ruddock, 'Alien Hosting in Southampton in the Fifteenth Century', *The Economic History Review 16*, no. 1 (1946): 30–37; Ian W. Archer, 'Responses to Alien Immigrants in London c. 1400 – 1650', in *Le migrazioni in Europa: secc. XIII-XVIII, ed. Simonetta Cavaciocchi* (Firenze: Le Monnier, 1994), 755–74; Jim L. Bolton, *The Alien Communities of London in the Fifteenth Century: The Subsidy Rolls of 1440 & 1483–4* (Stamford, CT: Richard III & Yorkist History Trust in association with PWatkins, 1998); Giorgia Nordio, 'La colonia mercantile veneziana nella Londra di metà Quattrocento:

attività commerciale e movimento anti-alien', in *Atti del congresso internazionale "Politiche del credito. Investimento, consumo e solidarietà"*, ed. Gemma Boschiero and Barbara Molina (Asti: Cassa di risparmio di Asti, 2004), 222–40.

91 '*La vostra Magnificienzia è consuetta al viazo de Allesandria e non molto praticha a lettere di chanbio perché de li non se adopera e del viazo di Ponente serva el contrario perho ne ho qualque chognizion che tanto è a mi aver da uno mio debittor una lettera de chanbio quantto una sentenzia fatta. Chotidianamente de qui se vende a termene di nave et galie ett venutti i tenpo è in facultà del credador senza sentenza con sonvenzion di consoli intrometter i beni del debitor. Io potria adur infiniti chaxi a vostra magnificienzia a propoitto di questo, ma son zerto la esegirà quantto li richiedo*'. ASVe, MdC, folder 29, reg. 2, letter to Francesco Marcello, consul in Damascus, 20 August 1483.

92 Eliahu Ashtor, 'Banking Instruments between the Muslim East and the Christian West', *The Journal of European Economic History* 1, no. 3 (1972): 553.

93 ASVe, MdC, folder 29, reg. 2, letter to Francesco Giustinian in Candia, 22 November 1482; Toma Zivran in Modon, 13 August 1483.

94 ASVe, MdC, folder 29, reg. 2, letter to Girolamo Tiepolo in London, 6 July 1482.

95 ASVe, MdC, folder 29, reg. 2, letter to Alvise Malipiero in Constantinople, 25 October 1483; Toma Zivran in Modon, 20 November 1483.

96 The information is provided in Giovanni Foscari's will and in a letter from his brother, which mentions Giovanni Foscari's trip to Genoa for the renewal of the contract (for three years). ASVe, GrM, folder 251, file 13 and folder 246, unnumbered papers, 1476.

97 A detailed analysis of exports, imports, measurements, and tariffs can be found in: Di Pasi, *Tariffa de pexi e mesure*, 145–47 (Damascus), 183 (Honain), 185 (Tunis), 185–87 (Bruges), 189–91 (England).

98 The presence of a local mediator could certainly have hindered the freedom of trade, although this potential obstruction was offset by the substantial concessions granted to the Venetian nation in Bruges. Peter Stabel, 'Venezia e i Paesi Bassi: contatti commerciali e stimoli intellettuali', in *Il Rinascimento a Venezia: e la pittura del Nord ai tempi di Bellini, Durer, Tiziano*, ed. Bernard Aikema, Beverly Louise Brown, and Giovanna Nepi Scirè (Milano: Bompiani, 1999), 31–33.

References

Abulafia, David. 'The Impact of Italian Banking in the Late Middle Ages and the Renaissance, 1300–1500'. In *Banking, Trade and Industry: Europe and Asia from the Thirteenth o the Twentieth Century*, edited by Alice Teichova, Ginette Kurgan-van Hentenryk, and Dieter Ziegler, 17–34. Cambridge: Cambridge University Press, 1997.

Adams, Julia. *The Familial State: Ruling Families and Merchant Capitalism in Early Modern Europe*. Ithaca, NY: Cornell University Press, 2005.

Andreoni, Luca, David Do Paço, Luca Mocarelli, and Giulio Ongaro. 'The Grain Trade and Minorities in the Early Modern Italian Peninsula and Beyond: An Introduction'. *Business History*, Advance online publication (2023). https://doi.org/10.1080/00076791.2022.2159383.

Archer, Ian W. 'Responses to Alien Immigrants in London c. 1400–1650'. In *Le Migrazioni in Europa: Secc. XIII-XVIII*, edited by Simonetta Cavaciocchi, 755–74. Firenze: Le Monnier, 1994.

Archetti, Gabriele. *Tempus vindemie: per la storia delle vigne e del vino nell'Europa medievale*. Brescia: Fondazione civiltà bresciana, 1998.

Ashtor, Eliahu. 'Banking Instruments between the Muslim East and the Christian West'. *The Journal of European Economic History* 1, no. 3 (1972): 553.

Bihr, Alain. *Le premier âge du capitalisme (1415–1763)*. Vol. 2. Lausanne, Paris: Éditions Page 2-Syllepse, 2019.

Blanchard, Ian. 'International Capital Markets and Their Users, 1450–1750'. In *Early Modern Capitalism. Economic and Social Change in Europe, 1400–1800*, edited by Maarten Prak, 107–24. Abingdon, Oxon, New York: Routledge, 2001.

Bolton, Jim L. *The Alien Communities of London in the Fifteenth Century: The Subsidy Rolls of 1440 & 1483–4*. Stamford, CT: Richard III & Yorkist History Trust in association with PWatkins, 1998.

Caferro, William P. 'Warfare and Economy in Renaissance Italy, 1350–1450'. *The Journal of Interdisciplinary History* 39, no. 2 (2008): 167–209.

Cipolla, Carlo M. *Le avventure della lira*. Milano: Edizioni di comunità, 1958.

Dameron, George. 'Feeding the Medieval Italian City-State: Grain, War, and Political Legitimacy in Tuscany, c. 1150–c. 1350'. *Speculum* 92, no. 4 (2017): 976–1019.

De Roover, Raymond. 'Cambium Ad Venetias: Contribution to the History of Foreing Exchange'. In *Studi in onore di Armando Sapori*, I:629–48. Milan: Istituto Editoriale Cisalpino, 1957.

De Roover, Raymond. *Money, Banking and Credit in Mediaeval Bruges. Italian Merchant-Bankers Lombards and Money-Changers: A Study in the Origins of Banking*. Cambridge, MA: The Mediaeval Academy of America, 1948.

Derville, Alain. *Villes de Flandre et d'Artois: (900–1500). Villes de Flandre et d'Artois: (900–1500)*. Villeneuve d'Ascq: Presses universitaires du Septentrion, 2002.

Di Pasi, Bartholomeo. *Tariffa de pexi e mesure. Qui comincia la utilissima opera chiamata taripha la qual tracta de ogni sorte de pexi e misure conrispondenti per tuto il mondo*. Venice: Albertin da Lisona Vercellese, 1503.

Dobb, Maurice. *Studies in the Development of Capitalism*. New York: International Publishers, 1946.

Dumolyn, Jan, and Bert Lambert. 'Cities of Commerce, Cities of Constraints. International Trade, Government Institutions and the Law of Commerce in Later Medieval Bruges and the Burgundian State'. *Tijdschrift Voor Sociale En Economische Geschiedenis* 11, 4(2014): 89–102.

Epstein, Stephan R. 'The Late Medieval Crisis as an "Integration Crisis"'. In *Early Modern Capitalism. Economic and Social Change in Europe*, edited by Maarten Prak, 25–50. London, New York: Routledge, 2001.

Fantacci, Luca. 'The Dual Currency System of Renaissance Europe'. *Financial History Review* 15, no. 1 (2008): 55–72.

Feniello, Amedeo. 'Un capitalismo mediterraneo. I Medici e il commercio del grano in Puglia nel tardo Quattrocento'. *Archivio Storico Italiano* 172, no. 3 (2014): 435–512.

Fredona, Robert, and Sophus A. Reinert. 'Italy and the Origins of Capitalism'. *Business History Review* 94, no. 1 (2020): 5–38.

Fusaro, Maria. 'The Burden of Risk: Early Modern Maritime Enterprise and Varieties of Capitalism'. *Business History Review* 94, no. 1 (April 2020): 179–200.

Gervais, Pierre. 'Capitalism and (or) Age of Commerce: The Peculiarities of Market Exchange in the Early Modern Era'. *Revue de la Société d'études Anglo-Américaines des XVIIe et XVIIIe siècles* 77 (2020): Online. https://journals.openedition.org/1718/5818.

Guidi Bruscoli, Francesco. 'Le tecniche bancarie'. In *Rinascimento italiano e l'Europa. Commercio e cultura mercantile*, edited by Franco Franceschi, Richard A. Goldthwaite, and Reinhold C. Mueller, 543–66. Treviso: A. Colla, 2007.

Gullino, Sofia. 'Northern Grain and the Flemish Nation in Genoa: The Structural Consequences of a Famine (1585–1616)'. *Business History*, Advance online publication (2021). https://doi.org/10.1080/00076791.2021.1979518.

Harris, Neal, and Gerard Delanty. 'What Is Capitalism? Toward a Working Definition'. *Social Science Information* 62, no. 3 (2023): 323–44.

Hocquet, Jean-Claude. *Le sel et la fortune de Venise. II. Voiliers et commerce en Mediterranée*. Villeneuve-d'Ascq: Publications de l'Université de Lille III, 1978.

Hunt, Edwin S., and James M. Murray. *A History of Business in Medieval Europe, 1200–1550*. Cambridge, New York: Cambridge University Press, 1999.

James, Margery Kirkbribe. *Studies in the Medieval Wine Trade*, edited by Elspeth M. Veale. Oxford: Clarendon Press, 1971.

Joseph A. Schumpeter. *The Theory of Economic Development*. Oxford: Oxford University Press, 1949.

Lane, Frederic C. *Andrea Barbarigo. Merchant of Venice*. Baltimore, MD: Johns Hopkins University Press, 1944.

Lane, Frederic C. 'Recent Studies on the Economic History of Venice'. *The Journal of Economic History* 23, no. 3 (1963): 312–34.

Lane, Frederic C., and Reinhold C. Mueller. *Money and Banking in Medieval and Renaissance Venice*. Vol. 1. Coins and Moneys of Account. Baltimore, MD: The Johns Hopkins University Press, 1985.

Mallett, Michael Edward. *The Military Organization of a Renaissance State: Venice, c. 1400 to 1617*. Cambridge: Cambridge University Press, 1984.

Marsilio, Claudio. *Dove il denaro fa denaro: gli operatori finanziari genovesi nelle fiere di cambio del 17. secolo*. Novi Ligure: Città del silenzio, 2008.

Marx, Karl. *Capital. A Critical Analysis of Capitalist Production*. Vol. 3. London: Swan Sonnenschein, Lowrey Co., 1889.

Menger, Carl. *Principles of Economics, I, General Part*. Glencoe: Free Press, 1950.

Mill, John Stuart. *Principles of Political Economy: With Some of Their Applications to Social Philosophy*. Vol. 1. London: J. W. Parker and Son, 1848.

Mueller, Reinhold C. *Money and Banking in Medieval and Renaissance Venice, 2. The Venetian Money Market: Banks, Panics, and the Public Debt, 1200–1500*. Baltimore, MD: The Johns Hopkins University Press, 1997.

Mueller, Reinhold C. 'The Role of Bank Money in Venice 1300–1500'. *Studi Veneziani, n.s.*, 3 (1979): 47–96.

Munro, John H. 'Il bullionismo e la cambiale in Inghilterra, 1272–1663: politica monetaria e pregiudizio popolare'. In *L'alba della banca: le origini del sistema bancario tra medioevo ed Età moderna*, edited by Roberto Sabatino Lopez (Or. ed. Los Angeles, 1979), 193–270. Bari: Edizioni Dedalo, 1982.

Munro, John H. 'South German Silver, European Textiles, and Venetian Trade with the Levant and Ottoman Empire, c. 1370 to c. 1720: A Non-Mercantilist Approach to the Balance of Payments Problem'. In *Relazione Economiche Tra Europa e Mondo Islamico, Seccoli XIII - XVIII*, edited by Simonetta Cavaciocchi, 905–60. Florence: Le Monnier, 2006.

Neal, Larry, and Jeffrey G. Williamson, eds. *The Cambridge History of Capitalism. Volume 1, The Rise of Capitalism: From Ancient Origins to 1848*. Cambridge: University Press, 2014.

Nordio, Giorgia. 'La colonia mercantile veneziana nella Londra di metà Quattrocento: attività commerciale e movimento anti-alien', in *Atti del congresso internazionale "Politiche del credito. investimento, consumo e solidarietà"*, edited by Gemma Boschiero and Barbara Molina, 222–40. Asti: Cassa di risparmio di Asti, 2004.

O'Connell, Monique. 'Sinews of Rule: The Politics of Officeholding in Fifteenth-Century Venetian Crete'. *Renaissance Studies* 15, no. 3 (2001): 256–71. https://doi.org/10.4000/1718.5818.

O'Connell, Monique. 'The Venetian Patriciate in the Mediterranean: Legal Identity and Lineage in Fifteenth-Century Venetian Crete'. *Renaissance Quarterly* 57, no. 2 (2004): 466–93.

C'Connell, Monique. 'Venice Outside the Lagoon: Politics and Local Administration in Fifteenth Century Venetian Crete'. Ph.D. Thesis, Northwestern University, 2002.

Pacioli, Luca. *Summa de arithmetica, geometria, proportioni et proportionalita*. Florence: Paganino de Paganini, 1523.

Pacioli, Luca. *Summa de arithmetica, geometria, proportioni et proportionalita*, edited by Jeremy Cripps. Seattle, WA: Pacioli Society, 1994.

Palermo, Luciano. 'Sulla teoria e sulla funzione della moneta nel XIV secolo'. *Mélanges de l'École française de Rome - Moyen Âge*, no. 128–2 (1 January 2016). https://doi.org/10.4000/mefrm.3390.

Paviot, Jacques. 'Les portugais à Bruges au XVe siècle'. *Arquivos do centro cultural Calouste Gulbenkian* 38 (1999): 1–122.

Piketty, Thomas. *Capital in the Twenty-First Century*. Cambridge, MA: The Belknap Press of Harvard University Press, 2014.

Romani, Marina, and Rachele Scuro. 'Grain Trade in Early Modern Mantua and Venice: The Role of Ashkenazi and Italian Jews'. *Business History*, Advance online publication (2022). https://doi.org/10.1080/00076791.2022.2103543.

Rose, Susan. *The Wine Trade in Medieval Europe 1000–1500*. London: Bloomsbury, 2011.

Rosolino, Riccardo. 'Justice in the Marketplace. The Politics of Grain Supply in Early Modern Sicily'. *Social History* 37, no. 2 (2012): 187–203.

Ruddock, Alwyn A. 'Alien Hosting in Southampton in the Fifteenth Century'. *The Economic History Review* 16, no. 1 (1946): 30–37.

Sangster, Alan. *De Raphaeli: Venetian Double Entry Bookkeeping in 1475*. Stirling: Lomax Press, 2018.

Sayous, André-Émile. 'Observations d'écrivains du XVIe siècle sur les changes et notamment sur l'influence de la disparité du pouvoir d'achat des monnaies'. *Revue économique internationale* IV (1928): 289–320.

Smith, Adam. *An Inquiry into the Nature and Causes of the Wealth of Nations*. Vol. 2. London: Strahan and Cadell, 1776.

Spufford, Peter. *Money and Its Use in Medieval Europe*. Cambridge: Cambridge University Press, 1988.

Stabel, Peter. 'Venezia e i Paesi Bassi: contatti commerciali e stimoli intellettuali'. In *Il Rinascimento a Venezia: e la pittura del Nord ai tempi di Bellini, Durer, Tiziano*, edited by Bernard Aikema, Beverly Louise Brown, and Giovanna Nepi Scirè, 30–43. Milano: Bompiani, 1999.

Stahl, Alan M. *Zecca: The Mint of Venice in the Middle Ages*. Baltimore, MD: The Johns Hopkins University Press in association with the American Numismatic Society, 2000.

Tazzara, Corey. 'Port of Trade or Commodity Market? Livorno and Cross-Cultural Trade in the Early Modern Mediterranean'. *Business History Review* 94, no. 1 (April 2020): 201–28.

Tognetti, Sergio. 'I mercanti-banchieri fiorentini e il ruolo di Venezia come piazza finanziaria europea nel tardo Medioevo. In margine al lavoro di R. C. Mueller'. *Archivio storico italiano* 157, no. 2 (580) (1999): 351–56.

Trivellato, Francesca. 'Renaissance Florence and the Origins of Capitalism: A Business History Perspective'. *Business History Review* 94, no. 1 (2020): 229–51.

Tucci, Ugo. 'Il commercio del vino nell'economia cretese'. In *Venezia e Creta. Atti del convegno internazionale di studi, Iraklion-Chanià, 30 Settembre-5 Ottobre 1997*, edited by Gherardo Ortalli, 183–206. Venice: Istituto Veneto di Scienze, Lettere ed Arti, 1998.

Varanini, Gian Maria. 'Le strade del vino. Note sul commercio vinicolo nel tardo Medioevo (con particolare riferimento all'Italia settentrionale)'. In *La civiltà del vino: fonti, temi e produzioni vitivinicole dal Medioevo al Novecento: atti del convegno, Monticelli Brusati - Antica Fratta, 5–6 ottobre 2001*, edited by Gabriele Archetti, 635–63. Brescia: Centro culturale artistico di Franciacorta e del Sebino, 2003.

Wallerstein, Immanuel Maurice. *The Modern World-System. I, Capitalist Agriculture and the Origins of the European World-Economy in the Sixteenth Century.* New York: Academic Press, 1974.

Zerbi, Tommaso. *Moneta effettiva e moneta di conto nelle fonti contabili di storia economica.* Milano: C. Marzorati, 1955.

Zug Tucci, Hannelore. 'Un aspetto trascurato del commercio medievale del vino'. In *Studi in memoria di Federigo Melis*, 3:311–48. Napoli: Giannini editore, 1978.

5 Agent and Intermediaries

The principal-agent relationship in medieval Venice was a crucial aspect of the city-state's commercial success. Remaining sedentary and resident near the Rialto port, Venetian merchants required an intermediary, an agent, to advance their interests in distant lands and to inform them as comprehensively as possible. As discussed in previous chapters, whether addressing the organization of family businesses or the creation of commodities and supply chains, the presence of agents was indispensable. It is equally clear, however, that in the preindustrial context, where physical distances were significantly greater than today and communication was slower, the limited presence of institutions and services to facilitate trade could lead to frictions between principals and agents. These relationships were susceptible to disruption due to various factors, including differences in training and commercial practices, conflicts of interest, or misinterpretations of directives originating from Venice.

One of the most important means of communication between the participants in the international trade of the Middle Ages, and essential for understanding the relations between them, is the commercial correspondence. These documents were central to facilitating the principal-agent relationship, enabling the principal (resident merchant) to communicate with agents operating in distant ports and markets. Merchant letters served as a vital means of exchanging information, allowing the principal to stay informed about market conditions, commodity prices, and business opportunities, while also acting as a mechanism of control and oversight over the agents' actions. Furthermore, these letters created an extensive communication network that spanned great distances, ensuring the effective circulation of essential information between markets. Several factors shaped the relationship between principal and agent, such as kinship, training, citizenship, and the capacity to control and legally reprimand a cheating agent. These factors will be explored in greater detail in the subsequent sections of this chapter.

Merchant Letters and Their Role

Before exploring the roles of agents and intermediaries and their relationships with the principal, it is essential to understand the primary communication tool between these parties: the commercial letter. This tool was indispensable for those

DOI: 10.4324/9781032628103-6

operating in different locations. The commercial letter addressed a principal challenge in these relationships—distance, which Fernand Braudel famously referred to as '*l'espace, ennemi numéro 1*' (distance, the first enemy).[1]

Letters have been central to numerous economic and social studies due to their rich content, which facilitates the analysis of both the timing and the routes through which information was disseminated.[2] This information transcends mere commodities or tangible goods, embodying actions that are continually redefined in the process of their transmission.[3] This aspect allows for sociological analyses of commercial letters, which can reconstruct the intricate relationships within mercantile realities—an approach especially valuable for studying intercultural trade.[4] These relationships facilitated control over these social groups by transmitting information that curtailed opportunistic behaviours, thus acting as effective tools for the enforcement of contracts. This enforcement relied on an informal reputation control system, known as '*fama*', with merchant letters serving as its most potent tool.[5] While such control was often less necessary in environments like the Republic of Venice where formal institutions acted as deterrents,[6] the minimization of risk, as illustrated in the case study of Marco Bembo, was primarily achieved through the careful selection of main agents, predominantly via familial and kinship ties.[7] In the relationship between the resident merchants and agents, business correspondence was so central that it was prominently highlighted in medieval merchant manuals. Benedetto Cotrugli, a 15th-century merchant and writer, encapsulated the significance of letters in international trade with these words:

> The merchant must be as diligent with the pen in recording his affairs in the books as he is in responding to letters; and let him never neglect to reply to any letter, however trivial it may seem, for every letter brings something, either now or in the future, and this is unfailing. Just as Pliny says that there is no book so worthless that one cannot find something of value in reading it, so there is no letter that does not yield some benefit, either directly or indirectly.[8]

Maintaining commercial correspondence constituted a significant portion of a merchant's work, demanding extensive time and effort. This critical task began with the gathering of information, followed by the composition of letters, their meticulous replication, transcription into official registers, and the dispatch of multiple copies, emphasizing its central role in the operations of mercantile companies. The exchange of information was crucial for mercantile firms of any size, and the value of this information is highlighted by the significant efforts made to disseminate it. The scope of a company's business letter repertoire could vary and often reflected the scale of its operations. Unfortunately, few complete archives of medieval commercial letters have survived in the Republic of Venice, making the case of Marco Bembo a notable exception.[9] In the letterbook of his company, 180 documents that he sent as a resident merchant are recorded, along with additional missives sent in his roles as an agent of the family firm and executor of wills, encompassing letters, *addenda*, and commissions.[10] Moreover, 211 missives are noted as dispatched within the same letterbook. While this number is exceptional for the surviving sources from 15th-century Venice, it remains relatively modest when compared to other cases. For instance, the correspondence of Marco Datini, a merchant from Prato in Tuscany, whose archive contains approximately 150,000 letters,[11] 125,000 of which are commercial in nature, received between the 1360s and the 1410s.[12] This comparison, frequently highlighted throughout this volume, illustrates the disparities in the size of these enterprises and the variation in the preservation of medieval mercantile documentation across different Italian contexts.[13]

In the letters of 15th-century Venetian merchants, such as Marco Bembo, there was a notable absence of the formality and standardization that characterized the letters of Jewish merchants and would become typical of correspondence in later centuries.[14] While crucial for the operations of mercantile companies, commercial letters at that time did not possess *de facto* legal standing.[15] Although they could be used in court to support one's case, documents that had already gained a recognized public and legal status and exhibited more standardization, such as accounting records, bills of exchange, and commissions, were generally preferred. Notably, excerpts from these letters frequently appeared both in the registers of Venetian courts—such as the *Petizion*, which is a primary source of information on mercantile litigation in 15th-century Venice—and within the commercial letters themselves.[16] Why might excerpts from accounting records and bills of exchange be included within letters? Merchants diligently updated their accounting books to encompass transactions conducted by agents in foreign markets for various reasons: legal compliance, mercantile practices such as the periodic closing of financial periods, and effective capital flow management.[17] The request for copies of accounts would intensify if there were concerns about an agent's transparency, thereby reinforcing the notion that accounting served as a binding instrument with intrinsic evidential value. In instances where discrepancies were found between the agents' accounts and the ledger, the causes were investigated, and an official request was issued to correct the accounts in the agent's ledger.[18] Accounting, therefore, functioned as a language that guaranteed transparency in business operations and enhanced trust among partners, principals, and agents.[19]

The Nature of Information in Business Correspondence

The subjects addressed in the letters were diverse, typically encompassing four key areas: familial, where updates about the household and relatives were shared; personal, which included assessments of agents and intermediaries and their operations; commercial and financial; and the broader realms of politics, diplomacy, or general economics (extending beyond the scope of an individual company's activities). While family-related information might appear less significant, it actually fulfilled a critical dual purpose. Firstly, in environments where small- and medium-sized businesses often equated 'family' with 'business', details concerning the well-being of the family unit, the health of loved ones, and household affairs were crucial. These updates reinforced the agents' sense of belonging, especially those stationed in foreign ports, and provided reassurances about the smooth—or otherwise—running of domestic matters. This aspect is illustrated in a letter from Alvise Foscari to his brother Giovanni, who was travelling between Tripoli and Damascus at the time, in which he reports the sudden death of their nephew Nicolò Cocco in Venice in the autumn of 1472. The event profoundly shocked Alvise due to its abruptness, leaving the nephew with not enough time to make a will. In his letter, Alvise expresses his deep distress and sorrow over the nephew's death, who besides being a family member was also a business partner (Nicolò had entrusted him with goods for a trip to Flanders).[20] The second reason for sharing family-related information was that it enabled the agent, often a family member, to stay informed about developments at the company's headquarters, allowing them to manage their local actions and resources more effectively. This type of communication also encompassed issues such as tax payments, the repayment of forced loans (which were quite common during wartime), or the need to secure funds for a family member's dowry.[21]

Additionally, other considerations were factored into these communications, such as the trustworthiness of individuals engaged in trade or requests to verify rumours heard about the reputation of someone in local markets.[22] This type of information, which straddles the line between personal, familial, and commercial realms, held significant importance in decisions related to the selection of agents or the continuation of partnerships with commission agents. These decisions were critical for establishing and maintaining the support networks of Venetian family businesses, since, as we will explore later in the chapter, the actions of commission agents could dictate the success or failure of a company.[23] Requests for information were typically quite direct and could include evaluations of past transactions or citizenship, thereby assessing the feasibility of pursuing a suspected cheater with the full authority of Venetian institutions within their territory. For instance, when initial issues arose with his agent in Modon, Tomado Zivran, Marco Bembo promptly instructed his nephew Zuane, who was then in Candia, to gather information on a certain Niccolò Dacho. Although Bembo had never met Dacho personally, he had heard of his reputable standing as a factor. However, Bembo wanted to confirm this information through local contacts before proceeding with any actions.[24] This inquiry was not made impulsively; it was informed by a series of troubling experiences Bembo had encountered with agents in Greece, particularly those in Thessaloniki, Manfredo de Zuane and Gerino Paxin. His frustration had even led him to express cautionary remarks about all Greek traders, advising meticulous verification of information as Greek merchants were reputed to disparage one another.[25] As a result, Bembo exercised increased caution in his subsequent interactions within the Greek region.[26] The boundary between personal and family information was not always clear, especially in Venice where personal and business realms often overlapped. Take, for example, a marriage—a matter typically classified as private. But what if the marriage involved a debtor who, by marrying, became a Venetian citizen and thereby subject to the jurisdiction of the Venetian magistrates? This scenario applied to Pallamides from Thessaloniki, a spice intermediary who initially pursued Bembo in a local court over a financial dispute. However, after his marriage and subsequent acquisition of Venetian citizenship, Pallamides consented to the mediation of Venetian authorities, who effectively resolved the issue.[27] Alternatively, consider the simpler scenario of a family member's marriage facilitating the expansion of kinship ties, thereby potentially extending the reach of the family enterprise. As illustrated in Chapter 1, such dynamics were evident in the cases of Giovanni Foscari and Alvise Michiel. Both individuals were intricately connected—commercially and politically—to the families of their respective spouses, Paola Gritti and Zilia Corner, exemplifying the strategic alliances formed through marital ties within Venetian society.

However, the paramount role of commercial letters was indubitably in the domains of commerce and finance. These letters facilitated actions in the markets, provided inquiries about pricing and business trends, issued orders, and noted shipments of goods (some of this information was so sensitive that it was encrypted). They also conveyed updates on interest rates, the values of currencies, and the movements of bills of exchange. The management of supply and commodity chains, speculative activities, and the practice of maintaining positions on bills of exchange for extended periods were all made feasible solely through this medium, which ensured a steady flow of vital information. As we will explore, the timeliness of this information greatly enhanced its value. The genesis of these communications was closely linked to the division of labour within Venetian firms, necessitating that the merchant resident in the city of origin maintain communication and oversight over his commissioned agents and employees. (Figure 5.1)[28]

These inquiries and requests are also intertwined with information regarding local and international political developments that could influence commercial activities. This includes the progress of wars, policies enacted by authorities, and dynamics within the European and Mediterranean courts. For instance, Marco Bembo's letters provide insights into the European and Mediterranean political landscapes marked by significant successions, such as those in England and the Ottoman Empire, which precipitated policy shifts or even civil wars.[29] A notable example is the ascension of Bayezid II, who succeeded Mehmed II. Following a contentious struggle for the throne, Bayezid II assumed control over the economy, extending export privileges to various merchants, a move that had substantial implications for trade dynamics. In this regard, Bembo instructed his nephew, Alvise Malipiero, to investigate the inclinations of the new court. He sought to ascertain whether the new sultan would maintain his father's lavish consumption patterns or, conversely, inaugurate a period of austerity within the court:

> I doubt that this Lord will follow in his father's footsteps, who, having seen the death of Mehmet Pasha and other lords, now does not seek to economize and reduce expenses. This will be detrimental to trade and to those involved, and there will not be the consumption that there was in the past.[30]

However, there was also the case of the succession to the throne in England: hindered by the Ferrara war, which was stifling the Venetian economy, Bembo dispatched Girolamo Tiepolo to London with jewels (three pendants, valued between 10,000 and 12,000 ducats) and included observations on the consumption habits of the English court as opposed to those of the Italian courts. Bembo described the jewels as 'ostentatious and suited for foreigners, yet of great value and exquisite beauty', appropriate for a noble of the court or, ideally, the king himself.[31] Bembo elaborated further, advising Tiepolo on the optimal strategy for approaching the king. The initial approach should involve a gift, preferably of wine catering to English tastes (malvasia or something sweet) to facilitate entry to the court. Once entry was secured, he recommended not presenting the jewels immediately, but rather their designs (which Bembo enclosed in the same letter).[32] He suggested explaining to King Edward V that, should the designs be to his liking, Bembo would be delighted to send the actual jewels to the court for his approval. From there, it would simply be a matter of negotiating the best price. Bembo adopts a pedagogical tone in his correspondence with Tiepolo, likely due to Tiepolo's lesser experience in high-end markets such as London. Bembo's mastery of these sophisticated marketing strategies likely stemmed from his experiences while travelling as an agent for the family firm in the 1470s, during which he visited major ports, often centres of royal courts. He remarks that jewellers like Domenico de Piero, who regularly engage with eminent clients including the Duke of Milan, the King of Hungary, the Holy Roman Emperor, and King Ferdinand of Naples, employ these tactics to ensure their jewels fetch their full worth, thereby securing profits for themselves and their intermediaries. Bembo further notes that while he is dispatching the jewels to London, he is aware that the Italian market offers greater profitability. He posits that sales to figures such as Pope Paul or the Duke of Milan could command higher prices than those achievable at the English court. However, current

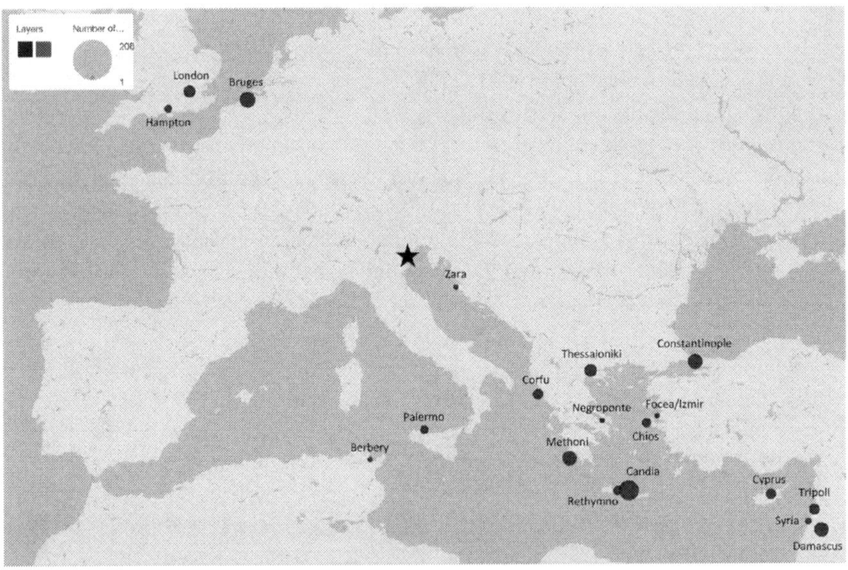

Figure 5.1 Destinations of Marco Bembo's letters from July 1482 to September 1484.

Source: ASVe, MdC, folder 29, reg. 2.

wartime conditions have precluded these avenues. Regrettably, shifts in the English court, particularly the replacement of the young Edward V by his uncle Richard III, disrupted the intended sale. As a result, the jewels were securely returned to Venice, enclosed in a letter, awaiting more auspicious circumstances in the Italian courts.[33]

The use of business letters for pedagogical purposes is particularly evident when targeting younger or novice merchants entering a market. This practice aligns with the Venetian system of educating young individuals in merchant practices, wherein the youngest and least experienced members of families were often dispatched to foreign markets to learn the trade first hand.[34] This educational approach will be further explored and elaborated upon in the subsequent paragraph.

The Circulation of Business Information

For centuries, commercial letters served as the primary method of exchanging information and were integral to the development of the capitalist system alongside accounting and financial instruments. These letters disseminated information about market trends, prices, and rates to dozens, if not hundreds, of people, thereby enabling them to exert greater control over capital flows and reducing the uncertainties associated with international commerce.[35] While some scholars argue that capitalism emerged when economic information became publicly accessible—particularly with the advent of economic newspapers, which were presumed to offer more comprehensive and timely updates,[36]—the reality is that information circulated no faster than it did via commercial letters until the Industrial Revolution brought about a significant acceleration in the speed of information dissemination.[37] Throughout the modern era, advancements in navigation and land transportation only marginally decreased travel times. As a result, the speed at which both letters and the information contained in pamphlets and periodicals moved from one market to another remained largely unchanged.[38] Calculating the transmission times of information contained within commercial letters presents several challenges. The primary issue pertains to the documentation itself: the exact date of a letter's receipt is seldom mentioned. On the rare occasions it is recorded, the details highlight that the recipient did not necessarily compose a reply immediately.[39] This lead to significant discrepancies, which can vary from a reply drafted on the day the letter is received to one composed as much as two months later.[40] The reasons for these discrepancies in response times varied and were influenced by both the urgency of the information needing transmission and the practical feasibility of dispatching the letter, whether by sea or land. Particularly in the winter months, the capability to send letters was significantly curtailed. Overland, the Alpine passes were often closed or impassable, while maritime routes faced similar disruptions. Winter typically hindered or minimized navigation, especially for longer journeys such as oceanic crossings or open-sea voyages in the Mediterranean, a phenomenon Marco Bembo described as 'the great freeze'.[41] Further complications arose from weather conditions, such as adverse winds or heavy rains, and wartime disruptions, which drastically reduced the availability of vessels and significantly compromised the

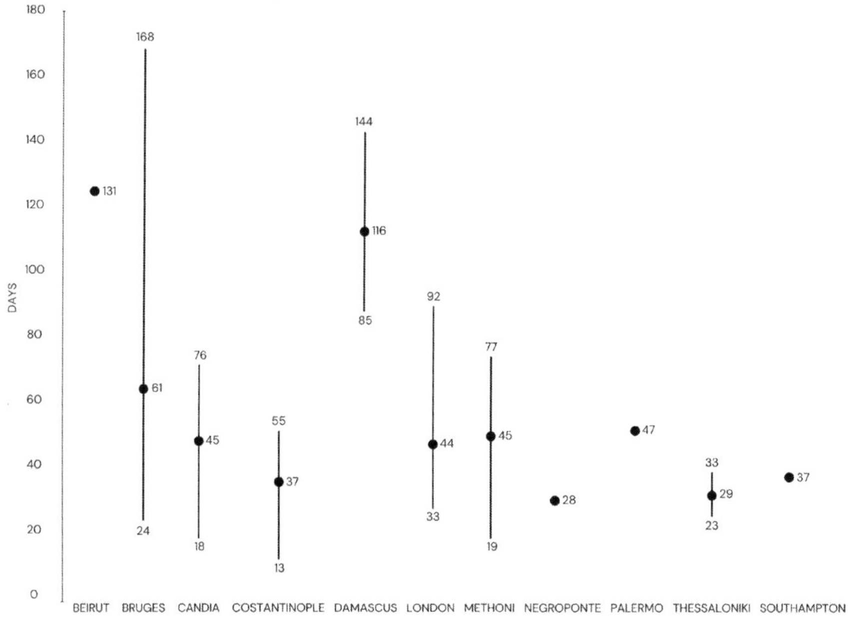

Figure 5.2 Maximum, minimum, and average transmission times of information by Marco Bembo's correspondents across Mediterranean and European ports, 1482–84.

security of communication routes within the Peninsula.[42] For instance, during the peak of winter between December 1482 and January 1483, a letter from London reached Venice in just over a month. Conversely, during the summer and autumn months, a letter from Constantinople took as long as 114 days to arrive in Venice after being sent. Subsequent letters written between August and September 1483 required 45 and 47 days, respectively, to make the same journey (Figure 5.2).[43] The factors that could either accelerate or delay the circulation of information were numerous and often unpredictable, particularly when tied to the dynamics of war, as was the case for Bembo. This element stood apart from the regular cycles of trade fairs and navigation that typically shaped Venetian economic life.[44] The pattern of Marco Bembo's letter-writing reflected the merchant's increasing challenges in securing safe transmission for his communications. At the onset of the conflict, before King Ferdinand had enacted the Adriatic blockade, Bembo's letters were strategically timed to coincide with the departures of reliably scheduled galleys and ships in March, April, July, and September. However, from September 1483 onwards, as anti-Venetian patrols intensified in the Mediterranean,[45] Bembo's letter-writing became much more frequent and consistent. This shift was a strategic adaptation to ensure that his letters were always ready to be sent whenever a trustworthy individual and a secure vessel were available. This approach aimed to avoid the significant delays or potential loss of letters due to messengers being obstructed by war or adverse weather conditions, and ships being commandeered for military service, which would otherwise require the letters to be rewritten and another passage to be found (Figure 5.3).[46]

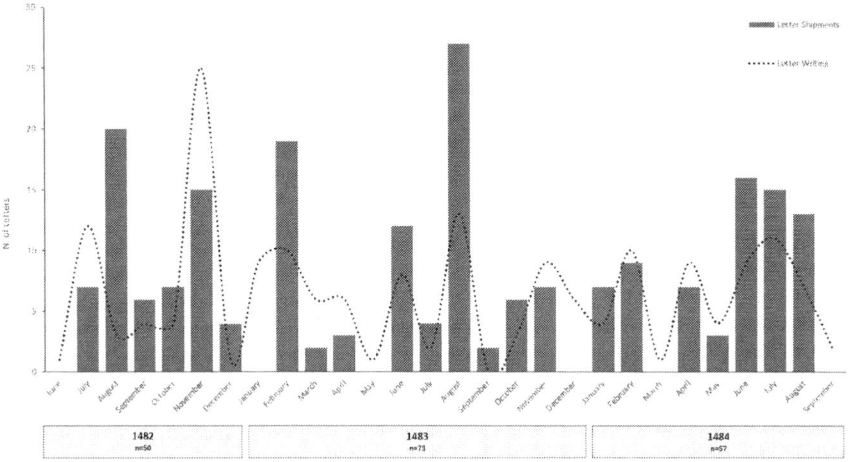

Figure 5.3 Dispatch and correspondence of commercial letters by Marco Bembo from Venice to his correspondents, 1482–84.

The challenge of securing transmitted information extended beyond commercial interests; it was also a governmental concern. The state relied exclusively on armed state galleys for sending official documentation, such as judicial records, which necessitated not only reliable passage but also a high degree of discretion.[47]

Discretion was a crucial aspect of mercantile communication, yet ensuring that information reached its intended recipient without interception was inherently challenging. One common issue was the potential for carriers to withhold the letters, accessing the information themselves. To mitigate this risk, merchants often sent multiple copies via different routes or employed encryption. For instance, in the correspondence of the Foscari brothers, after the initial courtesies and general information about pricing, they encrypted subsequent paragraphs. This practice ensured that only those with the appropriate cipher key, excluding even contemporary readers like us, could access the contents.[48] In other instances, the information contained in a letter could be shared in casual conversations, subsequently spreading through various other letters, thus disseminating the news to new actors and markets. A notable example occurred in the autumn of 1502 when news reached Venice of the Portuguese navigating around the Cape of Good Hope. This development was perceived by the Venetians as a substantial threat to their spice trade. The news, which today would be deemed a significant revelation, involved the opening of a new trade route that would enable, as it indeed did, the entrance of new players in the spice market and lead to lower prices for Eastern goods across the Continent. This information reached Italy, particularly Venice, through letters from its consuls and merchants scattered across the Mediterranean. The news then spread throughout Northern Italy from a letter originating in Venice and entrusted to Gabriello da Bergamo. Unable to keep such consequential news to himself, he revealed the letter to Nicolò Machiavelli, who on 16 November wrote from Imola to his government, informing them of these significant developments.[49] Assuming that the information contained within the letter was not disclosed during its transportation, as was the case with Machiavelli, potential leaks could still occur at the destination, facilitated by the recipients of the letters. This risk was inherently linked to the system of commissioned agents. As outlined in Chapter 1, these agents did not operate exclusively for one entity. Typically, they represented both their own *fraterna* and other Venetian operators. The agents for Marco Foscari and Alvise Michiel, for example, all operated on a commission basis. As we will explore in the following paragraph, these family firms, like most other Venetian businesses, did not employ exclusive, salaried factors. Instead, they favoured a relationship model that offered greater flexibility in the markets, though this approach also increased the risk of information leakage.[50]

How concerned were merchants with the secrecy of the information they transmitted? And which types of information were deemed most sensitive? In Marco Bembo's collection of 180 letters, references to the secrecy or confidentiality of communications and provided information are infrequent, typically related to commercial agreements designed to secure priority access to specific types of merchandise, or to concise letters that contained minimal information because they were sent via uncertain routes.[51] For instance, one case of required secrecy involved correspondence sent to Candia to a local wine producer, Querini, who owned vineyards capable of producing fine sweet wine. The aim was to monopolize his production, thereby excluding other wine traders who had previously sourced from him (such as the Contarinis) or those potentially interested in his products (like the Foscarinis). It was imperative that such a strategy remain confidential until the supply was officially secured through a formal agreement, leading Bembo to instruct his agent that 'the letter for Querini must not leave your hands'.[52]

The infrequent mentions of secrecy or discretion in handling information in Bembo's letters can be interpreted in two ways: either he assumed that the information would inevitably be shared during their transit from Venice to various destinations or he believed that entrusting the letters to secure routes would ensure their confidentiality. The true answer is neither simple nor obvious. From the perspective of the letter recipients, it seems unlikely that resident merchants would share confidential information with a commissioned agent without expecting some level of discretion. However, there was always a risk that the agent might use the information to benefit their own family business or other merchants they represented, as we will in the next paragraph. Regarding the transportation and chain of custody of these missives, it was crucial to carefully select whom to entrust with the letters to guarantee what is known as a 'safe passage' for the information.[53] A 'safe passage' could be secured either by an individual aboard the vessel who, due to their relationship with the merchant or agent, personally vouched for the security of the information; or it could be through a journey on a ship whose crew had demonstrated reliability in the past or had a strong reputation for trustworthiness. In both instances, ensuring a safe passage demanded considerable effort from both principals and agents. The trustworthiness of the ship or its crew needed to be complemented by the necessity for swift and frequent transits, a requirement that became even more challenging during wartime when the availability of ships was markedly reduced. The safeguarding of the information depended heavily on

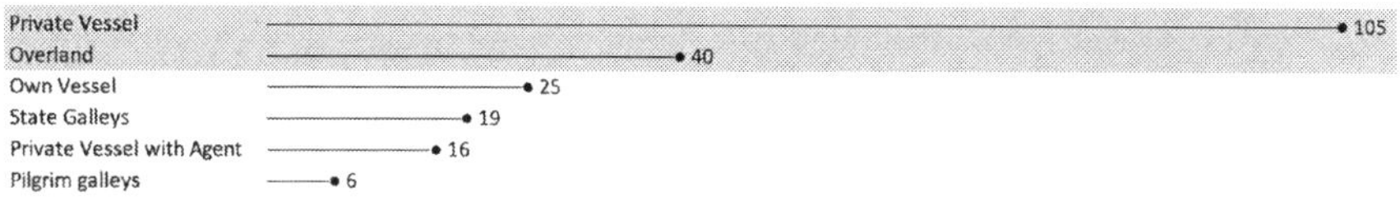

Figure 5.4 Modes of dispatch for outgoing letters by Marco Bembo as recorded in the copybook.

Source: ASVe, MdC, folder 29, reg. 2.

developing a network that provided meticulous attention to the handling of the letters and maintained strict confidentiality of their contents. Implementing a network of 'safe passages' was a complex task that necessitated detailed data compilation about individuals and ships. This network was incrementally constructed based on the ongoing exchange of information between the sender and recipient, recorded in each missive sent. Each letter catalogued the personnel and vessels involved in transporting the various copies, and the responses logged which letters were received, by whom, and when. This initial assessment of the communication and information flow was vital for refining the network, enabling modifications by removing or adding nodes based on the reliability of deliveries and the integrity of the letters. The routes Bembo established for the letters between 1482 and 1484, during the War of Ferrara, showcased a diverse array of pathways (Figure 5.4). Regarding Marco Bembo's letters, approximately 20% of the total were transported overland to destinations such as Flanders and England, with a couple of instances directed towards Greek territories like Thessaloniki and Modon, typically entrusted to couriers or foot messengers. For Mediterranean ports, the preferred method was by sea, predominantly via private ships. The selection of a specific ship for mailing a letter generally relied on personal trust in the ship's captain or on the presence of a passenger who could ensure the letters reached their intended recipient. This was often the case with prelates (such as the Monsignor Vicar of Modon returning to Crete from Venice)[54] or Bembo's own agents. When an especially trustworthy individual was departing on a ship, they were given as many letters as possible to distribute at various ports of call or close to the destination. For example, in August 1483, when his nephew Zuane Malipiero departed for Candia, he was tasked with distributing letters across the Eastern Mediterranean, from Thessaloniki to Damascus. The amount of letters and information dispatched was extensive enough to cover more than two months of business activities, with the next batch of letters to the Levantine markets sent between October and November of that year.[55] The decision to dispatch letters via private vessels or public galleys was dictated by a variety of factors. On the one hand, the security offered by galleys was enhanced because they were operated by semi-public officers and were state-chartered and armed (see Chapter 2). On the other hand, it is important to note that galleys, which were used in only 12% of cases, were significantly more expensive than private vessels, necessitating a careful balance between security, efficiency, and cost. Moreover, during periods of war, galleys were frequently requisitioned for combat, which could impose additional constraints on shipping options.[56]

The assurance of security and, most importantly, the certainty in the circulation of information played a fundamental role in overseeing the principal-agent relationship. This assurance served as a vital tool in managing intermediaries operating within foreign ports. These intermediaries, as previously highlighted, held significant importance for businesses structured around familial models, forming the backbone of their operational strategies. Ensuring the smooth flow of information among these key players was not only essential for maintaining trust and reliability but also for navigating the complexities of international trade with precision and efficacy.

Agents and Intermediaries

No business operates in isolation: regardless of the industry, every enterprise requires the support of various professionals, a notion that holds particularly true in international trade. In medieval times, family businesses relied on a diverse array of staff both at their domestic headquarters and abroad. Domestically, operations were supported by servants, scribes, and local artisans, while internationally the businesses depended heavily on commissioned agents and intermediaries. These agents not only represented the company on foreign markets but also actively promoted its commercial interests in strategic regions. As discussed in Chapter 1, the equal participation of siblings in managing the company's capital could complicate affairs, leading to misunderstandings regarding debts, credits, and the maintenance of business records.[57] In the cases of the three companies we have examined, a clear corporate hierarchy is evident, each dominated by one sibling or a parent figure. For instance, Alvise Michiel acted as the sole partner of his company, supported by his child, Silvestro, and his brothers-in-law who served as agents for the firm[58]; Giovanni Foscari was the principal partner in his *fraterna*, with his brother Agostino serving as a travelling partner and another brother, Pietro, who was the Bishop of Padua, therefore providing the needed political support to the family[59]; Marco Bembo, initially a travelling partner, ascended to the role of resident partner and the de facto manager of the family business following his brother's death, to whom he had previously reported via letters.[60] In these three family businesses, which were small to medium market operators in Venice, there was a heavy reliance on commissioned agents overseas and intermediaries both local and of Venetian origins. Within this framework, the critical nature of maintaining robust relationships with their agents and intermediaries becomes clear. Such relationships required a careful balance between maintaining control and fostering trust, often rooted in shared interests and mutual dependence.[61]

The 'agency relationship' between a resident merchant and a commissioned agent or intermediary is dynamic where one party is critically dependent on the other for the execution of business tasks. In medieval international trade, this agent—whether commissioned on a fee basis or employed as a salaried staff member—functions in foreign markets, primarily to further the interests of the principal, who is usually the resident merchant.[62] Interestingly, this relationship often exhibits a reciprocal nature; for instance, agents depend on the principals for the essential capital needed to carry out their daily operations. Theoretically, this arrangement promises mutual benefits, with each party fulfilling their designated roles diligently.[63] However, in practical terms, these relationships are fraught with complexities and seldom unfold smoothly. Challenges typically arise when principals are unable to directly monitor and control their agents' activities—imagine a Venetian patrician attempting to supervise a family member stationed abroad. This situation introduces significant hurdles in terms of remote management and enforcement.[64] While managing local partners within the merchant's own market may be comparatively straightforward, perhaps even involving the leverage of institutional forces in places like Venice, ensuring that agents operating abroad strictly adhere to their commitments poses a more daunting task. Principals expect their agents to comply with agreed terms, send back detailed and accurate reports, and maintain the highest standards of product quality.[65] Achieving these goals is central for maintaining the health and reputation of the business.[66] Despite the theoretical ideals of agency relationships, the reality often falls short. The distance, both geographical and cultural, added to the inherent challenges of communication and legal enforcement across borders, makes the consistent realization of these objectives difficult. This discrepancy between expectation and reality can lead to tensions and, in some cases, severe business disruptions. As such, every businessman must navigate these complexities with a combination of strategic planning, robust communication protocols, and, when possible, the development of trust-based relationships that transcend mere contractual obligations. These efforts are essential for bridging the gap between the theoretical benefits of international trade partnerships and the practical challenges they present.

But we know that in reality, these ideal outcomes rarely materialized as planned, making it essential for the principal to devise and implement strategies that would foster as much cooperation from the agents as possible. This task often proved challenging, necessitating a substantial investment of time and resources. Principals had to carefully balance incentives, establish clear communication channels, and occasionally intervene to resolve conflicts or misunderstandings, as we will see in this paragraph.[67] This effort was not just about maintaining smooth operations but also about building a reliable network of agents who could be trusted to act in the best interest of the business, even when direct oversight was not feasible. Such strategic planning and diligent management were crucial for mitigating risks associated with remote operations and ensuring the long-term success of international trade ventures.

Managing the Relationships with the Agents

In the cases considered here, the agents of the resident merchants were all commission-based. Why did merchants like Bembo or Michiel rely on commission agents instead of hiring exclusive agents, whom they could fully control and pay a salary? Hiring salaried agents was not unknown in Venice and was primarily the prerogative of the larger mercantile companies that wanted a permanent presence in the same location, almost like a subsidiary of the 'House'.[68] In such scenarios, it made sense to employ a salaried factor who could not only manage business activities locally but also oversee any additional agents and intermediaries, ensuring a cohesive operation.[69] For small- and medium-sized Venetian family businesses, the decision against employing salaried agents involved multiple factors. These firms often operated with more limited resources and preferred the flexibility that commission-based agents offered. Commission agents, while perhaps less controlled, could operate across a broader network without necessitating a fixed salary, reducing the firm's financial burden during fluctuating trade cycles. Furthermore, these agents were motivated by performance-based earnings, which could potentially drive greater initiative and results in diverse markets. However, this approach also came with its challenges. Relying on commission agents required robust monitoring mechanisms to ensure alignment with the company's objectives and the maintenance of quality standards. It also demanded a high degree of trust and effective communication, qualities that were crucial for maintaining long-term relationships with these agents. Thus, while the use of commission agents offered flexibility and cost efficiency, it also required careful strategic management to balance the benefits against the potential risks of reduced direct control.[70]

One of the critical factors influencing the decision between employing a commissioned agent or a salaried one was the business volume and networking needs of small companies.[71] Justifying the expense of a fixed salary for a factor, which around the early 1500s was approximately 120 ducats per year,[72] required a business volume substantial enough to generate commissions exceeding the salary costs—something that small- and medium-sized enterprises often found challenging. This situation was particularly pronounced in sectors where business transactions were not large enough in scale or frequency to sustain such overheads. For example, consider the case of Girolamo Longo, who served as an agent in Alexandria for Alvise Michiel from 1470 to 1476. During the years 1470 and 1471, Longo managed to acquire, mostly through barter, a diverse range of goods including spices (pepper and cloves), textiles, leathers, and olive oil, amounting to a total of 11,500 ducats.[73] Assuming a commission rate of 2% (and setting aside the complexity that some transactions were made with Silvestro Michiel, which would necessitate a division of commission and hence reduce individual earnings since it would not impact the overall business profitability), Longo would have earned approximately 115 ducats in commissions annually. This commission would barely cover his (estimated) annual salary, not accounting for other potential costs associated with his deployment overseas such as living expenses, travel, and incidentals, which would need to be borne by the company.[74] This tight margin makes it clear why smaller firms might hesitate to employ salaried agents unless the expected turnover and profit margins were sufficiently high to justify such an investment. Moreover, in a dynamic and often unpredictable market, relying on commission-based agents could provide firms with the flexibility to scale operations up or down according to market conditions without the financial burden of fixed salaries during lean periods. This strategy not only helped manage costs but also aligned agent incentives with company success, as agents would be motivated to maximize transactions to increase their earnings.[75]

The same financial considerations applied to Bembo, particularly with his most active agent, Francesco Giustinian, who was stationed in Candia. According to Bembo's calculations, Giustinian held between 4,000 and 5,000 ducats worth of merchandise in stock. Assuming optimistically that he managed to sell all of it within the year, the transactions would generate about 80 to 100 ducats in commissions.[76] For small businesses like Bembo's, therefore, it was financially impractical to offer a salary that exceeded the potential earnings from commissions on individual deals. This was especially true considering that commission-based selling incentivized agents who had become increasingly proficient in such transactions. This is why Marco Bembo consistently stressed in his correspondence that strong immediate performance would undoubtedly lead to an expansion of business activities in the future. He believed it was worthwhile for agents to exert considerable effort and aggressively compete on behalf of their principal, who, in return, would likely provide more substantial earnings and strengthen their business relationship over time.[77] Furthermore, Bembo understood that ensuring a substantial profit, which needed to benefit every link in the product's sales chain, was not just a strategy but a promise he made to his commission-based agents. This guarantee of profitability was crucial not only for motivating agents but also for sustaining a robust and loyal network, essential for the long-term success of his venture in the volatile Venetian trade environment. This approach helped maintain a cohesive operation where each participant's interests were aligned with the success of the enterprise, thus creating a mutually beneficial business ecosystem.[78]

Employing a salaried agent was particularly advantageous for larger companies that could benefit from having an individual who was wholly accountable to the 'House' and capable of managing other employees, such as additional agents or intermediaries. This type of employment often made the agent function like a foreign subsidiary for the Venetian House, resembling a corporate holding, a structure that was notably present among Tuscan companies.[79] In practice, this setup provided the agent specific privileges of access to Venetian companies, which in the context of family-run firms could become problematic as it implied overly close involvement with family business matters. As seen, for small- and medium-sized Venetian businesses, employing commissioned agents was more advantageous. It avoided the financial commitment of a fixed salary since these agents were compensated based on the successful completion of transactions, enhancing flexibility in foreign markets. This flexibility was crucial as it allowed companies to easily switch agents or employ multiple agents in the same market depending on business needs and market conditions. But even more importantly, this model facilitated the use of agents who were part of other Venetian firms, thereby fostering potential familial alliances and new business partnerships, expanding the company's operational scope and influence. This strategy of utilizing commissioned agents was intertwined with the familial and marital politics characteristic of Venetian *fraterne*, which often merged with their commercial and political interests.[80] As discussed in Chapter 1, these strategic familial alliances through marriage or business partnerships were common and central for expanding influence and securing business advantages. This approach was exemplified by Alvise Michiel with his commissioned agents, the Corner brothers, who assumed their roles after the untimely death of his eldest son, Silvestro. Similarly, Marco Bembo's nephews, the Malipiero brothers, became integral to the *fraterna*'s network, especially following the death of Lorenzo, further solidifying the strategic use of family and business connections to sustain and expand business operations.

Identity, Hierarchies, and Training

The network of agents and intermediaries employed by Venetian merchants was notably complex and hierarchical, comprising individuals engaged either temporarily for specific transactions or more permanently as enduring contacts for the resident merchant.[81] In the late 15th-century archival documents of Venice, the distinction between these two types of agents is somewhat blurred, as the terms agents, factor (*fattore*) and clerk (*commesso*) are frequently used interchangeably in commercial letters and accounting records. The key differentiator between these roles lies in the reasons for their selection and the specific responsibilities they held within the company. One category of agents was those appointed for a single journey or a brief period, occasionally acting merely as intermediaries for isolated transactions. Commonly, these agents were Venetian merchants or ship captains operating under the Venetian flag,[82] charged with the oversight of designated quantities of goods loaded onto ships. These goods were typically consigned to them through an '*aricordo*', a formal agreement drafted by the resident merchant, which detailed their obligations to sell these goods. The duration of their assignment could vary greatly depending on the volume of merchandise handled. For instance, Francesco Marcello was entrusted by Alvise Michiel with a shipment of fabrics (*soantone*) and alum for a voyage to Alexandria. Marcello managed this cargo for several months, demonstrating the temporary nature of such assignments, before ultimately transferring the goods to Marco Corner.[83] Consider the case of tin that Marco Bembo entrusted to Francesco Zisberto in Beirut. Zisberto was exceptionally well-versed in the local market dynamics, enjoying strong connections with both the local merchant groups and governmental institutions.[84] His proactive approach often involved visiting local courts to renegotiate prices or relocating goods to alternative markets like Damascus if he perceived better sales opportunities there.[85] Individuals like Zisberto essentially served as brokers, enabling small Venetian companies to sustain their presence in markets where they lacked permanent agents or to manage transactions that exceeded the expertise of resident merchants or available local agents.[86] These brokers, often referred to as '*sensali*', played a fundamental role in facilitating operations in specific locations or in conducting business with particular communities. Their versatility and wide-ranging skills were indispensable for navigating complex market landscapes and for bridging the gap between Venetian businesses and foreign economic spheres. They were ubiquitous across various sectors, engaging in diverse activities such as managing the German community in the *Fondaco dei Tedeschi*, mediating in currency exchanges, and more.[87] Although he did not provide exhaustive details, Alvise Michiel noted the activities of several such brokers, particularly those operating in regions such as Apulia, the Alexandria marketplace, and Syria. These brokers were specialised in the mediation of deals involving a range of commodities, including cotton, pepper, oil and brazilwood. The brokers were typically compensated with a fee ranging from one to two percent of the transaction value. They occupied a pivotal role in the economic chain due to their ability to leverage extensive networks, thereby facilitating the smooth flow of goods and services.[88] This brokerage system was not just a facilitative mechanism but a critical component of the international trade infrastructure, ensuring that small Venetian businesses could compete and thrive in international markets.

Concerning agents connected to resident merchants through familial ties, these individuals often constitute a distinct group with responsibilities that include strategic, 'big picture' functions. They are typically travelling agents who moved from one market to another, either supporting or overseeing the local commissioned agents and intermediaries, and more broadly coordinating business activities across various markets. (Refer to Tables 5.1 and 5.2 for details.) A notable example of such an agent is Andrea Corner, who was not only an agent for Alvise Michiel but also his brother-in-law, being the brother of Alvise's wife, Zilia. Andrea played a fundamental role in coordinating two of Alvise's major business endeavours during the 1470s, specifically in the oil and textiles sectors. By travelling between markets such as Alexandria, Apulia, and the Venetian mainland (Verona), Corner ensured

Table 5.1 The agents of Alvise Michiel (1470–81) in various foreign ports

Location	*Agent's name*	*Year(s)*	*Kinship relationship*
Alexandria	Girolamo Longo	1470	
	Girolamo Longo and Silvestro Michiel	1470	
	Andrea Corner	1471	Brother in law
	Francesco Marcello	1472	
	Marino Corner	1480	Brother in law
	Marco Corner	1481	Brother in law
	Francesco Michiel	1481	
Berbery	Marco Zulian	1471	
	Benedetto Bon	1474–77	
	Benedetto Soranzo	1476–77	
Flanders	Alberto Contarini	1471–74	
	Domenico Bembo	1471–77	Brother in law
	Marco Corner	1476–78	Brother in law
Damascus	Lorenzo di Priuli	1470–72	
	Nicolò Contarini	1474	Cousin
Apulia	Andrea Corner	1471–72; 1479	Brother in law
	Bonaventura di Arnafi	1475	
	Bonaventura de Magni	1475–77	
	Fantino Arimondo	1477	
Palermo	Domenico Bembo	1477	Brother in law
Syria	Giacomo Malipiero & Co.	1478	
Verona	Andrea Corner	1473–74	Brother in law

Table 5.2 The agents of Marco Bembo (1482–84) in various foreign ports

Location	*Agent's name*	*Years*	*Kinship relationship*
Berbery	Girolamo da Mosto	1484	
Flanders	Alberto Contarini	1482	
	Giacomo Van Chlei	1482–84	
Candia	Francesco Giustinian	1482–84	
	Zuane Malipiero	1483–84	Nephew
Cyprus	Zuan Confetto	1482–84	
Constantinople	Alvise Malipiero	1482–84	Nephew
	Piero Malipiero	1484	
Damascus	Antonio Negro	1482	
	Vielmo di Anzelieri	1483	
	Francesco Anzelieri	1484	
London	Girolamo Tiepolo	1482–84	
Modon	Zivran Toma	1482–84	
Negroponte	Alvise Malipiero	1484	Nephew
Palermo	Antonio Aiatta	1482	
Thessaloniki	Manfredo de Zuane	1482	
	Cristoforo Ambrosani	1483–84	
Southampton	Cristoforo Ambrosi	1482–84	
Tripoli	Martino Malipiero	1482–84	

that there were adequate supplies of oil—a critical commodity—to support the purchase of textiles and, importantly, metals for export to the Mediterranean markets, as detailed in Chapter 3. Andrea assumed this role after the death of Alvise's son, Silvestro, in 1470. Silvestro, during his active years, had managed complex transactions that spanned multiple markets. He directly interacted with Venetian communities in these markets and negotiated with local merchants, ensuring the smooth flow of goods and maintaining the firm's competitive edge in the challenging and dynamic environments of international trade.

In the Bembo family enterprise, Alvise and Zuane Malipiero, nephews of Marco Bembo, occupied roles akin to central managerial positions. Their relationship with Marco was extraordinarily close—so much so that Marco noted in his correspondence that his bond with them transcended the typical familial connections of uncle and nephews, resembling more a paternal relationship.[89] He even went so far as to declare that his legacy would one day belong to them, highlighting the depth of his trust and the integral role they played in his life and business. This profound connection formed the foundation of a trust-based managerial relationship, which persisted despite occasional disputes and the exchange of sternly worded letters to the two nephews. Marco Bembo's unwavering trust in them was such that he charged them with the oversight of other agents across the Eastern Mediterranean. He explicitly instructed those being supervised by Alvise and Zuane to treat them as though they were Marco himself, emphasizing that they should comply with their decisions without hesitation. This directive illustrates the extent of autonomy and authority he vested in them, effectively making them his proxies in the region. Marco Bembo's delegation of such significant responsibilities to Alvise and Zuane not only highlights the trust and reliance he placed in family ties but also indicates his strategic approach to maintaining control over his business operations from afar.[90] By positioning trusted family members in key oversight roles, he ensured that his business philosophy and operational directives were implemented consistently, even in his physical absence. This arrangement helped to mitigate risks associated with distance management and maintained a cohesive strategy across the diverse and geographically dispersed aspects of the Bembo trading operations.

The close relationship was also possible with agents who were not part of one's own family circle but who possessed a particular characteristic or expertise that made them crucial for business objectives. This was the case, for example, with the agent in Candia, Francesco Giustinian. Francesco was of Genoese origin and managed all of Bembo's affairs on the Island, including the trade of wine and other goods such as cheeses and, most importantly, fabrics. From the letters, Francesco appears to be an agent with scarce experience in international trade, whose success is sometimes questioned due to his reserved, elusive, and shy nature, which Bembo tries to change by using words of esteem and, above all, encouragement:

> Do as you see best, for my orders with you have always been generous, and you have been able to dispose of my things as if they were your own, and I have never contradicted what you have done. But you are colder than ice and need my words to be what warms you up.[91]

It is surprising how Bembo, who emerges from the letters as having an open, sociable, and quite frank personality, could choose someone so different and with limited experience to manage such an important market as that of Candia.[92] The answer seems to be linked to a shared interest: textiles. Both were indeed interested in drapery: Francesco was a draper who even went as far as to build workshops for Bembo in Candia[93]; Bembo himself owned a second-hand cloths shop in Venice and in 1483 even expanded his interest to the production of wool cloths, establishing a woollen workshop in Padua (with a rather ambitious production target of about 300 cloths per year). The first cloths produced in Padua were sent precisely to Candia, explaining to the agent that he leaves it to him to decide the best price, trusting his experience.[94]

A crucial factor in selecting an agent, in addition to familial connections or shared interests, was the ability to communicate effectively. This communication wasn't only limited to correspondence, which required the use of a common language like Venetian,[95] but also extended to proficiency in accounting language. These communication skills were vital for accurately conveying complex business concepts, such as double-entry bookkeeping and the complexities of managing currency and weight conversions across various markets.[96] The dissemination of these strategic skills was achieved through two primary channels: remotely, via written letters, and in person, through direct interaction with the resident merchant. The resident merchant typically exhibited greater experience than the younger agents and demonstrated a more profound comprehension of the subtleties inherent to international trade. This level of expertise was of the utmost importance for navigating the various dimensions of international trade, ensuring that all transactions were conducted with precision and integrity. Such direct mentorship and the ongoing exchange of detailed financial information helped to mitigate risks associated with international dealings, particularly the risk of fraudulent activities by agents. By fostering a culture of transparency and continuous learning, companies could maintain high standards of accountability and performance among their agents. This approach not only safeguarded the firm's assets but also reinforced the reliability and reputation of the business in the competitive world of international trade.[97] Particularly with his first nephew, Marco is proactive in providing guidance, often delivering his advice directly and unequivocally. He does not hesitate to sternly reprimand him when his actions fall short of expectations. From instructing on the precise order in which goods should be loaded onto ships to detailing the proper procedures for requesting local authorities to purchase wheat (to be imported to Venice and benefit from government incentives), Bembo is thorough in his oversight.[98] He actively dispenses orders and shares insights, emphasizing the importance of strict adherence to these protocols. Bembo's approach also extends to correcting mistakes, as seen when he severely scolds his nephew over a significant oversight—a merchant's error concerning a shipment of camlet cloths that arrived via their ship. Bembo reproached him for failing to communicate crucial details about the type and quantity of cloths involved.

> Similarly, the batch of camlets that arrived via our ship, for which I must reproach you severely for not informing me about what kind of camlots these were and their quantity. Try to manage your affairs with greater diligence than you have previously and proceed with more maturity, as you will see, I am one who does not keep quiet,

he admonishes.[99] This rigorous and sometimes harsh mentorship is indicative of Bembo's commitment to grooming his nephew for more significant responsibilities within the family business. He insists on meticulousness and a mature approach to business dealings, stressing that oversight and communication are paramount for the successful management and growth of their commercial activities. Bembo's direct and assertive style shows his belief in proactive, rather than reactive, management, which serves as a crucial learning curve for his nephew in facing the complex world of international trade.

The mistakes for which the uncle reproached his nephews seemed quite serious, especially within a context where mercantile training was initiated from a young age. In Venice, this educational process started typically around the ages of 14–15, when young men were sent to live and work within the businesses of established Venetian merchants in foreign markets. This immersive experience facilitated a deep understanding of international commerce from a young age.[100] This scenario was exemplified by Girolamo Michiel, the second son of Alvise, who in 1481 was entrusted to his uncle, Marco Corner, as he set off for Alexandria for on-site training.[101] Meanwhile, another son, Francesco, remained in Venice where he began his commercial education directly under his father's guidance, who entrusted him with 1,500 ducats in 1482 to invest in the local oil trade.[102] However, such training extended beyond Venice natives. It was also available to those born elsewhere who sought to learn the art of trade in Venice. This group included children of Venetians residing abroad, like Cristoforo Ambrosi, whose son Bembo placed under the tutelage of Paolo Tiepolo, a well-regarded mentor.[103] It also encompassed young relatives of the agents of Venetian merchants, such as the nephew of Toma Zivran, who sought lodging in Venice to learn advanced commercial techniques and network with merchants active across Europe.[104] This Venetian education provided a standardized knowledge base that not only familiarized non-native merchants with the Venetian market and trading style but also integrated them into a network that enhanced their reputations and enabled them to engage with Venetian counterparts on equal terms. The techniques mastered by Bembo exemplify the continual professional development of merchants who, through their travels and the robust networking opportunities provided by the Venetian market, acquired innovative techniques and strategies. These advancements enabled them to penetrate or establish new markets.

Acknowledging the significance of agents and intermediaries in Venetian commerce, it is vital to analyse how these relationships were cultivated and maintained over time. The initial phase involves a careful selection process, where the identities and potential influence of the agents are evaluated to ensure alignment with the merchant's business objectives and cultural practices. This step is crucial for establishing a foundation of trust and mutual understanding, which is essential for the long-term success of their partnerships. Beyond the initial selection, the ongoing management of these relationships is equally important. This includes regular assessments and adjustments based on performance, market conditions, and evolving business strategies. Additionally, the resolution of conflicts plays a critical role in sustaining these relationships. Effective conflict resolution strategies not only prevent disruptions in trade but also strengthen trust and cooperation between the merchant and the agent. By examining these aspects, we gain insights into the complex network of interactions that underpinned the success of Venetian merchants in their international trade endeavours.

Managing Agents, Communication, and Strategies

Managing agents and intermediaries involved deploying a suite of strategic approaches designed to balance control with trust, aiming to secure optimal cooperation from individuals who might operate in markets far from Venice, often outside its jurisdiction. The variability of these strategies was significant, tailored to accommodate the specific dynamics of each relationship: with family circle agents, communication could be more direct and often carried a pedagogical tone, while relationships with non-kin required a more cautious approach and a carefully calibrated communication style. In cases involving Venetian agents or those operating within Venetian territory, it was feasible to leverage the threat of institutional enforcement to correct behaviours perceived as unsuitable.[105] Conversely, this approach was less effective with agents outside Venetian jurisdiction or those who were not Venetian. Here, alternative motivational strategies were necessary, such as the potential to damage an agent's reputation to enforce compliance or rectify behaviours. The degree of trust or mistrust expressed in written communications depended on a complex interplay of factors. These included the availability of formal institutions capable of addressing and penalizing unscrupulous behaviour, the use of informal mechanisms like social or professional reputation to discourage cheating, and the calculated risk involved in extending trust to relatively unknown individuals. Each communication thus carried strategic considerations, weighing the potential benefits against the risks of conferring too much trust prematurely. This nuanced approach helped Venetian merchants deal with the complexities of international trade, ensuring they maintained influence and control over their far-reaching networks.[106]

Communicating with Agents

Commercial letters are invaluable in illustrating how resident merchants managed their relationships with agents, employing both motivation and reprimands as management tools. Marco Bembo's use of language in these correspondences was stratified into three main levels.[107] The primary level revolved around the concept of trust. In Bembo's letters, trust was portrayed as an exceedingly positive attribute, frequently employed to motivate and compliment agents. It could be expressed both formally and informally. For instance, phrases like 'I trust you as I trust myself', commonly found in these letters, not only indicated a significant degree of trust but also served as standard encouragement, urging agents to apply their logic and understanding of commerce to secure the best deals. When agents demonstrated exemplary performance, achieving noteworthy sales or acquisitions, a more assertive and less formal tone was used to express trust and appreciation. The second fundamental concept in Bembo's correspondence was honour. Honour came into play primarily during problematic situations, such as when agents failed to respond to letters, neglected to send financial statements, or when discrepancies in information aroused suspicions of misconduct. Unlike trust, which was communicated positively and used as an incentive tied directly to an agent's performance, references to honour were connected to the agent's reputation. Reputation, synonymous with one's professional esteem, was at risk in situations of misconduct. In such instances, Bembo would emphasize that a compromised reputation could threaten their standing in the business community, noting that 'a good reputation is worth more than any treasure'. This linkage highlights the critical role of reputation in international trade, where trust and honour are not merely personal attributes but essential assets that underpin the viability and integrity of commercial relationships (Table 5.3).

While various forms of communication served to convey trust, they were ultimately anchored in the last level of language, which is linked to the control that could be exercised over agents. The greater the ability to verify an agent's actions through both institutional or informal channels, and to cross-reference the information the principal received, the more direct and candid the language used in the

Table 5.3 Analysis of tone and terminology in Marco Bembo's letters

Terminology	*Negative tone*	*Positive tone*
Trust	1	68
Trust and honour	1	4
Honour	20	6
Other hints	26	69

Figure 5.5 The linguistic style and tone observed in Marco Bembo's letters (1482–84).

correspondence. This relationship between verification and communication style is illustrated in Figure 5.5. The agents who faced the sternest reprimands, evident in half of the correspondence, were the nephews, Alvise and Zuanne Malipiero. Operating in strategically important markets—Alvise in Constantinople and Zuanne in Crete—they were frequently admonished and meticulously guided by their uncle. He consistently employed a mix of incentives and penalties, a classic carrot-and-stick approach, to manage their performance and ensure alignment with the business's goals. Conversely, Marco Bembo's interactions with another agent, Francesco Giustinian, who worked in Candia alongside Zuanne, showcased a markedly different approach. In his letters to Francesco, Bembo never resorted to harsh tones or severe words, a stark contrast to his communications with his nephews, whom he occasionally described as naïve, inexperienced, and displaying 'beastly' behaviour. This divergence in communication styles underlines how Bembo adapted his approach based on the individual agent's reliability, performance, and perhaps personal relationship with him, reflecting a nuanced strategy to maintain control and foster effective working relationships across his network of agents.

The relationship with Giustinian is so important but fragile that Bembo utilizes all his adeptness in writing to express his esteem and his intentions for a long-term collaboration. This contrasts sharply with his approach to his nephews, with whom he does not feel compelled to employ such diplomatic communications. Despite the nephews occasionally causing financial losses through missed opportunities, their collaboration with Bembo is never in question. So confident is he in this familial bond that he instructs Alvise to return to Venice, leaving his brother in Constantinople to learn the trade, to groom him into a merchant, while Alvise will be given new assignments in Flanders and England. With his nephews, Marco does not feel the need to sugarcoat his words to gain compliance; the familial relationship itself ensures their loyalty and continued collaboration. This dynamic is further exemplified when he instructs the new agent in Constantinople, Piero Ambrosani, to heed whatever Alvise says as he represents Bembo's own interests, essentially making Alvise an extension of himself.[108] It is clear that for agents within the family circle, mistakes or dishonest actions do not result in market sanctions but rather in familial disapproval.[109] This family governance framework ensures that even in the face of errors, the agency relationship remains robust and unquestioned. The alignment of personal and business interests, reinforced by strong family ties, creates a protective and preferential environment for these agents, shielding them from the harsher consequences typically experienced by external agents. This familial advantage ensures continuity and loyalty, which are crucial for maintaining stable and effective business operations across distant markets.

In the case of agents like Francesco Giustinian in Candia and Toma Zivran in Modon, the enduring nature of their relationships with the resident merchant added a layer of stability. This long-term association accrued significant benefits, such as a robust stock of reputational value and tangible assets that could be leveraged in potential legal actions. The sustained duration of these relationships and the clear commitment from the resident merchant to uphold them were fundamental in fostering a stable and predictable environment. Over time, this stability becomes a mutual benefit, reinforcing trust and dependability between the merchant and the agent. It allows both parties to focus more on growth and less on oversight, leading to a more efficient operation. This enduring trust and the infrastructure of support it creates are essential for navigating the complexities of distant markets and the inherent challenges of international trade. Consider the case of Candia: after a year marked by sluggish business performance, which Bembo attributed to the timid nature of Francesco Giustinian, he decided to intervene.[110] To address this, Bembo sent his nephew, Zuanne Malipiero, to Candia. At that time, Zuanne was not working as Bembo's agent; he was actively involved in Venice, managing his own family firm's interests. However, upon his uncle's request—and with Bembo's assurance that he would oversee Zuanne's affairs in Venice in his absence—Zuanne departed for Candia in August 1483 to support the reserved Giustinian. Bembo was explicit with Giustinian from the outset: Zuanne's role was to assist in wrapping up ongoing transactions, not to replace him.[111] Giustinian was reassured that he would continue to handle his business affairs on the Island over the long term. While this arrangement appeared clear and settled, it did not take long for challenges to emerge. Within a few months, the relationship between Zuanne and Giustinian began to sour. The problems were attributed to personal disagreements and a clash in business philosophies, leading to significant tension. Giustinian felt so troubled by the situation that he wrote to Bembo, requesting a face-to-face discussion to clarify their misunderstandings, and he planned to travel to Venice for this purpose. This situation raises questions: was Giustinian inherently insecure and fearful, or was there a deeper communication failure on Bembo's part? Reviewing the outgoing correspondence directed to Candia over various months, it becomes clear that despite his reassurances, Bembo ceased direct communication with his agent Francesco Giustinian following his nephew Zuanne's arrival in Candia. While Bembo typically sent two letters per month to Francesco up until August 1483, this frequency declined sharply after Zuanne's arrival. In fact, no letters were sent to Francesco from January to June 1484, until Bembo needed to address and justify his actions to Giustinian. In his response, Bembo expressed his eagerness to spend time with him in Venice and to show him around the city. He reassured Giustinian of his continued esteem and trust in his abilities, reaffirming his intention to keep him as a commissioned agent. Bembo assured that any issues between the two in Candia would be personally resolved by him through correspondence, and his decisions would be based solely on his operational needs. Despite these reassurances, Giustinian continued to feel marginalized. From the content of unavailable letters, it appears that he urged Bembo to make a definitive decision and effectively recall Zuanne from Candia. In an effort to preserve the relationship with his agent and maintain stability in Candia, Bembo, while never openly showing favouritism in his letters, opted to reassign his nephew. He sent Zuanne to Modon to oversee Toma Zivran, another agent whose performance had been questioned based on reports from another Greek merchant who was also vying to become Bembo's agent.[112]

Effective communication with agents is crucial in sustaining successful business relationships. A lapse or error in communication from the principal's side can lead to significant misunderstandings, potentially disrupting operations and damaging trust. Such was the situation encountered with Giustinian, where miscommunications led to considerable complications. This reinforces the necessity for transparent, uniform, and intelligible discourse between merchants and their proxies to guarantee that both parties are in concordance and that misinterpretations are diminished, thereby sustaining the probity and efficacy of commercial operations across geographical distances.

Overseeing Agent Operations

Managing relationships with agents was highly complex and demanded a nuanced approach that balanced support with oversight. These relationships often involved mutual support, such as assisting agents with their affairs in Venice, and handling their mistakes or instances of bad faith. The objective was to develop effective control mechanisms, whether through providing favours to secure loyalty, issuing reprimands for unmet agreements, or managing the consequences of a failed agency relationship.

One of the most effective strategies for creating a sense of indebtedness—both economically and morally—between the principal and the agent was for the principal to take care of the agent's affairs in Venice. This practice was quite common and could encompass various actions such as advancing money, paying dowries, handling sales, or honouring bills of exchange. For instance, at the request of his brothers-in-law, the Corner brothers, who were engaged in a voyage to Alexandria, Alvise Michiel promised to manage their family's affairs. Leveraging his experience, he specifically committed to advancing 2,000 ducats for his sisters-in-law's dowries. To fulfil this promise, Alvise purchased four-fifths of a house with a warehouse in San Samuele, along the Grand Canal. This property was part of the inheritance left by their father, Antonio Corner, to his son Nicolò, who also became the trustee for his younger sisters, Lucrezia and Marisa. After receiving approval from the *Giudici dell'Esaminador*, the Venetian officials responsible for overseeing property sales, the money was used to settle the dowries with Vitale Miani and Nicolò Pisani.[113] Why did Alvise purchase only four-fifths of the house? It is likely that this transaction was not a genuine sale but rather a loan that required collateral to secure such a significant financial outlay. Nicolò retained the remaining fifth of the house and transferred its value, 300 ducats, via a bill of exchange to his new brother-in-law, Nicolò Pisani. This arrangement exemplifies the deep intertwining of familial and business interests. For Michiel, this substantial financial commitment was significant, especially in a context where he did not have sons old enough to serve as his agents and had to rely on his brothers-in-law.[114] Thus, this loan was a strategic investment in securing their loyalty and ensuring their effective cooperation in future business endeavours, highlighting the intricate balance between familial loyalty and business pragmatism. By supporting his brothers-in-law financially and managing their affairs in Venice, Alvise not only strengthened family bonds but also ensured that his agents remained indebted and loyal to him. This strategy reduced the need for constant monitoring and allowed for a more stable and trustworthy business operation. It also underlines the importance of integrating family and business to create a robust support network that could be relied upon in the competitive and often unpredictable world of international trade.[115] Moreover, this practice of intertwining family and business interests created a framework where personal relationships could be leveraged for professional gain. By ensuring his relatives' financial stability and future prospects, Alvise secured their loyalty and commitment, making them more likely to act in his best interest, which also increased the security and stability of the company. This method of fostering strong, reliable ties through personal investment was a cornerstone of Venetian mercantile success, demonstrating how deeply personal relationships were embedded in the fabric of commercial strategy.

Another method to control the actions of one's agents was by managing their finances and business operations directly. This approach was particularly challenging and could only be implemented under specific conditions, such as within a family business where the agents were very young and still gaining experience. This was the case with the Malipiero brothers, nephews of Marco Bembo. From Marco's earliest letters, it becomes clear that while Alvise, the eldest brother, was stationed in Constantinople—later joined by his younger brother Marino in 1483—the business in Venice was managed by their brother Zuane. Missing from this equation is their eldest brother, Lorenzo, who appears to have passed away by this time and Piero, who only in the last letter is mentioned as Alvise and Zuane's brother. At one point, Bembo needed to bolster support for Francesco Giustinian in Candia.

As we have seen earlier, he requested Zuane, the only nephew still in Venice, to take on this role. Marco was very direct in his letters about Zuane's assignment: Candia would not be a long-term post for him, as the Malipiero family's business primarily involved trade with the West. Marco had plans to send Alvise to the Western markets upon his return from Constantinople.[116] Therefore, Zuane's journey to Candia was at his uncle's explicit request, with the understanding that Marco would oversee the family's affairs in Venice during Zuane's absence. Bembo's detailed instructions and strategic planning demonstrate his meticulous approach to managing his business and family interests. By taking personal responsibility for the nephews' business dealings in Venice, Marco aimed to maintain seamless operations and protect the family's economic interests while Zuane, Alvise and Marino were abroad. This arrangement also highlights the strategic depth in Marco's approach. By ensuring that family members were placed in key roles, he not only maintained control over distant operations but also cultivated their skills and loyalty. Zuane's temporary assignment in Candia was a strategic move to support Giustinian while simultaneously preparing Zuane for future responsibilities in the family business. Marco's willingness to manage his nephews' affairs in Venice reflects his dedication to their professional development and the long-term success of their commercial endeavours.[117]

The uncle's influence on the actions of the Malipiero brothers is significant. While he assists his nephews with paying tithes and recovering debts, he also demands transparency from them.[118] In a particularly notable letter to his nephew who had left for Candia at his request, Bembo addresses several concerns. He accuses his nephew of being arrogant and thinking he knows more than those with more experience, from whom he refuses to learn. Bembo contrasts this with his own approach, emphasizing that he continues to learn despite his age. Bembo admonishes his nephew not to use his business and network for personal gain. Regarding a deal made with the scribe employed on Bembo's ship, he writes, 'If you must use my trading for your profit, tell me, because with my permission, you will have the freedom to do so. But taking it upon yourself is not a gesture I like, because it is not fair'.[119] With these words, Bembo sets a clear boundary for his nephew's actions and addresses a potential conflict of interest: the information and resources that Bembo possesses can only be used by his agents to the extent that he permits. Anything beyond that is not done 'in fairness', and Bembo warns his nephew that if he continues with this attitude, he will have no choice but to remove him from his business dealings.

The relationship with agents outside the family circle required a different approach, involving varied tones and language, and support provided through commercial actions, such as managing their affairs or settling their debts. For instance, Marco Bembo assisted Francesco Giustinian by settling his debts. Bembo did this not only by directly providing textiles to the creditor but also by offering to take goods from Giustinian—in this case, cheese—which he would then resell to settle the debt in cash when the creditor refused to accept more goods as payment. Moreover, Bembo actively sought new clients for Giustinian. On Bembo's recommendation, two Venetian brothers, the Viaro, decided to utilize Giustinian's expertise.

This situation highlights the dual significance of the agency relationship for both the agent and the resident merchant. The agent's good performance and loyalty to the resident merchant enhanced the agent's integration into the resident's network, making them an increasingly central figure while also attracting new clients.[120]

The close relationship between control and trust is evident not only in the tone of the letters but also in the cross-referencing of correspondence between various individuals in the same location. This often involves requesting support from other Venetian merchants in foreign markets, not so much for daily activities, but for handling shipments of goods that the agent might struggle to place through their own networks. This assistance is typically sought from more experienced merchants who are well-acquainted with both the local and international markets. However, this support is not fully disclosed to the agent. Instead, the agent is simply informed that they can seek advice from this trusted person.[121] In these interactions, we see the delicate balance between showing confidence in the agent and protecting the principal's interests. The principal employs a trusted merchant behind the scenes to favour their business while maintaining the agent's perception of autonomy. This approach ensures that the agent feels valued and supported while the principal's interests are safeguarded by an experienced merchant who can intervene if necessary.[122] Additionally, the selection of these more experienced merchants for support raises important considerations. Why were these merchants not asked to serve as agents themselves? In Marco Bembo's case, the merchants he contacts for support often belong to the local Venetian elite and hold official positions. For example, in Candia, Marino Dolfin, one of the two chamberlains of the Island, was a key contact. Bembo had offered his services to Dolfin in Venice, creating a reciprocal arrangement—*do ut des*—that primarily benefited Bembo. This strategy reveals a multilayered approach to managing business relationships: by securing the assistance of influential and experienced merchants, Bembo not only strengthened his agents' capabilities but also reinforced his own network of support. These elite merchants, often involved in official capacities, provided a reliable back-up for his agents, ensuring that even if an agent struggled, there was a safety net in place to protect the business's interests.[123]

This type of request fits into the context of a commercial system that did not expect agents or intermediaries to be experts in all phases of trade or responsible for the entire commercial cycle. Instead, they were expected to operate to the best of their abilities within their specific roles and to know when to leverage the expertise of more skilled artisans and merchants in particular fields. The separation of professional competencies and responsibilities in different phases of the commercial process is evident in some of Marco Bembo's letters to his correspondents. For example, Bembo instructed ship patron Andrea Malluxatto to depart from Venice to Constantinople with his goods, making stops in Modon and Corfu along the way. Even though Corfu was not exactly on the route, Malluxatto was to coordinate with local agents and intermediaries, leaving the requested goods and picking up whatever might be useful in Constantinople. Upon arrival in Constantinople, he was to leave the ship's cargo with Alvise, Bembo's nephew, and then personally travel, accompanied by Alvise's young servant who spoke Turkish and Greek, through the countryside to purchase wheat, which he would then transport back to Venice. To motivate Andrea and clarify individual responsibilities, Bembo explained that the success of the venture depended on everyone performing their best within their area of expertise:

> You must be diligent in ensuring the well-being and benefit of the ship because by doing so, you also secure your own profit. The ship's benefit consists of three things: one, quick navigation; two, saving costs—these are your responsibilities. The third is to ensure a good outcome for the cargo, which is my responsibility. And since you are the patron of the ship, I want you to have every liberty to do what you consider profitable and beneficial for the ship because being on site, you will be able to decide better than I, who am far away.

With these words, Bembo emphasized the importance of each person's role within the commercial process and the necessity of utilizing local expertise to achieve the best possible outcomes. By clearly delineating responsibilities and empowering his agents and intermediaries, Bembo ensured that each phase of the commercial operation was handled by those best equipped to do so, thereby optimizing the overall efficiency and success of his business ventures.[124]

The trust that Bembo often expressed for his agents and intermediaries was driven by an important factor: distance. This raises the question of how much of this trust was genuine and spontaneous, as it often was with family agents who could be easily controlled, and how much was born out of necessity—relying on the goodwill of a stranger to advance his interests. As we have seen, one effective incentive for persuading someone to cooperate and accommodate his needs was for the resident merchant to offer reciprocal services to his correspondents, thus exercising at least some degree of power and control over the relationship.[125] When these measures proved insufficient, Bembo resorted to threats, either formally by threatening legal action or informally by threatening to ruin their reputation within the Venetian community. This dual approach—combining kind words, which Bembo referred to as 'sweet words' or 'caresses', with more coercive strategies—allowed medieval merchants to bind and control their partners and agents effectively.[126] These agents and partners had a vested interest in demonstrating their cooperation with a member of one of the most powerful commercial communities of the time. By leveraging both positive reinforcement and potential sanctions, merchants like Bembo managed to maintain a delicate balance of trust and control, ensuring that their business interests were safeguarded even from afar. This strategy highlights the complexities of managing long-distance trade relationships in the medieval period and underscores the importance of trust, reciprocity, and strategic oversight in sustaining these vital connections.

The ability to move the right pieces, speak appropriately with partners, and respect the orders and timelines set by the resident merchant falls under what is known as the 'practice' that the resident merchant expects their agents to have or develop. Many conflicts with agents arise precisely due to the lack of this practice.[127]

Conflicts with agents or partners were something the principal sought to minimize and resolve amicably through lengthy negotiations whenever possible. In two years of correspondence with his agents, Bembo mentions only three conflicts that ended up in court. The first involved a dispute over the quality of wine exported from Candia to Flanders in 1479, blaming the producer for not properly overseeing the transfer process.[128] The second case concerned a debt owed by a Greek merchant, resolved extrajudicially.[129] The third case involved two factors: Manfredo de Zuane, a merchant, and Gerin de Paxin, his agent, from Thessaloniki.[130]

Bembo's relationship with Manfredo and Gerin was relatively cordial. In a letter sent in July 1482, Bembo expressed complaints about the quality of certain goods they had sent and their slow pace in selling his products, subtly threatening, 'so that I do not have to regret dealing with you'. However, in a letter to Andrea Alberga in Candia, his former servant, Bembo revealed his true feelings about the two: Manfredo and Gerin were slow and, more importantly, delayed sending the proceeds of their sales to Venice. Therefore, Bembo asked Alberga to go to Thessaloniki before returning to Venice and, under the pretext of collecting timber for the wine barrels from Candia stored in their warehouse, to withdraw all Bembo's business that the two were still handling. The issue was related to Bembo's capital, which the two had kept tied up in their warehouse for two years, amounting to about 1,000 ducats, and which they were not circulating.[131] In the letter entrusted to Andrea Alberga to be delivered by hand to Manfredo, Bembo expressed surprise that an established merchant like Manfredo would entrust his affairs to a rascal, a fool as Bembo called him, like Gerin, emphasizing, 'Merchants do not want to entrust their capital to others for three years just to see the returns'.[132]

The letter was entrusted to Andrea Alberga because Manfredo had not communicated with Bembo for a year, which was unacceptable behaviour. In subsequent dispatches, Bembo made sure to send copies of the letter to his nephew Alvise Malipiero in Constantinople, instructing him to make multiple copies and send them to Thessaloniki through various routes. Bembo also provided Alvise with a detailed list of the goods in Manfredo's possession: broadcloths, wet and trimmed, five pieces; Brescia cloths, five pieces; narrowcloths, 15 pieces; caviar, 11 kegs; fish, six barrels; and soaps, 51 cases.[133] He instructed Alvise to give this list to his young servant before sending him to Thessaloniki. Bembo wrote, 'so that if Manfredo outright refuses to do his duty, we can rightfully claim what is mine. You may entrust this matter to some of our reputable merchants there'. Despite these efforts, Manfredo continued to ignore Bembo, who only received updates about the situation through Andrea Alberga. Alberga promised to fulfil Bembo's expectations, but the lack of direct communication from Manfredo remained a significant issue. Bembo reiterated his threats: if Manfredo did not comply voluntarily, he would escalate the matter to the *Provveditori*, the Venetian magistrates.

The situation reached a critical point in the spring of 1483. Frustrated by the ongoing delays and lack of cooperation, Bembo decided to pursue legal action. He instructed his nephew Alvise, who was stationed in Constantinople, to send Piero Ambrosani, armed with a letter from the Bailo and the Signoria, to Thessaloniki. Ambrosani was tasked with collecting the 1,000 ducats owed by Manfredo and

Gerin.[134] By involving the Bailo and the Signoria, Bembo leveraged the authority of the Venetian government to enforce his claims, demonstrating the importance of official channels in resolving commercial disputes that could not be settled informally.[135] This situation also highlights the intricate balance of trust and control that merchants like Bembo had to maintain with their agents, especially those operating far from home. Ensuring that agents understood their responsibilities and the consequences of failing to meet them was crucial for the smooth operation of his extensive trade network. Naturally, to secure the cooperation of the authorities, Bembo had to substantiate his claim. He did this by using several letters from the two men, in which they had promised lucrative deals in wool and cotton but had ultimately failed to deliver. At this stage, he could only send copies of these documents because he did not have a secure means to send the originals.

How did this international effort to reprimand the two men who held 1,000 ducats of Bembo's capital end? Through Piero Ambrosani, Bembo managed to have the two imprisoned and was eventually able to send the original documents to continue the legal action. A few months later, in April 1484, the matter was handed over to Piero Malipiero, the future agent in Constantinople. Malipiero seems to be more seasoned than his brother, as he first obtained a collection order from the Ottoman court, known as the *Porta*, which was countersigned by the Bailo. He then forwarded this order to Anzolo da Canal, a Venetian merchant residing in Thessaloniki. Canal, in turn, hired a Jewish collector, Luquda Zidimari, who retained 10% of the recovered debt as his fee.[136] Despite never setting foot in the Ottoman Empire again, Bembo successfully leveraged the right contacts between Constantinople and Thessaloniki. These contacts were Venetian merchants well-integrated into the local milieu and adept at dealing with local institutions. This network allowed Bembo to secure payment of his debt. One of these contacts in Constantinople proved so trustworthy that he was later hired as an agent when Alvise was expected to return to Venice in the autumn of 1484 to take over the family business. However, Alvise never got to see his uncle again, as Marco Bembo died in September 1484. The responsibility of communicating Marco's inheritance arrangements to the nephews fell to Marco's widow, the wife of Lorenzo Bembo, Andriana Vendramin.

Renaissance merchants like Bembo had to handle a complex web of trust, legal manoeuvring, and strategic alliances. The success of Bembo's efforts was not just a matter of financial acumen but also of knowing how to utilize a network of trusted individuals who could act on his behalf across different jurisdictions. It highlights the importance of having reliable intermediaries and the intricate balance between trust and enforcement in the commercial relationships of the time. Bembo's ability to recover his capital, even from afar, stresses the effectiveness of his strategies and the strength of his connections within the Venetian commercial network. This network enabled him to exert influence and secure his interests across vast distances and different legal jurisdictions, enhancing his control over his trade and business operations, even when he could not personally oversee them.

Furthermore, this episode demonstrates the critical role of trust and reputation in international trade during the medieval period. Merchants like Bembo had to carefully balance trust and control, ensuring that their agents were reliable while also having mechanisms in place to enforce compliance. The use of local intermediaries, familiar with the legal and commercial practices of their regions, was vital for navigating these challenges effectively. In the broader context, Bembo's experience marks the importance of strategic alliances and legal recourse in maintaining commercial integrity. His ability to mobilize support from influential figures within the Venetian and Ottoman domains reflects his strategic foresight and the strength of his professional relationships. This not only ensured the recovery of his assets but also reinforced his standing within the Venetian commercial community, illustrating the interconnected nature of trade, law, and personal networks in the medieval economy.

Notes

1 Fernand Braudel, *The Mediterranean and the Mediterranean World in the Age of Philip II*, vol. 1 (New York: Harper & Row, 1972), 355.

2 Pierre Sardella, *Nouvelles et spéculations a Venise au debuts du 16. siècle*, Cahiers des annales (Paris: Armand Colin, 1948); Federigo Melis, 'Intensità e regolarita nella diffusione dell'informazione economica generale nel Mediterraneo e in Occidente alla fine del medioevo', in *Histoire économique du monde mediterraneen, 1450–1650, Mélanges en l'honneur de Fernand Braudel* (Toulouse: Privat Éditeur, 1973), 389–424.

3 Pierre Jeannin, 'La diffusion de l'information', in *Fiere e mercati nella integrazione delle economie europee secc. XIII-XVIII, Atti della trentaduesima Settimana di studi e altri convegni dell'Istituto Internazionale di Storia Economica F. Datini (8–12 Maggio 2000)*, ed. Simonetta Cavaciocchi (Florence: Le Monnier, Istituto internazionale di storia economica 'F. Datini', 2001), 231–62; Wolfgang Kaiser and Gilbert Buti, 'Moyens, supports et usages de l'information marchande à l'époque moderne', *Rives nord-méditerranéennes* 27 (2007): 7–11; Johann Petitjean, 'Processus et procédures de diffusion de l'information sur la guerre turque en Italie (fin XVIe -début XVIIe siècle)', in *Les formes de l'échange: Communiquer, diffuser, informer, de l'Antiquité au XVIIIe siècle*, ed. François Brizay, Histoire (Rennes: Presses universitaires de Rennes, 2012), 319–34.

4 S. D. Goitein, *A Mediterranean Society: The Jewish Communities of the Arab World as Portrayed in the Documents of the Cairo Geniza*, vol. 1: Economic Foundations (Berkeley: University of California, 1967); Philip D. Curtin, *Cross-Cultural Trade in World History* (Cambridge : Cambridge University Press, 1984); Francesca Trivellato, *The Familiarity of Strangers: The Sephardic Diaspora, Livorno, and Cross-Cultural Trade in the Early Modern Period* (New Haven, CT, London: Yale University Press, 2009).

5 Avner Greif, 'Reputation and Coalitions in Medieval Trade: Evidence on the Maghribi Traders', *The Journal of Economic History* 49, no. 4 (1989): 857–82; Avner Greif, 'Contract Enforceability and Economic Institutions in Early Trade: The Maghribi Traders' Coalition', *The American Economic Review* 83, no. 3 (1993): 525–48; Avner Greif, 'Contracting, Enforcement, and Efficiency: Economics beyond the Law', in *Annual World Bank Conference on Development Economics*, ed. M. Bruno and B. Pleskovic (Washington, DC: The World Bank, 1997), 239–65; Yadira González de Lara, 'The Secret of Venetian Success: A Public-Order, Reputation-Based Institution', *European Review of Economic History* 12 (2008): 247–85.

6 Douglass C. North, 'Institutions', *Journal of Economic Perspectives* 5, no. 1 (1991): 97–112; Greif, 'Contract Enforceability and Economic Institutions in Early Trade';

Isabella Cecchini and Luciano Pezzolo, 'Merchants and Institutions in Early-Modern Venice', *The Journal of European Economic History* 41, no. 2 (2012): 89–114.

7 For the importance of kin, see: Luciano Pezzolo, 'The via Italiana to Capitalism', in *The Cambridge History of Capitalism, I, The Rise of Capitalism: From Ancient Origins to 1848*, ed. Larry Neal and Jeffrey G. Williamson (Cambridge: Cambridge University Press, 2014), 266–313.

8 '*Et tanto vuol essere diligente alla penna, tanto in notare alli libri le faconde sue, quanto nel rispondere alle lettere ; et mai lassare alcuna per trista che la sia, che non li facci la risposta, perche ogni lettera li porta qualche cosa, ò di presente, ò di futuro, et questo non falla; che cosi come dice Plinio, che non è si vil libro, nel quale leggendo non truovi qualche cosa di buono. Cosi non è nessuna lettera, la quale non habbia qualche frutto, ò diretto, ò indiretto*'. Benedetto Cotrugli, *Della mercatura et del mercante perfetto. Libri quattro di M. Benedetto Cotrugli raugeo* (Venice: All'Elefanta, 1573), 74.

9 Bernard Doumerc, 'Par Dieu écrivez plus souvent! La lettre d'affaires à Venise à la fin du Moyen Age', *Publications de l'École Française de Rome* 190, no. 1 (1994): 99–109; Georg Christ, 'A Newsletter in 1419? Antonio Morosini's Chronicle in the Light of Commercial Correspondence between Venice and Alexandria', *Mediterranean Historical Review* 20, no. 1 (1 June 2005): 35–66; Franz-Julius Morche, 'The Letters of Others: Marino Morosini and His Curious Newsshest on the Battle of Maclodio', in *Cultures of Empire: Rethinking Venetian Rule, 1400–1700: Essays in Honour of Benjamin Arbel*, ed. Georg Christ and Franz-Julius Morche, The Medieval Mediterranean (Leiden, Boston, MA: Brill, 2020), 90–122.

10 ASVe, MdC, folder 29, reg. 2. These letters are also listed in Freddy Thiriet, 'Les lettres commerciales des Bembo et le commerce vénitien dans l'Empire Ottoman à la fin du XVe siècle', in *Studi in onore di Armando Sapori*, vol. II (Milan: Istituto Editoriale Cisalpino, 1957), 911–33; Alessio Sopracasa, 'Passage au Levant. Le « voyage » de Candie-Constantinople de la compagnia Bembo dans la seconde moitié du xve siècle: organisation et séjour', *Cahiers d'études italiennes* 25 (2017), https://doi.org/10.4000/cei.3499.

11 Giampiero Nigro, *Francesco di Marco Datini: l'uomo, il mercante*, (Firenze, Prato: Firenze University Press; Fondazione Istituto internazionale di storia economica "F. Datini", 2010); Angela Orlandi, 'Networks and Commercial Penetration Models in the Late Medieval Mediterranean: Revisiting the Datini', in *Commercial Networks and European Cities, 1400–1800*, ed. Andrea Caracausi and Christof Jeggle (London: Pickering & Chatto, 2014), 81–106.

12 Information on the composition of the archive, one of the richest for medieval and modern Italy, here: http://datini.archiviodistato.prato.it/l-archivio/descrizione/.

13 Francesca Trivellato, 'Renaissance Florence and the Origins of Capitalism: A Business History Perspective', *Business History Review* 94, no. 1 (2020): 229–51.

14 While, for example, Hebrew and Islamic letters tended to follow a certain modularity. See Kaiser and Buti, 'Moyens, supports et usages de l'information marchande à l'époque moderne'; Jessica L. Goldberg, 'Mercantile Letters', *Jewish History* 32, no. 2/4 (2019): 397–410.

15 Maura Fortunati, *Scrittura e prova: i libri di commercio nel diritto medievale e moderno* (Roma: Fondazione Sergio Mochi Onory per la storia del diritto italiano, 1996), 82–86, 94–105.

16 Among the many cases in Marco Bembo's letters, some stand out by reporting details not only about transactions for alum but also about the litigation that occurred at the local qadi court, in addition to a reference to a letter of commission by Tommaso Spinola, of which Bembo possessed a copy. ASVe, MdC, folder 29, reg. 2, letter to Antonio Negro in Damascus, June 1482.

17 Marco Bembo himself explains these reasons to his agents on several occasions. ASVe, MdC, folder 29, reg. 2, letter to Zuan Confetto in Cyprus, 22 November 1482; Andrea Alberga in Candia, 22 November 1482; Manfredo de Zuane in Thessaloniki,

22 November 1482; Giacomo Van Chlei in Bruges, 16 November 1482; Alvise Malipiero in Constantinople (addendum), 12 November 1482, 11 December 1482, 17 February 1483. The request is particularly repeated toward the agent in Modon, Toma Zivran, that Bembo believes might be cheating him. ASVe, MdC, folder 29, reg. 2, letters to Toma Zivran in Modon, 31 January 1483, February 1483, 19 March 1483, 19 November 1483, 3 April 1484 and 4 Semptember 1484.

18 ASVe, MdC, folder 29, reg. 2, letter to Alberto Contarini in Bruges, 23 April 1483; Girolamo Tiepolo in London, 14 June 1483; Piero Anbrosani in Thessaloniki, 18 August 1483; Zuane Malipiero, 18 April 1484; Francesco Giustinian in Candia, 10 June 1484.

19 Gaëlle Lapeyrie, 'L'écriture comptable comme langage spécifique des marchands (France Méridionale, début XVIIe siècle)', in *Langues et langages du commerce en Méditerranée et en Europe à l'époque moderne*, ed. Gilbert Buti, Michèle Janin-Thivos, and Olivier Raveux (Aix-en-Provence: Presses Universitaires de Provence, 2013), 207–26.

20 ASVe, GrM, folder 189, file 1, letter to Giovanni Foscari in Damascus from Alvise Foscari in Venice, 19 December 1472.

21 ASVe, MdC, folder 29, reg. 2, letter to Zuanne Malipiero in Candia, 15 December 1483; ASVe, MG, folder 15, reg. 2, cc. 50 *dare*, 151 *dare*.

22 For the role of gossips and reputation, see Ana Sofia Ribeiro, *Early Modern Trading Networks in Europe: Cooperation and the Case of Simon Ruiz*, (Abingdon, Oxon, New York: Routledge, Taylor & Francis Group, 2016), 164–80.

23 Thomas Max Safley, *Family Firms and Merchant Capitalism in Early Modern Europe: The Business, Bankruptcy and Resilience of the Hoechstetters of Augsburg* (Abingdon, Oxon, New York: Routledge, 2019), 101–29.

24 ASVe, MdC, folder 29, reg. 2, letter to Zuane Malipiero in Candia, August 1484.

25 ASVe, MdC, folder 29, reg. 2, letter to Alvise Malipiero in Thessaloniki, 10 June 1484.

26 The letters were sent to different agents, as the task to recuperate the merchandises, bartered by the two as these were their own, fell on different people across the months. Bembo never saw the capital back, as he died before the ordeal was over. ASVe, MdC, folder 29, reg. 2, letter to Francesco Giustinian in Candia, 5 September 1482; Andrea Alberga in Candia, 22 November 1482; Manfredo de Zuane in Thessaloniki, 22 November 1482; Manfredo de Zuane and Gerino de Paxin, 15 February 1483; Alvise Malipiero in Costantinople and Negroponte, 29 April 1483, 17 June 1483, 25 October 1483 and 24 July 1484; Piero Ambrosani in Thessaloniki, 4 and 18 August 1483.

27 ASVe, MdC, folder 29, reg. 2, letter to Francesco Giustinian in Candia, 22 November 1482.

28 Francesca Trivellato, 'Merchants' Letters across Geographical and Social Boundaries', in *Correspondence and Cultural Exchange in Europe, 1400–1700*, ed. Francisco Bethencourt and Florike Egmond (Cambridge: Cambridge University Press, 2007), 80–103.

29 ASVe, MdC, folder 29, reg. 2, letters to Giacomo Van Chlei, a Bruges, 23 April 1483 (on the peace with the King of France); Girolamo Tiepolo in London, 23 Aprile 1483 and 14 June 1483 (for the succession to the English trone); Alvise Malipiero in Constantinople, 17 February 1483 (on the civil war for the Ottoman throne); Andrea Tron in Rettimo, 16 July 1482; Francesco Giustinian in Candia, 11 July 1483; addendum for Toma Zivran in Modon, 19 August 1483; Zuan Malipiero in Candia, 19 November 1483; Alvise Malipiero in Negroponte, 25 July 1484 (on the Ferrara war).

30 '*dubitto che quell Signor non Siegi le vestigie del padre, che avendo morto Machomett, Bassà et altri Signori, che a hora non attendi al sparagno et mininuir le spexe, che questo sarà in dano dela marchandanttia et in dano di quelle, et non serà quel consumamento era per el passà*'. ASVe, MdC, folder 29, reg. 2, letter to Alvise Malipiero in Constantinople, 17 February 1483 and March 1483.

31 '*è chossa vistoxa e da oltramontani pluittosto che di gran valuta e molto bella*'. ASVe, MdC, folder 29, reg. 2, letter to Girolamo Tiepolo in London, 23 April 1483.

32 The jewellery consisted of a pendant featuring a shield-shaped sapphire weighing 110 carats, with a 30-carat pearl underneath (the design is 2.5 times smaller than the actual jewel); another pendant adorned with a natural 8-carat diamond, an emerald with a table cut, and a ruby also with a table cut on the upper part; and a third pendant showcasing a 9-carat pearl surrounded by five other pearls, each weighing 5 carats. ASVe, MdC, folder 29, reg. 2, letter to Girolamo Tiepolo in London, 23 Aprile 1483, 14 June 1483 and 30 August 1483.

33 ASVe, MdC, folder 29, reg. 2, letter to Girolamo Tiepolo in London, 23 April 1483, 14 June 1483 and 30 August 1483.

34 Ugo Tucci, 'Il patrizio veneziano mercante e umanista', in *Mercanti, navi e monete nel Cinquecento veneziano* (Bologna: Edizioni Il Mulino, 1981), 15–42; Michele Cassandro, 'Istruzione tecnica e cultura umanistica. per una psicologia del mercante tra Medioevo e prima Età moderna', *Studi Storici Luigi Simeoni* LVI (2006): 85–108.

35 Giorgio Doria, 'Conoscenza del mercato internazionale e sistema informativo: il know-how dei mercanti finanziari a Genova tra XVI e XVII secolo', in *La repubblica internazionale del denaro tra 15. e 17. Secolo*, ed. Aldo de Maddalena and Hermann Kellenbenz (Bologna: Il Mulino, 1986), 57–121; Kaiser and Buti, 'Moyens, supports et usages de l'information marchande à l'Epoque moderne'; Wolfgang Kaiser and Biagio Salvemini, 'Premessa', ed. Wolfgang Kaiser and Biagio Salvemini, *Quaderni Storici* Special issue 'Informazioni e scelte economiche', no. 1 (2007): 3–18.

36 John J. McCusker and Cora Gravesteijn, *The Beginnings of Commercial and Financial Journalism: The Commodity Price Currents, Exchange Rate Currents, and Money Currents of Early Modern Europe* (Amsterdam: NEHA, 1991); John J. McCusker, 'The Demise of Distance: The Business Press and the Origins of the Information Revolution in the Early Modern Atlantic World', *The American Historical Review* 110, no. 2 (2005): 295–321.

37 This perspective is discussed in Trivellato, 'Merchants' Letters across Geographical and Social Boundaries'.

38 Trivellato.

39 ASVe, MdC, folder 29, reg. 2, letter to Cristoforo Ambrosi in Southampton, 6 July 1482 (37 days after the writing of Ambrosi's missive).

40 ASVe, MdC, folder 29, reg. 2, letter to Girolamo Tiepolo in London, 19 March 1483 (in response to a letter written on the 11th of December and received shortly after the 13th of January).

41 '*il grande giello*'. ASVe, MdC, folder 29, reg. 2, letter to Alvise Malipiero in Costantinople, November 1483.

42 ASVe, MdC, folder 29, reg. 2, letter to Alvise Malipiero in Constantinople, 29 April 1483; Francesco Giustinian in Candia (*addendum*), 22 November 1482; Girolamo Tiepolo in London, 14 June 1483; Vielmo Anzelieri in Damascus, 20 August 1483; Francesco Marcello in Damascus, 20 August 1483. See also: Georg Christ, *Trading Conflicts: Venetian Merchants and Mamluk Officials in Late Medieval Alexandria* (Leiden, Boston, MA: Brill, 2012), 190, 17n.

43 ASVe, MdC, folder 29, reg. 2, letter to Girolamo Tiepolo in London, 19 March 1483; Alvise Malipiero in Constantinople, 25 October 1483.

44 Gino Luzzatto, 'Vi furono fiere a Venezia?', in *Studi di storia economica veneziana* (Padova: CEDAM, 1954): 201-209; Jeannin, 'La Diffusion de l'information'.

45 Francesca De Pinto, 'Storia di una guerra "italiana": Ferrara 1482–1484', in *Ancora sui poteri, relazioni, guerra nel regno di Ferrante d'Aragona. Studi sulle corrispondenze diplomatiche II*, ed. Alessio Russo, Francesco Senatore, and Francesco Storti (Naples: FedOAPress, 2020), 281–304.

46 ASVe, MdC, folder 29, reg. 2, letters to Girolamo Tiepolo in London, 6 July 1482; Francesco Giustinian drappiere in Candia, 31 January 1483; Girolamo Tiepolo in London, 19 March 1483; Tomado Zivran in Modon, 13 August 1483.
47 ASVe, MdC, folder 29, reg. 2, letters to Alvise Malipiero in Constantinople, 22 November 1482. Marco also explains that because he would only trust authentication to a secure channel, he sends only the copies of documents to non-secure channels: ASVe, MdC, folder 29, reg. 2, letter to Alvise Malipiero in Constantinople, 30 July 1483.
48 ASVe, GrM, folder 189, file 1, letter to Giovanni Foscari by Alvise Foscari, April 1473.
49 Archivio di Stato di Firenze, *Legazioni di Nicolo Macchiavelli*, n. 1, letter 13, mentioned in Sardella, *Nouvelles et spéculations a Venise au debuts du 16. siècle*, 34.
50 Frederic C. Lane, *Andrea Barbarigo. Merchant of Venice* (Baltimore, MD: Johns Hopkins University Press, 1944), 97; Trivellato, *The Familiarity of Strangers*, 167–69.
51 ASVe, MdC, folder 29, reg. 2, letter to Alvise Malipiero in Costantinople, 22 November and 11 December 1482.
52 '*fa ogni chossa che la posta dell Querini non tte esqua di le mano*'. ASVe, MdC, folder 29, reg. 2, letter to Francesco Giustinian in Candia, 16 July 1482.
53 Safe passages were not reserved solely for letters containing sensitive content, such as important information or official documents, but also for more valuable goods, such as jewellery. For goods of lesser value, however, especially those transported within the Mediterranean during the good season, thus with minimal risk of cargo loss, one could afford to be more flexible in selecting the passage and even attempt to save by not insuring the cargo. ASVe, MdC, folder 29, reg. 2, letters to Alvise Malipiero in Constantinople, 22 November 1482, 11 December 1482, 3 April 1484 (the latter in Negroponte); addendum to Francesco Giustinian in Candia, 22 November 1482; Minolò Michiel, Bailus in Corfu, 31 January 1483; Girolamo Tiepolo in London, 15 October 1483.
54 ASVe, MdC, folder 29, reg. 2, letter to Toma Zivran in Modon, 7 June 1483.
55 ASVe, MdC, folder 29, reg. 2, letter to Nicolò Michiel in Corfu, 25 October 1483; Alvise Malipiero in Constantinople, 25 October 1483; Piero Ambrosani in Thessaloniki, 25 October 1483; Tomado Zivran in Modon, 25 October 1483; Zuane Malipiero in Candia, 20 November 1483; Francesco Giustinian in Candia, 20 November 1483; Andrea Tron in Rethymno, 20 November 1483; Tomado Zivran in Modon, 20 November 1483.
56 ASVe, MdC, folder 29, reg. 2, letter to Contarini Alberto in Bruges, 6 July 1482; Tomado Zivran in Modon, 3 April 1484; Girolamo Tipolo in London, 14 June 1483.
57 Lane, *Andrea Barbarigo. Merchant of Venice*, 85–90.
58 Stefania Montemezzo, 'Strategie familiari e commercio internazionale: i Michiel da San Barnaba', *Studi storici Luigi Simeoni* 65 (2015): 29–40.
59 Giuseppe Gullino, 'Il clan dei Foscari: politica matrimoniale e interessi familiari (secc. XIV-XV)', *Studi veneziani*, no. 54 (2007), https://doi.org/10.1400/99775.
60 Thiriet, 'Les lettres commerciales des Bembo'; Sopracasa, 'Passage au Levant'.
61 Xavier Lamikiz, 'Social Capital, Networks and Trust in Early Modern Long-Distance Trade. A Critical Appraisal', in *Merchants and Trade Networks in the Atlantic and the Mediterranean, 1500–1800. Connectors of Commercial Maritime Systems*, ed. Manuel Herrero Sanchez and Klemens Kaps (Abingdon, Oxon: Routledge, 2017), 39–61; Ribeiro, *Early Modern Trading Networks in Europe*, 140–63.
62 Frederic C. Lane, 'Family Partnerships and Joint Ventures in the Venetian Republic', *The Journal of Economic History* 4, no. 2 (1944): 178–96. For an overview of the principal-agent theory, see Sean Gailmard, 'Accountability and Principal–Agent Theory', in *The Oxford Handbook of Public Accountability*, ed. Mark Bovens, Robert Goodin, and Thomas Schillemans (Oxford University Press, 2014) (online edition), https://doi.org/10.1093/oxfordhb/9780199641253.013.0016.

63 Russell Hardin, 'The Street-Level Epistemology of Trust', *Politics & Society* 21, no. 4 (1993): 505–29; Edwin S. Hunt and James M. Murray, *A History of Business in Medieval Europe, 1200–1550* (Cambridge, New York: Cambridge University Press, 1999), 54–60.
64 Ricardo Court, '"Januensis Ergo Mercator": Trust and Enforcement in the Business Correspondence of the Brignole Family', *The Sixteenth Century Journal* 35, no. 4 (2004): 987–1003.
65 For the role in information in business management, see Michael E. Porter, 'How Information Gives You Competitive Advantage', *Harvard Business Review* 63, no. 4 (1985): 149–60; Mark Casson, *Information and Organization: A New Perspective on the Theory of the Firm*, new edition (New York, Oxford: Oxford University Press, 1997), 3–34, 117–45; Cátia Antunes, 'Free Agents and Formal Institutions in the Portuguese Empire: Towards a Framework of Analysis', *Portuguese Studies* 28, no. 2 (2012): 173–85; Ribeiro, *Early Modern Trading Networks in Europe*, 140–63.
66 ASVe, MdC, folder 29, reg. 2, letter to Francesco Giustinian in Candia, 11 July 1483.
67 The relationship between principal and agent and their level of cooperation can be analysed through the lens of game theory, as done by Avner Greif, *Institutions and the Path to the Modern Economy: Lessons from Medieval Trade* (Cambridge: Cambridge University Press, 2006), 407–20.
68 Lane, 'Family Partnerships and Joint Ventures in the Venetian Republic'.
69 Lane, *Andrea Barbarigo. Merchant of Venice*, 89–90.
70 Greif, 'Contracting, Enforcement, and Efficiency'; Court, 'Januensis Ergo Mercator'; González de Lara, 'The Secret of Venetian Success: A Public-Order, Reputation-Based Institution'; Ribeiro, *Early Modern Trading Networks in Europe*, 25–34.
71 Francisco Apellaniz, 'Venetian Trading Networks in the Medieval Mediterranean', *The Journal of Interdisciplinary History* 44, no. 2 (2013): 157–79; Bart Lambert, 'Making Size Matter Less: Italian Firms and Merchant Guilds in Late Medieval Bruges', in *The Company in Law and Practice: Did Size Matter? (Middle Ages-Nineteenth Century)*, ed. Dave De ruysscher, Albrecht Cordes, Serge Dauchy, and Heikki Pihlajamäki (Brill Nijhoff, 2017), 34–48.
72 Lane, 'Family Partnerships and Joint Ventures in the Venetian Republic', 184.
73 ASVe, MG, folder 15, reg. 2, cc. 5, 9, 10, 11, 24.
74 Lane, 'Family Partnerships and Joint Ventures in the Venetian Republic', 184–85.
75 Lane, 'Family Partnerships and Joint Ventures in the Venetian Republic'; Apellaniz, 'Venetian Trading Networks in the Medieval Mediterranean'.
76 ASVe, MdC, folder 29, reg. 2, letter to Francesco Giustinian in Candia, 22 November 1482.
77 ASVe, MdC, folder 29, reg. 2, letter to Toma Zivran in Modon, 16 September 1482, February 1483, 7 June 1483, (*addendum*) 19 August 1483; Girolamo Tiepolo in London, 1 October 1482, 16 November 1482; Piero Ambrosani in Thessaloniki, November 1483, 4 August 1483; Francesco Giustinian in Candia, 16 July 1482, 31 January 1483.
78 *'un'altra volta non arette chauxa de infrixarve ma gadagnando lassar che ognun vadagni'*. ASVe, MdC, folder 29, reg. 2, letter to Francesco Giustinian in Candia, 22 November 1482.
79 Lane, 'Family Partnerships and Joint Ventures in the Venetian Republic'; Raymond De Roover, *The Medici Bank: Its Organization, Management, Operations and Decline*, Business History Series (New York University. Graduate School of Business Administration) (New York: Univ. Press, 1948); Richard A. Goldthwaite, 'The Medici Bank and the World of Florentine Capitalism', *Past and Present* 114 (1987): 3–31; Edwin S. Hunt, *The Medieval Super-Companies. A Study of the Peruzzi Company of Florence* (Cambridge: Cambridge University Press, 1994); Angela Orlandi, 'Le prestazioni di una holding tardo medievale riflette attraverso alcune teorie di management e la social network analysis', in *Innovare nella storia economica: temi e metodi*

(Prato: Fondazione Istituto internazionale di Storia economica F. Datini, Società Italiana degli Storici economici, 2016), 117–48.

80 Pezzolo, 'The via Italiana to Capitalism'.

81 Apellaniz, 'Venetian Trading Networks in the Medieval Mediterranean'.

82 Gino Luzzatto, 'Navigazione di linea e navigazione libera nelle grandi città marinare del Medio Evo', in *Studi di storia economica veneziana* (Padova: Cedam, 1954): 53–58; Renard Gluzman, 'What Made a Ship Venetian? (Thirteenth to Sixteenth Centuries)', in *Cultures of Empire: Rethinking Venetian Rule, 1400–1700: Essays in Honour of Benjamin Arbel*, ed. Georg Christ and Franz-Julius Morche, The Medieval Mediterranean (Leiden, Boston, MA: Brill, 2020), 293–328.

83 ASVe, MG, fodler 15, reg. 2, cc. 19 *avere*, 86 *dare*.

84 Christ, *Trading Conflicts*, 241.

85 ASVe, MdC, folder 29, reg. 2, letter to Antonio Negro in Damascus, June 1482; Vielmo Anzelieri in Damascus, 15 February 1483.

86 Christ, *Trading Conflicts*, 205.

87 Gigi Corazzol, 'Varietà notarile: scorci di vita economica e sociale', in *Storia di Venezia: dalle origini alla caduta della Serenissima. VI. Dal Rinascimento al Barocco*, ed. Gaetano Cozzi and Paolo Prodi (Rome: Istituto della Enciclopedia Italiana, 1994), 775–91; Michela Dal Borgo, 'Neo-convertiti aspiranti sensali (1569)', *Quaderni di studi arabi* 15 (1997): 163–65; Sergio Baldan, 'I senseri dei pellegrini e l'organizzazione dei viaggi da Venezia per la Terra Santa', *Studi Veneziani, n.s.* LXXIV (2016): 15–46; Isabella Cecchini, 'Instabilità finanziaria e intervento pubblico: Venezia 1600–1630', in *Le crisi finanziarie: gestione, implicazioni sociali e conseguenze nell'età preindustriale / The Financial Crises: Their Management, Their Social Implications and Their Consequences in Pre-Industrial Times, Atti della XLVII Settimana di studi, Istituto Internazionale di Storia Economia F. Datini* (Firenze: Firenze University Press; Fondazione Istituto internazionale di storia economica "F. Datini", 2016), 471–88.

88 ASVe, MG, folder 15, reg. 2, cc. 4 *dare*, 7, 12 *dare*, 13 *dare*, 17 *avere*, 18 *avere*, 30 *avere*, 31 *avere*, 34 *avere*, 36, 114, 117 *avere*, 123 *avere*, 131 *dare*, 132 *dare*, 141, *dare*.

89 ASVe, MdC, folder 29, reg. 2, letter to Zuane Malipiero in Candia, 3 April 1484.

90 ASVe, MdC, folder 29, reg. 2, letter to Piero Malipiero in Constantinople, 23 August 1484; Toma Zivran in Modon, 4 September 1484. The network of agents depicted in commercial letters is more nuanced and layered than that provided by accounting records. In accounting, it is indeed possible to identify, quantitatively, who the agents were and who the partners were, but it is less straightforward to understand the underlying structure of the firm's operations because personal information is not mentioned in the account books. In letters, however, it is possible to comprehend the hierarchies and identities of the nodes in the network of merchants' agents and intermediaries, thanks to the information available within the letters, both in the case of direct communication and through information provided to third parties.

91 '*Fatte chome megllio ve par, che senpre l'ordene mio con vui è stato largo e di le chosse mie avette posutto dar chome delle vostre, ne mai ve ho chontraditto a quello avette fatto. Ma vui siette pllui fredo che uno giazo ett bixogna le mie parolle siano quelle ve schallda'*. ASVe, MdC, folder 29, reg. 2, letter to Francesco Giustinian in Candia, 3 June 1483.

92 Christ, *Trading Conflicts*, 202–03.

93 ASVe, MdC, folder 29, reg. 2, letters to Francesco Giustinian in Candia, 16 July 1482 and 22 November 1482.

94 ASVe, MdC, folder 29, reg. 2, letter to Francesco Giustinian in Candia, 11 July 1483; letter to Zuane Malipiero in Candia, August 1484.

95 Francesco Guidi Bruscoli, 'Creating Networks through Languages: Italian Merchants in Late Medieval and Early Modern Europe', in *Commercial Networks and European Cities, 1400–1800*, ed. Andrea Caracausi and Christof Jeggle (London: Pickering & Chatto, 2014), 65–79.

96 Doria, 'Conoscenza del mercato internazionale e sistema informativo'; Andrea Caracausi, 'Formazione mercantile, conoscenza del diritto e idiomi politici', in *Formazione alla politica, politica della formazione a Venezia In Età Moderna*, ed. Andrea Caracausi and Antonio Conzato (Roma: Viella, 2013), 141–57.

97 Trivellato, *The Familiarity of Strangers*, 153–67; Christ, *Trading Conflicts*, 198.

98 ASVe, MdC, folder 29, reg. 2, letters to Alvise Malipiero in Constantinople, 30 July 1483; Zuane Malipiero in Candia, 3 April 1484.

99 '*per el simelle, la tavola di zambelotti vegnutta con ell nostro, che per Dio ho grandementte a inproperartte che non ai scritto che zanbelotti sono e che quantità. Zercha de zettero vardar meglio ai fatti tuo che non ai fatto per el passà ett prozieder con pllui maturittà che son de quelli se lamentta, chome ben intenderai*'. ASVe, MdC, folder 29, reg. 2, letter to Alvise Malipiero in Costantinople, 12 November 1482.

100 Doria, 'Conoscenza del mercato internazionale e sistema informativo'; Caracausi, 'Formazione mercantile, conoscenza del diritto e idiomi politici'. The training of young merchants was a key concern of contemporary manuals. Benedetto Cotrugli, *Della mercatura et del mercante perfetto. Libri quattro di M. Benedetto Cotrugli raugeo* (recently translated: Benedetto Cotrugli, *The Book of the Art of Trade*, ed. Carlo Carraro and Giovanni Favero (Cham: Palgrave Macmillan, 2017). This is one of the earliest manuals on commerce, originally published in the mid-15th century, which inaugurated a highly successful publishing trend that flourished in the centuries to come, exemplified by the renowned Luca Pacioli, *Trattato di partita doppia, Venezia 1494*, ed. Annalisa Conterio (Venezia: Albrizzi, 1994); Luca Pacioli, *Summa De Arithmetica, Geometria, Proportioni Et Proportionalita*, ed. Jeremy Cripps (Seattle, WA: Pacioli Society, 1994).

101 ASVe, MG, folder 15, reg. 2, cc. 152 *dare*.

102 ASVe, MG, folder 15, reg. 2, cc. 154 *dare*.

103 ASVe, MdC, folder 29, reg. 2, letter to Cristoforo Ambrosi in Southampton, 6 July 1482.

104 ASVe, MdC, folder 29, reg. 2, letter to Toma Zivran in Modon, 19 August 1483.

105 John W. Pratt and Richard J. Zeckhauser, 'Principal and Agents: An Overview', in *Principals and Agents: The Structure of Business*, ed. John W. Pratt and Richard J. Zeckhauser (Boston, MA: Harvard Business School Press, 1985), 1–36; Greif, 'Contracting, Enforcement, and Efficiency'; Cátia Antunes, 'Free Agents and Formal Institutions in the Portuguese Empire'.

106 D. Good, 'Individuals, Interpersonal Relations and Trust', in *Trust: Making and Breaking Cooperative Relations*, ed. Diego Gambetta (New York: Basil Blackwell, 1988), 31–48; Court, 'Januensis Ergo Mercator'; Lamikiz, 'Social Capital, Networks and Trust in Early Modern Long-Distance Trade. A Critical Appraisal'.

107 For the etiquette in early modern commercial letters, see Trivellato, *The Familiarity of Strangers*, 177–93.

108 ASVe, MdC, folder 29, reg. 2, letter to Piero Ambrosani in Thessaloniki, November 1483.

109 Lane, 'Family Partnerships and Joint Ventures in the Venetian Republic'; Julia Adams, *The Familial State: Ruling Families and Merchant Capitalism in Early Modern Europe* (Ithaca, NY: Cornell University Press, 2005), 80–97; Avner Greif, 'Family Structure, Institutions, and Growth: The Origins and Implications of Western Corporations', *American Economic Review* 96, no. 2 (2006): 308–12; Sebouh Aslanian, 'The Circulation of Men and Credit: The Role of the Commenda and the Family Firm in Julfan Society', *Journal of the Economic and Social History of the Orient* 50, no. 2/3 (2007): 124–71.

110 ASVe, MdC, folder 29, reg. 2, letter to Zuan Malipiero in Candia, 19 November 1483.

111 ASVe, MdC, folder 29, reg. 2, letters to Francesco Giustinian in Candia, 3 June 1483, 4 August 1483, 19 November 1483.

112 ASVe, MdC, folder 29, reg. 2, letter to Francesco Giustinian in Candia, 10 June 1484 and 31 July 1484.

113 ASVe, MG, folder 15, reg. 2, c. 151.
114 ASVe, MG, folder 15, reg. 2, cc. 58, 150, 151.
115 Ribeiro, *Early Modern Trading Networks in Europe*, 123–29.
116 ASVe, MdC, folder 29, reg. 2, letter to Alvise Malipiero in Constantinople, 11 December 1482, 17 February 1483, 29 April 1483, 25 October 1483.
117 ASVe, MdC, folder 29, reg. 2, letter to Francesco Giustinian in Candia, 3 June 1483, 17 June 1483.
118 ASVe, MdC, folder 29, reg. 2, letter to Zuane Malipiero in Candia, 15 December 1483.
119 '*ett se dei ell mio marchandanttar a tuo profitto, dimello, perche quando con lizenzia mia el festi ne aresti libertà. Ma tuortella da tti non me piaze el verso neanche de iustizia*'. ASVe, MdC, folder 29, reg. 2, letter to Zuane Malipiero in Candia, 20 November 1483.
120 ASVe, MdC, folder 29, reg. 2, letter to Francesco Giustinian Malipiero in Candia, 11 July 1483.
121 ASVe, MG, folder 15, reg. 2, cc. 108, 128.
122 ASVe, MdC, folder 29, reg. 2, letters to Marino Dolfin in Candia, 16 July 1482; Francesco Giustinian in Candia, 22 November 1482.
123 ASVe, MdC, folder 29, reg. 2, letters to Francesco Giustinian in Candia, 23 January 1483. In other instances, Bembo tries to leverage the Venetian officials on oreign markets: Marino Dolfin in Candia, 16 July 1482; Francesco Giustinian in Candia, February 1483; Alvise Malipiero di Paolo in Constantinople, 29 April 1483; Francesco Giustinian drapier in Candia, 29 July 1482; Alvise Malipiero in Constantinople, 30 July 1483.
124 '*Voglli esser sollizitto al ben ett a uttele di la nave, perché chusi fazendo ell sarà anche tuo. Ett l'uttelle suo consiste in 3 chose: l'una nel presto navichar e l'allttro in ell sparagno ett questo ttocha a tte. La tterza è in darlli con parttido e questo a mi aspetta. Ett perché sei pattron della ditta, vogllio tu abi ogni libertta in far quello te par sia profitto ett uttele de ditta nave perché esendo tu sul fatto meglllio saperai deliberar che io esendo lunttano*'. ASVe, MdC, folder 29, reg. 2, arichordo for Andrea Malluxa, 22 November 1482.
125 ASVe, MdC, folder 29, reg. 2, letters to Francesco Giustinian in Candia, 23 January 1483; Tomado Zivran in Modon, February 1483; Francesco da Mosto, i.e., Girolamo, on a ship to Barbary, June 1483.
126 ASVe, MdC, folder 29, reg. 2, letters to Francesco Giustinian in Candia, 23 January 1483 and February 1483; Alvise Malipiero in Constantinople, 17 June 1483.
127 ASVe, MdC, folder 29, reg. 2, letters to Francesco Giustinian in Candia, 29 July 1482; Francesco da Mosto, i.e., Girolamo, on a ship to Barbary, June 1483; Zuan Malipiero in Candia, 20 November 1483; Andrea Malluxà, ship's captain, 22 November 1482; Alvise Malipiero in Constantinople, 29 April 1483.
128 ASVe, MdC, folder 29, reg. 2, letter to Francesco Giustinian in Candia, 23 January 1483.
129 ASVe, MdC, folder 29, reg. 2, letters to Francesco Giustinian in Candia, 22 November 1482; Andrea Alberga in Candia, 22 November 1482.
130 ASVe, MdC, folder 29, reg. 2, letters to Manfredo de Zuane in Thessaloniki, 16 July 1482 and 22 November 1482; Gerino de Paxin in Thessaloniki, 15 February 1483.
131 ASVe, MdC, folder 29, reg. 2, letter to Alvise Malipiero in Constantinople, 12 November 1482.
132 '*I marchadantti non vuol mandare el suo in man de alltri per star 3 ani per aver el retratto. Ell vall pllui una bona fama che ogni ttexauro*'. ASVe, MdC, folder 29, reg. 2, letter to Manfredo de Zuane in Thessaloniki, 22 November 1482.
133 ASVe, MdC, folder 29, reg. 2, letter to Alvise Malipiero in Constantinople, 12 November 1482.
134 ASVe, MdC, folder 29, reg. 2, letters to Piero Malipiero in Constantinople, 18 April 1484; Piero Ambrosani in Thessaloniki, November 1483.

135 For the role of public institutions, see Greif, *Institutions and the Path to the Modern Economy*, 91–110.
136 ASVe, MdC, folder 29, reg. 2, letter to Piero Malipiero in Constantinople, 18 May 1484.

References

Adams, Julia. *The Familial State: Ruling Families and Merchant Capitalism in Early Modern Europe*. Ithaca, NY: Cornell University Press, 2005.

Apellaniz, Francisco. 'Venetian Trading Networks in the Medieval Mediterranean'. *The Journal of Interdisciplinary History* 44, no. 2 (2013): 157–79.

Aslanian, Sebouh. 'The Circulation of Men and Credit: The Role of the Commenda and the Family Firm in Julfan Society'. *Journal of the Economic and Social History of the Orient* 50, no. 2/3 (2007): 124–71.

Baldan, Sergio. 'I senseri dei pellegrini e l'organizzazione dei viaggi da Venezia per la Terra Santa'. *Studi Veneziani, n.s.* LXXIV (2016): 15–46.

Benedetto Cotrugli. *Della mercatura et del mercante perfetto. Libri quattro di M. Benedetto Cotrugli raugeo*. Venice: All'Elefanta, 1573.

Braudel, Fernand. *The Mediterranean and the Mediterranean World in the Age of Philip II*. Vol. 1. New York: Harper & Row, 1972.

Caracausi, Andrea. 'Formazione mercantile, conoscenza del diritto e idiomi politici'. In *Formazione alla politica, politica della formazione a Venezia in Età moderna*, edited by Andrea Caracausi and Antonio Conzato, 141–57. Roma: Viella, 2013.

Cassandro, Michele. 'Istruzione tecnica e cultura umanistica. per una psicologia del mercante tra Medioevo e prima Età moderna'. *Studi Storici Luigi Simeoni* LVI (2006): 85–108.

Casson, Mark. *Information and Organization: A New Perspective on the Theory of the Firm*. New edition. New York, Oxford: Oxford University Press, 1997.

Cátia Antunes. 'Free Agents and Formal Institutions in the Portuguese Empire: Towards a Framework of Analysis'. *Portuguese Studies* 28, no. 2 (2012): 173–85.

Cecchini, Isabella. 'Instabilità finanziaria e intervento pubblico: Venezia 1600–1630'. In *Le crisi finanziarie: gestione, implicazioni sociali e conseguenze nell'età preindustriale / The Financial Crises: Their Management, Their Social Implications and Their Consequences in Pre-Industrial Times, Atti della XLVII Settimana di studi, istituto internazionale di storia economia F. Datini*, 471–88. Firenze: Firenze University Press; Fondazione Istituto internazionale di storia economica "F. Datini", 2016.

Cecchini, Isabella, and Luciano Pezzolo. 'Merchants and Institutions in Early-Modern Venice'. *The Journal of European Economic History* 41, no. 2 (2012): 89–114.

Christ, Georg. 'A Newsletter in 1419? Antonio Morosini's Chronicle in the Light of Commercial Correspondence between Venice and Alexandria'. *Mediterranean Historical Review* 20, no. 1 (1 June 2005): 35–66.

Christ, Georg. *Trading Conflicts: Venetian Merchants and Mamluk Officials in Late Medieval Alexandria*. Leiden, Boston, MA: Brill, 2012.

Corazzol, Gigi. 'Varietà notarile: scorci di vita economica e sociale'. In *Storia di Venezia: dalle origini alla caduta della Serenissima. VI. Dal Rinascimento al Barocco*, edited by Gaetano Cozzi and Paolo Prodi, 775–91. Rome: Istituto della Enciclopedia Italiana, 1994.

Cotrugli, Benedetto. *The Book of the Art of Trade*, edited by Carlo Carraro and Giovanni Favero. Cham: Palgrave Macmillan, 2017.

Court, Ricardo. '"Januensis Ergo Mercator": Trust and Enforcement in the Business Correspondence of the Brignole Family'. *The Sixteenth Century Journal* 35, no. 4 (2004): 987–1003.

Curtin, Philip D. *Cross-Cultural Trade in World History*. Cambridge: Cambridge University Press, 1984.

Dal Borgo, Michela. 'Neo-convertiti aspiranti sensali (1569)'. *Quaderni di studi arabi* 15 (1997): 163–65.

De Pinto, Francesca. 'Storia di una guerra "italiana": Ferrara 1482–1484'. In *Ancora sui poteri, relazioni, guerra nel regno di Ferrante d'Aragona. Studi sulle corrispondenze diplomatiche II*, edited by Alessio Russo, Francesco Senatore, and Francesco Storti, 281–304. Naples: FedOAPress, 2020.

De Roover, Raymond. *The Medici Bank: Its Organization, Management, Operations and Decline*. Business History Series (New York University. Graduate School of Business Administration). New York: Univ. Press, 1948.

Doria, Giorgio. 'Conoscenza del mercato internazionale e sistema informativo: il know-how dei mercanti finanziari a Genova tra XVI e XVII secolo'. In *La Repubblica internazionale del denaro tra 15. e 17. secolo*, edited by Aldo de Maddalena and Hermann Kellenbenz, 57–121. Bologna: Il Mulino, 1986.

Doumerc, Bernard. 'Par Dieu écrivez plus souvent! La lettre d'affaires à Venise à la fin du Moyen Age'. *Publications de l'École Française de Rome* 190, no. 1 (1994): 99–109.

Fortunati, Maura. *Scrittura e prova: i libri di commercio nel diritto medievale e moderno*. Roma: Fondazione Sergio Mochi Onory per la storia del diritto italiano, 1996.

Gailmard, Sean. 'Accountability and Principal–Agent Theory'. In *The Oxford Handbook of Public Accountability*, edited by Mark Bovens, Robert Goodin, and Thomas Schillemans (online edition). Oxford University Press, 2014. https://doi.org/10.1093/oxfordhb/9780199641253.013.0016.

Gluzman, Renard. 'What Made a Ship Venetian? (Thirteenth to Sixteenth Centuries)'. In *Cultures of Empire: Rethinking Venetian Rule, 1400–1700: Essays in Honour of Benjamin Arbel*, edited by Georg Christ and Franz-Julius Morche, 293–328. The Medieval Mediterranean. Leiden, Boston, MA: Brill, 2020.

Goitein, S. D. *A Mediterranean Society: The Jewish Communities of the Arab World as Portrayed in the Documents of the Cairo Geniza*. Vol. 1: Economic Foundations. Berkeley: University of California, 1967.

Goldberg, Jessica L. 'Mercantile Letters'. *Jewish History* 32, no. 2/4 (2019): 397–410.

Goldthwaite, Richard A. 'The Medici Bank and the World of Florentine Capitalism'. *Past and Present* 114 (1987): 3–31.

González de Lara, Yadira. 'The Secret of Venetian Success: A Public-Order, Reputation-Based Institution'. *European Review of Economic History* 12 (2008): 247–85.

Good, D. 'Individuals, Interpersonal Relations and Trust'. In *Trust: Making and Breaking Cooperative Relations*, edited by Diego Gambetta, 31–48. New York: Basil Blackwell, 1988.

Greif, Avner. 'Contract Enforceability and Economic Institutions in Early Trade: The Maghribi Traders' Coalition'. *The American Economic Review* 83, no. 3 (1993): 525–48.

Greif, Avner. 'Contracting, Enforcement, and Efficiency: Economics beyond the Law'. In *Annual World Bank Conference on Development Economics*, edited by M. Bruno and B. Pleskovic, 239–65. Washington, DC: The World Bank, 1997.

Greif, Avner. 'Family Structure, Institutions, and Growth: The Origins and Implications of Western Corporations'. *American Economic Review* 96, no. 2 (2006): 308–12.

Greif, Avner. *Institutions and the Path to the Modern Economy: Lessons from Medieval Trade*. Cambridge: Cambridge University Press, 2006.

Greif, Avner. 'Reputation and Coalitions in Medieval Trade: Evidence on the Maghribi Traders'. *The Journal of Economic History* 49, no. 4 (1989): 857–82.

Guidi Bruscoli, Francesco. 'Creating Networks through Languages: Italian Merchants in Late Medieval and Early Modern Europe'. In *Commercial Networks and European Cities, 1400–1800*, edited by Andrea Caracausi and Christof Jeggle, 65–79. London: Pickering & Chatto, 2014.

Gullino, Giuseppe. 'Il clan dei Foscari: politica matrimoniale e interessi familiari (secc. XIV-XV)'. Studi veneziani, no. 54 (2007). https://doi.org/10.1400/99775.

Hardin, Russell. 'The Street-Level Epistemology of Trust'. *Politics & Society* 21, no. 4 (1993): 505–29.

Hunt, Edwin S. *The Medieval Super-Companies. A Study of the Peruzzi Company of Florence*. Cambridge: Cambridge University Press, 1994.

Hunt, Edwin S., and James M. Murray. *A History of Business in Medieval Europe, 1200–1550*. Cambridge, New York: Cambridge University Press, 1999.

Jeannin, Pierre. 'La Diffusion de l'information'. In *Fiere e mercati nella integrazione delle economie europee secc. XIII-XVIII, Atti della trentaduesima Settimana di studi e altri convegni dell'Istituto Internazionale di Storia Economica F. Datini (8–12 Maggio 2000)*, 231–62. Florence: Le Monnier, Istituto internazionale di storia economica 'F. Datini', 2001.

Kaiser, Wolfgang, and Gilbert Buti. 'Moyens, supports et usages de l'information marchande à l'époque moderne'. *Rives nord-méditerranéennes* 27 (2007): 7–11.

Kaiser, Wolfgang, and Biagio Salvemini. 'Premessa', edited by Wolfgang Kaiser and Biagio Salvemini. Quaderni Storici Special issue 'Informazioni e scelte economiche', no. 1 (2007): 3–18.

Lambert, Bart. 'Making Size Matter Less: Italian Firms and Merchant Guilds in Late Medieval Bruges'. In *The Company in Law and Practice: Did Size Matter? (Middle Ages-Nineteenth Century)*, edited by Dave De ruysscher, Albrecht Cordes, Serge Dauchy, and Heikki Pihlajamäki, 34–48. Brill Nijhoff, 2017.

Lamikiz, Xavier. 'Social Capital, Networks and Trust in Early Modern Long-Distance Trade. A Critical Appraisal'. In *Merchants and Trade Networks in the Atlantic and the Mediterranean, 1500–1800. Connectors of Commercial Maritime Systems*, edited by Manuel Herrero Sanchez and Klemens Kaps, 39–61. Abingdon, Oxon: Routledge, 2017.

Lane, Frederic C. *Andrea Barbarigo. Merchant of Venice*. Baltimore, MD: Johns Hopkins University Press, 1944.

Lane, Frederic C. 'Family Partnerships and Joint Ventures in the Venetian Republic'. *The Journal of Economic History* 4, no. 2 (1944): 178–96.

Lapeyrie, Gaëlle. 'L'écriture comptable comme langage spécifique des marchands (France Méridionale, début XVIIe siècle)'. In *Langues et langages du commerce en Méditerranée et en Europe à l'époque moderne*, edited by Gilbert Buti, Michèle Janin-Thivos, and Olivier Raveux, 207–26. Aix-en-Provence: Presses Universitaires de Provence, 2013.

Luzzatto, Gino. 'Navigazione di linea e navigazione libera nelle grandi città marinare del Medio Evo'. In *Studi di storia economica veneziana*. Padova: Cedam, 1954.

Luzzatto, Gino. 'Vi furono fiere a Venezia?' In *Studi di storia economica veneziana*. Padova: CEDAM, 1954.

McCusker, John J. 'The Demise of Distance: The Business Press and the Origins of the Information Revolution in the Early Modern Atlantic World'. *The American Historical Review* 110, no. 2 (2005): 295–321.

McCusker, John J., and Cora Gravesteijn. *The Beginnings of Commercial and Financial Journalism: The Commodity Price Currents, Exchange Rate Currents, and Money Currents of Early Modern Europe*. Amsterdam: NEHA, 1991.

Melis, Federigo. 'Intensità e regolarità nella diffusione dell'informazione economica generale nel Mediterraneo e in Occidente alla fine del medioevo'. In *Histoire économique du monde méditerranéen, 1450–1650, Mélanges en l'honneur de Fernand Braudel*, 389–424. Toulouse: Privat Éditeur, 1973.

Montemezzo, Stefania. 'Strategie familiari e commercio internazionale: i Michiel da San Barnaba'. *Studi storici Luigi Simeoni* 65 (2015): 29–40.

Morche, Franz-Julius. 'The Letters of Others: Marino Morosini and His Curious Newsshest on the Battle of Maclodio'. In *Cultures of Empire: Rethinking Venetian Rule, 1400–1700: Essays in Honour of Benjamin Arbel*, edited by Georg Christ and Franz-Julius Morche, 90–122. The Medieval Mediterranean. Leiden, Boston, MA: Brill, 2020.

Nigro, Giampiero. *Francesco di Marco Datini: l'uomo, il mercante*. Firenze: Prato: Firenze University Press; Fondazione Istituto internazionale di storia economica "F. Datini", 2010.

North, Douglass C. 'Institutions'. *Journal of Economic Perspectives* 5, no. 1 (1991): 97–112.

Orlandi, Angela. 'Le prestazioni di una holding tardo medievale riflette attraverso alcune teorie di management e la social network analysis'. In *Innovare nella storia economica: temi e metodi*, 117–48. Prato: Fondazione Istituto internazionale di Storia economica F. Datini, Società Italiana degli Storici economici, 2016.

Orlandi, Angela. 'Networks and Commercial Penetration Models in the Late Medieval Mediterranean: Revisiting the Datini'. In *Commercial Networks and European Cities, 1400–1800*, edited by Andrea Caracausi and Christof Jeggle, 81–106. London: Pickering & Chatto, 2014.

Pacioli, Luca. *Summa de arithmetica, geometria, proportioni et proportionalita*, edited by Jeremy Cripps. Seattle, WA: Pacioli Society, 1994.

Pacioli, Luca. *Trattato di partita doppia, Venezia 1494*, edited by Annalisa Conterio. Venezia: Albrizzi, 1994.

Petitjean, Johann. 'Processus et procédures de diffusion de l'information sur la guerre turque en Italie (fin XVIe -début XVIIe siècle)'. In *Les formes de l'échange: Communiquer, diffuser, informer, de l'Antiquité au XVIIIe siècle*, edited by François Brizay, 319–34. Histoire. Rennes: Presses universitaires de Rennes, 2012.

Pezzolo, Luciano. 'The via Italiana to Capitalism'. In *The Cambridge History of Capitalism, I, The Rise of Capitalism: From Ancient Origins to 1848*, edited by Larry Neal and Jeffrey G. Williamson, 266–313. Cambridge: Cambridge University Press, 2014.

Porter, Michael E. 'How Information Gives You Competitive Advantage'. *Harvard Business Review* 63, no. 4 (1985): 149–60.

Pratt, John W., and Richard J. Zeckhauser. 'Principal and Agents: An Overview'. In *Principals and Agents: The Structure of Business*, edited by John W. Pratt and Richard J. Zeckhauser, 1–36. Boston, MA: Harvard Business School Press, 1985.

Ribeiro, Ana Sofia. *Early Modern Trading Networks in Europe: Cooperation and the Case of Simon Ruiz*. Abingdon, Oxon, New York, NY: Routledge, Taylor & Francis Group, 2016.

Safley, Thomas Max. *Family Firms and Merchant Capitalism in Early Modern Europe: The Business, Bankruptcy and Resilience of the Hoechstetters of Augsburg*. Abingdon, Oxon, New York, NY: Routledge, 2019.

Sardella, Pierre. *Nouvelles et spéculations a Venise au debuts du 16. siècle*. Cahiers des annales. Paris: Armand Colin, 1948.

Sopracasa, Alessio. 'Passage au Levant. Le « voyage » de Candie-Constantinople de la compagnia Bembo dans la seconde moitié du xve siècle: organisation et séjour'. *Cahiers d'études italiennes*, no. 25 (2017). https://doi.org/10.4000/cei.3499.

Thiriet, Freddy. 'Les lettres commerciales des Bembo et le commerce vénitien dans l'Empire Ottoman à la fin du XVe siècle'. In *Studi in onore di Armando Sapori*, II:911–33. Milan: Istituto Editoriale Cisalpino, 1957.

Trivellato, Francesca. 'Merchants' Letters across Geographical and Social Boundaries'. In *Correspondence and Cultural Exchange in Europe, 1400–1700*, edited by Francisco Bethencourt and Florike Egmond, 80–103. Cambridge: Cambridge University Press, 2007.

Trivellato, Francesca. 'Renaissance Florence and the Origins of Capitalism: A Business History Perspective'. *Business History Review* 94, no. 1 (2020): 229–51.

Trivellato, Francesca. *The Familiarity of Strangers: The Sephardic Diaspora, Livorno, and Cross-Cultural Trade in the Early Modern Period*. New Haven, CT, London: Yale University Press, 2009.

Tucci, Ugo. 'Il patrizio veneziano mercante e umanista'. In *Mercanti, navi e monete nel cinquecento veneziano*, 15–42. Bologna: Edizioni Il Mulino, 1981.

Conclusion

This volume has examined the presence and success of small- and medium-sized family businesses in Renaissance international trade, using the Republic of Venice as a case study. It highlights the adaptive strategies these family businesses employed during periods of adversity, such as wars. The analysis of organizational methods within Renaissance Venetian family firms reveals how they leveraged public institutions and forged networks. These networks effectively balanced the roles of family members and foreign agents, enabling these enterprises to compete in a complex and competitive commercial landscape.

Why, then, have we specifically chosen to focus on small- and medium-sized enterprises? Within the Renaissance Venetian context, acknowledged as one of the nurseries of the capitalist system, it was these smaller enterprises that predominantly upheld the economic structure. Frequently, scholarly attention shifts towards larger corporations, where the manifestations of early capitalism are more conspicuous.[1] This neglect of smaller enterprises often stems from a dearth of documentation or their less conspicuous nature. However, a thorough understanding of these smaller entities is vital, as they offer essential insights into the broader economic fabric of the period. Our analysis delves into how institutions may have either supported or obstructed these businesses, thus playing a decisive role in shaping the contours of economic development during this era.

The Family Model and the Role of Public Institutions

In this book, we initially address the issue of the role of primarily public institutions and their influence on the activities of small- and medium-sized Renaissance commercial enterprises. These institutional interventions proved critical within a business environment predominantly characterized by nuclear family structures. Such analysis is of particular relevance in historiographical debates where the Italian Republics, including Venice, are frequently compared to guilds due to these unique features. Moreover, this discussion intersects with a broader debate that has explored the impact of both formal and informal institutions on economic development from the medieval period to the early modern age. This analysis sheds light on the nuanced ways in which institutions could either foster or hinder economic activities, thereby influencing the trajectory of economic development.[2]

DOI: 10.4324/9781032628103-7

Venetian business enterprises were deeply embedded in both family and state structures, often involving close relatives, such as brothers and sons, as partners in *fraterne*. These enterprises managed not only commercial ventures but also familial assets and estates, blurring the lines between personal and business finances.[3] The operational dynamics of a family firm included shared ownership of merchandise and real estate, as well as the collective management of both business and household expenses. Detailed ledger entries from the Michiel family illustrate the seamless integration of personal and business expenditures, encompassing items such as food, property upkeep, and familial gifts alongside commercial transactions. The Venetian family businesses of Alvise Michiel, Marco Bembo, and Giovanni Foscari engaged in a variety of economic activities, including long-distance trade and real estate investments. Their operations reflect a complex and adaptive approach to managing resources and navigating the competitive landscape of Renaissance commerce.[4]

To fully understand the operations of small- and medium-sized commercial enterprises in the Venetian Renaissance, it is essential to delineate the influence of public institutions on their activities. While familial connections provided significant support, mercantile documentation demonstrates the profound impact of public institutions on merchants' decision-making and strategies. The Venetian State did not adopt a neutral or passive stance with regard to its economic engagement. The Venetian State's proactive and interventionist approach encompassed the establishment of public navigation routes, the appointment of consuls and ambassadors abroad, the implementation of customs control, taxation, and the mandate for public appointees to submit their activities to the Senate for review.[5] This close relationship between the government, controlled by merchant noble families, and family firms led to a symbiotic dynamic. The ability of Venetian merchants to adapt to and exploit state interventions was crucial for their commercial success, illustrating a model of economic resilience and innovation with enduring historical significance. State interventions significantly influenced merchant behaviour, prompting both compliance with and circumvention of regulations. These interventions were crucial in a business landscape dominated by nuclear family structures, where the interplay between public initiatives and private interests ensured the enduring viability of family enterprises amidst growing commercial challenges. For instance, Giovanni Foscari was able to leverage public and private navigation systems to his advantage, effectively utilizing the public navigation infrastructure.[6] Similarly, Marco Bembo capitalized on government incentives for grain imports to generate profit during a war period. Among the many services offered by the government, a special relevance has the consuls, who acted as local extensions of the central government, serving both regulatory and supportive functions for the overseas engagements of Venetian family firms. Additionally, the public shipping system emerges as a crucial state initiative that merged public and private maritime efforts. This collaboration ensured streamlined transportation of goods, facilitating planning and reducing costs for merchants. The analysis reveals how merchants took advantage of state policies and interventions, shedding light on the underlying motivations and effects of these governmental actions.[7]

The Venetian state exercised significant control over both regional and international trades, employing it as a powerful tool characteristic of preindustrial states. In this context, commerce was regarded as a privilege rather than a right, with merchants allowed to participate in trade solely with the explicit consent of public authorities. These authorities themselves comprised members from the commercial class, effectively merging state regulatory frameworks with the interests of the mercantile aristocracy. This integration of governance and commercial interests shaped the economic landscape of Venice, influencing its trade policies and practices.[8] As observed, all three *fraterne* considered here had political representation, either through direct family connections, as with the Foscari and Michiel families, or through marital ties, as with the Bembo family. It is noteworthy that the state's control over the commercial sector can be described as corporatist, as it implemented exclusionary policies against foreigners and a significant segment of Venice's society, preventing them from actively participating in the city's international trade.[9] The complex classification of citizenship determined the level of commercial privileges, with higher tiers granting comprehensive commercial rights, including international trade.

This examination not only enriches our understanding of Venetian economic history but also offers broader insights into the dynamics of preindustrial trade and the delicate equilibrium between private enterprise and public authority. An illustrative example of these dynamics can be found in the correspondence of Marco Bembo. His proactive measures, which involved utilizing his network of agents and capitalizing on institutional frameworks, underline the complex interplay between public roles and private interests among Venetian merchants. This case highlights how merchants browsed the intertwined realms of government regulation and commercial ambition.

Strategies and Management

In this volume, we have explored the strategies and management tools that, in a commercially and politically fragmented world, allowed companies to remain competitive in international markets. The case studies reveal a sophisticated approach to financial management and investment in international trade. The adoption of advanced accounting practices and the strategic use of partnerships and consortia proved essential for navigating the complexities of preindustrial commerce. This analysis not only highlights the distinctive characteristics of Venetian merchant practices but also places them within a broader context of international trading traditions, offering a comprehensive understanding of historical business strategies.[10]

The ledgers of Giovanni Foscari provide invaluable insights into the financial strategies and investment practices of Venetian merchants, stressing the importance of partnerships and the distribution of shares in managing maritime ventures. Venetian merchants employed several strategies for investing in maritime trade, including leasing cargo space, chartering ships, and forming temporary consortia. These approaches facilitated risk distribution and enabled the participation of multiple investors in a single voyage. Giovanni Foscari's ledgers reveal detailed records of expenses and transactions related to his role as a galley patron, illustrating the financial commitments and collaborative efforts involved in maritime trade. The evolution of accounting practices, particularly double-entry bookkeeping, was fundamental in managing these complex activities.[11] The adoption of these methods facilitated meticulous tracking of assets and liabilities, ensuring the accuracy of records. Venetian accounting ledgers, exemplified by those maintained by the Michiel and Foscari families, demonstrate systematic transaction recording and the critical importance of keeping accounts current for effective business management. Moreover, these detailed records were essential for resolving conflicts when they arose, serving as reliable references that could support or settle disputes.

Like any business model, the *fraterna* approach offered several advantages, including complete control over business decisions and the preservation of family wealth. However, it also presented challenges, particularly in managing the responsibilities and financial activities of multiple family members. Comparative analysis of Armenian and Indian merchant practices illuminates different approaches to business organization, risk management, and the utilization of familial connections in trade. For example, Armenian merchants typically operated through a network of trusted agents dispersed across various regions, which allowed them to mitigate risks through diversification and localized knowledge. On the other hand, Indian merchants often depended on extensive kinship ties and community support, providing a robust framework for managing credit and resolving disputes. These comparative perspectives highlight the diverse ways in which family-based commercial enterprises have adapted to their respective economic environments, leveraging familial ties to bolster their business resilience and success.[12]

The Role of Agents

This book has elucidated the critical role of agents and intermediaries for small- and medium-sized enterprises, particularly when an extensive family network offers limited agent resources. Initially, it is imperative to comprehend the roles, capabilities, and functions of agents within the family. Following this, it becomes essential to understand the dynamics involving agents outside the family core, focusing on their management to ensure the highest level of collaboration in business relationships. This approach not only emphasizes control but also aims to cultivate trust, forming a delicate balance vital for successful commerce.

Despite the integration of family and business interests, individual family members could undertake independent ventures, eventually offering their services to multiple resident merchants as commission agents. As we observed particularly in Chapter 5, whether the agents were Venetian or foreign, it was essential for resident merchants to develop communication and management strategies that ensured maximum transparency and loyalty.[13] These relationships between merchants operating from Venice and their agents required meticulous record-keeping to prevent disputes and maintain clear financial boundaries, regardless of whether the agents were commission-based or belonged to the same *fraterna*. The goal was to maintain a clear separation between personal and family capital. Notable examples include family members like Silvestro Michiel, whose independent trading activities were recorded in the family's ledgers, as discussed in Chapter 1. The fraterna model facilitated the consolidation of family wealth and resources, with individual fortunes often built through commissions and personal ventures.

In medieval Venice, merchants stationed near the Rialto port relied heavily on agents to advance their interests in distant markets. These agents were vital for gathering market information, overseeing transactions, and ensuring the enforcement of contracts. Agents and intermediaries played a crucial role in Venetian commerce, facilitating transactions and representing the company in foreign ports. Their roles could be temporary, handling specific transactions, or more permanent, acting as enduring contacts for the resident merchant. The distinction between these roles was often blurred, with terms like 'agent' and 'clerk' used interchangeably. The key differentiator was the reason for their selection and the specific responsibilities they held within the company. Some agents were chosen for their expertise in particular markets, while others were selected based on familial ties or shared interests.[14] However, the medieval context presented significant challenges, including vast distances, slow communication, and limited institutional support. Relationships between principals (resident merchants) and agents were susceptible to disruption due to differences in training, commercial practices, conflicts of interest, or misinterpretations of directives originating from Venice. These factors necessitated robust communication and management strategies to ensure successful commercial operations.[15]

In the case studies, we observed an arrangement characterized by fluid dynamics within merchant networks, where the length and nature of an agent's engagement could shift significantly based on the business's needs and the trust placed in the agent. This flexibility allowed Venetian merchants to adapt quickly to changing market conditions and opportunities, ensuring their ventures remained agile and responsive to the demands of international trade. This model not only facilitated commerce but also fostered a system of repeated collaborations and trust-building, crucial for the long-term success and expansion of their trading operations.[16] Familial relationships often played a unique role in the structure of Venetian trading enterprises, as familial ties brought a deeper level of trust and commitment, which was crucial for managing the complex aspects of international commerce. Their deep-rooted connections within the family and comprehensive understanding of the business objectives allowed the agents to execute strategies that balanced short-term transactional needs with long-term goals, enhancing the firm's ability to adapt to the rapidly changing conditions of global markets. In this regard, as seen with the incident involving Marco Bembo's agent in Candia, Francesco Giustinian, and the arrival of a new actor, the nephew of Marco Bembo, Zuane Malipiero, the delicate balance required in managing distant business operations and the potential complications that can arise from introducing new dynamics into established relationships is relevant, and highlights the importance of clear communication and understanding individual temperaments in the complex dance of international trade and relationship management.[17]

One important strategy to secure agents and partners was to reciprocate services or favours. Reciprocity in business could be directly requested by agents or partners, as seen in the Michiel case, or proposed unilaterally. In the latter scenario, a morally indebted situation created by the resident merchant could foster a strong relationship. An example of this dynamic emerges from the commercial letters of Marco Bembo to his agents and partners in the Mediterranean and European ports. Bembo often announced that he had taken care of debt settlements or tax payments, or, as in Alvise Michiel's case, provided the necessary funds for his agents' family affairs, such as dowries for female family members. Why did these merchants perform such acts when the agents did not request them? These actions were likely attempts to create a stronger, almost morally indebted relationship with agents who had no familial ties to the merchant. This aimed to secure the agents' loyalty, which was a precious and costly commodity. The Bembo case highlights the challenge of securing agent loyalty: despite institutional support from courts and consuls and the adoption of informal strategies, it remained difficult to maintain good relations with foreign market representatives. This difficulty likely drove many Venetian merchants to choose family members as agents, as social factors made family members more likely to behave correctly and be more controllable by resident merchants.[18]

The management of agents and intermediaries by merchants illustrates the intricate balance of authority, mentorship, and planning required to run a successful family business in the competitive world of international trade. Their methods ensured that, even while dispersed across various regions, the family's business operations remained cohesive and aligned with broader goals. A key component of this strategy was the distinct approach to non-family agents, which was crucial for maintaining effective business relationships. By making non-family agents feel valued and supported, merchants fostered loyalty and enhanced the overall stability of their operations. This delicate balance of power and trust was essential for ensuring smooth trade activities. Merchants combined direct support with indirect mechanisms to safeguard their interests while creating a supportive environment for their agents, enabling them to operate confidently and efficiently.[19] In the case of Marco Bembo, his meticulous instructions and delegation of tasks exemplify the depth needed for managing long-distance trade. Bembo understood that empowering his agents and granting them autonomy was crucial for the successful execution of complex trade operations. This balance between guidance and autonomy not only motivated his agents but also allowed for flexible and adaptive management in a rapidly changing commercial environment. Through these methods, Bembo tried to maintain control over his expansive trade network, with the only aim to protect his business interests.

Trade and Capital

Finally, this book delves into the early forms of commercial capitalism, aiming to interpret these through the lens of the tools and practices employed by small- and medium-sized commercial enterprises. It strives to understand these forms by examining the actions of individuals who did not consider themselves capitalists and operated outside of a capitalist framework, yet who still made use of its tools and concepts.

The analysis of strategies that merchants adopted to ensure the reproduction of capital during periods of restricted circulation, such as wars, is particularly insightful. In these challenging contexts, merchants devised inventive methods to invest capital in the form of goods. A notable strategy was the development of commodity chains that utilized local resources. For example, the production of Feltre woollen cloths, which were then finished and dyed in Venice, exemplifies this approach. These cloths were subsequently exported to markets in Apulia and the Mamluk territories. This strategy not only maintained trade flows during conflicts but also bolstered local production and processing activities, contributing to the economic resilience of the region.[20]

Other crucial commodities for capital circulation included pepper, olive oil, metals, and wine. Pepper, a highly demanded spice in Europe, saw its trade significantly impacted by wars, as evidenced by the fluctuations in pepper imports and sales during the conflict with the Ottomans recorded in the Michiel ledger. Olive oil, essential for both household and industrial uses, played a critical role in Venice's economy, prompting extensive investment in the trade of Apulian olive oil by Michiel. Copper and tin, important imports from Central Europe, were utilized in various manufacturing processes in Venice before being exported. The continued trade of these metals during wartime ensured ongoing commercial activity. Wine also played a central role, with notable involvement from Marco Bembo and usage by Giovanni Foscari. Beyond its intrinsic value, wine facilitated trade by enabling Venetian merchants to establish and maintain influential networks across Europe. It also functioned as a form of currency, allowing merchants to engage in complex trade negotiations and social exchanges, transcending straightforward commercial transactions.[21] Giovanni Foscari's detailed account logs reveal the strategic use of wine in diplomatic and commercial contexts. Wine was allocated for various purposes, from galley consumption and facilitating textile purchases to serving as diplomatic gifts. But also the use of wine to enter the English court suggested by Marco Bembo to his agent in London stresses its utility in smoothing commercial operations and fostering relations with customs officials and local nobility.

Venetian merchants were adept at adapting their strategies to changing market dynamics. For example, the Michiel family firm diversified its trading portfolio to include a mix of high-value and essential goods, ensuring a balanced trade flow even during conflicts. This adaptability was key to maintaining Venice's central role in Mediterranean trade, in a period that marked the early stages of capitalist practices within a predominantly non-capitalist economy. In this context, we sought to understand what capital meant for economic agents who did not identify as capitalists and did not operate in a capitalist setting. In the Renaissance, capital took various forms and definitions, including physical goods, manufacturing processes, or currency.[22] Thanks to the case studies, it is clear that Renaissance merchants' idea of capital referred to investments, personal net worth, or the monetary value of assets, which were controlled using tracking instruments such as double-entry bookkeeping. Merchants believed that capital would be damaged by inaction, so their primary aim was to keep it circulating. The creation of commodity chains of low-value materials proved useful in this regard. The dynamic nature of capital involved transforming monetary investments into goods and then back into money, often through enhancement or transportation processes. Venetian merchants invested in product adaptation to meet market demands and facilitate further investments. Examples include cloth dyeing and wine blending, where initial capital invested in raw materials was enhanced through additional processing. This approach generated surplus value, crucial for multiplying wealth and sustaining business operations.

Financial instruments like letters of exchange were also important in managing capital flow. These tools allowed merchants to conduct transactions without physically transferring money, reducing the risks and costs associated with transporting large sums. The system of bills of exchange enabled international trade, providing a flexible method for payments and credit across borders and a collateral for partnerships and investments. Investing in essential commodities like grain and wine provided reliable returns and ensured the mobilization of capital. The continuous circulation of capital, whether in monetary form or goods, was crucial for generating profits. The strategies merchants employed to keep capital in motion, including leveraging financial instruments and investing in stable commodities, were at the centre of their activities. This approach not only ensured capital growth but also created new commercial opportunities and relationships.[23]

To conclude, the question posed in the introduction—how did Venetian family businesses manage to operate in an increasingly competitive market that required the use of various complex tools?—can be answered by summarizing the key factors involved.

Firstly, the advantages of family management played a crucial role, allowing for strong flexibility and readiness to adapt to contingencies. These businesses could rely on trusted agents from within the family, ensuring loyalty and alignment with the family's commercial objectives. Additionally, they included foreign agents eager to integrate into the Venetian network, thereby expanding their reach and influence in international markets. This blend of internal and external agents provided a robust network of contacts and expertise, essential for navigating the complexities of trade.

Secondly, the support and opportunities provided by the Venetian State were instrumental. The State facilitated access to international trade for its merchants through various means, including public navigation routes, diplomatic support, and a well-regulated market environment. Despite this support, the trade environment remained exclusive, as access was tightly controlled socially and economically. This exclusivity ensured that only those belonging to the patriciate or with significant standing and capability could participate, thereby reducing competition.

For this reason, a significant portion of the work of family businesses relied on commission agents, who represented the Venetian companies in foreign markets. These agents were the face of the Venetian enterprises abroad, responsible for managing transactions, gathering market intelligence, and maintaining relationships with local merchants and officials. The dynamic between the resident merchants and their agents was a delicate balance of trust and control. Merchants had to ensure their agents remained loyal and effective, often through a combination of incentives and oversight.

The agents' role was critical in ensuring the circulation of the merchant's capital. They developed and implemented commercial strategies that capitalized on the varying opportunities available across different markets and commodities. For instance, they had to be adept at leveraging local market conditions, negotiating favourable terms, and adapting to the shifting dynamics of international trade. The success of these strategies depended heavily on the agents' ability to act decisively and responsibly on behalf of the resident merchants.

In summary, the successful operation of Venetian family businesses in a competitive market was due to a combination of internal trust within the family, strategic use of foreign agents, and the supportive yet controlled environment provided by the Venetian state. This intricate balance allowed these businesses to browse the complexities of international trade. The adaptability and foresight of these merchants, coupled with a strong support network and a favourable regulatory environment, were key to their ability to compete in the landscape of Renaissance commerce.

Notes

1 Federigo Melis, 'L'archivio di un mercante e banchiere trecentesco: Francesco di Marco Datini da Prato', *Moneta e credito* 7, no. 25 (1954): 60–69; Raymond De Roover, *The Medici Bank: Its Organization, Management, Operations and Decline*, Business History Series (New York University. Graduate School of Business Administration) (New York: Univ. Press, 1948); Richard A. Goldthwaite, 'The Medici Bank and the World of Florentine Capitalism', *Past and Present* 114 (1987): 3–31; Edwin S. Hunt, *The Medieval Super-Companies. A Study of the Peruzzi Company of Florence* (Cambridge: Cambridge University Press, 1994); Angela Orlandi, 'Networks and Commercial Penetration Models in the Late Medieval Mediterranean: Revisiting the Datini', in *Commercial Networks and European Cities, 1400–1800*, ed. Andrea Caracausi and Christof Jeggle (London: Pickering & Chatto, 2014), 81–106.

2 Michael N. Pearson, 'Merchants and States', in *The Political Economy of Merchant Empires. State, Power and World Trade, 1350–1750*, ed. James D. Tracy (Cambridge: Cambridge University Press, 1991), 41–116; Avner Greif, 'Family Structure, Institutions, and Growth: The Origins and Implications of Western Corporations', *American Economic Review* 96, no. 2 (2006): 308–12; Sheilagh Ogilvie, *Institutions and European Trade: Merchant Guilds, 1000–1800* (Cambridge: Cambridge University Press, 2011).

3 Frederic C. Lane, 'Family Partnerships and Joint Ventures in the Venetian Republic', *The Journal of Economic History* 4, no. 2 (1944): 178–96; Ugo Tucci, 'La psicologia del mercante veneziano', in *Mercanti, navi e monete nel Cinquecento veneziano* (Bologna: Edizioni Il Mulino, 1981), 43–94.

4 Stefania Montemezzo, 'Strategie familiari e commercio internazionale: i Michiel da San Barnaba', *Studi storici Luigi Simeoni* 65 (2015): 29–40.

5 Gino Luzzatto, 'Navigazione di linea e navigazione libera nelle grandi città marinare del Medio Evo', in *Studi di storia economica veneziana* (Padova: Cedam, 1954): 53-58; Frederic C. Lane, 'Venetian Merchant Galleys, 1300–1334: Private and Communal Operation', *Speculum* 38, no. 2 (1963): 179–205; Maria Pia Pedani, 'Consoli veneziani

nei porti del Mediterraneo in Età moderna', in *Mediterraneo in armi (secc. XV-XVIII)*, vol. 1, ed. Rosella Cancila (Palermo: Mediterranea, 2007), 175–205; Claire Judde de Larivière, *Naviguer, commercer, gouverner: économie maritime et pouvoirs à Venise (XVe-XVIe siècles)* (Leiden: Brill, 2008).

6 Stefania Montemezzo, 'Galley Routes and Merchant Networks between Venice and the North Sea in the Fifteenth Century', in *Commercial Networks and European Cities, 1400–1800*, ed. Andrea Caracausi and Christof Jeggle (London: Pickering & Chatto, 2014), 153–69.

7 Frederic C. Lane, 'The Role of Governments in Economic Growth in Early Modern Times', *The Journal of Economic History* 35, no. 1 (1975): 8–17.

8 Andrea Caracausi, Giovanni Favero, and Paola Lanaro, 'A Political Economy? Some Preliminary Thoughts on Economic Privileges in Early Modern Venice', in *Die Ökonomie Des Privilegs, Westeuropa 16.-19. Jh./L'économie Du Privilège, Europe Occidentale XVIe-XIX Siècles.*, ed. Guillaume Garner (Frankfurt am Mainz: Vittorio Klostermann, 2016), 365–95.

9 Anna Bellavitis, '«Per cittadini metterete...»: La Stratificazione della società veneziana cinquecentesca tra norma giuridica e riconoscimento sociale', *Quaderni Storici* 89 (1995): 359–83.

10 Lane, 'Family Partnerships and Joint Ventures in the Venetian Republic'; Frederic C. Lane, 'Venture Accounting in Medieval Business Management', *Bulletin of the Business Historical Society* 19, no. 5 (1945): 164–73, https://doi.org/10.2307/3111058; Stefania Montemezzo, 'Fra pubblico e privato: la fraterna veneziana nel commercio del secondo Quattrocento', *Ricerche di storia economica e sociale* III (2017): 7–34.

11 Montemezzo, 'Galley Routes and Merchant Networks between Venice and the North Sea in the Fifteenth Century'.

12 Sebouh Aslanian, 'The Circulation of Men and Credit: The Role of the Commenda and the Family Firm in Julfan Society', *Journal of the Economic and Social History of the Orient* 50, no. 2/3 (2007): 124–71.

13 Gunnar Dahl, *Trade, Trust, and Networks: Commercial Culture in Late Medieval Italy* (Lund: Nordic Academic Press, 1998), http://archive.org/details/tradetrustnetwor0000dahl; Xavier Lamikiz, 'Social Capital, Networks and Trust in Early Modern Long-Distance Trade. A Critical Appraisal', in *Merchants and Trade Networks in the Atlantic and the Mediterranean, 1500–1800. Connectors of Commercial Maritime Systems*, ed. Manuel Herrero Sanchez and Klemens Kaps (Abingdon, Oxon: Routledge, 2017), 39–61.

14 Ricardo Court, '"Januensis Ergo Mercator": Trust and Enforcement in the Business Correspondence of the Brignole Family', *The Sixteenth Century Journal* 35, no. 4 (2004): 987–1003; Avner Greif, 'Contracting, Enforcement, and Efficiency: Economics beyond the Law', in *Annual World Bank Conference on Development Economics*, ed. M. Bruno and B. Pleskovic (Washington, DC: The World Bank, 1997), 239–65.

15 John J. McCusker, 'The Demise of Distance: The Business Press and the Origins of the Information Revolution in the Early Modern Atlantic World', *The American Historical Review* 110, no. 2 (2005): 295–321; Lamikiz, 'Social Capital, Networks and Trust in Early Modern Long-Distance Trade. A Critical Appraisal'.

16 D. Good, 'Individuals, Interpersonal Relations and Trust', in *Trust: Making and Breaking Cooperative Relations*, ed. Diego Gambetta (New York: Basil Blackwell, 1988), 31–48.

17 Pierre Jeannin, 'La Diffusion de l'information', in *Fiere e mercati nella integrazione delle economie europee secc. XIII-XVIII, Atti della trentaduesima Settimana di studi e altri convegni dell'Istituto internazionale di Storia economica F. Datini (8–12 Maggio 2000)* (Florence: Le Monnier, Istituto internazionale di storia economica 'F. Datini', 2001), 231–62; Wolfgang Kaiser and Gilbert Buti, 'Moyens, supports et usages de l'information marchande à l'époque moderne', *Rives nord-méditerranéennes* 27 (2007): 7–11.

18 Lane, 'Family Partnerships and Joint Ventures in the Venetian Republic'; Court, 'Januensis Ergo Mercator'.
19 Avner Greif, 'Reputation and Coalitions in Medieval Trade: Evidence on the Maghribi Traders', *The Journal of Economic History* 49, no. 4 (1989): 857–82; Yadira González de Lara, 'The Secret of Venetian Success: A Public-Order, Reputation-Based Institution', *European Review of Economic History* 12 (2008): 247–85.
20 Katherine Barbieri and Jack S. Levy, 'Sleeping with the Enemy: The Impact of War on Trade', *Journal of Peace Research* 36, no. 4 (1999): 463–79.
21 Hannelore Zug Tucci, 'Un aspetto trascurato del commercio medievale del vino', in *Studi in memoria di Federigo Melis*, vol. 3 (Napoli: Giannini editore, 1978), 311–48; Ugo Tucci, 'Il commercio del vino nell'economia cretese', in *Venezia e Creta. Atti del convegno internazionale di studi, Iraklion-Chanià, 30 Settembre-5 Ottobre 1997*, ed. Gherardo Ortalli (Venice: Istituto Veneto di Scienze, Lettere ed Arti, 1998), 183–206.
22 Ian Blanchard, 'International Capital Markets and Their Users, 1450–1750', in *Early Modern Capitalism. Economic and Social Change in Europe, 1400–1800*, ed. Maarten Prak (Abingdon, Oxon, New York: Routledge, 2001), 107–24; Pierre Gervais, 'Capitalism and (or) Age of Commerce: The Peculiarities of Market Exchange in the Early Modern Era', *Revue de a société d'études anglo-américaines des XVIIe et XVIIIe siècles* 77 (2020): Online. https://journals.openedition.org/1718/5818.
23 Richard Britnell, 'Commerce and Capitalism in Late Medieval England: Problems of Description and Theory', *Journal of Historical Sociology* 6, no. 4 (1993): 359–76; Blanchard, 'International Capital Markets and Their Users, 1450–1750'; Luciano Pezzolo, 'The via Italiana to Capitalism', in *The Cambridge History of Capitalism, I, The Rise of Capitalism: From Ancient Origins to 1848*, ed. Larry Neal and Jeffrey G. Williamson (Cambridge: Cambridge University Press, 2014), 266–313.

References

Aslanian, Sebouh. 'The Circulation of Men and Credit: The Role of the Commenda and the Family Firm in Julfan Society'. *Journal of the Economic and Social History of the Orient* 50, no. 2/3 (2007): 124–71.

Barbieri, Katherine, and Jack S. Levy. 'Sleeping with the Enemy: The Impact of War on Trade'. *Journal of Peace Research* 36, no. 4 (1999): 463–79.

Bellavitis, Anna. '«Per cittadini metterete…»: La stratificazione della società veneziana cinquecentesca tra norma giuridica e riconoscimento sociale'. *Quaderni Storici* 89 (1995): 359–83.

Blanchard, Ian. 'International Capital Markets and Their Users, 1450–1750'. In *Early Modern Capitalism. Economic and Social Change in Europe, 1400–1800*, edited by Maarten Prak, 107–24. Abingdon, Oxon, New York: Routledge, 2001.

Britnell, Richard. 'Commerce and Capitalism in Late Medieval England: Problems of Description and Theory'. *Journal of Historical Sociology* 6, no. 4 (1993): 359–76.

Caracausi, Andrea, Giovanni Favero, and Paola Lanaro. 'A Political Economy? Some Preliminary Thoughts on Economic Privileges in Early Modern Venice'. In *Die ökonomie des privilegs, Westeuropa 16.-19. Jh./L'économie du privilège, Europe Occidentale XVIe-XIX siècles*, edited by Guillaume Garner, 365–95. Frankfurt am Mainz: Vittorio Klostermann, 2016.

Court, Ricardo. '"Januensis Ergo Mercator": Trust and Enforcement in the Business Correspondence of the Brignole Family'. *The Sixteenth Century Journal* 35, no. 4 (2004): 987–1003.

Dahl, Gunnar. *Trade, Trust, and Networks: Commercial Culture in Late Medieval Italy*. Lund: Nordic Academic Press, 1998. http://archive.org/details/tradetrustnetwor0000dahl.

De Roover, Raymond. *The Medici Bank: Its Organization, Management, Operations and Decline*. (New York University. Graduate School of Business Administration). New York: Univ. Press, 1948.

Gervais, Pierre. 'Capitalism and (or) Age of Commerce: The Peculiarities of Market Exchange in the Early Modern Era'. *Revue de La Société d'études Anglo-Américaines Des XVIIe et XVIIIe Siècles* 77 (2020): Online. https://journals.openedition.org/1718/5818.

Goldthwaite, Richard A. 'The Medici Bank and the World of Florentine Capitalism'. *Past and Present* 114 (1987): 3–31.

González de Lara, Yadira. 'The Secret of Venetian Success: A Public-Order, Reputation-Based Institution'. *European Review of Economic History* 12 (2008): 247–85.

Good, D. 'Individuals, Interpersonal Relations and Trust'. In *Trust: Making and Breaking Cooperative Relations*, edited by Diego Gambetta, 31–48. New York: Basil Blackwell, 1988.

Greif, Avner. 'Contracting, Enforcement, and Efficiency: Economics beyond the Law'. In *Annual World Bank Conference on Development Economics*, edited by M. Bruno and B. Pleskovic, 239–65. Washington, DC: The World Bank, 1997.

Greif, Avner. 'Family Structure, Institutions, and Growth: The Origins and Implications of Western Corporations'. *American Economic Review* 96, no. 2 (2006): 308–12.

Greif, Avner. 'Reputation and Coalitions in Medieval Trade: Evidence on the Maghribi Traders'. *The Journal of Economic History* 49, no. 4 (1989): 857–82.

Hunt, Edwin S. *The Medieval Super-Companies. A Study of the Peruzzi Company of Florence*. Cambridge: Cambridge University Press, 1994.

Jeannin, Pierre. 'La Diffusion de l'information'. In *Fiere e mercati nella integrazione delle economie europee secc. XIII-XVIII, Atti della trentaduesima Settimana di studi e altri convegni dell'Istituto internazionale di Storia economica F. Datini (8-12 Maggio 2000)*, edited by Simonetta Cavaciocchi, 231–62. Florence: Le Monnier, Istituto internazionale di storia economica 'F. Datini', 2001.

Judde de Larivière, Claire. *Naviguer, commercer, gouverner: économie maritime et pouvoirs à Venise (XVe-XVIe siècles)*. Leiden: Brill, 2008.

Kaiser, Wolfgang, and Gilbert Buti. 'Moyens, supports et usages de l'information marchande à l'époque moderne'. *Rives nord-méditerranéennes* 27 (2007): 7–11.

Lamikiz, Xavier. 'Social Capital, Networks and Trust in Early Modern Long-Distance Trade. A Critical Appraisal'. In *Merchants and Trade Networks in the Atlantic and the Mediterranean, 1500–1800. Connectors of Commercial Maritime Systems*, edited by Manuel Herrero Sanchez and Klemens Kaps, 39–61. Abingdon, Oxon: Routledge, 2017.

Lane, Frederic C. 'Family Partnerships and Joint Ventures in the Venetian Republic'. *The Journal of Economic History* 4, no. 2 (1944): 178–96.

Lane, Frederic C. 'The Role of Governments in Economic Growth in Early Modern Times'. *The Journal of Economic History* 35, no. 1 (1975): 8–17.

Lane, Frederic C. 'Venetian Merchant Galleys, 1300–1334: Private and Communal Operation'. *Speculum* 38, no. 2 (1963): 179–205.

Lane, Frederic C. 'Venture Accounting in Medieval Business Management'. *Bulletin of the Business Historical Society* 19, no. 5 (1945): 164–73. https://doi.org/10.2307/3111058.

Luzzatto, Gino. 'Navigazione di linea e navigazione libera nelle grandi città marinare del Medio Evo'. In *Studi di storia economica veneziana*, 53–58. Padova: Cedam, 1954.

McCusker, John J. 'The Demise of Distance: The Business Press and the Origins of the Information Revolution in the Early Modern Atlantic World'. *The American Historical Review* 110, no. 2 (2005): 295–321.

Melis, Federigo. 'L'archivio di un mercante e banchiere trecentesco: Francesco di Marco Datini da Prato'. *Moneta e credito* 7, no. 25 (1954): 60–69.

Montemezzo, Stefania. 'Fra pubblico e privato: la fraterna veneziana nel commercio del secondo Quattrocento'. *Ricerche di storia economica e sociale* III (2017): 7–34.

Montemezzo, Stefania. 'Galley Routes and Merchant Networks between Venice and the North Sea in the Fifteenth Century'. In *Commercial Networks and European Cities, 1400–1800*, edited by Andrea Caracausi and Christof Jeggle, 153–69. London: Pickering & Chatto, 2014.

Montemezzo, Stefania. 'Strategie familiari e commercio internazionale: i Michiel da San Barnaba'. *Studi storici Luigi Simeoni* 65 (2015): 29–40.

Ogilvie, Sheilagh. *Institutions and European Trade: Merchant Guilds, 1000–1800*. Cambridge: Cambridge University Press, 2011.

Orlandi, Angela. 'Networks and Commercial Penetration Models in the Late Medieval Mediterranean: Revisiting the Datini'. In *Commercial Networks and European Cities, 1400–1800*, edited by Andrea Caracausi and Christof Jeggle, 81–106. London: Pickering & Chatto, 2014.

Pearson, Michael N. 'Merchants and States'. In *The Political Economy of Merchant Empires. State, Power and World Trade, 1350–1750*, edited by James D. Tracy, 41–116. Cambridge: Cambridge University Press, 1991.

Pedani, Maria Pia. 'Consoli veneziani nei porti del Mediterraneo in Età moderna'. In *Mediterraneo in armi (secc. XV-XVIII)*, 1. edited by Rossella Cancila, 175–205. Palermo: Mediterranea, 2007.

Pezzolo, Luciano. 'The via Italiana to Capitalism'. In *The Cambridge History of Capitalism, I, The Rise of Capitalism: From Ancient Origins to 1848*, edited by Larry Neal and Jeffrey G. Williamson, 266–313. Cambridge: Cambridge University Press, 2014.

Tucci, Ugo. 'Il commercio del vino nell'economia cretese'. In *Venezia e Creta. Atti del convegno internazionale di studi, Iraklion-Chanià, 30 Settembre-5 Ottobre 1997*, edited by Gherardo Ortalli, 183–206. Venice: Istituto Veneto di Scienze, Lettere ed Arti, 1998.

Tucci, Ugo. 'La psicologia del mercante veneziano'. In *Mercanti, navi e monete nel Cinquecento veneziano*, 43–94. Bologna: Edizioni Il Mulino, 1981.

Zug Tucci, Hannelore. 'Un aspetto trascurato del commercio medievale del vino'. In *Studi in memoria di Federigo Melis*, 3:311–48. Napoli: Giannini editore, 1978.

Sources

Unpublished Sources

Archivio di Stato di Venezia
Archivio privato Gradenigo rio Marin, folder 189.
Archivio privato Gradenigo rio Marin, folder 246.
Archivio privato Gradenigo rio Marin, folder 250, reg. 2.
Dieci Savi alle Decime in Rialto, Filze, Redecima 1514, 67, San Simeon Piccolo 7.
Giudici di Petizion, Sentenze a giustizia, reg. 150.
Giudici di Petizion, Sentenze a giustizia, reg. 195.
Maggior Consiglio, Regina, reg. 23.
Miscellanea di carte non appartenenti ad alcun archivio, folder 8.
Miscellanea di carte non appartenenti ad alcun archivio, folder 29, reg. 2.
Miscellanea Gregolin, b. 15, reg. 2.
Notarile, Testamenti, folder 1186 (notary Domenico Groppi).
Segretario alle voci, reg. 6.
ASVe, Senato, Deliberazioni, Incanti di galere, reg. 1 (1469–1489).
Senato, Dispacci antichi rettori ed altre cariche al Senato, folder 1.

Index

Note: **Bold** page numbers refer to tables; *italic* page numbers refer to figures and page numbers followed by "n" denote endnotes.

Made in the USA
Las Vegas, NV
19 September 2026

3b7ddeae-39fe-41eb-9c33-f71d0e3fd7acR01